Living with AIDS in Uganda

Living with AIDS in Uganda

Impacts on banana-farming households in two districts

AWLAE SERIES No. 6

Monica Karuhanga Beraho

Wageningen Academic
Publishers

ISBN 978-90-8686-064-7

First published, 2008

Wageningen Academic Publishers
The Netherlands, 2008

Acknowledgements

I am highly indebted to several individuals and organizations without whose support it would not have been possible to accomplish my PhD studies.

This PhD study was funded by the Netherlands government through AWLAE (African Women Leaders in Agriculture and Environment), a program of Winrock International, for which am deeply thankful. I am also grateful to the study leave granted to me by Makerere University and to my colleagues in the Department of Agriculture Extension Education who took over my teaching and administrative duties. Special thanks go to other friends in the Faculty of Agriculture for their friendship and the words of encouragement that they always had for me: Peter Ebanyat, Margaret Najjingo Mangheni, Christopher Bukenya, Florence Kyazze, Edward Semakula, Frank Matsiko, Paul Kibwika, Joyce Kikafunda and Robina Sonko. To Peter, Margaret and Pastor Jooga thanks for standing with me in prayers during those many times that I needed your support.

My profound gratitude is due to the management and support staff of the AWLAE Scholars PhD program who were key in facilitating administrative aspects of my PhD work: Anke Niehof, Lisa Price, Antine Hardon, the late Julia Gitobu, Margaret Lubale, Norah Muthike, Riet van de Westeringh, and Hedy Munro. To Anke and Lisa am sincerely grateful for your tireless effort in starting such a novel program that I could benefit from. Special thanks to Anke for your wisdom, patience and commitment to ensuring successful implementation of the AWLAE program. All financial and other support was always received on time. Assistance, warmth and friendship from other staff of the Sociology of Consumers and Household Group is also gratefully acknowledged. Special thanks to Juanwen Yuan and Hom Gartaula with whom I shared offices. To Marian Koster, thanks so much for the friendship and warmth we shared and for taking time to comment on all my chapters despite your own busy schedule. I benefited very much from your critical input. Dinie Verbeek thanks for organizing my work and have it ready for submission in time.

To my friends and colleagues in the first cohort of AWLAE scholars, Doris Kakuru, Faith Nguthi, Lydia Ndirangu, and Caroline Nombo and those in the pipeline, Gaynor Paradza, Hirut Bekele, Kidist Gebreselassie, and Susana Akrofi, I am grateful for the friendship, laughter, care and support that we shared. To the other AWLAE scholars that I interacted with, Corrie Du Preez, Joyce Challe, and Mariame Maiga, thanks for the encouragement and friendship. All this support helped me to keep focused on the goal to work hard and finish my PhD program. To the WUR Ugandan friends during my last year in Wageningen: Enoch Kikulwe, Richard Mugambe, Judith Tukahirwa, Ruth Mubeezi, Meshach Katusimeh, Christine Ampumuza, and Racheal Namuli, thanks for creating such a supportive and enjoyable environment away from home. I thank you for the many ways in which you blessed my stay in

Wageningen. Special thanks go to Richard Mugambe, Robert Kyakanda and Farai and Busi Maphosa for the spiritual support and special friendship.

I would like to express my sincere appreciation to all those who assisted me in my research process. Special thanks go to Steven Yiga and Saul Kusemererwa for the tireless effort they put into organizing the data collection process. I would like to thank the respondents for their time and willingness to share their experiences with me. I thank Jairus Muhere and Basil Mugonola for the data management process. I am very grateful to Enoch Kikulwe, Edward Kato and Kidist Gebreselassie for their technical assistance with the statistical analysis, Moses Musinguzi for drawing the maps of the study area and Andrew Akrofi and Ed Hall for editorial assistance. My gratitude also goes to Mike Jacobs of Wageningen Academic Publishers for the work put into production of this book.

To my dear mother-in-law, Joyce Kobuyonjo, while am greatly indebted to your support, I have no words that can describe how grateful I am. For more than two years, you left your home to take care of my children and home during the time I was in Wageningen pursuing my PhD studies. Thanks for the care and comfort that you gave to the children and my husband; it gave me the peace and strength to complete my studies. Thanks for the words of wisdom and encouragement at those times when I would have given up. Without you I know I wouldn't have finished my program in time. I will forever be grateful to your support. To my other relatives and in-laws thanks for the different ways in which you supported my family during the period of my studies abroad. Special thanks to Steven and Patience Mugarura, Sam and Grace Tayebwa, Simon Nuwagaba, Ruth Kenyangi and Pamela Asiimwe.

I am highly indebted to my promoter Prof. dr. Anke Niehof for the technical guidance, tireless review and re-reading of my work because you wanted it to be excellent. I also thank you for your understanding and patience despite some of my shortcomings, without you, this project would have been impossible to accomplish. To my co-promotor Dr. Paul Hebinck, I am very grateful to the valuable critical input that you always brought into our discussions. Your contributions have enriched many of the ideas presented in this book. I also thank you and Anke for believing in me and always making me feel that I could do even better. I am proud to have been one of your students.

To my darling husband and friend Emmanuel Beraho, no words can express my sincere gratitude for the love, understanding and support that you have continued to give me throughout this PhD process and for shouldering all the parental responsibilities. Thanks for all the sacrifices you made for your own studies and work and for being there for the children and for me. To my dear children Namara, Ainomugisha, Ninsiima, Kamukama and Kansiime-Ruhanga, thanks for the many ways in which you continued to express your love for me. I also thank you for the patience despite missing me so much. The thought of you was a great source of motivation and strength to complete my studies. In honour, I dedicate this book to you, your Daddy and Nywokwenkuru.

Finally, and most important, I thank the Almighty God who gave me the wisdom, good health and strength to successfully complete my studies. All glory and honour be given to Him, for indeed He is a good and faithful God.

Table of contents

Acronyms

ACP	AIDS Control Programme
AE	Adult Equivalent
ANOVA	Analysis of Variance
ARV	Anti Retro Viral
AWLAE	African Women Leaders in Agriculture and Environment
CBO	Community Based Organization
CEDO	Community Extension Development Officers
CHAI	Community HIV/AIDS Initiative
CIS	Corrugated Iron Sheet
CMD	Cassava Mossaic Disease
CRS-Uganda	Catholic Relief Services-Uganda
CU	Consumer units
DFID	Department for International Development
DRC	Democratic republic of Congo
FAO	Food and Agriculture Organization
FGD(s)	Focus Group Discussion(s)
FLE	Family Life Education Unit
FNP	Food and Nutrition Policy
GDI	Gender Development Index
GDP	Gross Domestic Product
GLM	General Linear Model
GOU	Government of Uganda
HBC	Home Based Care
HH	Household
HIPC	Highly Indebted Poor Countries
HIV/AIDS	Human Immune-deficiency Virus / Acquired Immune Deficiency Syndrome
IMF	International Monetary Fund
INIBAP	International Network for Improvement of Banana and Plantain
KARI	Kawanda Agricultural Research Institute
KII	Key Informant Interview
LC	Local Council
MAAIF	Ministry of Agriculture Animal Industry and Fisheries
MADDO	Masaka Diocese Development Organization
MAHCOP	Mobile AIDS Care Counselling and Orphans Programme
MFPED	Ministry of Finance Planning and Economic Development
MFS	Mobile Farm School
MLWE	Ministry of Lands Water and Environment
MOH	Ministry of Health
MRC	Medical Research Council
MYFG	Mobile Young Farmers Groups

NAADS	National Agricultural Advisory Services
NACP	National AIDS Control Programme
NARP	National Agricultural Research Policy
NCWLA	National Community of Women Living with HIV/AIDS
NEMA	National Environment Management Authority
NGO	Non-Governmental Organization
NSF	National Strategic Framework
NTAE	Non-Traditional Agricultural Export
OLS	Ordinary Least Squares
OVC	Orphan and Vulnerable Children
PAE	Per Adult Equivalent
PEAP	Poverty Eradication Action Plan
PIPs	Policies Institutions and Processes
PLWHA	People living with HIV/AIDS
PMA	Plan for the Modernization of Agriculture
PMTCT	Prevention of Mother to Child Transmission
PMU	Programme Management Unit
PRSP	Poverty Reduction Strategy Paper
ROSCAs	Rotating Savings and Credit Associations
SAPRI	Structural Adjustment Participatory Review Initiative
SD	Standard Deviation
ACDI-VOCA	Agricultural Cooperative Development International and Volunteers in Overseas Cooperative Assistance
SE	Standard Error
SPSS	Statistical Package for Social Scientists
STD	Sexually Transmitted Disease
STIs	Sexually Transmitted Infections
TASO	The AIDS Support Organization
TB	Tuberculosis
TFR	Total Fertility Rate
TLU	Total Livestock Unit
TOTs	Training of Trainers
UAC	Uganda AIDS Commission
UBOS	Uganda Bureau of Statistics
UDHS	Uganda Demographic and Health Survey
UFNP	Uganda Food and Nutrition Policy
UGX	Uganda Shillings
UHSBS	Uganda HIV/AIDS Sero-Behavioural Survey
UN	United Nations
UNAIDS	The Joint United Nations Programme on HIV/AIDS
UNDP	United Nations Development Program
UNFPA	United Nations Population Fund
UNHS	Uganda National Household Survey

UNICEF	United Nations Children's Education Fund
UNIFEM	United Nations Development Fund for Women
UNRISD	United Nations Research institute for Social Development
UPE	Universal Primary Education
UPPAP	Uganda Poverty Participatory Programme
UWESO	Uganda Women's Efforts to Save Orphans
VTC	Voluntary Training and Counselling
WB	World Bank
WFP	World Food Programme
WINROCK	WINROCK Institute for Agricultural Development

Glossary

Okusaka	Work for food
Mugaga	Rich person
Muno Mukabi	A friend in need
Mupakasi	Labourer - *Kupakasa* Work for cash (labouring)
Muyaye	Delinquent street boy
Mailo	Mile land
Kibanja	Residential and cultivation tenancy (inheritable) usually on milo land (plural-*Bibanja*)
Mutaka	Land owner (plural-*Bataka*
Kanzu	Initial fee paid to acquire a *kibanja*
Busuulu	Land rents calculated according to size of *Kibanja*
Envujjo	Commodity rents according to type of produce obtained
from land	
Lukiiko	Buganda Parliament
Matooke	Name for one of the beer types of banana
Bogoya	Name for desert types of banana
Sukari- Ndizi	Name for desert types of banana (apple banana)
Mbidde	Local name for one of the beer types of banana
Kayinja	Local name for one of the beer types of banana
Omubisi	Banana wine
Mwenge muganda or *tonto*	Local alcoholic drink made from banana
Waragi	Alcoholic drink made from banana
Nabusa	Local name of a type of cooking banana cultivar
Nakitembe	Local name of a type of cooking banana cultivar
Kibuzi	Local name of a type of cooking banana cultivar
Kivuvu	Local name for one of the beer types of banana
Gonja	Plantain
Ficus natalensis	Bark cloth tree
Kawunga or posho	Maize bread
Akalo	Millet bread
Boda boda	Bicycle or motorcycle used as 'taxi

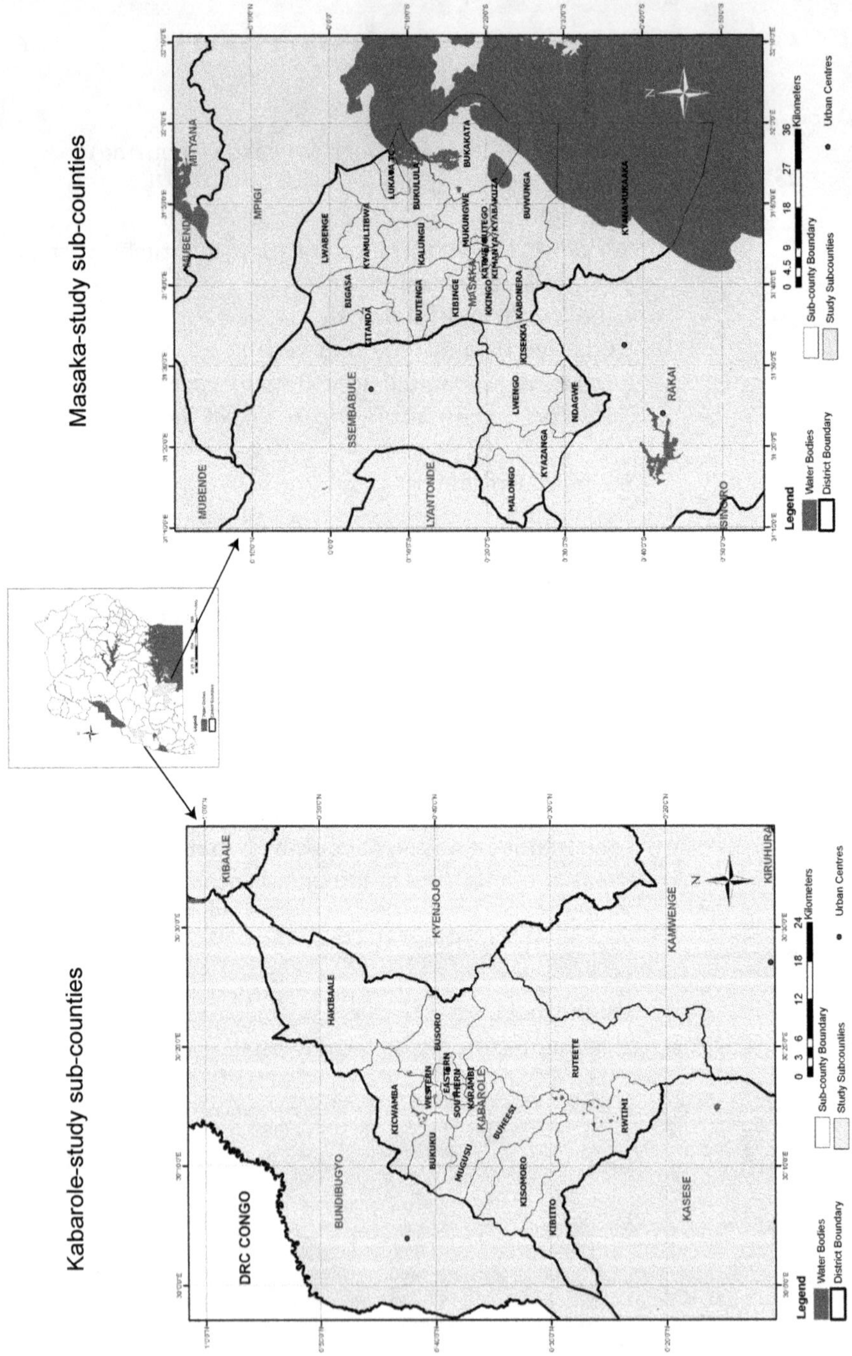

Map of Uganda showing study areas by district.

Chapter 1

Introduction and background

This chapter introduces the research on which this thesis is based, its rationale and objectives. The research was conducted in rural Uganda, among banana-farming households in a high HIV/AIDS-prevalence area. In section 1.3, this context will be discussed and profiled. Section 1.4 explains why the research focused on banana-farming households. The end of this chapter presents the thesis outline.

1.1 Justification and rationale for the research

Jessica's story that is narrated below reflects the processes and problems that are the subject matter of this thesis. Jessica lives in a village called Mbirizi, about 40 km from the town of Masaka, along the Masaka-Mbarara highway in Uganda.

Case 1.1. Jessica's story

It was four o'clock in the afternoon when we arrived at Mbirizi. Jessica Nakanwagi had just returned with some food after finishing weeding her neighbour's banana plantation and was preparing for the evening meal - the only meal of the family of seven. They have been eating only one meal a day for four months since the previous season's crop failed due to drought.

Jessica is fifty-two and has been widowed for about twenty years. Her husband died of natural causes and left her a very young family of five children (three boys and two girls) that she has raised single-handedly under very difficult conditions. The only property her husband bequeathed was the one-acre piece of land that she lives on. Her only income is through manual labour in other people's gardens and remittances from her eldest son Kavuma, who now is bedridden with AIDS. This income allowed for educating her children only up to primary grade seven.

"Jobs are difficult to come by in this place. After seventh grade, Kavuma was just roaming in the trading centre looking for work and I feared that he would become a '*muyaye*' (street boy). I had no land to give him so that at least he could grow some maize or vegetables and get some money. I therefore approached my brother, who lives in Masaka, to take Kavuma in and give him some work in his garage. My brother obliged and Kavuma went to live and work with his uncle. My son worked very hard and his uncle loved him and put him in charge of purchasing spare parts. This involved travelling to Kampala, Nairobi or Mombassa in Kenya. My son never forgot us or the problems he had left home. He would send me money to maintain the home and educate his siblings. After the other two boys finished primary seven, Kavuma took them to Masaka and got them casual employment because it would be difficult to continue paying their school fees since he had got married and had a young family of his own. School for the girls was also a problem. After their primary grade five, I could no longer pay for their education. The eldest was 16 years at that time and I was worried that she would get pregnant. At that time, I thought I was lucky to marry off my daughter to a local trader in the nearby district of Rakai. People told me that the trader was very industrious and had a lot of money."

Jessica said that the past five years had been the most difficult years of her life. "Then Satan in the form of '*buno obulwadde obwaja*' [Literally, 'this disease (AIDS) that came'] visited me. My youngest son died at the beginning of 2002 from AIDS. His elder brother, married with two boys, died a few months later from the same disease. His wife brought me their two boys [now aged three and four] in 2004 because she was very sick and could not take care of them. We buried her in July 2004. My eldest daughter, Nankya died of AIDS in 2003, a year after her husband's death. They left three children and we agreed as a clan that Namusoke [Jessica's only living daughter] should go to live in her sister's home and we would take care of the children and the property. None of Nankya's in-laws had been spared by the AIDS scourge that ravaged Rakai district. The pain of losing three children and the responsibility that has come with it – five orphans, and now waiting for Kavuma to die despite the five tortuous years of futile care, is nothing comparable to anything that I have ever experienced, not even the hardship of raising five children with nothing! I don't think I have a heart; mine got rotten long time ago from pain! I am just a moving object."

Kavuma came back home five years ago with three sons (now of ages nine, eight and six) and has been bedridden ever since. Jessica told us that when Kavuma started falling sick without getting better, his wife ran away and left him with their three children because she didn't want to be stigmatized as being an HIV/AIDS-widow. During this period, he was hospitalized in Masaka referral Hospital for at least six times and the shortest time that he had stayed in hospital was two months. "Taking care of him (Kavuma) has been difficult, especially because of the hospital bills and the transportation costs to seek medical care. I also have to pay the person who brings us food when he is hospitalized. Food in towns is very expensive, so someone brought me raw food which I could prepare myself and, in that way, I managed to minimize the costs and save some money to buy eggs and milk for Kavuma."

Jessica then told us how she has been unable to take Kavuma to hospital for the past six months. Instead, she had been buying painkillers from a local drug shop. As the discussion went on, she told of how they sold everything that could be converted to cash, like the household items that Kavuma had brought from town. This included a 14-inch black-and-white television set, a radio and a bicycle, as well as her three goats. Now there was nothing left to sell. She then pointed to the banana plantation a few meters away, "You can see for yourself the effect of months of neglect on the bananas and other crops. It is difficult to look after such a patient single-handed and also manage to weed one's garden. Although the situation was worse when Kavuma was hospitalized, things are not very different when we are back home. The care he needs also leaves little time to attend to my gardens. I now find it better to earn some cash or food from weeding my neighbours' gardens whenever I can spare time because the food from my gardens cannot sustain us – the yields are so low due to poor management. One of the neighbours is good to me. She gives me food whenever I have nothing to give the patient or the children. She says I weed her bananas very well." Indeed, Jessica did not need to elaborate on the poorly managed banana plants and the small maize and bean gardens overgrown with weeds which we could see around the house.

Kavuma's condition had been deteriorating. He said he was in severe pain and was insisting that his mother take him to hospital. Moreover, Kavuma was now too weak to use public transportation and would need a hired vehicle – something they cannot afford. We had a vehicle and offered to take Kavuma to Hospital, but Jessica had to refuse; she had another problem. Since Namusoke had moved to Rakai to take care of her late sister's children, Jessica had no one to take care of her home while she took Kavuma to hospital. This meant that Kavuma would have to wait for at least two to three days before he could be taken to hospital. Jessica had to first get someone to lend her money, then travel to Rakai and ask her daughter Namusoke to come and take care of the home and Kavuma's young children who are younger than Jessica's other grand children in Rakai. Only then could she take Kavuma back to hospital. She alluded to the fact that going back to the hospital was futile, but she had to do it so that her son would not feel neglected in his last days on earth. We asked her how the debt would be covered, and she answered *"Simanyi, tulilabireyo!"*, which means *'I don't know, we will see when that time comes.'* First things first, to her, solving the problem at hand was what mattered. Future problems would be dealt with in their own time.

A week later, we were told that Kavuma had passed away before his mother could get someone to lend her the money she needed to take him to the hospital.

This story provides a glimpse into the life of a 52 year old widow, traumatized by the deaths of her three children and five years of nursing a fourth one that also died. She cares for five orphans, under 10 years of age with one acre of land as her only resource. There were signs that the household was food insecure, so one wonders what would happen if the household was to experience another hardship, such as a drought?

To Jessica, the battle with AIDS is also a battle for daily survival. On the one hand, she cares for a chronically sick patient suffering from one ailment after another and, at the same time, looks for food for the household. On the other hand, she tries to reassure her orphaned grand children that all will be well.

Many households are in similar situations, if not worse, and they experience AIDS and its impacts in different ways. Both between and within households, AIDS means something different for men and women, the married and unmarried, young and old, the affected and non-affected and the rich and poor. AIDS also changes the way people use resources and negotiate social relations in the process of livelihood generation. For Jessica, for example, AIDS means reduced resources and a daily struggle to generate a livelihood, while for Kavuma, AIDS means personal deprivation of good health, dependence on others and helplessness. This underscores the relevance of not only understanding how HIV/AIDS impacts households, but also how it impacts individual household members, their positions and relationships.

Furthermore, because livelihoods are generated within a given social and institutional context, this context influences the way people live and deal with HIV/AIDS. Therefore, to reduce the prevalence and the impact of HIV/AIDS, we must know how AIDS is understood by individuals within institutions that can mitigate the impacts of AIDS. This is exemplified by the following statement made by the former Ugandan Minister of Agriculture, Dr Kisamba-Mugerwa at the IP/FAO workshop of March 2003.

> *Despite Uganda's efforts to reduce HIV/AIDS prevalence in the last ten years, and the introduction of anti-retroviral drugs on the market, the disease is greatly affecting the agricultural sector [...] there is a close link between HIV, poverty, poor nutrition and household food and livelihood insecurity, which is directly undermining government's efforts in realizing the economic empowerment of rural people.*

To ministers and policy makers, HIV/AIDS mean something much different than to individuals living with AIDS or having affected relatives as seen in Jessica's situation. To ministers and policy makers, AIDS is an issue of labour shortage because AIDS affects skilled manpower of prime age. It decimates productive labour and, thereby, reduces government revenues. This, in turn, undermines the government's efforts to implement its programmes.

However, with or without AIDS, rural households have always experienced all sorts of adversity and crises such as drought, floods, famine, disease and poverty. These crises have always been more or less a rural phenomenon. So what makes AIDS so much more devastating? Although the epidemic was first recognized in Uganda about quarter of a century ago, it remains a crisis requiring ongoing emergency attention as was the case twenty years ago. What effects can be observed as a result of HIV/AIDS that makes it stand out as a unique shock? Which groups or households are particularly vulnerable to these effects and why? To what extent are these households able to cope, if at all? What can remedy the situation?

What theory and methodology have the social sciences to offer to answer those questions? The 'livelihood' approach has become increasingly popular as a way of conceptualizing, in a holistic manner, the activities poor people undertake and the interacting factors and processes (risks and opportunities) that influence their livelihood. The livelihood approach departs from structural approaches to poverty - both macroeconomic and basic needs approaches - that tend to portray people as mere victims of structural constraints. It focuses on the idea that poor people are endowed with agency and that they can actively shape their lives by means of material and non-material assets, depending on the context in which they live (De Haan & Zoomers, 2005). A number of frameworks, for example the DFID's sustainable livelihood framework, adopted in this study, have been developed to show the linkages between various factors and processes that influence the way individuals construct their livelihood. The usefulness of such theoretical frameworks in investigating a complex livelihood issue such as AIDS is explored in Chapter 2.

The above set of un-answered questions provided the motivation to pursue further studies when the Netherlands Ministry of Foreign Affairs (Department of Development Cooperation) provided funding to support twenty African women scholars for PhD studies in the Netherlands. The funds were channelled through the African Women Leaders in Agriculture and Environment Programme (AWLAE), a programme of WINROCK International that aims at creating a critical mass of professional women that will be able to influence policy in their organizations in ways that support women in agriculture. The above questions also fitted in well with the strategic themes of gender, HIV/AIDS and food security of the AWLAE programme.

1.2 Research problem and objectives

The HIV/AIDS epidemic is undoing decades of economic and social development in sub-Saharan Africa and is causing rural disintegration. Its impacts on rural populations - their livelihoods, their farming systems and food security - have been especially severe (FAO, 1995). This is partly due to the fact that HIV/AIDS mainly affects people in their most productive age (Ntozi & Nakanaabi, 1997). The epidemic is, therefore, likely to further undermine food security, poverty eradication interventions and consequently all other efforts aimed at achieving the Millennium Development Goals (MDGs) of halving the number of poor and hungry in the world by 2015.

The effects of the epidemic could be reduced if governments had effective policies or could effectively target those affected. Existing policies are ineffective because governments do not have sufficient information to target those who most need resources and support. Accurately identifying and measuring the impacts of HIV/AIDS on rural households is essential to developing effective policies and mitigation strategies.

Since its outbreak in the early 1980s, AIDS has become the most studied infection in human history (Farmer, 1996:263) and the information gathered and knowledge accumulated on its impacts at macro, community and household levels continue to grow. However, while biomedical knowledge of HIV/AIDS and its treatment have advanced remarkably, social research and analysis lags (Marais, 2005). And, given that AIDS presents socio-cultural dimensions that are not addressed by clinical solutions, the biomedical paradigm alone is unlikely to adequately address HIV/AIDS-related impacts (Hunter, 1990; Bond & Vincent, 2002). AIDS generates a way of life that mobilizes clusters of social relationships, a way of life that informs and is informed by local knowledge. AIDS is as much a social and cultural condition as it is a medical one (Bond & Vincent, 2002). In Uganda, like in other parts of the world, the initial focus was on biomedical research and the sexual behaviour of individuals.

While there has been a considerable increase in the number of AIDS-related studies with a socioeconomic focus[1], these studies have not adequately addressed two crucial social processes. First, households and communities in many instances tend to be pictured as homogeneous entities. Yet, in addition to the socio-cultural and economic context, the progression of HIV/AIDS impacts is likely to vary in different households and for different individuals within the same household. This depends on a variety of factors such as household size and composition, life cycle, dependency ratio, household assets and resources, the person who gets affected or dies and the type of syndromes exhibited. Second, few AIDS-related studies have examined how social differentiation or gender relations within AIDS-affected households influence the way individuals and households respond to the effects of the disease: the livelihoods they pursue, how they deal with other adversity. Indeed, much AIDS literature has identified AIDS as one of the vulnerability causing factors. However, beyond this, there is the need to understand how vulnerability due to HIV/AIDS interacts with a barrage of other adversity or how HIV/AIDS-related vulnerability reconfigures existing gender and other social inequities.

[1] Since the establishment of The Working Group on the Socioeconomic, Cultural and Legal Impact of AIDS in 1990, there has been an increase in the number of AIDS-related studies with a socioeconomic focus. Examples of some of the studies done include AIDS in relation to women and children, orphans, and infant mortality (Wakhweya *et al.*, 2002; Anderson *et al.*, 1990; Chin, 1990; Hunter, 1990; Prebble, 1990); family and household (Ntozi, 1997; Ntozi & Nakanaabi, 1997; Seeley *et al.*, 1993); communities (Seeley *et al.*,1991); agriculture (FAO, 2003; Asingwire, 2001; FAO, 1995; Barnett & Blaikie, 1992).

This study, therefore, looks beyond AIDS-as-the-disease, to include other perspectives (social differentiation, gender, and locality) and meanings as understood by those affected. The study contributes to understanding different inter- and intra-household 'phenomena' in AIDS affected rural livelihoods. The main objectives of this study, therefore are to:

1. Contribute towards the livelihood conceptual framework by focusing on the role of social differentiation in livelihood generation and in dealing with livelihood shocks, and
2. Identify critical factors that need to be taken into consideration in the development of relevant policies for HIV/AIDS-affected agriculture-based households or those that are at risk.

Given these two general objectives, the study specifically examines how the effects of HIV/AIDS on banana-farming households influence household resource use and consequently the food and livelihood security of rural farmers in the study area, while applying a gender perspective. In the process, the relevance of the sustainable livelihood framework in gaining such insights is also examined. Furthermore, the study examines the effects of HIV/AIDS on the agriculture extension agency and community based organizations because these effects influence the effectiveness of these organizations to address the impacts of HIV/AIDS on communities.

Given the complexity of livelihood processes, the research adopted a multi-methodology strategy and was conducted in the districts of Masaka and Kabarole, Uganda. Although the household is the unit of analysis, it has not been treated as a closed and stable entity but rather with a flexibility that allows resources, relations among persons and processes therein to be captured.

1.3 Country profile: background

1.3.1 Geography, climate and population

Uganda is a land-locked country in Eastern Africa located at the equator between latitudes 1° 30' South and 4° North and stretching from 29° 30' East to 35° East. It has a total geographic area of about 241,038 square kilometres, of which open water and swamps constitute 17 percent (Ministry of Lands Water and Environment (MLWE), 2002). It is bordered by the Sudan in the north, the Republic of Kenya in the east, the Democratic Republic of Congo (former Zaire) in the west and Tanzania and Rwanda in the south. The country's geographic features range from extensive plains to high snow-capped mountains, but most of the country lies at an altitude of 900 to 1500 m, with an average altitude of 1200 m. By virtue of its location across the Equator, its climate is generally equatorial with two rainy seasons annually which, however, merge as you move away from the Equator towards the semi-arid North East (MLWE, 2002). The southern part of the country is, therefore, generally well watered with two rainfall peaks occurring in March-May and August-November without any pronounced dry season in between. In the north, there is a marked dry season from November to March. Precipitation varies from 700mm in semi-arid areas of Kotido district in the North East to 1500 mm/yr in the high rainfall areas on the shores of Lake Victoria, around the highlands of Mount Elgon in the east, the Ruwenzori Mountains in the southwest, Masindi in the west and Gulu in the north (National Environment Management Authority (NEMA, 1998). Mean annual rainfall is estimated at 1180 mm. The mean annual temperature over most of the country is between 18 °C and 35 °C, while the corresponding minimum range is 8 °C to 23 °C. Relative humidity is high, ranging between 70 and 100 percent, and the mean monthly evaporation rates are between 125 and 200 mm.

According to the 2002 census, the 2002 population of Uganda was 24.2 million, with a national average population density of 123 inhabitants per km^2. Between 1991 and 2002, the country's population grew at an average annual growth rate of 3.2 percent with an overall increase of 7.5 million over the period. This is said to be the highest inter-censual increase ever registered in Uganda (UBOS, 2006). The total population of the country is estimated at 27.4 million (as of end 2006) of which 14 million are females and 13.4 million males. The rural population comprises of 87 percent (UBOS, 2006). The proportion of adults aged 15-59 infected with HIV is 6.3% while that of children below 5 years is 0.7 percent.

The high population growth is attributed to the high fertility levels and a declining infant and child mortality as observed from the Uganda Demographic and Health Survey (Ministry of Health and ORC Macro, 2000/1). The level of fertility in Uganda has been consistently high over a long period of time (UNFPA, 1995; UNFPA, 2005; UNFPA, 2006). At a total fertility rate (TFR) of about seven children per woman, the estimates in the UNFPA reports are consistent with those obtained from the 1995 and the 2000/01 UDHS. This high fertility level has been attributed to, among other things, the early age at which Ugandan women begin child bearing, low contraceptive prevalence rates and a high-unmet need for family planning among some social groups. However, some cultural, social and economic factors that have maintained a high desire for many children have also been associated with Uganda's high fertility rates (Nuwagaba, 1994).

1.3.2 Socio-economic conditions

In spite of the many years of civil, political and economic crisis experienced in the seventies and early eighties, Uganda's macroeconomic situation made a considerable turn around and the economy experienced impressive growth and underwent a series of structural shifts during the nineties. Real gross domestic product (GDP) grew by an average rate of 6.9 percent per annum since 1991 resulting in an average annual increase in real GDP per capita of 3.7 percent (which is high by any standards) and annual average inflation maintained below ten percent since 1994. As recent evidence from household surveys suggests, there is no doubt that growth is slowly reducing poverty across society. The proportion of people living below the income-based poverty line declined from 56 percent in 1992 to 35 percent in 2000.

While the growth figures may look very good for much of the 1990s, it is important to note that this has been from an extremely low base, and growth rates are not keeping up with the rapid population growth[2]. Furthermore, these figures say nothing about actual food security[3] or the distribution of income and resources within national boundaries. Underlying this impressive picture of economic growth there is a serious regional and rural-urban imbalance. The lowest income groups are concentrated in the rural areas, with the Northern and Eastern regions of the country being poorer than the other regions. Further inequality is seen in the distribution of income between sectors with growth in the agricultural sector (where the majority of the poor are occupied) lagging considerably behind the other sectors (for example, the services and industry sectors) during the past five years (UBOS, 2006; UBOS, 2003b). The poor performance of the agriculture sector raises concerns and indicates that the extent to which growth is broad-based is limited: individuals in half of the 46 percent of households that are active in cultivating food crops are below the poverty line, whereas the overall average of the population below this line is 35 percent (UBOS, 2003b). It is also noteworthy that despite the decline in poverty, the total population below the poverty line dropped only marginally from 9.8 million to 9.2 million over the same period of 1992-2000 (UBOS, 2003b). Using a broader definition of poverty, information obtained during the Uganda Participatory Poverty Assessment Programme (UPPAP) indicates that people in rural communities believe that poverty is increasing (MFPED, 2000)[4].

Poverty in Uganda is not gender-neutral and distribution, impacts and responses between men and women exist. As a social category, women are poorer than men. For example, the ratio of female-earned income to male-earned income for Uganda in 2003 was 0.67 and the GDP per capita figure of US $ 1,169 for women was lower than the national average of US $ 1,457 (UNDP, 2005). The gender-related development index value (GDI) for Uganda ranks 109th (out of 140), with a value of 0.502 (UNDP, 2005). In terms of other development indicators, life expectancy for males is 48.8 years and for females 50.0 years while the proportion of illiterate

---

[2] Uganda's annual population growth rate of 3.4% is higher than the average for Sub- Saharan Africa of 2.1% (UNDP, 2004).

[3] Available agricultural and population statistics data indicates that average per capita food production in 1999-2002 was 35% less than what it was in 1970-1972 (World Bank, 1993; UBOS, 2001). Therefore, the country's food production has not been keeping pace with population growth.

[4] During the poverty assessment studies, poor people defined poverty as lack of access to services, powerlessness, lack of alternatives in the face of adversity, lack of control over ones life in addition to low incomes and lack of material assets.

males is 21 percent as against 41 percent for females (UNFPA, 2005). Although girls and boys enjoy relative parity in terms of primary school enrolment, a number of studies have revealed a marked gender bias against girls' enrolment in secondary schools (Kakuru, 2006; UNIFEM, 2000).

As UNDP and UNAIDS argue, poverty aggravates socio-economic, cultural, and biological factors that predispose girls and women to increased risk of infection. "A lack of control [by poor women] over the circumstances in which intercourse occurs may increase the frequency of intercourse and lower the age at which sexual activity begins. A lack of access to acceptable health services may leave infections and lesions untreated. Malnutrition not only inhibits the production of mucus but also slows the healing process and depresses the immune system" (UNDP, 1992:4; UNAIDS, 2000).

Collins and Rau (2000) describe the relationship between poverty and HIV/AIDS as bi-directional. "On one hand, poverty is seen as a factor in HIV transmission and exacerbating the impact of HIV/AIDS while on the other, they argue that the experience of HIV/AIDS by individuals, households and even communities that are poor can readily lead to an intensification of poverty and even push some non-poor into poverty" (Collins & Rau, 2000:6). As discussed further below, HIV/AIDS continues to exacerbate the socio-economic problems facing the country with consequences of increased inequality and vulnerability among the poor and women.

1.3.3 The HIV/AIDS epidemic in Uganda

Uganda has been affected by the HIV/AIDS epidemic for almost a quarter of a century. The epidemic started on the shores of Lake Victoria in Rakai district (located in the south western part of the country), the initial epicentre of the illness. Thereafter, HIV infection spread quickly, initially in major urban areas and along highways. By 1986, HIV had reached all districts in the country, resulting in what is classified as a generalized epidemic. As in other countries in sub-Saharan Africa, unprotected sex with an infected person is still the most common means of HIV transmission (84%), although mother-to-child transmission has become an important route as evidenced by the number of children with AIDS at the end of 2002 (Uganda AIDS Commission [UAC] 2003). HIV/AIDS is the leading cause of death among individuals aged between 15 and 59 (Garbus & Marseille, 2003). It is estimated that about two million people were infected by HIV throughout the 25 years of the epidemic, of which about one million have died and another one million are living with the infection (UNAIDS, 2006). Results from the 2004 UHSBS indicate that just over 6 percent of Ugandan adults are infected with HIV and the prevalence among women is higher (8%) than among men (5%). Moreover, people living in urban areas have had higher prevalence relative to those in rural areas (Ministry of

Health and ORC Macro, 2006). Nearly 80 percent of those infected with the disease are between 15 and 45 years old, the most economically productive group and often fenders of families (UAC, 2003a). Since the beginning of the epidemic through 2001, two million Ugandan children (approximately 25% of all Ugandan children and 18% of all orphans in Sub-Saharan Africa) have been orphaned by AIDS (UAC 2003a). It is important to note that the severe health impacts of HIV/AIDS occur in a country that is already plagued by other health problems including high rates of malaria, tuberculosis, malnutrition, infant mortality, and maternal mortality.

Table 1.1 presents HIV prevalence by age and sex in 2004/2005. While 6.3 percent of the adults aged 15-59 were infected with HIV, prevalence among men and women was 5.2 percent and 7.3 percent respectively. Prevalence for both men and women increased with age until it reached the peak at 30- 34 (10.3%). For women, the peak prevalence of HIV was in the age group 30-34 (12.1%) while for men it was in the 40-44 age group (9.3%). HIV prevails in more women than men below the age of 49 years. However, for the age group 40-44, the female rate is marginally lower than the male rate. At ages 50-59, the pattern reverses and prevalence is slightly higher among men than women. The higher prevalence of HIV among older men presents great risks for young girls who go out with such men for survival sex.

HIV prevalence levels were higher among urban children compared to rural children. There are virtually no sex differentials in prevalence among children under five years, where prevalence is 0.7 percent for both sexes. However, HIV prevalence

Table 1.1. HIV prevalence by age and sex, 2004/2005.

Age	Percentage HIV positive		
	Male	Female	Both sexes
15-19	0.3	2.6	1.5
20-24	2.4	6.3	4.7
25-29	5.9	8.7	7.6
30-34	8.1	12.1	10.3
35-39	9.2	9.9	9.6
40-44	9.3	8.4	8.8
45-49	6.9	8.2	7.6
50-54	6.9	5.4	6.1
55-59	5.8	4.9	5.4
Total 15-49	5.2	7.3	6.3

Source: Statistical Abstract 2006 (UBOS, 2006).

among children below 18 months is one percent compared to 0.5 percent for those aged 18-59 months. The results also indicate that HIV prevalence is relatively higher among children with dead mothers.

As has been noted by Badcock-Walters (2001), one of the major impacts of AIDS will be a reversal in the gains that had been obtained in gender parity in schooling. This is because girls of high-school age are more vulnerable to the disease than boys of the same age and also because girl children in AIDS-affected households are likely to be the first to leave school to assist with domestic chores and save on school fees.

In her study on gender equality in education in Uganda, Kakuru (2006) found HIV/AIDS-affected households reduce time and investment in education. Girls become more burdened with domestic work and have less access to time and material needs for educational purposes than their male counterparts. Furthermore, the higher prevalence among women is likely to increase their susceptibility to other infections and diseases, thus reducing their capacity to engage in productive activities, leaving transactional sex as the only viable alternative to survival with consequences of increased HIV infections in this group.

A history of civil war and political conflict, economic collapse in the 1970s and early 1980s, migration, geographical positioning and extreme poverty have formed a lethal mixture that both fuelled the spread of HIV and increased the susceptibility of certain social groups to the disease (Haddad & Gillespie, 2001; Bond & Vincent, 2002). The consequences of the HIV epidemic have ranged from macro-economic effects to those directly affecting individuals. The micro- and macro-economic consequences are diverse but centre on the loss of critical human capital, reduced industry and private sector growth, as well as the diversion of government resources to the health sector for the control and prevention of HIV/AIDS with negative effects on economic growth and poverty reduction. It has been estimated that Uganda will have lost 14 percent of its agricultural labour force due to AIDS by 2020 (MFPED, 2004).

At community level, declining productivity in agriculture is eminent, and the death of prime-age adults has imposed unsustainable strains on the extended family structure due the massive burden of orphans. This has led to increasing numbers of households headed by grandmothers and children. At the household level, food insecurity, degraded livelihoods, increased vulnerability and adverse socio-economic impacts have been identified in many instances as causes and consequences of HIV/AIDS (MFPED, 2003).

For the agricultural sector, the overall impact of the epidemic has been deepening rural poverty, reduced ability of rural households to produce sufficient and nutritious foods, weakening of rural institutions to deliver services as well as the undermining of government initiatives and agricultural policies in terms of their effectiveness. It is noteworthy that small-scale and subsistence agriculture in sub-Saharan Africa (Uganda inclusive) is particularly vulnerable to the effects of HIV/AIDS because of its heavy dependence on household labour, which in most cases is that of women. Since the greater majority of the rural poor in the country depend on agriculture for their livelihoods, HIV/AIDS is likely to increase livelihood vulnerability.

Government response to the AIDS epidemic

The Government's response to the epidemic has been positive. Uganda's 'success' in confronting the epidemic owes much to the government's initial frankness in dealing with it on the international stage and identifying it as one of the areas needing foreign assistance (Barnett & Whiteside, 2002). The government also recognises the developmental challenges of the epidemic and has demonstrated great commitment to addressing them. As Coutinho (2003: cited in Garbus & Marseille, 2003)[5] observes, government's sustained commitment to the fight against AIDS is demonstrated by HIV/AIDS being among President Museveni's top three priorities, that is, "peace and security, economic empowerment and HIV/AIDS" since the NRM government came into power. Furthermore, HIV/AIDS control is one of the developmental priorities addressed in the country's Poverty Eradication Action Plan (PEAP) and the National Vision for 2025. In the PEAP, the agricultural sector has been identified as the engine for development. It is no wonder then that the agricultural sector, has been one of the leading sectors in AIDS mainstreaming in Uganda.

Government and public efforts in the early 80s were, however, ad hoc and slow. This resulted in lost opportunities to control the disease before it became generalized. However, in 1986, the government established the AIDS Control Programme (ACP) – the first national AIDS control programme in the world – in the Ministry of Health (MOH) as a step to control the spread of the epidemic. In its first four years, the ACP made significant progress in the areas of epidemiology, surveillance, health and AIDS education, and blood transfusion services. However, because the health sector coordinated all AIDS control interventions, the epidemic was initially addressed as primarily a health problem. As a consequence, there was limited participation by other government ministries and organizations because they felt that HIV/AIDS control was the responsibility of the MOH. At the same time there was a growing recognition on the part of the government that HIV/AIDS impacts transcended the sphere of public health and required the involvement of all spheres of public life in the country, comprising the public, civil society, NGOs, communities, and individuals.

[5] Dr. Alex Coutinho, is the Executive Director of Uganda's AIDS Support Organization.

Consequently, the multi-sectoral approach to HIV prevention and control, including care and support services, was adopted in 1990. There are three distinct elements in the approach. Firstly, it advocates the active involvement in AIDS control activities by all members of society, individually and collectively, with coordination at various administrative and political levels, down to the grassroots level. Secondly, the approach seeks to address not only HIV/AIDS prevention but also the active response to, and management of, all perceived consequences of the epidemic. Thirdly, the approach emphasizes organizational capacity building for sustainable activities among sectors and individual organizations. In line with this, a multi-sectoral coordinating body, the Uganda AIDS Commission (UAC), was created by statute of Parliament in 1992 and placed under the office of the President to coordinate the harmonised implementation of the multi-sectoral approach. Initially, twelve other ACPs were created by the UAC in selected key government ministries to institutionalize the multi-sectoral strategy. To date HIV/AIDS has been mainstreamed in all government ministries. For example, all government ministries have HIV/AIDS work plans, albeit being implemented to varying degrees and with varying impact. In addition to the multi-sectoral approach, the government has adopted a policy of openness about the epidemic as well as established mechanisms to ensure involvement of development partners and political leaders at all levels of governance in efforts to prevent the epidemic and mitigate its impacts.

Uganda government has been working with other partners to scale up preventive therapy and management of sexually transmitted diseases (STIs) and opportunistic infections (OIs), access to voluntary testing and counselling (VTC), prevention of mother to child transmission (PMTCT), anti-retro viral therapy (ART) as well as safe blood services. It also participated with success in advocacy for reduced prices for generic ARVs and establishment of necessary infrastructure for their effective administration. In 1999, the government participated in the first vaccine trial in Africa, and by putting a high-level HIV/AIDS coordination Unit in place, has been able to find donors to finance the implementation of a National Strategic Framework (NSF) for HIV/AIDS Activities as well as other projects. The NSF guides the implementation of all policies on HIV/AIDS and their mainstreaming into sector development policies (MFPED, 2004).

Agricultural sector response

The Ministry of Agriculture, Animal Industries and Fisheries (MAAIF) embarked on measures to mainstream HIV/AIDS in 1995. It established a coordination unit, the appointment of HIV/AIDS focal point officers in all units/agencies under MAAIF and the organization of awareness creation activities for them. This awareness creation for agricultural field staff has been initiated in some districts like Masaka and Kabarole. In addition, MAAIF has put several policies and strategies in place under the Agricultural Sector Response to HIV/AIDS, which it has been implementing since 2001 (and has recently undergone review following the revision of the National Strategic Plan). The policies have included Guidelines for Mainstreaming HIV/AIDS in the Agricultural Sector, the Agricultural Sector HIV/AIDS Policy (yet to be finalized) and the Uganda Strategy for Reducing the Impact of HIV/AIDS on Fishing Communities (UAC, 2006). Although the Plan for Modernization of Agriculture (PMA) was formulated prior to the design of the NSF for HIV/AIDS, most policies and statutes provided for by the PMA have foreseen in a need for mainstream HIV. The National Agricultural Advisory Services (NAADS) has also developed strategies to integrate HIV/AIDS information in its system. The National Agricultural Research Policy, NARP (2003) specifically states that HIV/AIDS must be considered in agricultural technology development and dissemination. The recently published Uganda Food and Nutrition Policy, FNP, (2003) also underscore the mutual linkage between HIV/AIDS and nutrition. In addition, to the policy framework, the ministry has facilitated development of the nutrition and HIV/AIDS booklets (Tanzarn and Bishop-Sambrook, 2003) and a Training Guide on HIV/AIDS for field extension agents. As a supplement to the nutrition handbook, health-boosting recipes for PLWHA have also been developed.

The above notwithstanding, great challenges remain in the effective implementation of these policies and guidelines, as well as in the management of resources mobilized for HIV/AIDS control. With regard to policy, Asingwire and Kyomuhendo's (2003) analysis of existing government policies on HIV/AIDS reveals a number of gaps. These range from the lack of a comprehensive consideration of all relevant aspects of HIV/AIDS control, to clarity in implementation strategy. Similar concerns were raised during the mid term review of the AIDS control programmes (UAC, 2003b). For example, many of the individuals in line ministries that are supposed to be responsible for the implementation of the NSF are not technically competent in HIV/AIDS, neither are they conversant with the contents of the NSF nor their related roles and responsibilities (UAC, 2003b). This incompetence on how to mainstream HIV/AIDS interventions in extension activities was confirmed by agricultural field staff in Masaka and Kabarole districts (personal communication).

Furthermore, while the establishment of focal point officers for AIDS in all sections and departments of the MAAIF is a useful mainstreaming strategy, Topouzis (2003) argues that there has been a tendency to situate these within "soft" units, such as the Family Life Education Unit (FLE) in MAAIF, rather than within "hard" units (such as livestock, crop production, fisheries and agricultural extension). As such, Topouzis notes, the FLE role was perceived as another project rather than efforts to mainstream HIV/AIDS into the Ministry's departments and programme activities.

In August 2005, the Global Fund to Fight AIDS, Tuberculosis and Malaria suspended the disbursal of money from all five of Uganda's Global Fund grants after financial irregularities were discovered within the Ministry of Health's special Programme Management Unit (PMU) (Global Fund Press Release, 24 August 2005). It was later reported in The Lancet (2006) that the management of Uganda's grants was generally poor, and that significant sums of money had been diverted to activities, bodies and items not related to combating AIDS, Tuberculosis or Malaria. Although the suspension was later lifted, Uganda has not received commitment for further funding beyond the initial five-year grant period. It is also important to note that the agricultural sector remains one of the most poorly funded ministries. Therefore, resources and technical capacity to mainstream HIV/AIDS interventions in the agricultural sector remain limited. Besides the limited funding, the lack of commitment among some heads of departments to prioritize HIV mainstreaming in their sector programmes has been noted as an additional constraint (Topouzis, 2003).

Finally, the limited availability of information to enable effective targeting of affected rural populations remains a challenge for agricultural professionals. Available research (including the East African region) to date provides inadequate information as to how HIV/AIDS is affecting the agricultural sector; its structure, cropping systems, relative costs of inputs and factors of production, technological and institutional changes, and supply and demand for agricultural products (Jayne *et al.*, 2005). Jayne *et al.* further argue that until these issues are clarified, policy makers will be inadequately prepared to forecast anticipated changes to the agricultural sector *or put effective policies in place* (own italics). Therefore, the effectiveness of any intervention in the agricultural sector is likely to depend on a clear understanding of the dynamics of the epidemic and how individual farmers and farming households in different localities have been affected and are responding to the epidemic.

Other organizations involved in addressing HIV/AIDS impacts

Civil society organizations: According to the Country AIDS Policy Analysis Project (2003), by September 2003, there were about 2,500 NGOs working on HIV/AIDS in Uganda. Key NGOs at national level included The AIDS Support Organization (TASO), National Community of Women Living with HIV/AIDS (NCWLA), National Guidance and Empowerment Network of People Living with HIV/AIDS in Uganda, AIDS Information Centre, Hospice Uganda, Uganda Network of AIDS Service Organizations, National Forum of PWHA Networks in Uganda, Uganda Youth Anti-AIDS Association, and Uganda Women's Effort to Save Orphans (UWESO). Faith organizations (mainly Catholic, Anglican and Moslem) which are now registered under the National NGO forum have also been instrumental in initiating HIV/AIDS prevention and support efforts. Of these, TASO, NCWLA and National Forum of PWHA Networks in Uganda had activities in the communities studied. In addition, African Youth Alliance for HIV/AIDS awareness and prevention, UNDP and UNICEF in Kabarole and MAHCOP and World Vision in Masaka, have been particularly active in HIV/AIDS-related efforts.

Major activities have included community awareness raising of AIDS, provision of VTC services, orphan support and home based care (HBC), as well as psychological support. In 2003, civil society provided about 80 percent of VCT and 90 percent of post-test counselling and care, almost all support and care to orphans and vulnerable children, as well as home based care services, with financing largely from external donors (Garbus & Marseille, 2003). In Masaka, MAHCOP and World Vision have provided critical support to AIDS orphans and other vulnerable children and PLWHA. However, inadequate financial, human, and institutional capacity continue to constrain implementation and scaling up of civil society activities, the result being concentration of activities in urban and peri-urban areas, with the greater majority needing these services in the rural areas being left out.

Specific activities targeting the agricultural sector have included: provision of agricultural extension services and training, provision of improved seeds (mainly maize, beans and vegetable) and other planting materials, provision of livestock (local and improved breeds of goats, pigs and heifers), food aid and to a limited extent, financial support in form of grants and credit.

Research organizations: Various organizations, both academic and research, have been involved in HIV/AIDS research activities. These include the Joint Clinical Research Centre, Uganda Cares, Uganda Virus Research Institute, the Academic Alliance for AIDS Care and Prevention in Africa and Makerere University. Others are the Uganda Medical Research Council Programme on AIDS, Mulago, Nsambya, and Mengo hospitals, Medical Research Centre (MRC) and Mildmay Palliative Care Centre. Most of these organizations collaborate with and get their funding from international partners. Apart from research they are also involved in provision of VTC, PMTCT, ART, palliative as well as HBC services. Among these, Uganda Cares and the MRC have activities in Masaka district. For Kabarole, Buhanga, Virika and Kabarole referral hospitals and partners are the main research institutions.

Most of the research conducted is in the medical field with very little on agriculture (Makerere University). While it is imperative that research in agriculture be increased, the non-research activities of these organizations have improved the health of HIV/AIDS-affected individuals and to some degree increased their ability to participate in productive activities.

Challenges to mitigation of HIV/AIDS impacts in Uganda

The main challenge facing HIV/AIDS mitigation measures are financial resources. Uganda is one of the poorest countries with an economy heavily dependent on external donor funding. The servicing of the civil war in the northern part of the country and rampant corruption also continues to divert resources from key service sectors like agriculture and health. Therefore, despite the strong political will and support, the resources allocated to HIV/AIDS prevention and control remain limited. As Garbus and Maiseille (2003) pointed out, the country faces challenges of mobilizing resources, expanding and sustaining prevention interventions, providing ART to all who need it, protecting the youth, maintaining prevalence declines while at the same time meeting donor/lender conditions.

Uganda's HIV/AID challenges have been associated with difficulties in monitoring of trends in areas of civil conflict, HIV/AIDS knowledge gaps among the communities, scaling up services in rural areas and reaching the underserved communities, and inadequate STI services, sexual and reproductive education for the youth. The challenges have also been associated with the increasing care and support burden, serving mobile populations and people in conflict areas, HIV/AIDS-related stigma and discrimination, local level coordination, and sustainability of interventions (Garbus & Maiseille, 2003).

1.3.4 The policy context

The State's vision and strategies for the reduction of poverty are articulated in the Poverty Eradication Action Plan (PEAP). Uganda was the first country to present a full Poverty Reduction Strategy Paper (PRSP) to the International Monetary Fund (IMF) and the World Bank (WB) in support of Uganda's successful application for debt relief under the highly indebted poor countries (HIPC) Initiative in April 1998 and under the enhanced HIPC in May 2000. Some of this money has been used in the prevention and control of HIV/AIDS and malaria.

The PEAP provides a comprehensive development framework for Uganda and guides the formulation of Uganda's government policies. It emphasizes a multi-sectoral approach in cognizance of the complex and multi-dimensional nature of poverty and the links between influencing factors. The goals of the PEAP are: fast and sustainable economic growth and structural transformation; good governance and security; increased ability of the poor to raise their incomes as well as increased quality of life for the poor. Under the PEAP, Government efforts are geared towards development in the rural areas where the majority of the country's poor are found. The agricultural sector has been identified as the engine for development. It is believed that stimulating agricultural growth and diversifying production among other things are essential for poverty reduction. The Plan for Modernisation of

Agriculture (PMA)[6], approved by the Cabinet in October 2000 is seen as providing opportunities to improve the welfare and quality of life of poor subsistence farmers through increased agricultural production and productivity, gainful employment, as well as sustainable use and management of natural resources. A key component of the PMA is the National Agricultural Advisory Services (NAADS) whose main objectives are to increase the availability of appropriate advice and information to all the farmer types in an equitable and cost effective manner as well as ensure availability of sufficient appropriate technologies to meet identified farmer needs.

1.3.5 The role of the agricultural sector

Uganda's economy is relatively reliant on the agricultural sector. Thus the role of the sector in national development and the livelihoods of the majority of the population cannot be over-emphasized. In spite of steady improvements in the growth of the services and industry sectors and a decline of twelve percent[7] points of agriculture's contribution to GDP just over the past decade, a large majority of people (69%) still depends on agriculture as the main source of income (UBOS, 2003a). The sector indirectly serves as a source of employment and income through activities such as agricultural processing, domestic trade and transportation, as well as being an important provider of raw materials to the manufacturing sector, particularly the agriculture-based industries. Apart from maintaining its share as the main sectoral employer within the economy, agriculture is also the main foreign exchange earner, with agricultural exports constituting over 50 percent of total exports (Abdalla & Egesa, 2005). The agricultural contribution to the GDP comes almost exclusively from about 3 million smallholder subsistence farmers, 80 percent of whom have less than two hectares of land (NEMA 2001; World Bank 1993). The hand hoe is the predominant technology for cultivation. Farming is mainly subsistence, substantial commercial agricultural farming being limited to tea and sugar production (the major large estate crops), and, more recently, horticultural flower farming. The agricultural sector is mainly dominated by food production, contributing 71 percent of agricultural GDP, while livestock products account for 17 percent, export crop five percent, fisheries[8] four percent and forestry three percent (MAAIF & MPFED, 2000). Only one third of the food crops grown is marketed compared to two thirds of livestock produced (MAAIF & MPFED, 2000). During the period 1992/93 to 2001/02 all sub-sectors of the agricultural sector in Uganda experienced growth rates of 3.5 percent and higher with the exception of the cash crop sub-sector, which declined in 1997/98 largely due to the adverse effects of the El Nino weather conditions

[6] The PMA and UFNP have been formulated within the context of the overall national development policy objective of eradicating poverty as spelt out in the Poverty Eradication Action Plan (PEAP). The PEAP formulated in 1997 and revised in 2000 and 2005 has the overall aim of reducing absolute poverty to 10 percent by 2017 (MAAIF & MFPED, 2000).

[7] Agriculture accounted for 38.7% of GDP in 2002/3, as compared to 51.1% in 1991/92.

[8] In Uganda, fishing is treated as an agricultural activity.

(Abdalla & Egesa, 2005). "Although the food crops sub-sector still dominates, the cash crop sub-sector including non-traditional[9] export crops is registering considerable growth due to the liberalization of agricultural produce marketing, and diversification of non-traditional agricultural export (NTAEs) crops" (NEMA,1998: xx). A key component of the PMA is the National Agricultural Advisory Services (NAADS) which represents Government of Uganda's new approach to the delivery of agricultural extension services.

The country has a diversity of agro-ecological zones allowing the production of a wide range of crops (e.g. banana, cereals, root crops, and pulses). Parsons (in NEMA, 1998) classified Uganda into five major farming system zones based on the following criteria: natural resource potential for agriculture, main agricultural activities, dominant crops and animal husbandry practices, social history and the presence of tsetse flies. The zones are: northern and eastern (cereal cotton, cattle; intensive banana, coffee); western (banana, coffee, cattle); West Nile (cereal, cassava, tobacco) and Afro-montane systems. This classification is not exhaustive and to some extent, was determined by colonial arrangements of supply zones for the various cash crops rather than purely agronomic potential (NEMA 1998:46). It is important to note that these farming systems are dynamic and because of a variety of factors have been changing. Some key factors that have been at play include increasing population density, soil fertility decline, pest infestation, and emergence of new producing areas and markets (NEMA, 1998). Barnett and Blaikie (1992) in their study on Uganda combine household level impact studies based on extensive fieldwork using a farming system classification. In mapping HIV prevalence, and adaptations to labour loss and other characteristics, they identified nine (out of 50) farming systems to be vulnerable to the HIV/AIDS pandemic in Uganda. The northern Mubende and western Luwero Districts, the northern Hoima District, Kabarole District, Kasese District, Southern Iganga District and Tororo District were classified as under serious threat. Southwestern Mubende District, northwestern Masaka District, and southern Hoima District were said to be under moderate threat. Although currently most of Uganda's farming systems are less vulnerable to the HIV-epidemic (Topouzis, 2000), current trends of increasing environmental degradation due to agricultural related activities could lead to increased vulnerability of affected farming systems (NEMA, 1998; 2001).

In the 1960s, the agricultural sector enjoyed positive growth rates averaging 10 percent per annum. During the 1970s and early 1980s, however, the sector experienced negative growth rates due to a series of policy and structural constraints (MAAIF and MFPED, 2000). This may be attributed largely to civil strife, armed conflicts,

[9] Uganda's agricultural exports are classified as traditional and non-traditional with the traditional exports comprising coffee, cotton, tobacco, and tea and the non-traditional agricultural exports (NTAEs) comprising items such as fish, hides and skins, simsim, maize, beans, flowers, among others.

disintegration of public infrastructure and services, economic mismanagement, the collapse of law and order, as well as foreign exchange scarcity for agricultural inputs (World Bank, 1993; MAAIF & MFPED, 2000). In addition, there were institutional constraints such as inefficient and ineffective government research and extension services and segmented, inefficient and discriminatory markets for capital, labour, land and agricultural inputs (MAAIF & MFPED, 2000). However, with the re-establishment of peace and security, combined with the Government's economic recovery programme introduced in 1987 and the Structural Adjustment Policies of the early 1990s, most of the above constraints have been removed. In spite of this, the agricultural sector still faces fundamental constraints to its continued growth. Some of the major ones are associated with poor marketing information and infrastructure, technology generation and dissemination constraints, financial and human resource constraints, environmental degradation, and the effects of HIV infection and AIDS.

One of the biggest challenges of the agricultural sector is ensuring sustainable food security and the growth of the agricultural sector in the face of the HIV/AIDS epidemic. This is particularly so given that the largest group of poor households in Uganda has consistently been those in agriculture, which are most vulnerable to the impacts of the epidemic (MFPED, 2004). Although Uganda is generally regarded as self-sufficient in food production and achieving self-sufficiency in food production has for long been one of the major food security strategies of the government, the situation is changing and different parts of the country are increasingly experiencing food shortages periodically. HIV/AIDS has been said to heighten vulnerability to food insecurity while, reciprocally, food insecurity heightens susceptibility to HIV exposure and infection (Gillespie & Kadiyala, 2005), with the cycle being particularly more devastating for women than men. Women, widows and female-headed households, male youths, households with large families, and people depending on vulnerable sources of income, such as fisher folk, nomads and small-scale farmers growing only one low-value crop, form the most vulnerable social groups in Uganda (MAAIF, 2002). HIV/AIDS-induced vulnerability is of particular importance to the understanding of intra-household dynamics with regard to labour availability and resource use and consequently the capacity of households to generate sustainable livelihoods in a context of limited resources, environmental shocks and rural poverty. For those who have tried to understand rural poverty in Africa, many phenomena seem to be related in one way or another. However, some causes and effects are more important than others. The challenge for this study is to understand why HIV/AIDS is unique and important by analyzing the ways in which HIV and AIDS reconfigures the vulnerability of agriculture-based livelihoods.

1.4 Rationale for selection of banana farming area

In 1993, FAO ranked banana as one of the four most important food crops in the world (FAO, 1993). Banana is the major staple food crop in large parts of Uganda (see Table 1.2). In addition, banana-farming systems comprise almost half of all farming systems in the country and banana offers high potential as a food security crop because harvesting is possible throughout the year (Masanza, 2003).

In the East African Highlands, banana is traditionally a main staple (Tibaijuka, 1983) as well as a cash crop (Price, 1995). Similarly, in Uganda, the crop is a staple food of Bantu ethnic groups (Masanza, 2003) and the surplus is locally traded as a regular source of income in the region (Davies, 1995). The highland cultivars found in East Africa account for 75% of production in Africa and constitute 20 percent of the world's banana production (INIBAP, 1989).

Table 1.2. Area planted and production for main food crops in Uganda, 2001-2006.

	Plantain	Pulses		Cereals			Root crops		
	Banana	Beans	G.nuts	Millet	Maize	Sorghum	Sweet potato	Irish potato	Cassava
Area Planted (x 1000 ha)									
2001	1,622	731	208	389	652	282	572	73	390
2002	1,648	765	211	396	676	285	589	78	398
2003	1,661	780	214	400	710	290	595	80	405
2004	1,670	812	221	412	750	285	602	83	407
2005 (Est.)	1,675	828	225	420	780	294	590	86	387
2006(Proj.)	1,677	849	231	429	819	308	584	90	379
Production (x 1000 MT)									
2001	9,732	511	15	584	1,174	423	2,515	508	5,265
2002	9,888	535	16	590	1,217	427	2,592	546	5,373
2003	9,700	525	14	640	1,300	421	2,610	557	5,450
2004	9,686	455	15	659	1,080	399	2,650	573	5,500
2005 (Est.)	9,045	597	159	672	1,170	449	2,478	585	5,031
2006 (Proj.)	9,391	594	185	692	1,285	493	2,511	612	4,927

Source: Ministry of Agriculture, Animal Industry and Fisheries (MAAIF) and Uganda Bureau of Statistics. (Statistical Abstract, 2006). Note: figures for 2005 are estimates while those of 2006 are projections.

Despite the importance of the crop, production of especially the predominant *Musa AAA-EA* has declined due to a complex of socio-economic and technical problems. Among the socio-economic production constraints are land shortage, poor farming methods, limited availability of production inputs, and poor marketing facilities, while the technical constraints include pests and diseases, soil nutrient deficiencies and lack of pest and disease tolerant varieties (Masanza, 2003). All these factors become important in a context of high HIV prevalence.

Further interest arose from the fact that the rural banana economy - especially banana marketing - is associated with mobility related HIV/AIDS risk factors. For example, the Masaka cohort study found that rural populations are very mobile, and this is strongly and positively correlated with both the prevalence and risk of HIV (Garbus & Marseille, 2003). The highway from Busia, a border town at the Kenya-Uganda border, through Kampala and to the Western part of the country goes through many banana-growing areas. Because of the big urban demand, traders travel from urban areas to rural areas to buy and convey bananas and other agricultural products to the urban centres. Some rich banana farmers in the rural areas are involved in the rural-urban banana trade. Some have their own trucks while others hire them.

These farmers and urban traders buy bananas from individual farmers or groups that market together. The high tropical temperatures and the lack of refrigerated trucks makes marketing problematic. The traders may require about a day to fill a ten-ton-size truck since the bananas are usually collected in smaller quantities from different farms. Even local traders buying from farmers and bulking the bananas at certain markets may require one or two days to get enough to fill a big truck depending on the season. With the high tropical temperatures, traders have to transport the bananas to the market before they ripen. Once the bananas ripen in transit they spoil and their value decreases drastically. This is particularly so for the cooking type that is mainly marketed green. Therefore, traders usually prefer to travel when the temperatures are cooler, that is, in the late evenings or at night with the objective of arriving in the urban centres very early in the morning to ensure that the bananas do not ripen. However, there are government restrictions on heavy trucks and buses moving at night. This means that most of the traders travel during the early part of the night and have to spend part of the night at one of the trading centres along the highway. This lifestyle has been found to lead to high risk of exposure to HIV/AIDS, and they are foci of HIV transmission. Additionally, local markets in the rural areas where farmers take their bananas and other produce for sale have also been associated with high sexual activity.

1.5 Thesis outline

The remaining part of this thesis is organized as follows. Chapter 2 discusses the livelihood approach (the main analytical tool used in the study), the concepts of livelihood and household, and the conceptual framework. It ends with the presentation of the research questions that I seek to answer in this thesis. Chapter 3 describes the research strategy and methodological considerations, followed by the research design and methods used in data collection. Chapter 4 describes the key demographic characteristics of the surveyed households and farms and the main source of livelihood in the study area. Chapter 5 discusses a number of case studies that illustrate the different strategies people employ in pursuance of their livelihoods, and, for those who are infected with HIV, the ways in which they respond to the effects of the epidemic. In Chapter 6, cluster analysis is used to identify and characterize households along livelihood strategies pursued. In addition to a description of the identified livelihood strategy options, a discussion of the key determinants of livelihood strategies in the two districts is presented. Chapter 7 discusses the effects of HIV/AIDS at household level. It presents an analysis of the ways in which HIV/AIDS increases vulnerability, and which households or groups are most affected. In Chapter 8, I first present the responses to and strategies used by individuals in different households in dealing with the effects of the epidemic. This is then followed by a brief overview on the effects of HIV/AIDS at community level, existing institutional and community initiatives for the prevention and control of HIV/AIDS-related effects and an analysis of their effectiveness. Chapter 9 discusses the key findings and conclusions of the study and implications for agricultural policies and programmes.

Chapter 2

Rural livelihoods: concepts and research framework

This chapter presents and discusses the theoretical framework used in the research. First, the concept of livelihood is discussed and subsequently that of the household, because livelihoods are anchored to households. In discussing the household as a unit of analysis, the usefulness of headship as an analytical category in this study is also presented. Then the livelihood framework is presented and each of its different elements - resources, mediating factors and processes, strategies, outcomes and the vulnerability context - are in turn discussed. In the review, I address some of the limitations of the concept and, where relevant, incorporate other theoretical elements to improve the analytical potential of the livelihood approach.

Given the high prevalence of HIV/AIDS in the study area, HIV/AIDS is looked at as being an important element of the internal vulnerability to the farming households, in addition to being part of the external vulnerability context. In applying the concept, food security is used as one of the key livelihood outcome indicators and the relevance of social differentiation and gender in shaping livelihoods is taken into account as well. In addition, the linkages between HIV/AIDS, gender, and food and livelihood security are presented. I end with a discussion of the conceptual framework elaborating on how the various concepts are interrelated, and the research questions that this thesis intends to answer.

2.1 The concept of livelihood

The concept of "livelihood", though relatively new, has been extensively discussed among academicians and development practitioners. According to Frankenberger and McCaston (1998), the concept has developed through the evolution of concepts and issues related to household food and nutritional security. However, the initial ideas behind the concept owe much to the work of Robert Chambers. A livelihood is described as comprising of the capabilities, assets and activities required for a means of living (Chambers & Conway, 1992) as well as the interaction between assets and transforming processes and structures in the context that individuals find themselves in (Carney, 1998). Building on the work of Chambers and others from the Institute of Development studies of the University of Sussex, Scoones (1998) came up with a definition of livelihood that tied it more explicitly to the notion of sustainability. Following a review of prevailing definitions of the concept, Ellis proposed the following definition of livelihood: "A livelihood comprises the assets (natural, physical, human, financial and social capital), the activities, and the access to these (mediated by institutions and social relations) that together determine the living gained by the individual or household" (Ellis, 2000:10).

From these and other definitions there is a consensus that livelihood is about the ways and means of "making a living" and that, essentially, livelihoods revolve around resources, institutions that influence access to resources, activities, and the way the resources are used.

The concept, however, also contains a process dimension that is not always made explicit in livelihood definitions. As Niehof (2004) argues, many livelihood definitions do not distinguish between the dimensions of process, activities, assets and resources, and outcomes. She therefore proposes the need to distinguish between the concepts of livelihood (the material means whereby one lives) from that of livelihood generation (the processes determined by the various activities that people undertake to provide for their needs) and livelihood outcomes. Thus, the concept of livelihood entails what people have or can claim, what they can do given that, the decisions and choices (with regard to the management and use of the resources and assets) they make given existing opportunities or constraints, and what they achieve in the process. Such a holistic approach to livelihood needs to go beyond looking at material well-being and also should include non-material aspects of well-being (de Haan & Zoomers, 2005; Long, 1997). As Wallman (1984) observes, a livelihood is equally a matter of the ownership and circulation of information, the management of social relationships, the affirmation of personal significance and group identity, and the tasks associated with meeting these obligations are as crucial to livelihoods as bread and shelter.

2.2 Household

The household is often used as the unit of analysis in livelihood research. Niehof (2004) refers to it as the locus of livelihood generation. Households are one of the basic units of human social organization and largely represent the arena of everyday life for a vast majority of the world's people (Clay & Schwartzweller, 1991). Narayan *et al.* (1999) have also described the household as the primary place where individuals confront and reproduce societal norms, values, power and privileges. Therefore, the day-to-day organization and management of activities within households is important for the social reproduction of any given society.

Despite their universal occurrence, it is noteworthy that households vary in form and function (Netting *et al.*, 1984), as well as over time and across cultural and social geography (Guyer & Peters, 1987). The African farm household has been described as "a diversified and multi-faceted economic entity that pursues numerous agricultural and non-agricultural enterprises. It operates within elaborate networks of credit, insurance, and contracts" (Doss, 1999:27). African farm households mesh strongly with wider networks of family and kin, making boundaries very fluid. Indeed, various studies have shown that household boundaries vary globally in relation to social and economic differences (Rudie, 1995).

The above notwithstanding, the concept of "household" is problematic and has received much criticism. The range of cross-cultural diversity of household forms, has led some anthropologists to challenge the validity of the "household" concept. Households are seen as shifting and flexible structures. Their boundaries are difficult to discern, having a multiplicity of family and household composition and social relations based on marriage and kinship, and they present a variety of conjugal and residential arrangements (Evans, 1991). Anthropologists have also questioned the conflation of families and households, arguing that while most households may be family based, households may also possess non-family members through adoption, or hiring domestic servants (cf. Pennartz & Niehof, 1999). Anthropologists further point to the danger of neglecting intra-household organization. Therefore, the notion that familial ties necessarily imply purely voluntary and altruistic interactions is rejected, pointing to the contractual nature of some household relations (Roberts, 1989).

Feminists have also criticized the economic household model (Kabeer, 1991). Many have argued for the need to problematize "the household" and cease treating it as a black box for which some combined utility function is assumed under the altruistic leadership of the household head. In addition, they argue that households are not homogeneous entities and there is need to take into account gender inequalities that exist, but are usually glossed over.

Furthermore, livelihoods and well-being are increasingly conceptualized as partly the outcome of negotiations and bargaining between individuals with unequal power within households; households are sites of conflicts as well as cooperation (Moser, 1993; Sen, 1990). Therefore keeping the lid on the black box has the danger of neglecting gender-based and/or age-related intra-household inequalities. In addition, attention has been drawn to the importance of external networks of relationships in intra-household decision-making and the general well-being of households and their members. As Guyer and Peters (1987) argue, the household is in fact both an outcome and channel of broader social processes.

Defining household membership in a context of much (labour) migration is another issue. As Netting and Wilk (1984) argue, "household" denotes common residence and economic cooperation for production, consumption and reproduction, but due to social transformations, household members now may also include those physically absent. Consequently, important members of households could be those who are not in residence but supply such households with necessary cash remittances and other key household necessities and services. This was found to be the case in the study area, where some of the men in male-headed households were engaged in various trades that required them to be away from their homes. They would occasionally either send or take home cash and other goods. Others had business premises in trading centers where they would live during the week and then go home at the weekends or whenever necessary to address household needs and obtain food. While these people are not always physically present as members of their households, they play an important role in decision making and provisioning for their household and the resident members looked up to them for support.

In spite of the validity of the critique of "the household", the empirical significance of household relationships in the daily management of resources, and as the routine context of people's lives suggests that the concept has a certain "facticity, despite its shifting guises" (Kabeer, 1994:14), which provides a rationale for retaining it. Moreover, as Cheal (1989) points out, a moral dimension to the household economy obliges household members to share resources and take care of dependants. On one hand. Pennartz and Niehof (1999:183) argue that "to members of a given household, the moral contents of domestic arrangements and their application in practice is contestable". But, on the other hand, they agree that the aspect of morality in kinship relationships and the domestic unit, particularly in relation to care provision and poverty, is crucial. They refer to the household as a context of "condensed morality" (Pennartz and Niehof (1999:206). This makes the concept particularly relevant in a situation of HIV/AIDS because of the high care-related demands of the epidemic.

In all societies, most people live in households of one kind or another. Evidence shows that this cohabitation involves, to some degree, a common understanding between the household members on the roles and responsibilities of different individuals as well as the rules guiding use and management of resources. This does not imply that resources are always pooled or that benefits and power are equally shared. Indeed, within the household a variety of interests, conflicts and alliances are subsumed. Moreover, gender and other intra-household differentiation factors influence decision-making, power, access and use of resources, to the disadvantage of some members. However, the key point here is that there is still a strong case for taking the household rather than the individual as a unit of analysis.

Nonetheless, households have a diversity of forms and comprise members that are differently related, and have varying agency and entitlements. This implies that any analysis at the household level needs to take into account the different needs, interests and individual strategies of its members. Furthermore, while seen as important production units, households are also social units and therefore need to be studied and understood in the context of underlying cultural norms and values (see Rudie, 1995).

In addition, the household as a unit provides a practical level for the operationalization of policy and development interventions. Moreover, in the context of the study areas, the household provides a production unit with which the inheritance of land and its utilization (a key resource in this study) are closely associated.

The following is the operational definition of the household as used in this study.

> *A household refers to a person or group of persons, family-based, who live together and/or eat together and/or jointly cultivate a common piece of land and/or pool resources from multiple sources and/or are answerable to the same head and/or depend on each other, all done with the overall objective of securing livelihood. This includes members of the household that may not be physically present sometimes, particularly the household head, but who are found to play a significant role in decision making, as well as supply the bulk of the cash and other household necessities. Members that have permanently migrated are not included but any regular income or support that they provide to the household is included as part of the household's resources.*

It is noteworthy that the livelihood framework is limited with regard to analysis of internal dynamics of households such as gender and power relations, gender inequalities and differential access to resources by different household members. Livelihood analysis is therefore combined with gender analysis during collection of qualitative data in order to capture intra-household dynamics.

One way of gauging gender differences in access to livelihood resources and options is to compare the conditions of female- and male-headed households. However, the usefulness of the category of "headship" and whether female-headed households are necessarily associated with poverty and vulnerability, has raised both conceptual and methodological concerns. First, conceptual concerns have been raised due to the fact that "female" is not a homogenous category. Second, aspects of female headship such as greater self-esteem on the part of women, more freedom to choose an occasional partner and a reduction in or elimination of physical and emotional abuse, among others, put female headship in a more positive light. The different studies[10] conducted over the last decade have yielded inconsistent conclusions. Nonetheless, as Dolan (2002:3) argues, "headship nevertheless remains a useful tool for understanding how gender identity might condition the capabilities, entitlements and subsequent opportunities of households. Households headed by women, for example, are typically endowed with varying amounts and types of resources and capabilities that equip them to respond to change and opportunities differently. As

---

[10] Examples of studies done include: Appelton, 1996; Chant, 1997; Fuwa, 2000; Quisumbing, Haddad & Peña, 2001.

a result, headship can provide a useful analytical device to identify how households adapt in the face of vulnerability." In my quantitative analysis, survey households were categorized into three groups: male-headed households, single-female-headed households and widow-headed households. The category of single-male-headed was not used because the households in this category were too few.

2.3 Components of the livelihood framework

Below in Figure 2.1 is the DFID's sustainable livelihood framework modified to include the linkages with HIV/AIDS, given the epidemic's high prevalence levels in the study area. The main elements of this livelihood framework include:

- Livelihood resources or assets: what people have or are entitled to have or can access.
- The external environment: That constitutes of policies, institutions and processes (PIPs) and the vulnerability context, within which livelihood generation takes place.

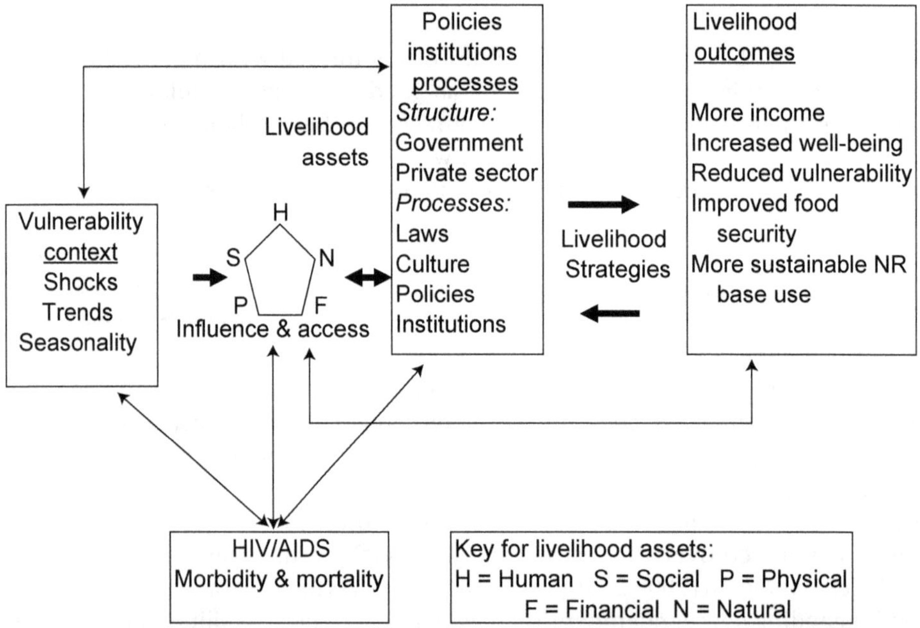

Figure 2.1. The traditional sustainable livelihood framework (adopted with modifications from DFID guidance sheets) (source: www.livelihoods.org/info/guidance_sheets_rtfs/Sect2.rtf, downloaded, June 17, 2007). The arrows within the framework are used to denote a variety of different types of relationships, all of which are highly dynamic. Although all arrows imply a certain level of influence, none of the arrows imply direct causality.)

- Livelihood strategies: the activities, decisions and choices people make to generate the means of household survival and long-term wellbeing.
- Livelihood outcomes or goals: the nature and quality of living resulting from the livelihood strategies pursued.

The livelihood framework attempts to explain in a holistic manner the way poor people generate a living. The assumption is that people are endowed with and/or have access to a range of livelihood resources that they draw upon to undertake a variety of activities in the process of livelihood generation. In this process, people strive to meet a range of livelihood outcomes (consumption and economic, material and non-material) while at the same time responding to arising opportunities as well as unforeseen challenges and events. The decisions that guide the activities undertaken or strategies used are partly driven by people's own preferences and priorities. They are also influenced by the vulnerability context (shocks, trends, seasonality) in which the people live; this context influences access to resources. In a similar manner, the structures, institutions and processes (PIPs) that are part of the external environment also influence the type of choices individuals make to generate a livelihood (cf. Farrington *et al.*, 1999).

Apart from the vulnerability context, on which people have no influence, all other arrows that denote relationships are bi-directional. So while the PIPs play a role in influencing people's access to resources, services and, consequently, their strategies, people sometimes consciously engage in activities that transform the social structures and processes that shape their lives. In the same vein, the type of livelihood outcomes realized will influence future livelihood strategies and the household resource base, be it through re-investment to create new resources or dis-saving to respond to crises (cf. Bebbigton, 1999). It is important to note that while in the framework, only positive livelihood outcomes are presented; not all strategies result in positive outcomes. Prevailing environmental conditions or household dynamics may result in outcomes that fall short of what was desired.

In the DFID sustainable livelihood framework, I have introduced HIV/AIDS and the levels at which its effects interact with the other elements of the framework. The high HIV prevalence levels in Masaka and Kabarole make HIV/AIDS part of the vulnerability context. However, at the household level, HIV/AIDS-related morbidity and mortality also increases the internal vulnerability of affected households. In the next part of this section, each element of the framework is discussed.

2.3.1 Assets and resources

In most livelihood literature, the term "asset" is used interchangeably with capital and resource. Largely, livelihood analysis focuses on the asset status of households basing on the belief that people require a range of assets to achieve desirable livelihood outcomes. Households and individuals are considered to possess assets which they seek to nurture and combine in ways that will ensure survival. A clear understanding of the configuration of the assets available to people, therefore, is an important step in livelihood analysis, in that it is an indicator of people's capacity to generate a viable living – both now and in the future – (see Corbett, 1988) as well as their potential resilience to shocks and stresses in the environment. Assets are the inputs to the livelihood system. They form the basic building blocks upon which individuals are able to undertake production, engage in labour markets and participate in reciprocal exchanges with other individuals (Ellis, 2000). Assets may be described as tangible or intangible, material or non-material stocks of value or claims that can be mobilized and utilized directly, or indirectly, to generate a livelihood (Chambers & Conway, 1992; Ellis, 2000; Swift, 1989). They include such things as land, crops, seed, labour, knowledge, experience, skills, cattle, money, jewelry, food stocks, social relationships, and so on. According to Niehof and Price (2001), the terms "asset" and "resource" are contextualized and situational terms, and assets can be converted into resources when the assets lose their static nature of being kept without use. For example, when kept for its value, livestock is an asset. However, when livestock is used in production activities, say plowing, or it is sold and the money used to hire extra agricultural labour, it becomes a resource. Therefore, assets may be seen as a form of saving or insurance that may be mobilized whenever the need arises to be sold or converted directly for consumption. Given the pivotal role of assets in livelihood generation, the way individuals and households balance their asset or resource acquisition and use is likely to have implications for livelihood and long-term security.

While there are different asset classifications, the most common is where assets are classified into five capitals: human, natural, physical, financial, and social (see Carney, 1999; Scoones, 1998), and sometimes represented as a pentagon as presented in DFID's Sustainable Livelihood Framework. (cf. Kollmair & Gamper, 2002, for the definition of the five "capitals"). It is important to point out that although assets are usually classified according to these five categories (and presented in a pentagon), representing individual or household assets and resources in this form may be misleading.

First and foremost, these categories are not mutually exclusive; some assets may belong to more than one category. One could argue, for example, that an element like livestock seen as financial capital by Kollmair (2002) could be categorized under physical capital. While land as a productive resource, for instance, is categorized under natural capital, it is equally a cultural and political resource. Another problem associated with the above categorization is that there are assets that do not fit in any of the five categories. Bebbington (1999), for example, has included "cultural capital" as a sixth capital. While in the livelihood framework, culture may be subsumed under social capital, the concept of social capital does not fully take into consideration all aspects of culture. For example, Gudeman (1986) argues that the process of livelihood construction must be regarded as culturally modeled implying that culture plays an important role in shaping people's choices, and livelihood options. Therefore, submerging culture under social capital only looks at culture as a resource and fails to take into consideration other aspects of culture (religion, norms, stigma, status) that define the cultural context and have structural effects (Brons *et al.*, 2007; Müller, unpublished). Yet as Müller further argues, culture is a key feature in the context of an epidemic such as HIV/AIDS that is mainly spread by sexual transmission (particularly in Sub-Saharan Africa) in determining individual and group behaviour. Therefore, flexibility in the definition of livelihood assets, but while at the same time capturing the full meaning of these assets is essential in analysis.

Time is another variable that does not fit in any of the five "capital" categories. As Engberg (1990:17) notes: "It cannot be accumulated or increased but the way it is used can be altered and organized". Assets are always in a state of constant change through use and ageing. For example, taking human "capital", education levels, skills and experience definitely change with time. While one's knowledge and experience may increase with age, yet the amount of labour output decreases. Another example is social capital, which with time may also grow or diminish. In a situation of HIV/AIDS, a household's access to social capital may depend on the social networks created by the household head. In the event of death, such social capital may diminish or be completely inaccessible. Time is therefore an important element in understanding livelihoods given the temporal dimension of household life cycle, livelihood strategies, decision making, asset creation and resource use. For example, the size and composition of households reflect phase in the life course (Ali, 2005; Pennartz & Niehof, 1999), which in turn determines their needs, labour potential, and to a great extent, their asset base and livelihood strategies.

Another type of time is seasonal time, which influences agricultural activities. There will be times of peak labour activity when availability of household labour is most crucial and this will have a bearing on the way labour and other assets are allocated across different activities. Time use is also gendered. The gender division of labour also means that different individuals in the household will have different amounts of time at their disposal, which too may have implications regarding the extent of involvement in different productive activities. Moreover, cultural norms and values as well as gender notions change with time. Time, is an integral part of livelihood generation and the economic, social, political and historical context for livelihood strategies needs to be given a temporal perspective (Ali, 2005). Having another dimension of the pentagon to cater for the time element may therefore improve asset analysis.

Secondly, the way the five "capitals" are presented gives an impression that assets are one-dimensional. This leads to a failure to capture other dimensions associated with an asset such as its status or quality, its location, or its substitutability. For example, two households may have the same acreage of landholding. But if one household is on marginal land and the other household is on fertile land, the second household will be better endowed with natural capital. Furthermore, in sub-Saharan Africa, a household may own small pieces of land in different locations. One piece of land is likely to be more useable and have higher value (if it were to be used as collateral). In such circumstances, it may be misleading to take the total land acreage of such a household if, for example, only half of the land is accessible and can be used for production or if the household has no capacity to productively utilize all the land they own. Additionally, given the patrilineal land inheritance system in Uganda, widows may have user rights over their late spouse's land but cannot make decisions on its sale. While, for example, land, in case of a severe stressful event, can be sold by a male-headed household, this may not be the case for widow-headed households.

Furthermore, the pentagon fails to highlight the multifunctional nature of assets. Empirical reality shows that different households vary in their asset base and that people attach different importance and meanings to different assets at different points in time. Land, for example, is an important productive resource in most rural areas. However, it is also an important cultural and political asset. While livestock like cattle maybe an important household resource, it may hold different meanings for different household members. For the male household head it may be a status symbol, for the male child a potential resource to be accessed for paying bride wealth and as part of his inheritance, while for the women and girls the livestock will be a source of milk like for everybody else in the household. It is noteworthy that asset endowments may sometimes be a liability. For example, being affiliated to some political organization may imply social capital when that political organization is in power, it may become a liability when another political organization takes power. Additionally, whereas women in female-headed households often complain about limited labour due to the lack of male labour, some women in male-headed households have complained of drunken husbands that do not help with agricultural work and spend the little money earned on drinking. All this points to the fact that the same asset may have different uses for different households in a community or individuals in a given household, therefore assets play different functions in people's livelihoods. Hence as Bebbington (1999:2022) argues assets transcend use value per se, and in his words:

> *A person's assets, such as land, are not merely means with which he or she makes a living: they also give meaning to that person's world. Assets are not simply resources that people use in building livelihoods: they are assets that give them the capability to be and to act. Assets should not be understood*

> *as things that allow survival, adaptation and poverty alleviation: they are also the basis of agents' power to act and to reproduce, challenge or change the rules that govern the control, use and transformation of resources.*

It is important to note that while this holistic approach to asset analysis is useful and needs to be done, it introduces challenges of capturing different capitals in the same terms and on the same scale to make useful comparisons between households or communities.

Finally, the term "capital" is also problematic because of the economic connotations, which give the impression that all assets or resources are like commodities purchased or sold off and that people's activities are entirely oriented towards material gain (cf. Arce & Fisher, 2003; Hebinck & Bourdillon, 2001; Whitehead, 2002). Although material gains are central and important to the notion of livelihood generation, livelihood strategies are not always defined in economic terms but also include other aspects of people's lives that are cultural, non-material and non-commoditized. Bebbington (1999:2034) observes that there is "a conjunction between place and the reproduction of cultural practices that are important inputs to and outputs of livelihood strategies". It is also important to note that not all assets are capital stocks that one would expect to yield flows of benefits over time. In this sense, the term "capital" is misleading. Despite this, however, the term and its classification into the "five vital" assets continues to be widely used in livelihood literature.

From the foregoing sections it becomes clear that defining and quantifying assets is fraught with difficulties. The dynamic nature of assets makes it difficult to capture the state and changing quality and quantity of these assets. Some assets can only be accessed if other assets are available. And asset analysis may exclude those who do not have any assets yet are the most vulnerable. Some, therefore, have challenged the usefulness of asset analysis arguing that, at best, it only offers superficial value. This notwithstanding, "assets" as basic inputs to livelihood generation are important and the concept of assets and their analysis as part of livelihood analysis remains relevant. The challenge for future research is the development of tools and indicators that will enable the capture of the various perspectives of people's assets. Assets are not static and as Ellis (2000:48) suggests, it is important that they are viewed in a dynamic sense: "It is not always the static level of a particular asset that is significant, it is more often the direction in which that asset is moving as a consequence of the impact of external pressures and trends on livelihoods". Furthermore, a simple description and assessment of an asset's worth does not fully capture the stream of financial returns, social utility and other benefits generated (Devereux, 1993:55), nor highlight the negative effects of asset depletion (Start & Johnson, 2004). Bebbington's words quoted above underscore the importance of taking a holistic outlook in the process of asset analysis.

"Work on food security and asset-based approaches reveal the central role that assets have in determining the ability of a livelihood to insure against risks and mitigate future shocks, to cope with them when they do occur and to adapt existing livelihood portfolios to gradual or sudden shifts in the terms" (Start & Johnson, 2004:18). In this study, I therefore seek to understand the type of assets owned and the role of different assets in livelihood generation for different groups of individuals and households. Furthermore, I examine how key assets have been changing (temporal perspective), and which assets have been affected and in what ways, particularly in the context of HIV/AIDS. In the analysis, differences in asset ownership by gender of household head and wealth and HIV/AIDS status of the household are explored. In this thesis, assets are looked at as the basic building blocks of livelihood generation. Specifically, household labour, land, and livestock were identified as key assets for investigation. Furthermore, given that consumption is the ultimate goal of livelihood activities, household expenditure on food and non-food items was also examined. Information on ownership of other household assets like bicycle, radio, motorcycle, and car, that have been found to be indicators of enhanced social status in Uganda (UBOS, 2003b) was also collected.

2.3.2 Human agency

Human resource represents the skills, knowledge, physical power and strength, and good health that together enable people to pursue different livelihood strategies and achieve their livelihood objectives (DFID, 2000). Humans are a critical resource to households and they are important for the mobilization, utilization and eventual conversion of the other resources into various livelihood outcomes. People directly use resources as inputs for livelihood generation turning them into functions, for example, earning a living, gaining social and material advancement, enjoying respect and security as well as creating other resources. However, the availability, quantity and quality of the human resource (labour) has a bearing on the type of occupations pursued by household members and consequently on the kind of livelihood generated.

Yet, the supply of household labour depends on a number of inter- and intra-household dynamics. According to Kollmair and Gamper (2002), those at household level include gender, age, household size, skill levels, leadership potential, health status, and so on. In addition, household labour requires time and investment in education and skills and experience to build up yet easily be lost when a household member becomes ill, handicapped or dies, or for some reason has to leave the household. A lack of or reduction in available household labour (active, skilled and healthy individuals) is likely to have significant implications for household self sufficiency and survival.

As Murray (2000) states "a livelihoods approach focuses on the agency and the capability of actors, on strengths rather than needs". The capabilities approach, which emphasizes what people are capable of doing and becoming (Sen, 1985; Dreze & Sen, 1989), is important to the notion of livelihood generation. Agency implies recognizing that people have the capacity to make choices and take control over their actions. Besides knowledge, skills and good health, people's capabilities also entail the wealth of experience acquired over the years, ability to negotiate, create and maintain social networks (associability), as well as the potential to improve these attributes. Nonetheless, while people have agency, it is not possible for them to have complete control over all factors that impinge on their livelihood. Moreover, the extent to which different individuals or groups can influence environmental factors and processes varies.

2.3.3 Access to resources

An analysis of a household's or community's resource status must consider whether individuals have access to and can use the resources, which individuals or groups have access and which ones do not, in what ways do people access resources and how do they put them to use. As recent literature stresses, it is not the issue of ownership that is usually at stake but rather that of access to a given resource. Therefore, while a number of resources at household or community level may exist, individual access to these resources for livelihood generation is another issue. Niehof and Price (2001) distinguishes resources according to the level at which they are accessible, owned or used, that is, at the individual level or collective level. Human resources, such as skills, are accessible at the individual level, while resources such as land, income, labour, and biodiversity are accessible at either the household or community level or both. Community level resources, particularly the natural resources, can only be accessed through entitlements (Swift, 1989). Chambers and Conway define access as "the opportunity in practice to use a resource, store or service or to obtain information, material, technology, employment, food or income" (Chambers & Conway, 1992:8). Access to resources is a prerequisite for the ability to use them and is often negotiated (Bebbington, 1999). In the entitlement literature the relationship between the rules and norms and rights of access to certain resources is discussed. Sen (1981) defines entitlements as "the set of different alternative commodity bundles that the person can acquire", the effective command or control over those bundles. Start and Johnson come to similar conclusions about the importance of access. Through their analysis of the differences between Sen's entitlement concept and other micro-economic models of livelihood, they observe that "very different sets of entitlements can be returned from similar initial endowments, the explanation lying in processes of access, production, transformation and exchange" (Start & Johnson, 2004:15).

According to Chambers and Conway (1992), claims and access are part of social capital. Niehof (2004) points out that social relationships play an important liaison function in the availability or usability of other assets and resources. Bebbington further emphasizes the importance of social "capital" by saying that theoretically access to other actors comes prior to access to material resources. As he argues, "for such relationships become almost *sine qua non* mechanisms through which resources are distributed and claimed, and through which the broader social, political and market logics governing the control, use and transformation of resources are either reproduced or changed" (Bebbington 1999: 2023, italics original). The example of a widow's limited rights to sell land during a stressful situation given in the section above is a case in point. Therefore, social relations play a crucial role in influencing people's access and use of resources by enhancing access to other actors or strengthening linkages with them. The actors include, for example, government, civil society, informal institutions, service agencies and individuals.

Individuals and groups of people possess differing potential access to resources. And both assets and access are gendered. For example, women have fewer rights than men regarding household and community resources and agricultural services (Pena *et al.*, 1996). They have limited access to land (Doss, 1999), and their plots are often less fertile and more distant from the homestead (Alwang & Siegel, 1994; Barnes, 1983; Jackson, 1985). They also face greater institutional biases than men in access to training (Baser, 1988; Saito & Weidemann, 1990) and technological inputs (Gladwin *et al.,* 1997). Similarly, widow- and child-headed households may have limited access to community resources compared to the male-headed households, given that they usually have low social standing in the communities and may be excluded from community networks. Moreover, individual access to resources is influenced by power relations within the household.

In her study on gender and livelihoods in Uganda, Dolan (2002) found that women in female-headed households experience fewer restraints in securing access to, and control over livestock and livestock products than women in male-headed households. None of the female heads interviewed in her study, for example, were limited by restrictions as to which animals they could maintain or sell or both, yet any claims to livestock by women in male-headed households were not guaranteed and depended upon marital negotiations and the leverage that the women could exert within their households. As Kabeer (1997) notes, rules that legitimize resource access and ownership may promote gender inequalities. Gender asymmetries in access to resources are likely to affect equitable distribution and efficient use of resources as well as the empowerment of the various users with implications for livelihood generation.

Therefore, while it is important to know who owns what resources there is need to go beyond this and consider who has what rights to access what resources, withdraw or exclude others from given resources, or who has the power to alienate others or transmit such rights (Schlager & Ostrom, 1992).

In most parts of the rural developing world, one of the structural causes of poverty is the lack of access to the vital means of production. A key resource of poor households tends to be family labour. Results of the 2002 census show that the adult population in Uganda (18-60 years) constituted about 39.4 percent of the total population while 56.1 percent was below 18 years of age, thus yielding a dependency ratio of about 1.4 (UBOS, 2003b). Rural household labour supply is further constrained by the reduction in child labour since the introduction of the Universal Primary Education (UPE)[11] program, low participation of adult males, the fact that female labour is already over-burdened with production and reproduction, and the increased care needs associated with HIV/AIDS in affected households.

Next to labour, the most important resource determining well-being of a rural community is land, its quantity, quality, access and terms of utilization. In Uganda, land continues to be an important resource, particularly for agricultural production, and in this sense the basic source of income for the majority of rural households (NEMA, 1998).

Ownership of livestock has also been found to be a very socially differentiating asset in rural Uganda (Tenkir, 2000). While access to land is through both informal and legal structures, access to livestock is determined by informal structures.

Access to resources is indeed influenced by a variety of factors and in this study an attempt is made at understanding the ways in which the HIV/AIDS epidemic restrains or enhances people's access to resources through its direct impacts on household resources as well as the way it impacts on other access mediating factors.

2.3.4 Policies, institutions and processes (PIP) and the vulnerability context

Livelihoods are shaped by a multitude of socio-economic, political, cultural and environmental factors. A clear understanding of the specific environmental context in which people live is fundamental to the understanding of livelihoods and as Beall and Kanji (1999) contend, the value of a livelihood approach diminishes, if these are ignored. The factors and processes in the environment are either exogenous or endogenous to the social norms and structures of which households are part

[11] The scheme provides access to free primary education for up to four children. Since its introduction in the 1997 academic year, the number of primary enrollments has doubled. Child labour is a very important source of family labour for poor households.

(Ellis, 2000). These factors and processes are usually dynamic and may be found to operate at global, regional or local scales or levels. They may also operate at other levels: the *social level,* which includes changing relationships and the structures of kinship, gender and age; the *cultural level,* which relates to customs, religion and other beliefs, local and external, customary laws such as inheritance and land tenure; the *economic level,* which involves investments, markets, prices, production technologies; the *political level,* which covers governance (tribal/state), policies and state laws, wars and conflict; the *institutional level,* which covers laws, resources and activities of the institutions; and the *natural environment,* which includes environmental resources/assets, state and cultural laws governing access to these resources.

Thus, diverse structures and institutions, often working in combination, shape the ways in which different people access, use and derive well-being. In the framework a distinction is made between the vulnerability context, over which people have limited control, and the PIP, which are the result of historical processes in which people can potentially participate. Not only do the vulnerability context and PIPs interact with the resource base of households and individuals, they also interact with each other. However, people also affect the vulnerability context, directly or indirectly by changing the PIP environment which in turn can influence the vulnerability context, even though their control over this environment may seem limited (cf. Brons *et al.*, 2007).

Policies, institutions and processes are the most important factors in the framework according to DFID. Ellis (2000) describes PIPs as comprising a diverse and complex range of issues associated with policies, social relations and processes as well as concerning issues of power, authority and participation. The PIPs in the livelihood framework are also referred to as transforming structures and processes. The structures constitute the organisations – both private and public – that set and implement policy and legislation, deliver services, purchase, trade and perform many functions that affect livelihoods. The processes determine the way in which structures and individuals operate and interact. Ellis (2000) defines the processes as comprising both social relations (gender, caste, class, age, ethnicity, and religion) and institutions (formal rules and conventions and informal codes of behaviour).

PIPs are important as they influence availability of resources and what individuals and households can do with such resources to shape their livelihoods. They influence access to (various types of resources, livelihood strategies, decision-making bodies and sources of influence), the terms of exchange between different types of resources, as well as returns (economic and otherwise) to any given livelihood strategy. Therefore, on the one hand PIPs offer opportunities that households can draw upon to enhance livelihood security, while on the other hand they may create circumstances that limit people's choices and chances of survival. For example, government investments in transport and communication infrastructures influence the availability of information, access to markets, and costs and returns to investment. Macroeconomic policies are likely to affect the rate of resource accumulation given their effects on input and output prices, as well as the type of available investment opportunities and their profitability or riskiness. Furthermore, institutions and cultural rules and regulations that regulate access to common resources also influence which individuals or groups will be able to access them.

The absence of appropriate structures (for example, agricultural extension organizations) and relevant policies leads to increased vulnerability of people. This has been found to be particularly so in remote rural areas where services such as agricultural extension, HIV/AIDS testing and counselling, as well as physical and market infrastructure, to mention a few, are lacking. Understanding PIPs and the way they interact with each other and with other elements of the framework allows the identification of constraints and opportunities that influence access to livelihood resources and the groups or individuals who are advantaged or marginalized by the existing structures and processes. Although the livelihood framework has been criticized for having a micro bias, the discussion on the PIPs emphasizes the micro-macro linkages (cf. Brocklesby & Fisher, 2003).

The relevance of the vulnerability context lies in its direct impact on people's resources and options. For example, shocks like floods or civil conflict directly erode or destroy people's resource base while trends such as rainfall variability or crop/animal disease and pest outbreaks affect the technical feasibility of potential investments in agriculture and accordingly the livelihood strategies chosen. Furthermore, seasonal shifts in prices, employment opportunities and food availability are one of the greatest and most enduring sources of hardship for poor people in developing countries. In this study, HIV/AIDS is an important part of the vulnerability context but at the same time it causes impacts on the vulnerability context, household resources as well as on the PIPs. This makes the relationships between HIV/AIDS and other elements in the framework highly complex. Nonetheless, the high prevalence levels in the study area imply that the environment presents high risks in terms of people's exposure to HIV and the associated impacts. The HIV/AIDS epidemic is therefore likely to increase poor people's vulnerability, making them less able to cope with other shocks and stresses. However, given differences in people's resource endowments, different people will experience impacts of HIV/AIDS (and the vulnerability context in general) differently as they try to cope.

It must be noted that not all trends are negative or increase vulnerability. Improvement of economic conditions, introduction of a new irrigation technology or disease resistant crop variety, for example, may be important for increasing people's opportunities and livelihood choices, particularly for the poor. However, even when trends move in the right direction, the poorest are often the least likely to benefit because they lack resources and may have limited or no capacity to make use of the available opportunities.

2.3.5 Livelihood activities and strategies

In the two preceding sections, the discussion has dwelt on people's entitlement to resources and the need to understand what determines access and use of resources by different individuals and households. However, resources (or their access) on their own cannot sustain a livelihood. Another important area in livelihood analysis, therefore, is the use of resources in the various activities that people engage in to obtain a living. Livelihood activities may be defined as the sets of actions through which individuals within households gain their means of living. Some activities, for example, farming, brewing, trading, crafts making, migratory labour, transport, and sex work are geared toward generation of a direct income. Other activities including childcare, social contracts in production, maintaining social and kinship relations and gift giving do not yield direct income but are important for social reproduction, help to secure access to and use of key resources, and contribute to social status and well being.

Livelihood activities may be divided into activities relating to production, reproduction, consumption and exchange. Productive activities refer to those activities that produce goods and services that are potentially tradable and therefore contribute to income.

Reproductive activities include those associated with household maintenance and well-being (childcare, cooking and cleaning), childbearing and the socialization of children. Sometimes they are extended to include community support activities like cleaning of community wells, care and support given to those bereaved, or participation in cultural ceremonies.

Consumption activities can be seen as activities that result in use or purchase of goods and services that are essential to the satisfaction of material needs such as food, clothing or medicine. The household is seen as the locus for livelihood generation and consumption.

Exchange activities have been described as those related to the transfer of goods, services or information between individuals, groups of individuals and institutions (may occur without necessarily involving the use of cash or reciprocity). Exchange activities include commercial trade, barter and gift sharing.

The reality for poor people is that survival and prosperity depends on the pursuit of diverse and multiple activities simultaneously by different household members

(Chambers, 1992) and sometimes in different localities. The nature, scope and effectiveness of these activities depends on availability of resources, the type and status of these resources, people's capability to create or access them, and the contextual risks and uncertainties that they have to cope with. In this thesis, I examine the livelihood portfolios of people in the study area by exploring the various combinations of income generating activities undertaken and resource use.

The concept of household strategies was at first applied to specific social groups – people in marginal positions/small businesses, peasants – who draw on a range of resources in the struggle to survive in risky environments, and the terms "survival" or "coping" strategies were coined to refer to such household strategies (Wallace, 2002). While the pursuit of multiple activities has always been seen as a way of spreading of risks and thus associated with survival among the poor, it is not only the poor that engage in multiple activities and strategies (Niehof, 2004). The better-off households do this as well, but in this case to make use of available income-generating opportunities to accumulate more assets or strengthen existing stocks. There is consensus now that the concept of livelihood strategies can be applied to various household types: rich and poor. As Barrett *et al.* (2001) assert, very few people collect all their income from any one source, hold all their wealth in the form of any single asset, or use their assets in just one activity. Analysis of strategies shows that there are multiple ways in which people construct livelihoods. Therefore, a broad range of causes and motivations, that differs between families at particular points in time, and within families at different points in time, prompt households and individuals to pursue different activities (Ellis, 1998).

Contemporary livelihood studies focus on the ways through which people devise various strategies to access resources and the activities they engage in to obtain or enhance their living. However, the concept of "household strategies", has attracted much debate. First, the word "strategy" gives the impression that individuals within households behave in a rationally strategizing manner and that they are always in charge or control of their lives, which is not necessarily true. There is now empirical evidence to show that households have a range of economic and non-economic goals which guide their actions, and that sometimes households do plan their activities while at other times they may not. As De Haan and Zoomers (2005:39) assert, household behaviour is not always deliberate "and human behaviour should not always be seen as conscious or intentional: much of what people do cannot be classified as strategic".

Secondly, the term has received much criticism from gender specialists whose studies have shown that the household cannot be considered a homogeneous unit with members having similar interests (Bagchi *et al.*, 1998; Guyer, 1981; Netting & Wilk, 1984). The term "household strategy" assumes a consensus within the household as to what the strategy is, or that it represents the interests of all household members

(Nelson & Smith, 1999, cited in Wallace, 2002). Gender and other intra- and inter-household factors influence the type and scope of livelihood strategies pursued, and are likely to play a significant role in either enabling or disabling livelihood choices. In this case it is unlikely that women's needs, interests and ensuing strategies would necessarily be in concordance with those of men. Besides, livelihoods are less likely to be organized in one locality and current trends towards individualization seem to accelerate the breakdown of households with men, women and children having different interests (De Haan & Zoomers, 2005; Hebinck & Smith, 2001).

However, the concept is not redundant. It remains relevant because it helps us to understand which resources are important to which groups of people and also how those resources are combined and used to obtain a living. Warde (1990) suggests a useful way of dealing with the definition problems. He proposes two definitions: a "strong" and a "weak" definition of strategy. The "strong" definition is that households really do sit and plan their activities (an idea he found unrealistic), and the "weak" definition states that a strategy of some sort can be inferred from a given set of livelihood outcomes (the definition that he himself uses). Whichever definition is found more appealing, the value of the concept of strategy will depend on information obtained from the households or individuals themselves regarding what they actually do and with what aim in mind, and how they do it. This would enable the researcher to make sense of the way in which livelihoods are generated. However as Schmink (1984:95) cautions, "The concept [...] of strategy can lose its meaning to the extent that it becomes a mere functionalist label applied *ex post* to whatever behaviour is found". With this in mind it is also important that the concept be used with such flexibility as to incorporate strategies of individual household members. For this study the "weak" definition of strategy was used.

The different ways and means through which individuals in a given household make use of resources at any given time is often referred to as a household's "livelihood strategy". However, in addition to activities that generate income or lead to investment of money into other resources, a livelihood strategy also encompasses many other kinds of decisions and choices, including cultural and social choices (Ellis, 1998). A review of recent literature indicates that people respond to risks and uncertainties as well as opportunities in a variety of ways. What is evident though is that these vary between a conscious choice to manage risks and make use of opportunities (making further investment, savings and accumulation) on the one hand and economic necessity or survival (responding to stress, shocks, vulnerability and poverty) on the other (Dolan, 2002; Ellis, 2000; Smith *et al.*, 2001; Bebbington, 1999). Such responses have been categorized as insurance strategies, coping strategies and adapting strategies[12], respectively. As Van der Geest and Dietz (2004:141) note, "Whether a certain response should be labeled as "coping" or "adapting" depends on the intensity, timing, effectiveness and sustainability of the response and most of all the reason why the household adopts that particular response (the motivation); and this differs per household, per livelihood system, per region and over time."

Diversification has also been identified as one of the livelihood strategies used by rural people. Ellis (2000:15) defines rural livelihood diversification as "the process by which rural households construct an increasingly diverse portfolio of activities and assets in order to survive and to improve their standard of living". Since it is generally recognized that poorer sections of the rural population diversify as a response to vulnerabilities, diversification can be understood as "a form of self-insurance" (Barrett *et al.*, 2001:322; Van der Geest & Dietz, 2004:137). However, as Niehof (2004) observes, diversification does not seem to be a transient phenomenon or just one associated with survival. It "may be associated with success at achieving livelihood security under improving economic conditions as well as with livelihood distress in deteriorating conditions" (Ellis, 1998:2).

Zoomers (1999, cited in De Haan & Zoomers 2005:39-40) argues that any given strategy should be conceived as a stage rather than a structural category. Furthermore, beyond intentional and unintentional behaviour, Zoomers also acknowledges structural components to be part of strategies arguing that one's geographical location, for example urban or rural, also influence one's life chances and outcomes. Thus in her classification of strategies, both intentional and structural elements are apparent. She distinguishes four categories, namely; (i) accumulation strategies involving long-term view of future resources, (ii) consolidation strategies aimed at stabilizing well-being, (iii) compensatory strategies to deal with sudden shocks, and (iv) security strategies to deal with situations causing vulnerability and leading to insecure livelihoods.

---

[12] Van der Geest & Dietz (2004:137) define insurance strategies as those activities undertaken to avoid future livelihood stress, food shortages and future entitlement failure, and include activities that vary income sources and spread them over time to avoid risks and those that create buffer stocks. Investing in food stores, livestock, saleable resources (valuable items like jewellery), human resources (children's education or acquiring skills) and social networks are given as examples of insurance strategies. Coping is a short-term response to an immediate and or unusual crisis or stressful situation and 'coping strategies', are defined as an 'involuntary response to disaster or unanticipated failure in major sources of survival' (Ellis, 2000). For a detailed discussion and critique on the concept of coping see (Davies, 1993; De Waal, 1989; De Waal *et al., 2005;* Rugalema, 1999; 2000). Whereas 'coping' is associated with "trying to preserve existing livelihoods in the face of disaster", 'adaptation' refers to the more rational response of "making permanent changes to the livelihood mix in the face of changing circumstances" (Davies & Hossain, 1997; Ellis 2000).

The main conclusions from the discussion above is that, first, whatever strategies are adopted, the aim is to obtain a certain standard of living and maintain or enhance capability and resources, or be able to cope with and recover from stress and shocks. Second, people make decisions about how their resources are used or which activities will generate better returns given the resources at their disposal. So people will adopt a given strategy (consciously or unconsciously) based on their personal capabilities and resources, priorities and preferences, past experience, existing opportunities as well as the prevailing physical and socio-economic context. It is also noteworthy, that in reality and at any particular point in time members of any given household may make more or less strategic decisions sequentially or simultaneously as they respond to different factors and processes and available opportunities in the environment (cf. Chambers, 1997).

While the concept of livelihood strategy has gained prominence in development practice in recent years, to operationalize it is not without challenges. Existing literature on the concept has shown that certain strategies seem to offer households higher returns on resources, thus leading to more sustainable livelihoods than others. Therefore, beyond mere identification of different mixes of activities undertaken by different households, operationalization of the concept would facilitate identification of distinct livelihood strategies that can be associated with either "improving" or "deteriorating" livelihoods, information that would be useful for policy and program development or implementation. Several different methods exist in the literature to characterize household livelihood strategies (Barrett *et al.*, 2005; Reardon *et al.*, 1992), with the classifications mostly being based on household incomes. This may be problematic given that the concept of livelihood strategies mainly focuses on people's behaviour and the decisions and choices they make to allocate resources to different activities and not on incomes derived thereof. For this study, therefore, livelihood strategies are inferred from the activities that people undertake and the resource endowments at their disposal. Where possible, especially with the case study subjects, the rationale behind different strategies is examined.

2.3.6 Livelihood outcomes

Desired positive outcomes of a livelihood include income security, food security, strengthened resource base, improved well-being (health, self esteem, respect, sense of control, maintenance of cultural assets), reduced vulnerability and sustainable use of natural resources. As Ellis (2000:30) notes "Outcomes are related to security, including the level and stability of income and degree of risk, and environmental sustainability, including soil quality, and biodiversity." Livelihood outcomes directly influence people's assets base and access to resources. Not all strategies engaged in by individuals or households lead to positive livelihood outcomes and well-being. Sometimes the strategies undertaken (particularly those resulting in depletion of key household resources) compromise the household's future capacity to cope with and recover from stress and shocks, or to provide for its members.

The quality of livelihood produced may be examined in terms of its sustainability (robustness of its resource base and ability to recover from stress) or its vulnerability (inability to cope with the uncertainties and shocks in the environment) (Niehof, 2004). A livelihood is said to be sustainable when it can cope with and recover from stresses and shock and maintain and enhance its capabilities and assets both now and in the future, while not undermining the natural resource base (Chambers & Conway, 1992; Scoones, 1998). The concept of sustainability, therefore, goes beyond a mere description of current livelihoods, to include the way these livelihoods (individual and aggregate) may affect the ability of other people to achieve their own livelihoods, both now and in the future. Accordingly, the poorest and often most vulnerable households that find themselves forced to adopt strategies which just enable them to survive but not to improve their welfare, can be said to have unsustainable livelihoods.

2.3.7 Vulnerability

Vulnerability has been interpreted, and defined, differently by different disciplines In general, vulnerability is the inability to cope with stress or adversity. Blaikie *et al.*, (1994:9) define vulnerability as "the characteristics of a person or group in terms of their capacity to anticipate, cope with, resist and recover from the impacts of natural hazard." According to Cardona (2004), vulnerability may be defined as an internal risk factor of the subject or system that is exposed to a hazard, corresponding to its intrinsic predisposition to be affected, or to be susceptible to damage. It therefore, represents the physical, economic, political or social susceptibility or predisposition of a community to damage in the case of a destabilizing phenomenon of natural or anthropogenic origin. For Devereux (2001), vulnerability is exposure to a threat in combination with susceptibility or sensitivity to the adverse effects of the threat. Therefore, beyond mere predisposition to exposure to an event or change, the concept also focuses on the inability to cope with the effects produced by that particular event or change. While the concept of vulnerability is often used as a synonym for poverty, the two are not the same (Moser, 1998)[13]. However, due to resource constraints the poor are among the most vulnerable (Dietz, 2000), but there are also rich households that may be vulnerable, for example in the case of HIV/AIDS-related mortality of a key breadwinner. Therefore, as Chambers (1989:1) notes, vulnerability is "not lack or want (poverty per se), but defencelessness, insecurity, and exposure to risks, shocks and stress".

---

[13] Most of the poverty literature presents the two concepts as very closely interlinked (cf. Banerjee & Newman, 1994). While Wisner (1993) argues that vulnerability is simply poverty, Devereux (2001) says that livelihood vulnerability is just one of the causes of poverty and not its symptom.

A distinction between physical vulnerability and social vulnerability is usually drawn (Brons *et al.*, 2007; Chambers, 1990; Watts & Bohle, 1993), whereby the former refers to exposure to stress and crises resulting from physical hazards, and the latter refers to the capacity of individuals and communities to respond to physical impacts. Factors and processes such as crop and animal pest and disease outbreaks, unreliable weather or markets, diminishing social support networks and poor road infrastructure, can be said to constitute the biophysical environment. In this sense, HIV/AIDS is part of the external vulnerability context of many rural livelihoods in sub-Saharan Africa (Blaikie *et al.*, 1994; Barnett *et al.*, 2000). At the same time, individual and household characteristics such as age, sex, education, health status, gender of headship, income, asset ownership, dependency ratio influence people's fall-back position and can be said to be linked with social vulnerability.

Vulnerability is a dynamic concept that involves a sequence of responses that occur after a given shock is experienced (Glewwe & Hall, 1998). The concept has two dimensions: susceptibility and sensitivity. According to Davies (1993), susceptibility refers to "bouncebackability", or the ease and rapidity by which a community or household or individual returns to a normal state after a crisis, while sensitivity refers to the magnitude of a system's response to an external event or the intensity with which shocks are experienced. "Bouncebackability" is dependant on the household or individual's capacity to deal with the crisis as well as the existence and magnitude of other shocks at the time of the new crisis. Winchester (1992) relates the level of vulnerability to household characteristics (like household size, age of household members, household asset base, and nature of support networks engaged in) and community characteristics (that is, the socio-economic and socio-political factors). Therefore, household resource base status, existing social support networks, prevailing socio-economic and political environment as well as government and private institutional support are important determinants of the capacity to effectively respond to a given the crisis and, consequently, the ability to bounce back.

The degree of vulnerability to different hazards and consequences, and thus the level of resilience or sensitivity, will vary for different individuals and among households depending on level of exposure to different risks and the capacity to respond. Farmers in different localities experience different vulnerabilities to varying degrees. The impact of climatic variability, for example, may particularly affect farmers in drought-prone areas. However, farmers in areas that are not drought-prone experience a crop disease outbreak, then the impact of the drought that would normally be inconsequential becomes significant.

Furthermore, As Dolan (2002) notes, gender identities also shape the options and rights individuals possess. Previous research has identified social characteristics such as gender, age, wealth status and education to be associated with vulnerability (Cutter, 1996). The fact that households are composed of individuals with varying degrees of agency, endowments, rights, and power implies both differential susceptibility and sensitivity. As Sen (2002) argues, vulnerability is gendered because of the gender hierarchies in the development process that result in differential ways in which women experience marginalization and discrimination compared to men. Furthermore, he sees social vulnerability as originating from exclusion because of a breakdown in social ties and, among other things, the lack of protection against hardship created by divorce, desertion, widowhood or old age (World Bank, 2000).

In many parts of sub-Saharan Africa, the high prevalence levels of the HIV epidemic has led to increased vulnerability through reduced productivity, capacities and opportunities. As Gillespie *et al.* (2001) point out, HIV/AIDS strips individuals, households, networks and communities of different forms of capital thus reducing their future capacity to cope with other shocks (cf. Barnett *et al.*, 2000; Blaikie *et al.*, 1994). For example, many studies on impacts of HIV/AIDS show that households are shifting labour and other resources from productive activities to those related to HIV/AIDS-related support and care, thereby jeopardizing short and long-term survival (Tabaijuka, 1997). HIV/AIDS-induced changes in household composition and structure are of particular importance in the study since they influence household labour availability for agricultural production and other income generating activities and, as a result, the capacity of households to generate sustainable livelihoods. The HIV epidemic, which has created a large number of orphans and child- and female-headed households, has been identified, as one of the main causes of increased vulnerability in Uganda (Bevan & Ssewaya, 1995).

2.4 Applying the livelihood approach

The livelihood approach is useful in that it facilitates our understanding of the various ways in which people construct a living: how people use and organize access to resources, deal and negotiate with institutions, react to rules, regulations and other changes in their institutional and physical environment as well as the ways by which they adapt or respond to changes in the environment. While livelihood analysis has been applied to rural areas, and often to farming, such analysis has also emphasized that besides farming, rural people make a living in other ways (Carney, 1998; Scoones, 1998; De Haan & Zoomers, 2005; Hebinck & Bourdillon, 2001; Whitehead, 2002). Despite the focus on the household as the unit of analysis in this study, the livelihood approach also facilitates linkage of relevant interactions at micro, intermediate and macro levels of development (Adato & Meinzen-Dick, 2002). It also facilitates an appreciation of how changes at any one level transform what is happening and what is possible at the micro level.

In this study I use livelihood analysis to investigate livelihoods of banana-farming households in the districts of Kabarole and Masaka where HIV prevalence is medium to high, respectively. Key questions focus on whether there are livelihood effects as a result of HIV/AIDS that can be observed and, if yes, what the effects are on household resources and strategies and their implications for household food and livelihood security.

Gillespie and Kadiyala (2005) note that HIV/AIDS heightens vulnerability to food insecurity while, reciprocally, food insecurity heightens susceptibility to HIV exposure and infection--with the cycle being particularly more devastating for women than men. In applying the livelihood concept, I used food security as one of the key livelihood outcome indicators.

Furthermore, because society is socially differentiated, the role of social differentiation in shaping livelihoods was taken into account as well (Francis, 2002; Hebinck *et al.*, 2007; Murray, 2002). In addition, a number of studies have shown that gender is a strong organizing principle within the household and the role that each household member plays has important consequences for the household's livelihood portfolio (Niehof & Price, 2001). Besides, the management of labour, income and resources is closely interlinked with household organization and the sexual division of labour (Kabeer, 1994; Moore, 1988). Also, because livelihood options are to some extent determined by the composition and internal dynamics of the households (Upton, 2004), the role of gender relations in influencing access to and use of resources and the nature of livelihood strategies pursued, is examined.

2.4.1 Food security

The concept of food security was developed in the 1970s and has evolved considerably (Hoddinott, 1999). At the time of the 1974 World Food Conference, food security was defined as the "availability at all times of adequate world food supplies of basic foodstuffs [...] to sustain a steady expansion of food consumption [...] and to offset fluctuations in production and prices" (Mechlem, 2004:633). In the 1970s, food security was mostly considered in terms of national and global food supplies.

The limitations of this focus came to light during the food crisis that plagued Africa in the early 1970s and again in the mid-1980s. It became clear that adequate food availability at the national level did not necessarily translate into food security at individual and household levels (Frankenberger, 2001). Sen's (1981) theory on food entitlement had a considerable influence on this paradigm change. He was able to show that people do not starve because of an insufficient supply of food, but because they possess insufficient command over, or access to, food (Sen, 1980; 1981). The household food security approach that evolved in the late 1980s emphasized both the availability of food and stable access to it, that is, food availability at the national and regional levels and stable and sustainable access at the local level were both considered essential to household food security (Frankenberger & McCaston, 1998).

During the same period, the temporal dimension of the concept also came to the fore. It refers to the time frame over which food security is being considered and describes the intensity and characteristics of household food insecurity. In Maxwell and Frankenberger (1992), a distinction is drawn between chronic food insecurity, the inability to "access" food on an ongoing basis, and transitory food insecurity, a temporary inability to meet food needs.

Different institutions, organizations and scholars have defined food security differently[14]. The definition of food security most widely used and accepted now is the definition adopted at the World Food Summit in 1996: "Food security, at the individual, household, national, regional and global levels is achieved when all people, at all times, have physical and economic access to sufficient, safe and nutritious food to meet their dietary needs and food preferences for an active and healthy life" (FAO, 1996). In addition to addressing elements of earlier definitions (availability, access and sufficiency) this definition also adds "safe" and "nutritious". It also recognizes the dietary needs and the importance of cultural factors (in terms of preferences), and sees food security as a means to reaching a broader goal of an active and healthy life, a key livelihood outcome. According to FAO, the definition also introduces the idea of adapted food, that is, of the "biological utilization" of food, which depends, *inter alia*, on cooking methods, ways of consuming food, and the state of a person's health (FAO, 2001). It is noteworthy that this definition also addresses food security as an issue from the individual to the global level.

The concept of food security, therefore, encompasses elements of production in relation to food availability and distribution, and access by all, as well as issues of consumption, in the sense that individual food needs are met. The above notwithstanding, availability and accessibility of food to meet household and individual food needs should also be sustainable.

Although food availability at the household level is a key issue, intra-household factors may prevent equitable and adequate access to food among different household members. Within the household, access to food by individuals is linked to their control over household income and other resources. As Maxwell & Frankenberger (1992) point out, it is misleading to assume that household members share common preferences with regard to the allocation and distribution of household resources and food. Due to differences in power relationships within the household, some

[14] Food security has been defined at global and national or sub-national level (Eicher & Staatz, 1990; Maxwell, 1988), household level (Calon, 1990; Van Braun *et al.*, 1996) and at individual level (Barraclough & Scott, 1988; World Bank, 1986).

individuals, for instance the head of the household, may have more power in determining the use of food resources (or other resources necessary for food acquisition). As pointed out by Pinstrup-Andersen (cited by Carletto, 1998), apart from availability (household supply) and ability to acquire food (household access), it is necessary to consider intra-household preferences and distribution (individual access). Cultural factors have also been found to deny some members of the household (particularly women and children) from getting an equitable share (Maxwell, 1996). In households where distribution is unequal, it is, therefore, possible that the total amount of food increases while some individuals experience no change in their food security. And, there may also be food secure individuals in food insecure households.

The concept of food security is understood in terms of three elements: availability, access, and adequacy. Although the household was the main unit of analysis, intra-household dynamics that influence food and resource allocation were also studied, as well as the wider environmental and institutional context that may also constrain the chances of a household to achiev food security.

"Availability" refers to own production and capacity to produce enough food. At the household level, availability is taken as the capacity of the household to produce the food they need.

"Access" refers to ability to obtain food either through own production, purchasing from the market, gathering from the wild, or through claims on and donations from kin and community support. Maxwell and Frankenberger (1992) define access as the entitlement to produce, purchase, exchange or receive food, with entitlement referring to the set of income and resource bundles over which households can establish control. This implies the need for stocks of food in the market as well as having the purchasing power created by saving money or other assets such as cattle and other possessions. Bohle (1993) describes the risk of food insecurity as having three dimensions: the risk of exposure to crises or shocks, the magnitude or consequences of crises and households' vulnerability to these crises. The latter dimension, he claims, is determined by the capacity of the household to cope with crises. For that reason, food security is related to risk, in a sense that there may be a possibility of entitlement failure to food in the present, future or both. A food secure household is able to procure enough food at present and in the future. Therefore, in addition to understanding a household's immediate access to food, the stability and sustainability of the channels through which the household ensures access to food need to be taken into consideration.

Most of the rural households in the study area depend largely on what they cultivate. Information was obtained on the agricultural activities of the household and their changes over a period of three years. This infomation included crop patterns, farming practices – particularly banana-farming practices – and the utilization of household resources including labour, land, capital. In addition to assessing food availability from own production, I looked at how households survive during times of food scarcity. Information was obtained on food purchases, more specifically on who buys food, food prices, as well as on household expenditures on non-food items. Finally, the household head's perceptions of food adequacy and sufficiency of food reserves/stocks to the next harvest were explored. The adequacy score – a mean rank explaining adequacy of a variety of foods consumed in each household – was used as a proxy for food (in)security, which in turn is used as an indicator for livelihood vulnerability. Information was collected on household food adequacy for 14 most commonly consumed foods.

2.4.2 Social differentiation

Access to resources is related to social differentiation, which is usually defined as the socially recognized differences between particular groups or categories of individuals (Juteau, 2003). It is linked to social stratification and, hence, to inequalities of power, status, wealth and prestige. Social differentiation is also linked to economic, political, and normatively determined processes that, among other things, affect the life chances of individuals (Juteau, 2003). Therefore, different social positions are characterized by unequal resources and opportunities to life chances. For instance, people of lower social categories will in most cases be associated with conditions of social disadvantage and relative deprivation such as dropping out of school school-age children; being unemployed; living in poverty; being homeless or in sub-standard housing; and contracting or dying from AIDS and other infectious diseases. Several authors have shown that livelihoods are rather heterogeneous and that livelihood analysis needs to take such differentiation into account (Bagchi *et al.*, 1998; Francis, 2002; Hebinck *et al.*, 2007; Murray, 2002).

There is evidence of increasing socio-economic differentiation in Uganda. Bevan and Ssewaya (1992) for example, cite case study evidence by ACTIONAID Uganda (1994) and Bazaara (1992) to this effect. "Growth, particularly in non-traditional food crops such as maize, may be accompanied by increasing rural differentiation and some people argue that, in some areas trade liberalization, the move into food crop sale for export and the lack of improvements in productivity, are increasing "land grabbing", wage labour and hence poverty" (Bevan & Ssewaya, 1995:82). This shows that the limited access to factors of production of poor farmers makes them enter into exploitative relationships with more well to do farmers for survival.

In the livelihood framework, factors associated with the external environment are often held responsible for social differentiation. Such factors include, but are not limited to, rapid economic and population growth; economic diversification; increased levels of education or illiteracy; structural adjustment programs; and proneness to certain vulnerabilities or shocks as in the case of high HIV prevalence. Analysis of livelihoods need to take this into consideration. Nonetheless, while different social groups may be differentiated by social, economic, political participation and cultural experiences, each category is also internally differentiated. Gender, age, religion, region, handicap and differential access to resources within a given social category affect life opportunities and chances for different individuals in different ways. In this study gender is considered an important differentiating variable given its relevance in understanding intra-household dynamics in a situation of HIV/AIDS.

2.4.3 A gender perspective

The term gender refers to socially constructed maleness and femaleness and varies both within and across cultures and over time. According to Kabeer (1999:4), "gender is taken to refer to the full ensemble of norms, values, customs and practices" that define differences between men and women in a given society. A gender analysis involves the investigation of the socially defined roles, responsibilities of and the relations between men and women in a given society. In so doing, the heterogeneous nature of men's and women's responsibilities and experiences and consequently differences in their interests and needs is revealed. As several anthropologists have pointed out, household relations play an important role in defining opportunities for social and economic well-being (Moore, 1988; Guyer, 1980,1988; Whitehead, 1981). Women's social status within the kinship system and household, for example, influences their capacity to access and mobilize resources as well as the types of livelihood opportunities that are open to them.

A gender perspective, therefore, imparts a multidimensional perspective on livelihood because it takes into account the multiple roles played by men and women in the household, the labour market and society, as well as factors that interrelate with gender, such as age and ethnicity (Clert, 1998 cited by Mujer & Desarrollo, 2004). It improves our understanding of how the household functions, since it reveals the hierarchies and inequalities in the power relations and the distribution of resources. A gender perspective also affirms the importance of taking into account the historical processes and micro-macro linkages that have shaped and continue to shape people's lives.

Traditionally, in many parts of Africa, there has been a strict division of labour by gender in agriculture (Hoddinott & Haddad, 1995; Saito, 1994)[15]. However, a

[15] Many studies examining time allocation across agricultural and non-agricultural tasks find that women work more hours than men do (Saito, 1994) and low-income women have longer working days than higher income women (Haddad *et al.*, 1997). Not only are women actively engaged in agricultural and wage-generating activities, but a substantial part of a woman's day is devoted to domestic production such as fetching water and fuel wood, preparing meals and child care (Haddad *et al.*, 1997).

number of authors have documented changes in gender roles (Alwang & Siegel 1994; Saito 1994). HIV/AIDS-related sickness and death is known to reduce labour as well as change its allocation within farming households. Women acquire headship and take over men's roles when men travel elsewhere to seek employment or die of HIV/AIDS. What is noteworthy, is that although the gender division of labour may be changing, men do not appear to take over women's agricultural activities, specifically the production of food for home consumption (Doss, 1999). Nonetheless, local conceptions of gender rights and responsibilities influence the type of activities undertaken (Dolan, 2002). As Dolan further argues the potential to exploit a particular asset or capitalize on a livelihood option is as much governed by the social meanings attached to particular tasks as to gender. Accordingly, "identifying the nature of gender relations not only provides a clearer picture of intra-household obligations and exchanges, but also shows us how livelihood strategies are negotiated, structured and legitimated through broader ideological processes" (Dolan, 2002:3).

Bravo (1998:63, cited by Mujer & Desarrollo, 2004) observes that women's intensive involvement in the domestic sphere, because of the sexual division of labour, causes "inequality of opportunities for women, as a gender, to gain access to material and social resources (ownership of productive capital, paid labour, education and training), and to participate in decision making in the main political, economic and social policies". He further argues that not only do women have fewer material assets, they also have fewer social and cultural assets, all of which increases their vulnerability. According to Ruspini (1996), women's narrower access to resources translates into deprivations in various social spheres, such as the labour market, the welfare or social protection system and the household. Social perceptions of the contributions of women to the household also affect their bargaining power and the level to which they will have access to resources within the household (Sen, 1990).

The fact that people have different agency and rights and resources implies that they will have different needs, interests and constraints. Moser (1993) has identified two types of needs: needs that arise as a result of either men and women's socially accepted roles (practical gender needs) and those that arise from women's subordinate position to men in society (strategic gender needs). Practical gender needs are a response to immediately perceived necessities, identified within a special context, such as provision of water, food, health, childcare and income (Moser, 1993). HIV/AIDS-related care needs have increased the burden of care in affected households with most of it falling women and girls. HIV/AIDS widowers who do not remarry also experience problems in having to take over the late spouse's roles (cooking and childcare, for example) which they were never socialized to do. Addressing practical gender needs is a response to basic needs and does not challenge the gender division of labour.

Moser goes on to describe strategic gender needs as those pertaining to the gender division of labour, and power and control over resources and including such issues like legal rights, domestic violence, and women's control over their bodies, and equal wages. Strategic gender needs are pertinent to the discussion of HIV/AIDS as a report on Uganda by Human Rights Watch (2003:21) shows:

> *Cultural perceptions of women's sexual and reproductive obligations in marriage rob women of bodily autonomy, while unequal property rights, the payment of bride price, and women's inability to take their children from the fathers' homes render women unable to leave abusive relationships. [...] Widows also face imposing obstacles: many are stripped of their property and left to struggle to support themselves and their children. These factors and more combine with violence, or the threat of violence, to create an environment within which women are trapped into having unprotected sex with HIV-positive men and are unable to seek information or treatment on HIV infection and AIDS.*

Meeting strategic gender needs has the potential to bring about transformation in women's position and a reduction in existing inequalities.

Gender needs arise as a consequence of the constraints men and women face in the process of livelihood generation. Kabeer & Tran Thi Van Anh (2002) developed a typology for assessing the nature of gendered constraints. These they have described as follows: *gender-specific constraints*: stemming from the specific nature of gender and power relations themselves, such as the allocation of labour and other resources for productive activities and household tasks, as well as access to services and markets, and the incidence of gendered violence; *gender-intensified disadvantages*: arising from the uneven and often inequitable distribution of resources between men and women, including cultural/religious conventions, and the social rules and norms that regulate property rights, inheritance practices and resource endowments; and *gender-imposed constraints:* resulting from biases and partialities of those individuals who have the authority and power to allocate resources, and these include provision of credit, information, agricultural extension and health care. As Seeley *et al.* (2004) rightly argue, understanding these constraints takes us beyond gender relations and sexual behaviour, to also focus on challenges individuals face in mitigating impacts of HIV/AIDS. And according to Whitehead (2001), the gendered constraint typology is helpful in identifying areas that might require policy intervention.

2.5 HIV/AIDS, rural livelihoods and gender

HIV/AIDS, rural livelihoods and gender issues are intimately linked. HIV/AIDS-related illness and death are major causes of and contributors to household livelihood and food insecurity, with differential impacts for men and women. This is understandable given the epidemic's attack on the most productive segment of society and existing gender inequalities in the agricultural sector. In Sub-Saharan Africa, for example, 80 percent of economically active women work in the agricultural sector and the share of female agricultural labour is increasing rapidly (World Summit, 2002)[16]. Yet, in spite of their crucial role in agriculture, many women in rural sub-Saharan Africa are disadvantaged with respect to access to cash, land, and other resources and related decision-making. For example, a 1988 study in four districts of Uganda found that "93 percent of the rural women were farmers; however, most of the land they cultivate is under the control of men, that is, husbands (63%) or male relatives (17%). Only seven percent of the women own the land they cultivate, ten percent borrow [...] 82 percent of this land was indicated to be customary or public land, eight percent freehold, while in ten percent of cases, it was not known by the respondents" (Sebina-Zziwa, 1995: 13). The same study found that while women provided over 70 percent of the agricultural labour on both cash and food crops, they had limited decision-making power over the proceeds. The decision on how to spend the income from food crops rested with women in 40 percent of the cases and with men and women jointly in 18 percent of the cases. With cash crops, women controlled the cash crop income by themselves in only 19 percent of the cases, with men making the decision on their own in 65 percent of the cases and joint decision-making occurring in 14 percent of the cases (Sebina-Zziwa, 1995). Other studies (Kharono, 2001) have generated similar information. Against this background, this section will highlight linkages between HIV/AIDS, rural livelihoods, and gender.

The HIV/AIDS epidemic has had far-reaching effects across all sectors of society, with those in the agricultural sector being especially severe due to the labour-intensive nature of activities in this sector. Seven million agricultural workers are estimated to have died from AIDS since 1985 in sub-Saharan Africa and FAO (2002) estimates that by 2020 this number will be 16 million. The heavy reliance on family labour – especially that of women – has made small-scale agriculture in sub-Saharan Africa particularly vulnerable to the adverse effects of HIV/AIDS-related labour loss with increasing likelihood of poverty and food insecurity. Consequently, there is reduced crop production and capacity to purchase inputs such as fertilizer and improved seed, delayed implementation of agricultural activities such as weeding, as well as reduced capacity to engage in other viable income generating activities. Ultimately, the household's agricultural production and both on-farm and off-farm income decline. This in turn results in the household's reduced capacity to produce enough food through own production and inability to purchase sufficient food and

[16] In Uganda, women produce over 70 percent of the country's food products (MAAIF, 2000) and provide 68 percent of the labour for food crop cultivation and 53 percent of the labour needed for cash crop cultivation (MAAIF, 2000; World Bank, 1993).

other goods associated with food security, with likely negative impacts on food and livelihood security.

HIV/AIDS not only threatens the capability of a household to function as an economic unit, but the entire social fabric of the family (and community) is potentially disrupted or dissolved (Mann *et al.* 1992). At the individual level, there are also close linkages between HIV/AIDS and nutrition. Poor nutrition reduces the body's resistance to opportunistic infections, thereby accelerating the onset of full-blown AIDS. At the same time, the progression of HIV/AIDS, associated with an increasingly weakening immune system and repeated infections, may lead to malnutrition. The chronic nature of the syndrome tends to lead to reduced appetite and/or chronic diarrhoea in affected patients, thus interfering with the body's absorption of nutrients. Yet AIDS and associated opportunistic infections increase the body's need for essential nutrients, which nutrients are usually inaccessible to many poor infected individuals, thus completing the cycle. Affected individuals experience challenges associated with a reduced ability, on one hand to access adequate and nutritious food and, on the other, to utilize the food for health outcomes.

At community level, the epidemic reduces agricultural productivity in both small subsistence and commercial farming. It also weakens rural institutions in their capacity to deliver services as professional staffs are affected. Furthermore, the combined impacts erode the economic performance of the economy. The epidemic undermines governments' efforts to implement national agricultural policies, as affected households may no longer be able to cultivate cash crops or participate in formal cooperatives that are promoted by the government. As Baylies (2002) notes, HIV/AIDS can be treated in its own right as a shock to household food security, but it has also such distinct effects that it is a shock like none other. The following paragraphs bring out the differential gender dimension of HIV/AIDS on household food security.

HIV/AIDS impacts are not gender-neutral but are mediated by socio-cultural landscapes (Gillespie *et al.* 2001 and UNDP, 2002) that make women more vulnerable to AIDS impacts than men (UNAIDS, 2004). Women are more susceptible to HIV-infection because of their physiological characteristics, and inequality and power imbalances between the different sexes in society. Official statistics show that HIV/AIDS disproportionately affects women (UNAIDS, 2004). In sub-Saharan Africa, for example, 57 percent of adults infected are women, 75 percent of young people infected are women and girls, and in almost every country prevalence rates for women are higher than for men (UNAIDS, 2004). Women and girls, often have limited power over their bodies, particularly regarding their sexuality, which makes protecting themselves difficult. Women's economic vulnerability may force them to engage in risky behaviour such as transactional sex for survival. As Tallis (2002:1) notes, "HIV/AIDS is not only driven by gender inequality; it entrenches gender inequality, putting women, men and children further at risk". Following the death of an adult, for example, some rural households may send children to urban areas to search for employment. In an urban setting, children may also be withdrawn from school and pushed into petty trade or begging on the streets in a bid to raise the necessary income to buy food. Also, males from poor households may be forced to migrate to other rural areas or urban centers in search of employment. In all these cases prolonged periods away from home increases people's risk of exposure to HIV. Girls are particularly vulnerable to exploitation given that they normally engage in domestic work that in most cases is beyond visible scrutiny by the public.

According to Sebina-Zziwa (1998), widowhood represents one of the crisis moments in a woman's life when her structural vulnerability and her dependence on her male relatives, is manifested. Widows suffer more than widowers following the death of a spouse. Inheritance customs, especially the traditional claiming of land and property by the deceased man's male family members, for example, has resulted in orphans and widows being dispossessed of their parent's or spouse's inheritance, thus increasing their vulnerability (UNDP, 2002; Wakhweya *et al.*, 2002). Wakhweya *et al.* (2002) further assert that disinheritance represents a major economic loss to orphans and their families given that it not only reduces assets and income opportunities in the short term but also has implications for children's long-term economic and food security. This coupled with stigmatization by in-laws results in some widows becoming poorer, deeply distressed and with no motivation to live (UNDP, 2002). In contrast, widowers stay with their properties and sometimes even acquire new partners. Widow-headed households also suffer from the direct loss of the spouse's farm labour and income, since men are the ones who usually work outside the home (UNDP, 1995; Wakhweya *et al.*, 2002). Moreover, premature death of a spouse also deprive the woman of the necessary time to build up a set of important social networks, such as access to community land, community groups, and/or microfinance groups, that can be used to exert power within the family (Gillespie *et al.*,. 2001). Therefore, if property rights for a whole range of assets are not clearly and equitably defined or are not enforced, women are likely to be less able to shape their own destinies, let alone be food secure. In such circumstances, though, widows from wealthier households may be better-off (in terms of resilience to HIV/AIDS impacts) than those from poor households.

Traditional gender roles have resulted in HIV/AIDS producing differential impacts with women and girls experiencing the heavier brunt. Because women are the traditional care providers, the burden of care for AIDS patients and AIDS orphans automatically falls on them (UNDP, 1995). In a study conducted by Wakhweya *et al.* (2002) 85 percent of single-parent orphan households were headed by females. The growing burden on women workers as they care for sick family members and orphans is likely to result in a reduction of the carrying capacity of households. Time spent in care provision also means time foregone to engage in (other) income generating activities with consequences of increased poverty, food insecurity and, possibly, engagement in high risk behaviours. As Opiyo (2001) points out, it appears that the rise of prolonged sickness and care due to AIDS has reduced the time available for women to engage in income-earning activities more so than for men. All this is likely to impact negatively on the nutritional value of the household food basket. It is worth mentioning that increased household workload and childbearing increase women's susceptibility to HIV, and the progression to full blown AIDS in case the woman is affected. Gender disparities and cultural practices also tend to render girls particularly exposed to exploitation and heavy responsibilities, especially in the areas of housekeeping and agricultural production (Jayne *et al.*, 2005). It is usually the girls who miss school or drop out of school, to care for younger siblings or a sick relative (Kakuru, 2006).

One of the other critical effects of HIV/AIDS is that the death of adults in prime productive age results in the loss of valuable knowledge and skills. There is an increasing number of households in high-prevalence areas that have experienced the loss of adult with key agricultural skills. In such households, the children are under pressure to help meet the household's food needs by engaging in agricultural activities. But these children lack or have limited knowledge of agricultural production and therefore farming is unlikely to be a viable livelihood activity. Desperate to survive, such children may leave home in search of work, a move that will further reduce household labour for agricultural production. These factors, whether singly or in combination, work together to exacerbate the already bad situation of food insecurity[17] in such households.

It can be concluded that there are significant linkages between HIV/AIDS, rural livelihoods, food security and gender. Gender disparities in property rights (which culminate into limited access to resources, bargaining power on the part of women, and livelihood opportunities) increase women's vulnerability to various shocks and risks in the environment including those associated with HIV/AIDS.

2.6 The research framework

On the basis of the discussions in the previous sections, this research assumes that issues related to AIDS or its effects, intra-household dynamics, and the social and institutional environment, all interact in a web of complex relationships to influence livelihood and food security of farming households.

[17] Available agricultural and population statistics data on Uganda indicates that average per capita food production in 1999-2002 was 35 percent less than what it was in 1970-1972 (UBOS, 2001; World Bank, 1993). This also needs to be viewed in the context of Uganda's high annual population growth rate of 3.4% (UNDP, 2004).

The arrows within the framework presented in Figure 2.2 are used to denote a variety of different types of relationships, all of which are highly dynamic. None of the arrows imply direct causality, although all imply a certain level of influence. The fact that the arrows are in two directions implies the potential of intra-household and environmental factors to modulate the impacts of HIV/AIDS. Full arrows indicate the relationships that were investigated in this study, dotted arrows those that are assumed but not investigated.

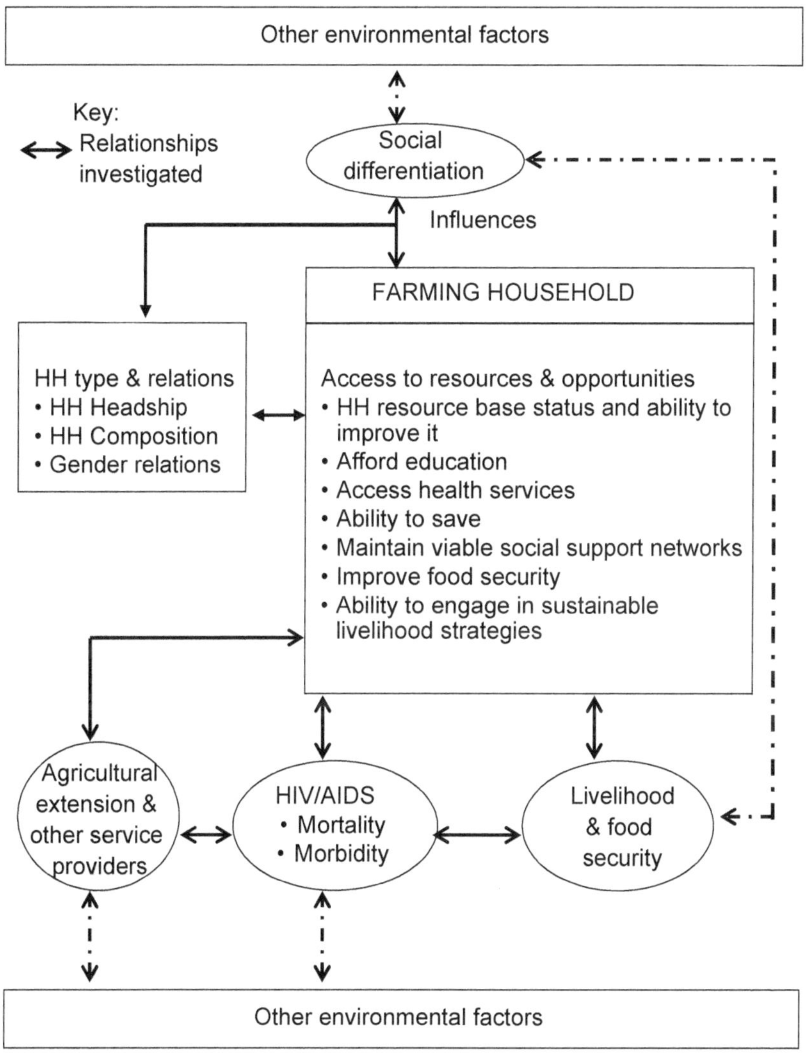

Figure 2.2. Research framework: relationships between HIV/AIDS, farming households and livelihood security.

The farming household is seen as the locus of livelihood generation. The framework posits that rural households possess a number of resources (such as land, crops, seed, labour, knowledge, cattle, money, social relationships, and so on), and given these resources and the capabilities of members, different activities are undertaken to earn a living and provide for food security. Because households are internally differentiated, access to resources varies between households and within households at different points in time. Additionally, social differentiation influences individual and household's access to resources and life opportunities, the type of livelihood strategies pursued, and consequently overall livelihood and food security. Farming households are seen to function and interact with the environment. The external environment not only affects household's activities and strategies but also the feasibility and net profitability of non-farm and farm activities. It does this through its influence on policies, land and labour markets, available technology and services, and access to resources. Accordingly, the environment is associated with risks and opportunities that the members of rural farming households have to cope with or take advantage of. Therefore, uncertainties and opportunities influence how material and social resources are managed and used, as well as the decisions and choices people make.

HIV/AIDS is one of the risk factors in the environment, representing an extreme source of livelihood and food security shock (Gillespie *et al.*, 2001). HIV/AIDS intervenes and affects farming households by directly affecting individuals within the household or indirectly through its impacts on social structures and institutions, which is why HIV/AIDS is a source of both internal and external vulnerability. Internal vulnerability is associated with HIV/AIDS-related mortality and morbidity effects on individuals within the household entailing resources being diverted from on-farm and off-farm activities to AIDS-related costs, thus reducing people's future capacity to cope with other shocks. External vulnerability is associated with risk of exposure to HIV/AIDS as well as HIV/AIDS-related mortality and morbidity effects on individuals in the support and service institutions. At the level of the household, it is assumed that the direct effects of HIV/AIDS morbidity and/or mortality influences household structure and composition, gender division of labour, as well as the access, use and status level of household resources, leading to reduced resources, productivity, and future capacity to respond to crises. Again, because households are internally differentiated and members have different priorities, needs and access to resources, they will accordingly experience different impacts as a result of HIV/AIDS. HIV/AIDS-related effects are also likely to influence inter-household social relations that are important in AIDS-related care.

Agricultural extension agencies and other organizations and institutions providing agricultural-related services are another part of the environment important in this study. The AIDS epidemic directly affects these organizations and their activities. In addition, the effects of AIDS on farming households may also influence the interactions between farming households and organizations providing agriculture-related services. For example, if we take the interaction between a given agricultural technology and the farming household, AIDS influences the outcomes of this interaction with likely consequences of changing the suitability of technology for the farming household and thus its relevance for livelihood generation. Depending on the type of technology, it may produce effects that will either augment or mitigate the effects of HIV/AIDS on farming households.

While death of any kind undoubtedly brings hardship and suffering to affected households, the magnitude of the social and economic consequences are assumed to vary significantly according to the extent to which the deceased tend to be primary breadwinners and core members of the household, as well as the household's *ex ante* resource levels. The main purpose of this study is therefore to examine the general patterns of the effects of HIV/AIDS on resource access and use among banana-farming households and associated implications for livelihood and food security. The specific research questions and sub-questions were formulated as follows.

1. How do banana farming households achieve and enhance their food and livelihood security?
    a. What resources do farming households have access to?
    b. How do rural households compose their livelihoods in order to survive?
    c. In what ways is access to resources and the type of livelihood pursued gendered?
2. What are the effects of HIV/AIDS-related mortality and morbidity on household resources, activities and overall livelihood and food security?
    a. What are the effects of HIV/AIDS on access to and use of household labour, income and land?
    b. What are the effects of HIV/AIDS on intra-household relations among banana farming households?
    c. In what ways are HIV/AIDS effects on household resources gendered?
    d. What are the effects of HIV/AIDS on household food and livelihood security?
    e. Which households are more vulnerable to HIV/AIDS effects and why?
3. What organizations and community support mechanisms are in place to deal with HIV/AIDS effects on the agricultural sector and household food security?
    a. What are the effects of HIV/AIDS at community level?
    b. What has been the response of MAAIF in mitigating the effects of HIV/AIDS?
    c. What is the role of agriculture extension in mitigating the effects of HIV/AIDS?
    d. In what ways are other community organizations and institutions addressing the effects of HIV/AIDS?
    e. In what ways can existing interventions be strengthened?

Chapter 3

Research design and methodology

The general objective of this study was to gain insight into the effects of HIV/AIDS on household labour and resources use in banana-farming households and the implications for food and livelihood security. Thus, the study analyses the way banana farmers engage in a portfolio of activities to meet a multiplicity of objectives. The analysis included how such objectives change over time, the constraints faced in the process of livelihood generation, the way the HIV/AIDS epidemic and other physical and environmental factors affect this process, and whether the HIV/AIDS-related effects on livelihoods are gendered.

This chapter presents the research approach used in the study and the different data collection methods employed to answer the research questions. The first section of this chapter discusses the research design and methodological issues, followed by an overview of the study area in section 3.2 and the different phases of the data collection process in section 3.3. Section 3.4 describes the methods used in data collection. The chapter concludes with a discussion on the methods of data analysis, ethical considerations and the problems encountered during the study.

3.1 Methodological considerations and research design

The study is descriptive in nature and a cross-sectional study design was employed. The nature of livelihood processes and in particular, intra-household dynamics and inter-household relations, lends itself to an approach that combines quantitative and qualitative research methods.

There has been an increasing appreciation among researchers of the importance of combining qualitative and qualitative data collection methods because it improves the accuracy and validity of the research findings (Ashley *et al.*, 2003; Pelto & Pelto (1978, cited in Scrimshaw, 1990). Scrimshaw (1990:88) stated, "the methodological concepts of validity and reliability provide a common foundation for the integration of quantitative and qualitative techniques".

In line with the above, I used a variety of research techniques appropriate for the collection of different kinds of data to capture various aspects, meanings and functioning of people's livelihoods. Hence, data related to demographic characteristics, resources use and change, livelihood activities and constraints, and perceptions of AIDS impacts for which it was important to understand the distribution over the study population, were collected through the survey. The survey also allowed for quantitative analysis and generalizations to be made. Qualitative ethnographic methods were used to explore, understand and interpret livelihood processes and how these have changed in a situation of AIDS; people's opinions and perceptions of these processes, power relations, as well as people's behaviour and experiences in responding to the effects of AIDS.

Because of HIV/AIDS-related stigma, an in-depth understanding of the epidemic's effects could also be best achieved by using the qualitative approach. This is supported by several proponents of qualitative research who argue that qualitative data preserves the chronological flow, assesses local causality and provides useful explanations that may not be arrived at by means of quantification methods (Crabtree & Miller, 1992; Miller, 2000; Strauss & Corbin, 1990).

Case study approach: Because the study design was cross-sectional, it meant that livelihoods would be looked at as a snap shot in time. However, people's livelihoods are dynamic and historical processes have an influence on the way current livelihoods are pursued. The case study approach was therefore selected to provide this temporal perspective to livelihood generation. Furthermore, because it is difficult to capture processes and issues of power and control in a survey, case studies provided the opportunity to do so. As Crabtree & Miller (1992) noted, a qualitative approach explores meanings, perceptions, relationships, associations and patterns based on personal experience of the phenomenon being investigated. According to them, case studies examine most if not all the aspects of a particular event (case or series of cases). Additional qualitative data were collected through interviews, group discussions and observations.

Gender perspective: Given the importance of gender in determining access to, and control over household assets and resources, the study was structured in such a way as to ensure generation of gender disaggregated data. An equal number of men and women's FGDs were conducted to ensure that views were enlisted from both men and women in each locality. This was also done during case study selection. Furthermore, key informants included both men and women to obtain perceptions and interpretation of issues from both perspectives. For analysis, household headship provided one of the analytical categories. Through a gender perspective, the study examined social relations between men and women and how this affects the gender division of labour, access, use and control of household resources, as well as differences in coping and survival mechanisms, and vulnerability to HIV/AIDS.

Validity and reliability issues: *Validity* refers to the "degree to which scientific observations measure what they purport to measure" Pelto & Pelto (1978:33, cited in Scrimshaw, 1990:88). *Reliability* (also referred to as replicability) is "the extent to which scientific observations can be repeated and obtain the same results" (Scrimshaw, 1990:89). The validity and reliability of research depends on the methodological approach used. Being aware of the limitation of surveys on one hand and case study approach on the other, a strategy to combine the two types of methods was used. "Qualitative methods are acknowledged to be accurate in terms of validity, while quantitative methods are considered to be better in terms of reliability or replicability" (Scrimshaw, 1990: 89).

In addition, the study design was such that in the process of data collection, triangulation of information from different research methods, techniques and sources was done. As Marshall and Rossman (1995:146) argue, "designing a study in which multiple cases are used, multiple informants or more than one data gathering technique can greatly strengthen the study's usefulness for other settings". Furthermore, the research procedures ensured that the various data collection methods were used correctly. These procedures included systematic area and subject sampling; selection of a large survey sample; pre-testing of survey instruments; careful selection and thorough training of interviewers[18]; supervision of interviewers and cross-checking data throughout the survey; careful and systematic selection of case study respondents; gender considerations in the selection of various respondents and focus group participants; gender considerations in the scheduling of interviews and FGDs; follow-up visits to clarify or obtain more information; and personally facilitating interviews and group discussions.

3.2 Description of the study area

The study was conducted in the two districts of Masaka and Kabarole in Uganda. The rationale for this selection was guided by the topic of the study, i.e. HIV/AIDS impacts among banana-farming households. Banana production is an important livelihood activity in the two districts. Furthermore, a review of HIV studies conducted in Uganda indicated that available micro-level studies of the effects of HIV/AIDS on rural households have mainly used a case study approach and have been undertaken in Rakai district, known to have high HIV prevalence. While providing valuable information, such studies are limited in their ability to extrapolate to the national level because the samples are usually small. For this reason two districts with differences in welfare and demographic characteristics, as well as HIV prevalence were selected. Based on data from the 2003 STD/HIV/AIDS Surveillance Report, Masaka was identified as a-high-prevalence area and Kabarole as a-medium-prevalence area (MOH, 2003). A brief description of the two districts is as follows:

[18] The interviewers or research assistants were trained for two days. Because the questionnaire was in English but the interviews had to be conducted in the local languages (Luganda & Rutoro), during the training the questions were translated into local language to ensure that each interviewer understood how to ask the questions. After the pre-test exercise, another training session to discuss difficulties encountered by the interviewers in and questions requiring further clarification was conducted. At the end of the day, the filled in questionnaires were checked for unclear responses and missing information.

Masaka

Masaka district is one of the oldest districts of Uganda and was part of Buganda Kingdom at independence. Originally, it consisted of Rakai, Kalangala and Sembabule, making it once the largest district in Uganda. Presently, Masaka has been reduced in size after Kooki, Ssesse islands and Sembabule sub-districts were elevated to district status. The district is located about 37km from the Equator towards the south, between 0º-25º South and 34º East. It is bordered by Sembabule district in the north west, Mpigi in the North, Rakai in the west and south and Kalangala district in the East. Average altitude is 115m above sea level and it has a total area of 4560 sq. km (of which 30 percent is water and swamps). Average rainfall is between 1100-1200mm while temperatures range between 10°-30°C.

The district has an estimated population of 876,474 persons (50.2% males and 49.8% females), of which 11 percent reside in urban areas. The population of children below 15 years is about 50 percent showing similarities with the national picture. The population density of 245 persons per square kilometre (2002 national census) is higher than the national average of 124. Furthermore, the district is estimated to have 175,631 households of which about one third are female-headed. The district has a diversity of ethnic groups of which the majority are Baganda followed by the Banyankole, Banyarwanda and Banyoro. But Buganda culture is dominant and the main language spoken is Luganda. The HIV prevalence rate for central region is 8.5 percent. Among the mentioned ethnic groups, Baganda with a prevalence rate of 8.2 percent (10.1% among women and 5.8 among men) and that for Banyankole at 6.9 percent (7.6% among women and 5.9 among men) are the highest (MOH and ORC Macro, 2006).

Predominantly, agriculture is the main source of household income with 74.3 percent deriving a livelihood from it. Bananas, maize, beans and cassava, sweet potatoes, and Irish potatoes, groundnuts, millet and yams constitute the main crops grown while coffee is the traditional cash crop. However, farmers also grow a variety of other crops, fruits and vegetables for cash (pineapples tomatoes, onions, cabbages). Less important sources of income include property rents, incomes from cottage industry, metal fabrication and rearing poultry. The majority of the cottage industries are agriculture-based, predominantly involved in processing of coffee (over 73%) and maize. The geographical location of Masaka District also favors its commercial sector and has led to up springing of about 50 trading centers along the highway running from Kampala to the western region of Uganda.

With regard to physical infrastructure, the district has six main tarmac roads going through it and a fairly good feeder and access road network. Nonetheless, infrastructure is inadequate in some rural areas and with some feeder roads impassable during the rainy season (for example, some parts of Kyazanga). Nine out of 23 sub-counties have electricity but only 0.61 percent of the population have access to electricity. MTN, CELTEL and Uganda Telecom cellular network companies provide telecommunication services. There are six local radio channels in addition to the national Radio Uganda and three providers of television services. The main educational institutions include 454 primary, 79 secondary, 13 each of tertiary and vocational and 2 nursing schools. Forty seven percent of the population are literate; of these the literacy rate for men (65%) is higher than that for women (59%). The district has four main health units[19] offering HIV testing and counseling services. Other health services include immunization with coverage at 52.6 percent and modern contraceptive prevalence at 15 percent of the target population.

Firewood is the predominant source of fuel. Although 78 percent of the villages have access to safe-water[20], some communities (for example, Kyazanga and Mbirizi where some of the surveyed villages were drawn) have a severe water problem. Nonetheless, the proportion of households with access to safe water in the district is higher than that recorded for the national average (61 %) during the 2002 national census.

Kabarole

Kabarole was part of Toro kingdom at independence. Following abolition of the kingdoms in 1967, it became a district composed of present-day Kasese, Kamwenge, Kyenjojo, Bundibujo and Kabarole districts. Under the 1974 Provincial administration, Toro district was sub-divided into the districts of Semiliki, Rwenzori and Toro. The latter became Kabarole in 1990, while the other two are the present day Bundibugyo and Kasese districts. In 2000, Kamwenge and Kyenjojo were carved out of Kabarole. The district is located in the western region of Uganda, between 0°15' and 1°00' N and 30°00' and 31°15' E. It is bordered by the districts of Bundibugyo in the west, Hoima and Kibaale in the north, Kasese and Kamwenge in the south and Kyenjojo in the east. Average altitude ranges from 915 m at Lake Kyoga to 3,556 m above sea level and the district has a total area of 1,816 sq km (of 0.87% is open water - mostly Lake George, making it the least endowed with surface water resources in the region). Average annual rainfall is between 750-1000mm while temperatures do not exceed 19°C.

The district has an estimated population of 359,180 (50.1% males and 49.9% females), of which 11.3 percent reside in urban areas. The population density of 200

[19] Masaka Hospital/Uganda Cares, Kinoni Health Centre, Kitovu Hospital, and TASO - Masaka. However, Kitovu Hospital has mobile VTC services in some selected sub-counties in the district. Masaka Hospital/ Uganda Cares have trained staff at sub-district level (Health center IVs), in preparation of starting mobile testing services to reach un served populations.

[20] Tap water, water from boreholes, protected springs and Gravity Flow schemes are regarded by Uganda Government as safe for drinking.

persons per square kilometre (2002 national census) is also higher than the national average of 124 persons per square kilometre. It has an estimated number of 70,421 households. The district has a rich diversity of ethnic groups, with nearly every tribe in the country being represented. However, Batoro, Batuku and Basongora form the dominant tribes (about 52%), followed by the Bakiga (28%), Bakonjo and Bamba. The major languages spoken are Rutooro, Rukiga and Runyankore. The HIV prevalence rate for Kabarole at 11 percent (District Development Plan document) is much higher than that reported for the whole of the western region (6.9%) by MOH and ORC Macro (2006). MOH and ORC Macro also showed that in 2004/05 the Batoro had the highest HIV prevalence – 14.8 percent (16.4% among women and 12.8 among men) – of all ethnic groups nationwide.

Like for other districts, agriculture is the main source of livelihood of the people in Kabarole. Food crops grown include cassava, bananas, maize, beans, sorghum, sweetpotato, and Irish potato, groundnuts, millet, yams, and soya bean. Passion fruits, pineapples, tomatoes, onions, and cabbages constitute the main fruit and vegetable crops grown. Coffee and tea (grown as an estate crop) are the traditional cash crops grown, though farmers get income from the sale of food crops as well. Other sources of income include bakeries and confectionery, agro-processing especially of tea, coffee and maize, industries producing soap, garments, and jaggery, lime and chalk, furniture production and saw milling.

The district has an inadequate feeder road network. In some places roads are in poor condition, while in others there is hardly any road link. The few roads with tarmac have been in a very bad state requiring repair. The road between Fort Portal and Mubende was not a tarmac road[21] by the time of the study. The western railway to Kasese that goes through the southern part of the district used to be an important means of cheap transport. However, the irregularity of the train service has deprived the district of a cheap link to urban markets. Access to electricity is limited to major urban centers. Like for Masaka district, MTN, CELTEL and Uganda Telecom cellular phone companies provide telecommunication services but there are only two radio broadcasting companies: Radio Uganda and Radio Toro. There is some limited use of solar and gas lighting. The main educational institutions include 130 primary, 30 secondary, three teacher training colleges and one national technical institute at Kichwamba. Buhanga, Virika and Kabarole referral hospitals are the three health units providing VTC services. Information on other health services and indicators was not available.

The predominant source of fuel is firewood. The level of safe water coverage (77.5%) is similar to that in Masaka district.

---

[21] The rehabilitation and building of the road links to Kasese and Mubende have been under way and are likely t be completed in 2007. This is going to greatly increase access to markets for agricultural produce.

3.3 Phases of the field work

The first phase involved a reconnaissance visit to the study area, conducted in December of 2003. Its main objectives were a familiarization with the research area and obtaining relevant district-level data for refinement of the research proposal. In addition, the data obtained was later used in sampling and selection of the villages in which the survey was conducted. In Phase 2, efforts were geared towards establishing rapport with relevant authorities and obtaining research clearance. It included an initial qualitative exploratory phase that started in September 2004 and lasted for three months. The data collected provided general information about the study area and insights about the HIV/AIDS situation. It also helped to identify factors that could be fuelling the epidemic. Additionally, the second phase was used to operationalize the concepts and determine relevant variables that were included in the questionnaire for the household survey. In this phase, community HIV-risk factors were also identified. These facilitated the selection of sub-counties for the study; no other data on HIV prevalence at sub-district level were available[22]. In Phase 3, a household survey was conducted during May-August 2005 in 26 villages in both districts. This was followed by preliminary analysis of the survey data to identify key issues that needed more in-depth investigation in order to adequately answer the research questions. This information facilitated development of selection criteria for the cases. The final phase (Phase 4) mainly focused on the use of in-depth interviews to investigate key processes and relationships using case studies drawn from the two districts. However, additional focus group discussions (FGDs) and key informant interviews were conducted to fill in missing information or whenever new questions arose. A summary of the four phases of the research process is presented in Figure 3.1.

3.4 Methods and techniques for data collection

Qualitative and quantitative data collection techniques were used for the study. Qualitative and quantitative methods provided a richer base for analysis. In this study, the two methodologies were viewed as complementary, each contributing to a better understanding and interpretation of the data generated and to the ultimate findings (Breitmayer *et al.*, 1993). The main data collection techniques included review of secondary data, focus group discussions, in-depth key informant interviews, survey, case study, as well as participant observation.

---

[22] Factors that guided selection of study areas at sub-district level: Presence of TASO and Kitovu Mobile HIV/AIDS programs, proximity to Rakai District (Epicenter of the Epidemic in Uganda), location along the Kampala Masaka highway.

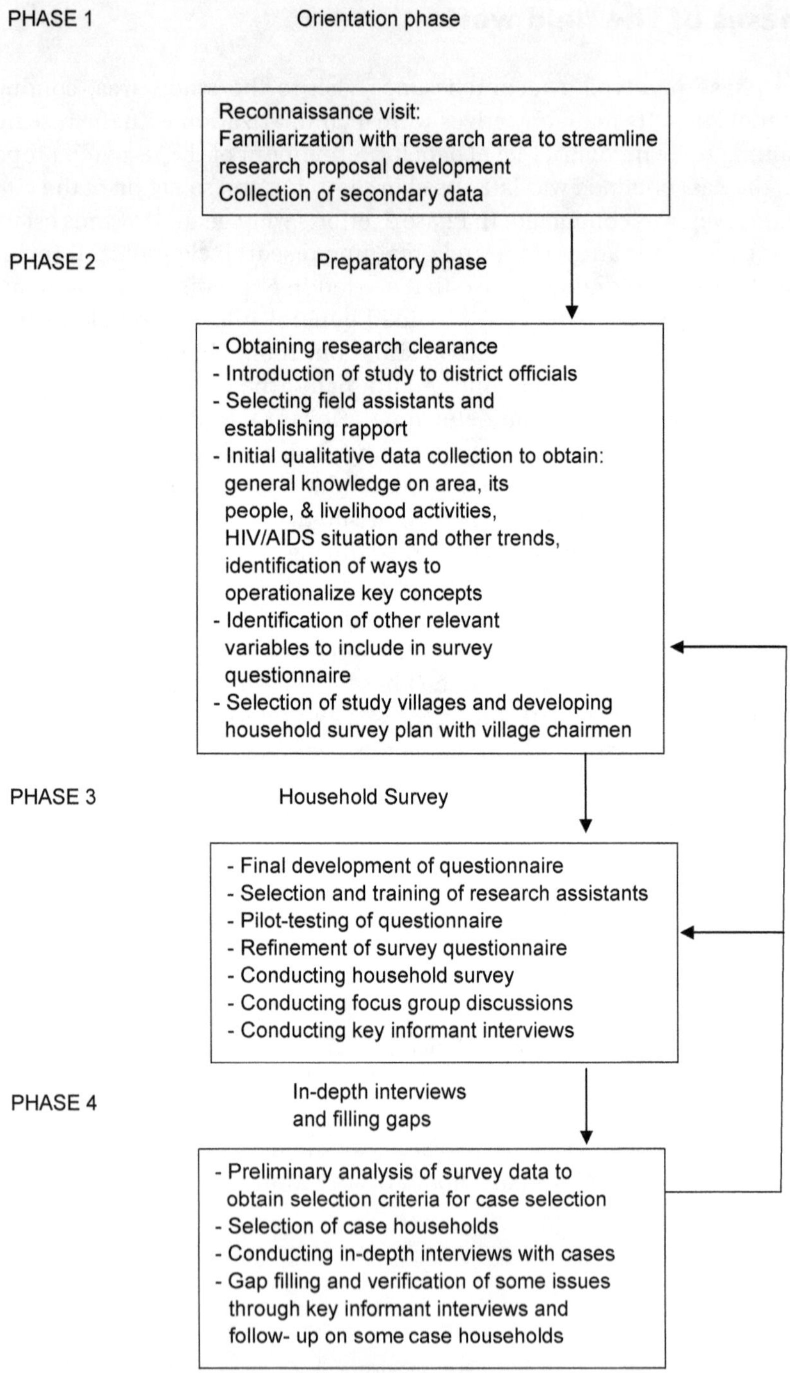

Figure 3.1. Phases of the research process.

3.4.1 Secondary data

A detailed content analysis of relevant reports and documents provided secondary data. These documents included extensive and diverse literature by local and foreign researchers, civil servants, civil society activists and journalists, and included both published and unpublished information. Use was also made of materials from the Uganda AIDS Commission, Uganda Bureau of Statistics (UBOS), National Agricultural Advisory Services (NAADS), the ministries of Finance, Agriculture, Health, Gender Labour and Social Development and their departments at district level, as well as Community Based Organizations (CBOs) and NGOs involved in the provision of HIV/AIDS-related care and support. Most of the information studied focused on ethnographic, physical and demographic characteristics of the study area, crop production and farming systems, HIV/AIDS community risk factors, perceived impacts of HIV/AIDS on agriculture-based livelihoods and existing support mechanisms, programs and policies on HIV/AIDS prevention and control.

3.4.2 Primary data

The methods and techniques used for collecting primary data included the following:

Household survey

In this study, a household is defined as a person or group of persons, family-based, who live together and/or eat together and/or jointly cultivate a common piece of land and/or pool resources from multiple sources and/or are answerable to the same head and/or depend on each other, all done with the overall objective of achieving livelihood security.

For the survey, this included members of the household that may not have been physically present at the time of the survey, particularly the household head, but who play a significant role in decision making, as well as supply the bulk of the cash and other household necessities. Members that had permanently migrated were not included but any regular income or support that they provided to the household was included as part of the household's resources.

A total of 650 banana farming households were sampled but information was collected from only 543 households (304 in Masaka and 239 in Kabarole districts), because some households were physically inaccessible (too remote) while others refused to participate. The survey method was used because of its appropriateness in answering the *what* and *how* questions with regard to the type of resources that households are endowed with, changes in these resources, effects of HIV/AIDS as well as the magnitude of household resource change in the period three years prior to the survey (cf. Babbie, 1995).

A draft questionnaire to address issues on which quantitative data was developed using focus group information collected during the reconnaissance visit and the preparatory phase. Through consultations with supervisors, the instrument was refined. The improved draft was pilot-tested among 20 banana-farming households in one of the villages in Masaka outside the sampled group, to avoid reporting bias but at the same time use a similar group of respondents in pre-testing the instrument.

Following the pre-test, the questionnaire was adjusted to improve clarity and relevance of some questions as well as the flow and sequencing of questions. However, prior to pre-testing the survey instrument, the following procedure was used to select the study villages and households to include in the sample.

Area Sampling: A multistage sampling technique was used in the selection of the study area. The two districts were purposively selected using the following criteria:

- Banana production as the main food and livelihood activity.
- HIV prevalence levels being high (Masaka) and medium (Kabarole).

Each district in Uganda has three levels of administrative units: the district level, county level and sub-county as the lowest level of governance. Sub-counties are further sub-divided into parishes and villages. For purposes of area selection, each district was stratified by the smallest administrative unit: a sub-county. For each district, three sub-counties were purposively selected on the basis of a high level of banana production and HIV/AIDS prevalence ranging from high, through medium to low prevalence (cf. section 3.2). High banana production was then used to purposively select one to three parishes per sub-county basing on the sub-county population. Finally, depending on the population of the sampled parishes and ease of accessibility, one to three villages were selected using simple random procedures. A total of 26 villages from 13 parishes in six sub-counties constituted the study areas for the household survey.

Subject sampling: Following the selection of the study villages, and with the help of the area extension officer, all the village chairmen[23] of the sampled villages in Masaka were invited to planning meetings. At the meetings, the objectives of the study and issues to ensure a smooth data collection process were discussed. The

[23] A village chairman is a locally elected leader in charge of a village also designated as Local Council I (LCI).

latter included the village chairmen's role in developing an inventory of all banana-farming households in each of their villages; mobilizing individuals to participate in group discussions and relevant logistics. A timetable was then drawn and agreed upon by all the chairmen. This process was repeated for Kabarole.

The chairmen were each required to develop an inventory of banana-farming households that had at least one-eighth of an acre under banana (i.e approximately 50 banana stools). However, a few non-banana-growing households were included in the survey.

After receiving the inventories, the population density of banana-farming households per village was used to calculate the required sample size. Depending on the number of banana-farming households with the specified acreage, 25 to 45 banana-farming households were selected per village. Four fifths of the required sample of banana-farming households were randomly selected. The other one-fifth was purposively selected and included banana-farming households that had a member who had had prolonged illness or HIV/AIDS-related illness or had lost an adult member due to HIV/AIDS, according to key informant information[24]. This was to increase the chances of including HIV/AIDS affected households given: (i) the difficulty and ethical implications of identifying such households beforehand and (ii) the absence of records on HIV/AIDS due to the non-existence of HIV testing facilities in the rural areas.

For each sample household, using the revised questionnaire, face-to-face interviews were conducted with the household head. However, the household head would consult with the spouse on matters that he or she was more versed with during the course of the interview. In about 40 households, the household heads were absent at the time of the survey and their spouses were interviewed instead. A total of 304 respondents in Masaka and 239 in Kabarole were interviewed.

Data collected: The following data was collected during the household survey: demographic information; household characteristics and resource use; banana farming practices and constraints; livelihood activities including household consumption and production activities, and constraints related to agricultural production; health of household members, including nature and type of illnesses experienced by members, effects of illness on livelihoods and ways of coping; food security and coping strategies; access to services; as well as changes in household assets, resources and production activities in the three years prior to the survey. A specific section answered by widows generated data on widow's perceptions of the

[24] The village chairmen have good knowledge of most households in their village and they are responsible for issuing death certificates.

effects of HIV/AIDS on household members' well-being and resources and ways in which widow-headed households are coping with the effects of the epidemic.

Focus group discussions (FGDs)

The focus group discussions provided an opportunity to gain a deeper understanding of the prevailing community operations as well as the socio-cultural and political environment in which the study was conducted. The technique brought out collective experience and opinion from a wide range of people. Twelve group discussions were conducted in phases 1 and 4 and another 26 FGDs were conducted as part of the household survey to obtain additional qualitative data to enrich the analysis and interpretation of the quantitative data. A total of 338 people (183 women, 9 girls, 10 boys and 136 men) participated in the group discussions. Of these, eight were mixed groups composed of male and female participants, 13 were of entirely male and another 13 only female participants, two groups were composed of children while another two groups were of AIDS-affected individuals. Table 3.1 summarizes the composition and specific topics discussed in the different FGDs.

The FGDs were conducted for 60 to 100 minutes with six to ten participants. Separate discussions were conducted for women and men except in a few situations (Table 3.1) when general information was required, and in one case, when a mixed group discussion was organized to deal with contradictions that had arisen during the separate group meetings. The segregation of the groups by gender was intended to provide a free environment for expression. Local leaders, agricultural extension staff, health personnel and community development workers facilitated selection of FGD participants. These included individuals (some of whom were household

Table 3.1. The composition and topics of FGDs.

Composition of group	Topics discussed and phase of study	Mska* Total groups	Krole* Total groups	Total males	Total females
Mixed (men & women)	*Orientation and preparatory phase:* Community resources/ opportunities Livelihood activities and strategies Food security status and indicators Major problems in the area HIV/AIDS: magnitude of problem HIV/AIDS initiatives in community Cultural norms	2	2	14	28

Table 3.1. Continued.

Composition of group	Topics discussed and phase of study	Mska* Total groups	Krole* Total groups	Total males	Total females
Men	*Survey:* Main sources of income Constraints in agriculture Livelihood and food security issues Effects of HIV/AIDS at various levels Access to services (extension, health, credit, markets) Household resource allocation and decision making	7	6	97	0
Women	*Survey:* Similar to those for men's group, and special constraints women face in livelihood generation	7	6	0	135
Children	*In-depth interview phase:* Effects of HIV/AIDS Access to services (health & education) and other community support Response/coping with AIDS	1	1	10	9
AIDS-affected	*In-depth interview phase:* Effects of HIV/AIDS Access to health services & ART, and other HIV/AIDS-related support Response/coping with AIDS Existing HIV/AIDS community support organizations	1	1	11	6
Mixed (men & women)	*In-depth interviews:* Division of labour and seasonal calendar Household resources allocation and decision making Characteristics of food secure HH Wealth ranking	2	2	14	14
Total		20	18	146	192

* Mska= Masaka; Krole= Kabarole.

heads that had participated in the survey) with local knowledge and experience with respect to the selected discussion topics. In addition to and for only two FGDs (one for HIV-infected men and one for HIV-infected women), participants were selected based on their self reported HIV/AIDS status.

Information obtained through focus group discussions included: livelihood activities and strategies, food security and vulnerability; banana farming practices and gender division of labour in agricultural activities; household resource access, use and control; gender relations; HIV/AIDS-related effects and coping mechanisms; cultural norms relating to reciprocity, collective action, exclusion; as well as the type and nature of informal and formal organizations supporting agriculture or AIDS-affected households or both.

Key informant interviews

There are different types of interviews that can be used in qualitative research (Fontana & Frey, 1994). They may be formal or informal and vary in depth with their use depending largely on the type of information required. Interviews with selected informants were conducted in a rather unstructured manner because the interview guidelines were not strictly followed, but rather, allowed the respondents to take the discussions in directions that interested them. However, I always tried to bring the conversation back to the central research themes.

(i) A total of 28 individuals (Table 3.2) were selected as key informants and they included: officials in the ministries of Agriculture and Health, government and private extension officers, district community development and administrative officers, CBO/NGO workers (Kitovu Mobile, TASO, World Vision, Uganda Cares, CHAI), agricultural researchers from Kawanda Agricultural Research Institute (KARI) and International Network for the Improvement of Banana and Plantain (INIBAP), local leaders, banana farmers and people living with HIV/AIDS. The rationale for conducting interviews with these people was to obtain expert information on specific issues relevant to the study, given their knowledge, experience and professional background.

The different key informants were purposively selected based on the following criteria:
(i) the government ministry officials, researchers and district/sub-district technical staff based on their expert knowledge and availability at time of interview;
(ii) representatives of community organizations based on position in organization, activities involved in, willingness to share experiences and availability at the time of interview; and local leaders by virtue of their position as leaders in the study areas and availability at the time of interview.

Table 3.2. Summary of sources of information, number in source category and data collection techniques.

Sources	How many	Data collection techniques
People (individuals and groups)	Heads of sampled households (543)	Household survey
	Men's, women's, children's, mixed and AIDS-affected groups (38)	Focus group discussions conducted separately for each category
	Agricultural extension staff –district and MAAIF (10) Health staff (4) Representatives of NGOs/ CBOs (10) Local leaders (4)	Formal and informal interviews for key informants
	Case study subjects (20)	In-depth interviews, life history and participant observation
Documents	Relevant academic literature National and district reports, CBO/NGO reports News articles,	Review and content analysis
Context	Field situation	Direct observations and photography

Case studies

The case study method was used to generate qualitative data to explore the dynamic and complex social relations and processes within and between banana-farming households in HIV/AIDS-affected households. Mitchell (1983:192) defines a case study as "a detailed examination of an event (or series of related events) which the analyst believes exhibits (or exhibit) the operation of some identified general theoretical principle." While case studies can be used for both generating and testing hypotheses (Flyvbjerg, 2006), Yin argues that case a study can be defined as an empirical inquiry that investigates a phenomenon within its real-life context (Yin, 2002). Using Yin's definition, case studies were used to examine the inter-relationship between HIV/AIDS and rural livelihoods. I examined a number of affected household to explore the ways in which HIV/AIDS influences resource access and use, changes in gender and social relations, causes vulnerability, reproduces inequalities, as well as the mechanisms through which it triggers off various downward spirals.

This method facilitated a deeper understanding and synthesis of issues such as culture, social relations, perceptions, attitudes and opinions of people in relation to HIV/AIDS and how these fuel the epidemic. In addition, the methodology provided insights on the challenges of generating sustainable livelihoods in a situation of poverty and HIV/AIDS and the strategies people use to deal with these challenges. In the process it was also possible to gain an "emic" perspective through interpretations of the different phenomenon by the people themselves. Furthermore, it was possible to explore how different individuals and groups are differently affected by the epidemic. As Mitchell (1983) argues, case studies serve to establish the validity of a particular theoretical principle, not by achieving statistical significance but through their ability to elaborate a theoretical principle, by confronting it with the complexity of empirical reality. Qualitative techniques used included open interviews, participant observation and in-depth life history interviews.

A total of 20 cases were studied. Some were used to explain a variety of issues in the thesis, while others were particular to specific topics. For some, the focus was on household strategies while for others, it was on specific individuals within the household and their individual strategies. Yet in others, life histories of individuals in certain households were looked at to identify processes that make some people more vulnerable to effects of the epidemic. Identification of case study households was facilitated by government health workers and workers of NGOs involved in HIV/AIDS treatment and support who had proof that the selected households had at least one affected member. Additionally, the household head or another member of the selected households were asked to confirm the HIV/AIDS status of their households with medical documents indicating proof of HIV positive diagnosis or medical forms indicating that an affected household member was on ARV treatment.

In some situations, however, I had to rely on self-reported status, when tests were conducted by the district referral hospitals or a known mobile HIV testing and counselling agency. In two cases, participants showed the different medications that they were on, and the labels indicated that it was ARV treatment.

Households to serve as case studies were purposively selected using the following criteria: first, HIV/AIDS affectedness i.e., households that had proof of HIV/AIDS morbidity and/or mortality and secondly, the selected households were banana farmers or had grown at least one-eighth of an acre of banana in the past. Preliminary analysis of the survey data had indicated correlations between magnitude of HIV/AIDS-related effects and gender of the household head, number of years since the occurrence of an HIV/AIDS related death of an adult bread winner, household asset status, and whether infected individuals were on ARV treatment or not. Therefore, these factors were used as additional selection criteria. In-depth interviews for cases study households were guided by a checklist.

Observation

Gittleson and Mookherji (1997) argued that observations provide a good opportunity to get detailed and real insight in actual situations including "actions, conversations, and physical descriptions". Observation as a technique was therefore used to get a better grasp on processes of livelihood generation, the type, nature, state and use of household assets, the way other environmental factors (including poverty) may work to intensify the impacts of HIV/AIDS, as well as have an increased appreciation of the emotional and psychological impacts associated with HIV/AIDS, i.e., fear, pain, disillusionment and hopelessness, among others. In addition, the technique was used to triangulate information collected with other methods and/or obtained from different data sources, particularly regarding gender division of labour for agricultural practices. A checklist was used as a guide to look out for factors and processes on which critical observations were necessary. The observions were recorded in a field note book. For the case study households, a tour around some of the fields to observe what was being grown or look at the state of the gardens was done. In addition to what was observed, information was also collected through listening to conversations and discussions during informal visits to the communities or whenever a women's group organized a repast for me.

3.5 Data analysis

Both quantitative and qualitative data analysis techniques were used. The adoption of a multi-methodology strategy was useful in the interpretation and understanding of the key research issues. Quantitative data was used to put figures on what existed and what was representative and provide a context for the cases. Qualitative data facilitated answering of the "how and why" questions by providing explanations (and sometimes even generating new questions) to the variations captured in the quantitative data, thus producing a richer analysis.

The household was selected as the unit of analysis (see Chapter 2). For purposes of quantitative analysis, survey households were categorized into three groups: one of male-headed households and two of female-headed households (single-female-headed and widow-headed households). The category of single-male-headed was not used because they were too few. During analysis, comparisons were drawn between the male-headed and the two types of female-headed households in Masaka and Kabarole districts while taking into account their wealth status. In addition, comparisons were drawn between the "HIV/AIDS-affected" and "non-affected" households. In their study, Barnett and Blaikie (1992) defined three distinct categories of HIV/AIDS-related impacts on households. *AIDS-afflicted* households are defined as those where a member of the household is either ill or has died from HIV/AIDS. *AIDS-affected* as those where no member is infected, but AIDS effects are indirect through, for example, diversion of resources to support an AIDS-afflicted household or by taking in orphans while *unaffected* households are those that have not experienced HIV/AIDS-related direct or indirect impacts. As is the case in the area in which Barnett and Blaikie (1992) carried out their field work, unaffected households are rare in Masaka and Kabarole. In this study, "affected households" are defined as households that were directly affected by AIDS and therefore had at least one member known to be HIV-positive at the time of the study or have died from (an) AIDS (-related) illness. Based on key informant information obtained from health personnel, households reporting morbidity or mortality due to Tuberculosis were included among "HIV/AIDS-affected households". Households that were not directly affected by AIDS are defined as "non-affected households" and included those where no member was suffering or had died from illness related to AIDS. In addition, a distinction was drawn between HIV/AIDS-related morbidity and mortality (which are attributed to the former causes) and morbidity and mortality attributed to other causes, based on self-reported information on diagnosis and cause of death. While information was collected on orphanhood, households supporting orphans were not included among affected households because in many cases the respondents were not sure or had no proof that orphanhood was HIV/AIDS-related. Nonetheless, the distribution of orphans by household headship and HIV/AIDS-orphan-related effects was examined. Orphans in this case were defined according to Uganda law as children under the age of 18 years of whom at least one parent is not alive (UBOS, 2004).

3.5.1 Quantitative data analysis

Survey data was first subjected to preliminary analysis using the Superior Performing Statistical Software (SPSS 12.1 version). Quantitative techniques such as descriptive statistics, General Linear Model (GLM) (Multiple Comparative Procedure) and nonparametric statistics were used to understand the relationships between different variables. Percentages were used to determine and explain proportions, while means were mainly used to determine differences in household asset ownership and use, farming practices, food adequacy as well as HIV/AIDS status.

GLM was used where there was one dependent variable and one or more independent ones. The F-test was used to determine if the mean values of the independent variable (or combinations of values for multiple independent variables) significantly differed between groups and, thus, did not occurr by chance. If the group means did not differ significantly it was inferred that the between group differences in the independent variable(s) do not have an effect on the dependent variable. Where the F-test showed that the between group means of an independent variable differed, multiple comparison tests of significance (one way analysis of variance or Chi Square) were used to assess which group means differed significantly from which others. GLM was, therefore, used to obtain group means for the following variables: (i) Household (HH) assets by household headship, (ii) mean HH asset change by household headship, (iii) mean adequacy food score by household headship, (iv) AIDS status by district and by household headship, (v) food security status by whether AIDS-affected HH and by district, (vi) mean change in HH incomes by whether AIDS-affected and by district, (vii) effects of ill health on agricultural production by household headship, and (viii) strategies employed during times of food scarcity by household headship and by district.

Additional multivariate analysis using the ordinary least squares method (OLS), multinomial logit (mlogit) and ordered logit (ologit) was done to take into account effects of various factors on people's livelihood and the way these factors interact with HIV/AIDS (see Appendix 1). First, cluster analysis was used to identify main livelihood strategies pursued by farmers in Masaka and Kabarole districts. This was then followed by the use of a mlogit to identify the determinants of a household's livelihood strategy. The choice of the mlogit model was based on its ability to perform better with discrete choice studies (McFadden, 1973; Judge *et al.*, 1985).

An OLS regression model was used to determine factors that influence per capita expenditure since the dependent variable is continuous and almost all farmers spend some money. Per capita consumption expenditure was used as a proxy indicator for livelihood security. Expenditure data is preferred over income data because "income data usually presents two disadvantages; (i) household survey income data, particularly self-employment income, may be unreliable; (ii) income data may not capture changes in living standards caused by increased income instability if consumption declines in response to greater uncertainty, for example, [when putting aside] precautionary savings" (Glewwe & Hall, 1998:184).

The adequacy score – a mean rank explaining adequacy of the various food categories for each household – was used as a proxy for household food security, which in turn was used as an indicator for livelihood vulnerability. Information was collected on household food adequacy for 14 most commonly consumed foods. The ranks ranged from 1 to 4, with 1 = inadequate, 2 = barely adequate, 3 = adequate and 4 = very adequate. From the adequacy ranks reported per food type, an aggregate mean food adequacy score for the 14 food types was calculated for each household. The mean adequacy ranks were further used to categorize households into three, i.e., food insecure, barely food secure, and food secure. The Wilcoxon signed-rank test, T, (Wilcoxon matched-pairs test) was used to compare the mean adequacy food score of households in the two study areas. Specifically, the Wilcoxon test factors in the size as well as the sign of the paired differences were done. A third model was then used to identify factors determining livelihood vulnerability in Masaka and Kabarole districts. In this case, an ordered choice model (ologit) was used since the outcomes were mutually exclusive and exhaustive and there was an ordering (hierarchy) among the responses (rankings) of the respondents (cf. Green, 2003).

It is noteworthy that although the major factors were analyzed separately, and attempts were made to control for variations in other factors as far as possible, interactions between factors influencing livelihood processes could be complex and therefore all the interactions could not be eliminated completely.

3.5.2 Qualitative data analysis

The data analysis started from the field and continued until the end of the research. It included both context and content analysis and was manually done.

Context analysis: The subjects' livelihoods were generated within a given environmental context, often characterized by insecurities, risk and opportunities. Therefore, to understand the ways in which livelihoods in different contexts were shaped, this environment was analyzed. To situate respondent livelihoods and link them to their historical context, the social, structural and institutional context that influences whether people construct secure livelihoods in a situation of AIDS (or not) was analyzed.

Content analysis: First, data from tape-recorded interviews were manually transcribed. Some of the data from group discussions, participant observations and interviews was analyzed and interpreted in the field or at the point of interaction with the respondents. Otherwise, for the greater bulk, a process of careful and systematic analysis of data collected from life histories and interviews was employed. This involved a process of data reduction and categorization to identify key themes and sub-themes, and was combined with reading and re-reading of the recorded material (O'Leary, 2004) to identify meanings, explanations and relationships between the concepts. In addition, continuous reflection on insights gained during the data collection process facilitated interpretation and linkage of livelihood outcomes and HIV/AIDS-related vulnerability.

3.6 Ethical considerations and problems encountered during data collection

Although it is sometimes indicated that stigma due to HIV/AIDS does not exist in Uganda, or that it has significantly declined, stigma was very evident in some of the study villages. Therefore, during the data collection process measures were necessary to avoid stigmatization of affected households. The survey sample was not stratified into affected and non-affected households. These two categories were compared later during data analysis. Additionally, interviews with affected households were private and not even the village chairman was aware of the times such households were visited.

The other ethical consideration involved the compensation of the participants' time and/or transport costs incurred to participate in the study. Participants of FGDs just received refreshments during the group discussions.

Access to information and respondents was particularly difficult in the household survey. Besides the ethical issue, there was also no data to facilitate stratification of households into HIV/AIDS-affected and non- affected. To increase the chances of having more HIV/AIDS affected households, a combination of sampling methods for subjects to include in the survey was done. All households in the sampling frame that were widow-headed or had lost an adult member due to prolonged illness in the three years prior to the survey or which were known to have a sick member with a history of prolonged illness were included in the survey. They constituted about one fifth of the sample.

In addition, obtaining production data was difficult given the lack of farm production records, limited recall on the part of farmers and sometimes the very small acreages involved. Sometimes, farmers reported number of plants grown instead of acreage. Estimation was very difficult because different farmers had different crop spacing. Because of being highly unreliable, yield data was not used for analysis.

The study was conducted during a period that followed a severe drought (almost two years of little to no rain in Masaka district and less than a year for Kabarole district). This is likely to have skewed the picture of household food security and data on household incomes/expenditure since the main source of household income is agriculture. Additionally, during the study period, prices of all goods rose as a result of increasing oil prices on the world market. Moreover, there had been a trend of increasing poverty in rural areas[25]. This presented the challenge of disentangling the effects of HIV/AIDS from other existing environmental stresses.

Furthermore, because of the high prevalence of HIV/AIDS and poverty, the people had high expectations from outsiders who carried out research in their communities, even when the research objectives were made clear to them. They hoped that the investigations were about identifying those most in need so that they could later benefit from programmes as had been the modus operandi used by certain NGOs working in the study communities. Consequently, many people wanted to participate in the FGSs or be selected for the survey so as to have their names and/or those of their children recorded. This made some respondents' information sometimes doubtful. The use of a variety of methods to triangulate information was helpful. To partly deal with the problem of bias during the selection of FGD participants, the local leaders were always told to select about twice as many people that were required for the FGD from which about ten (half) would then be randomly selected.

[25] Income poverty increased from 34% to 38% between 2000 and 2003, and inequality as measured by the Gini coefficient rose markedly from 0.39 to 0.43 (MFPED, 2004).

Chapter 4
Farming households and farming in the study areas

Agriculture presents the most important economic activity in Masaka and Kabarole and is largely dependent on small and medium scale farms with average land holdings of 2.5 ha. This chapter describes farming households in Masaka and Kabarole districts and the major livelihood activities, thus providing a context for understanding the way other livelihood strategies are integrated with farming and how they reinforce each other. The rest of the chapter is organized as follows: in section 4.1, demographic and other household characteristics of the surveyed households are presented. Section 4.2 presents agriculture production in the study area with particular emphasis on the land tenure systems and access to land, main food crops grown and animals reared, as well as access to markets and services. In section 4.3 the main constraints experienced by farmers in the two districts are discussed. Section 4.4 discusses the food security status of surveyed households and the chapter ends with concluding remarks in section 4.5. The discussions in this chapter mainly focus at the level of the household.

4.1 Demographic and household characteristics

A total of 650 households were sampled but information was collected from 543 households (304 from Masaka and 239 from Kabarole districts) because some households were physically inaccessible (too remote) while others refused to participate. Households are categorized into three groups; one of male-headed households and two of female-headed households, that is, single-female-headed and widow-headed households. Two of the households in Masaka district were child-headed and could not be included in the statistical analysis, but their data has been used in other ways. Of the 541 households, 72.1 percent are male-headed. For the female-headed ones, those headed by widows (18.7%) are about twice as many as those headed by single women (9.1%). The men and women interviewed were also of assorted religious and ethnic backgrounds with Catholic (48%), Anglican (29.9%), and Muslim (10.7%) being the dominant religious categories. Ethnic affiliation varied between the two districts with Baganda (60.4%) and Banyankole (19.8%) being the most common ethnic groups in Masaka, while in Kabarole it were the Batooro (64%) and Bakiga (25.9%).

4.1.1 Demographic characteristics

Demographic characteristics of respondents are presented in Tables 4.1 and 4.3 and their marital status in Table 4.2. Age of the household head is on average 42 years.

Table 4.1. Demographic characteristics by district.

Variable		Masaka (%)	Kabarole (%)	Overall (%)
Characteristics of Household Head				
Single-female-heads		9.9	8.4	9.2
Male-heads		66.6	79.1	72.1
Widow-heads		23.5	12.6	18.7
Never attended school		23	26	23
Attained lower primary		23	29	23
Attained upper primary		38	34	3
Attained secondary (1-4 years)		14	11	14
Attained upper secondary/tertiary		2	1	2
Household characteristics				
Households fostering orphans***		12.2	7.1	9.9
Households with school-going children		63	62	62
Housing:	Permanent house**	49.0	2.9	28.7
	Semi-permanent house	39.1	90.0	61.5
	Temporary house	11.8	7.1	9.8
		Mean (SD)	**Mean (SD)**	**Mean (SD)**
Age of Household Head (years)		43.9 (14.55)	42.4 (12.41)	43.2(13.67)
Household size		6.2 (2.72)	6.4 (2.56)	6.2 (2.65)
Economic dependency ratio***		2.79 (2.24)	1.75 (1.92)	2.30 (2.15)
Mean number of orphans/HH		1.38 (0.68)	1.31 (0.48)	1.36 (0.62)
Number of individuals supported outside HH		2.77(2.8)	2.87(2.14)	2.81 (2.57)
N		303	238	541

Source: Household survey; ***, **, *, implies significant difference at 1%, 5% and 10% level respectively.

Female household heads were likely to be older. As can be seen in Table 4.5, the mean age of widowed household heads at 49.5 years was significantly different ($p < 0.01$) from that of single female heads (43.5 years) and male heads (41.6 years). The age of respondents was not verified and is likely to be approximate. Total number of household members recorded from infancy to 96 years was 3,414.

Table 4.2. Respondent's marital status by household headship.

Marital status	Single-female-HH (frequency)	Male-HH (frequency)	Widow-HH (frequency)	Overall	
				frequency	%
Married with one partner	12	343	0	355	65.4
Married with more than one partner	1	20	0	21	3.9
Single	16	11	0	27	5.2
Divorced	6	0	0	6	1.1
Separated	15	6	0	21	3.9
Widowed	0	10	101	111	20.6
Total	50	390	101	541	100.0

Source: Household Survey.

Education of household members: Thirty-eight percent of household heads had at least 5 years of formal education, 23 percent never attended school[26]. There are no significant differences observed in the level of education of household heads between the districts. However, at the household level, the proportion of male household heads that had never attended school (18%) was significantly lower ($p<0.1$) compared to that of single female household heads (34%) and widowed ones (44%). Additionally, the proportion of household heads with post- primary education (>15%) was significantly higher ($p<0.05$) than that for both types of female heads (<5%). Sixty-four percent of all children of school-going age were in school[27].

But the proportion of school- age children in male-headed households was slightly lower ($p<0.1$) compared to that of children in households with female heads, implying that female-headed households may have had more children in school. This also implies that female-headed households have less access to child labour than their male counterparts. About 50 percent of all adults in the surveyed households had attained at least primary education, 22 percent secondary education and the same proportion never attended school.

[26] Comparing with 2002 national census statistics: 27 percent (18% males and 35% females) of the population aged 15 years and above had never attended school; only 43 percent (51% males and 36% females) of the same age category had completed primary education; and the overall literacy rate for persons aged 10 years and above was 68% (with 76% for males and 61% for females), UBOS (2004).
[27] In 2005/06, 84% of primary aged children were attending primary schools (DFID, 2007).

Table 4.3. Demographic characteristics by household headship.

Variable	SF-HH (%)	Male-HH (%)	W-HH (%)
Characteristics of Household Head			
Never attended school*	34.0^{a}	18.0^{b}	44.0^{a}
Attained lower primary	32.0	25.0	27.0
Attained upper primary*	28.0^{bc}	39.0^{b}	27.0^{c}
Attained secondary (1-4 years)*	4.0^{a}	16.0^{b}	3.0^{a}
Attained upper secondary/tertiary*	2.0	2.0	1.0
Household characteristics			
Households with one or more orphans	24.0	29.5	27.7
Households with school-going children*	66.0^{bc}	59.0^{b}	72.0^{c}
Housing: Permanent house**	58.0	63.3	57.4
Semi-permanent house	18.0	7.2	14.9
Temporary house	11.8	7.1	9.8
HH owning bicycle**	30.0^{a}	57.0^{b}	26.0^{ab}
HH owning radio**	50.0^{a}	79.0^{b}	50.0^{a}
	Mean (SD)	**Mean (SD)**	**Mean (SD)**
Age of Household Head*** (years)	$43.5(13.16)^{a}$	$41.6\ (13.63)^{a}$	$49.8\ (12.03)^{b}$
Household size	6.1 (2.43)	6.5 (2.70)	5.4 (2.39)
Economic dependency ratio	1.93 (2.01)	2.43 (2.19)	1.89 (2.03)
Number of orphans/HH	$1.14\ (0.38)^{a}$	$1.33\ (0.49)^{b}$	$1.42\ (0.72)^{b}$
Number of individuals supported outside HH	2.5 (1.41)	2.9 (2.81)	2.4 (1.48)
N	50	390	101

Source: Household survey. ***, **,*, implies significant difference at 1%,5%, and 10% level respectively. Superscripts with the same letter across the row are not significantly different. SH-HH = Single-female-headed, Male-HH = Male-headed and W-HH = Widow-headed.

Household size: Most households are male headed, the proportion being slightly higher in Kabarole. Household size varied between one and 15. The average household size was about six of which approximately 2 persons were adults (18 years and above), implying that about two thirds of household members are dependants.

The mean household size (6.3) among survey households was much higher than the national average[28] of 4.7 as reported in the 2002 National Census report (UBOS, 2003b). The mean number of children per household increased from 3.68 in 2002 to 3.85 in 2005 (with over 90 percent being attributed to new births[29]), while for the number of adults decreased from 2.58 to 2.43 over the same period ($p < 0.1$). This implies an increase in the dependency ratio and is a reflection of national trends. The 2002 population census shows that the population of children less than 15 years constituted about a half of the total population (49%), while another 4.5 percent were above 60 years of age, yielding a dependency ratio of 1.16 (UBOS, 2003b).

Although the demographic dependency ratio is usually used as an indicator of the economic burden of the employed portion of the population, it was not used here because some of the household members in the productive age group were found to be dependants. Instead, the economic dependency ratio was calculated, considering only people who were economically active while taking into account their age differences. Considering the economic dependency ratio[30], there was a significant difference ($p < 0.01$) between Masaka and Kabarole with households in Masaka district having a dependency ratio of 2.8 in Kabarole 1.8. This can be partly explained by the higher proportion of households fostering orphans in Masaka (12.2%) compared to those in Kabarole (7.1%), which was found to be significant ($p < 0.01$). Another possible explanation could be the relatively higher rate of migration observed among households in Masaka which was about one and a half times higher than that in Kabarole, which would imply that households in Masaka were more likely to have fewer adult members. Differences in the economic dependency ratio by household headship are statistically insignificant.

Relation to household head: The majority of the children (78%) were direct descendants of the household head and live with their biological parents, 12 percent with grandmothers, five percent with grandfathers, and the remaining five percent with other relatives. The rest live with other close relatives. About one tenth of respondents belonged to households fostering orphans (the proportion being slightly higher in Masaka), with each orphan household having on average one orphan, which is almost similar to the 13 percent level of orphanhood recorded in the 2002 census. While there are no significant differences in the proportion of households fostering orphans between the districts, differences were observed at household

[28] From the 2002 Census, the mean household size for the central region [including Masaka] was 4.2 and that for the Western region [including Kabalore] was 4.8 (UBOS, 2003b).

[29] This is similar to national trends. Uganda's population is characterized by high levels of fertility and this has not changed in the last twenty years.

[30] Active household members' labour contribution was calculated using the following factors: up to 14 years (× 0.6); 15 years (× 0.7);16 years (× 0.8);17 years and >65 years (× 0.9); 18-64 years (× 1).Then economic dependency ratio was calculated by dividing Number Economically active household members by the Household size.

level. About two thirds of the households fostering orphans were widow-headed households. This may be partly explained by the fact that children in widow-headed households are orphans because they had lost a father. It is likely that some of the orphans were from the widow's dead sons and daughters.

Besides orphans, respondents indicated providing support to an average of three persons outside the household, with no differences observed between the districts. Almost all people outside the household receiving support were very close kin, such as, children, parents, siblings or other spouses of the household head.

4.1.2 Other household characteristics and morbidity

All respondents live in their own houses with the majority of household in Kabarole having semi-permanent housing. The proportions of households with permanent houses is slightly higher in Masaka than in Kabarole (Table 4.1). Malaria is endemic in the study areas; therefore the degree of risk to malaria is high. Furthermore, respondents also indicated exposure to the risk of other infectious diseases like bacterial diarrhoea, respiratory tract infections and typhoid fever. Given the levels of HIV/AIDS prevalence in the study area, HIV/AIDS was mentioned as one of the leading causes of ill health and death. Respondents and focus group participants reported limited access to health services due to the high cost of medical services and drugs, or living a long distance from the health facilities. This is likely to result in higher rates of morbidity and increased susceptibility to other opportunistic infections which may also be expensive to treat.

4.1.3 Comparing the demographic characteristics of AIDS-affected and non-affected households

For purposes of analysis, HIV/AIDS affected households were selected using the following criteria: an affected household had at least one adult member with AIDS, and/or had lost a member due to HIV/AIDS and/or had a member who had TB or had died of TB. The proportion of affected households in the sample is 21.4 percent.

In Tables 4.4 and 4.5 the distribution and characteristics of HIV/AIDS-affected and non-affected households are presented. The proportion of affected households in Kabarole is significantly higher ($p < 0.01$) than in Masaka. Proportion of affected households among the two types of female-headed households is also significantly higher ($p < 0.01$) than that for male-headed HH.

Household heads in affected households are likely to be older (48.5 years) than those in non-affected households (42 years). Furthermore, differences are observed regarding the education levels of household heads with those in HIV/AIDS-affected

Table 4.4. Demographic characteristics by HIV/AIDS status.

Variable		AIDS-Affected HH(%)	Non-Affected HH(%)	Overall (%)
Characteristics of Household Head				
Single-female-heads***		14	8	9
Male-head**		47	79	72
Widow-heads***		39	13	19
Never attended school***		36	21	24
Attained lower primary*		32	24	26
Attained upper primary***		24	39	36
Attained secondary (1-4 years) **		7	14	13
Attained upper secondary/tertiary		1	2	2
Household characteristics				
Households with one or more orphans***		62	32	39
Households with school-going children		68	61	62
Housing:	Permanent house**	20	31	29
	Semi-permanent house	67	60	62
	Temporary house	13	09	10
District:***	Masaka District	16	84	56
	Kabarole District	28	72	44
		Mean (SD)	Mean (SD)	Mean (SD)
Age of Household Head*** (years)		48.7 (14.0)	41.8 (13.2)	43.58
Household size		6.4 (2.73)	6.3 (2.63)	6.30
Dependency ratio		2.97 (2.17)	3.39 (2.14)	1.26
Mean number of orphans/HH***		1.4(0.73)	1.3 (0.54)	2.56
N		116	425	541

Source: Household survey. ***, **, *, implies significant difference at 10%, 5% and 1% respectively.

households having lower education levels than those in non-affected ones (Table 4.4). However, there are no differences observed in household size and dependence ratios between HIV/AIDS-affected and non-affected households. Regardless of of being HIV/AIDS-affected or not, the dependency ratio of female-headed households is higher than that for male-headed households.

Table 4.5. HIV/AIDS status by district and by household headship.

HIV/AIDS status	Single-female HH		Male-HH		Widow-HH		Total	
	N	%	N	%	N	%	N	%
Masaka								
Non-affected	23	76.7	176	87.6	55	77.5	254	83.8
Affected	7	23.3	26	12.4	16	22.5	49	16.2
Kabarole								
Non-affected	10	50.0	161	85.2	0	0	171	71.8
Affected	10	50.0	27	14.8	30	100.0	67	28.2
Column total	50	9.2	390	72.1	101	18.7	541	100

Chi square value = 11.357; p=0.001.
Source: Household survey.

While there is no difference in the proportions of HIV/AIDS-affected households between the two districts, differences between household categories are observed. Household level analysis reveals that the proportion of affected widow-headed households (37.6%) is significantly higher than that of affected male-headed households ($p < 0.05$). In Kabarole district, all widow-headed households in the sample are affected by AIDS. Among HIV/AIDS-affected households, the proportion of female-headed households is significantly higher than that of their male counterparts ($p < 0.05$).

There is a clear and significant difference in the proportion of households fostering orphans (0.01). The proportion of AIDS-affected households with orphans and the mean number of orphan per households is significantly higher than that of non-affected households. The high incidence of HIV among widow-headed households may partly explain the equally higher incidence of orphans among HIV/AIDS-affected households (Table 4.4). Another study conducted in selected districts in Uganda by Wakhweya *et al.* (2002), revealed that eighty five percent of single-parent orphan households were headed by females, thus giving similar results.

4.2 Agricultural production in the study areas

4.2.1 Land tenure

For the respondents in Masaka and Kabarole, primarily land has an important symbolic significance because it defines one's cultural identity. Land inheritance is seen as a representation of a continuation of family from one generation to another. Therefore, despite the decline in land due to population increase, sons always have a claim on their father's land, however small. Moreover, for those who migrate to urban areas in search of greener pastures, if things do not work out, they return "home", which is the land of their ancestors. From the past and most importantly today, almost all households identify land as an essential resource by which one engages in economic activities for livelihood generation as well as participates in social and cultural activities of one's family and community. Land is the primary tangible resource of households by which individuals produce food and generate cash (through sale of crops and livestock products or renting-out).

Cash generated is used to acquire more land, animals, a radio, or bicycle, or consumer goods and services (clothes, supplementary foods, health care, and education) as well as meet kinship obligations and those to institutions (for example paying taxes to the state). Land is also used to negotiate, create, strengthen and maintain social relationships (intangible resources) which may be called upon in future when need arises. Therefore, and as is generally agreed in the literature (cf. Kamjathy & Nicholas, 2001), land is the primary resource of identity, shelter, wealth, social status, power and livelihood security for the residents of Masaka and Kabarole. Nonetheless, unequal land rights and inefficiencies in the allocation of land in the study areas exist. Barnett and Blaikie (1992:75) noted: "This inequality lies both in the pre-colonial society and in the ways in which colonialism affected that society." In the following part of this section, I will first discuss the land tenure systems found in the study area, highlighting their historical origin, and then go on to discuss issues of land access, ownership and utilization based on survey results.

Types of land tenure in Masaka and Kabarole

Land tenure refers to a set of rights which an individual or institution holds in land. In Masaka and Kabarole districts, four categories of land tenure exist: customary tenure, *mailo* tenure, freehold tenure and leasehold tenure.

Customary tenure: Customary tenure prevailed in Uganda before the coming of colonialists and land ownership was vested in different entities: the chief or ruler, the tribe, the clan, the family, and in a few cases, the individual (Bikaako & Ssenkumba, 2003). Customary tenure Customary tenure was characterised by local customary regulation and management and is broadly categorized into three: communal tenure, clan tenure and pastoral tenure. In Masaka and Kabarole (part of former Buganda and Toro kingdoms respectively) the communal tenure system prevailed and land ownership was vested in the ruler, either as an owner or a trustee. Although homesteads and cultivated fields were owned corporately, individuals enjoyed specific rights, for example rights to fields and agricultural products, among others. However, rather than ownership, an individual's rights in land involved rights to cultivate and use (derived from their membership of a kinship group or political status) and could also be passed on to one's heirs over successive generations (William, 2003).

As Bikaako & Ssenkumba (2003) note, while men with patrilineal customary tenure systems had absolute inheritance rights to the occupation, possession and use of land, these rights did not apply to women. According to Barnett and Blaikie (1992), within the "feudal" system of pre-colonial and early colonial Buganda, women (with a few exceptions of women from the royal household) gained access to land only by occupying a status *vis-à-vis* men. Under customary tenure decision making was vested in men and even where women were given land by their natal families, they were not allowed to alienate family property (Barnett & Blaikie, 1992; Kabonesa, 2002). In Toro however, some women could inherit land and property such as livestock as well as household status from their fathers if there were no sons (Bikaako & Ssenkumba, 2003). They further say that the idea that children irrespective of their sex should receive part of the father's property was upheld. Also because uxorilocal marriage was practiced in Toro, some women engaged in socially important roles that were often a preserve of men. Toro customary law also bound the chief to grant adult women (including widows) rights of occupation over customary land provided they proved that they had the means to construct houses on the land. Married women, however, except in the case of lease hold, would never be considered. If they were considered, they would normally get smaller portions than their sons (ibid). Unlike in Buganda, daughters in Toro could dispose of their lands, and if they married, husbands had no authority over such lands. Disposal of their land required their permission and these lands were returnable upon divorce.

Despite the introduction of other land tenure systems, customary tenure remains the most wide spread, covering 64 percent of total land area, Obol Ochola (1971, cited in Bikaako & Ssenkumba, 2003:238). As Kabonesa (2002) points out, for example, that although under the colonial government, most of the land in Toro became Crown land[31] the same customary laws of occupancy still applied to its allocation and use. In the pre-colonial era, under customary tenure the women had exclusive rights to cultivation in addition to owning the produce from the land that they were given upon marriage (Bikaako & Ssenkumba, 2003; *Sebina-Zziwa, 1995*). However, colonial legislation and policies undermined customary legal systems giving household heads (mainly men) more autonomy over decisions of land access and control, thus rendering women's user rights less permanent than before (Bikaako & Ssenkumba, 2003). Prior to the 1995 Constitution of Uganda, customary tenants were regarded as tenants at sufferance and could be evicted any time from occupied land by the state. The 1995 Constitution recognized customary land holding as a legal tenure

[31] This went on until 1969 when Crown land became public land.

thereby raising the status of customary tenants and the customary tenure system. Apart from protected or gazetted areas, tenants on former public land now enjoy security and may no longer be evicted. This has been reinforced by enabling a customary tenant to acquire a certificate of customary ownership and, within the provision and limitations of the certificate, usufruct rights over the land. Today, customary land tenure is more widespread in Kabarole district while *mailo* tenure is predominant in Masaka district.

Mailo tenure: To further establish their rule and have better control of areas that were perceived to be a threat, the British colonial administration introduced new land tenure systems. In Buganda, the *mailo* land tenure system was introduced and refers to land allotted under the 1900 Uganda Agreement. Under this Agreement, the *Kabaka* (King) royal family and several thousand Baganda chiefs and notables acquired 8,958 square miles of land, as freehold – known in Buganda as *mailo* (from the word "mile") – and the rest 9,000 square miles of "waste and uncultivated land" was allocated to the protectorate as Crown land[32] (Green, 2005). However, only 4,138 individuals in Buganda benefited from the land allocations (Bikaako & Ssenkumba, 2003). The 1900 Agreement, among other things, introduced the system of individualized land tenure and established land as a commodity that could be purchased or sold (William, 2003). The allocated land became legally inheritable and in the process the Agreement created a social and economic structure in Buganda constituting of the land lords and tenants. Formerly free peasants now had to pay for the land they were cultivating on. Therefore, for the majority of Baganda who never owned *mailo* land, one obtained user rights on a piece of land through entering into an agreement to purchase a *kibanja* (Plural: *bibanja*) from a freehold land owner or *mutaka* (plural: *bataka*) (Williams, 2003). However, *Milo* lands were subject to restrictions passed in subsequent legislation by the *Lukiiko* (Buganda parliament) and the 1967 Constitution[33]. Today, many households in Masaka as in other districts that were part of the Buganda kingdom, own *bibanja* and their tenure basically consists of rights for cultivation rather than ownership (cf. Williams, 2003). In present day Uganda, *mailo* land forms the largest share of freehold land since the 1969 Public Lands Act that made all former official estates in *mailo* tenure freehold estates. However, unlike the original freehold land owners,

---

[32] When the land was properly surveyed, it was found that there was considerably less than was originally estimated, thereby leaving the crown with only 8,307 square miles (West, 1972:59 cited by Green, 2005).

[33] First, the 1908 Buganda Land Law prevented *mailo* owners from disposing of their lands to those who did not belong to the protectorate, churches or other societies, except with the approval of the governor and the *Lukiiko*. Second, through the Land law, Succession Law and the 1927 *Busuulu* and *Envujjo* Law, relations between *mailo* owners and peasants on their land was specified. With the 1927 land reform, the rent and dues for the *bibanja* were established at extremely low rates that one could basically say that the peasants had "free" occupancy rights. Third, the 1967 Constitution also has a provision for the regulation of *mailo* lands, and vested ownership of, and control over, all minerals and water on *mailo* lands in the state.

the *mailo* owners' rights are subject to the customary and statutory rights of those persons in occupation of the land and their successors at the time that the tenure was created.

The *mailo* reforms improved opportunities for women's access to land in that women now could gain access to land by purchasing tenancy or by inheritance (West, 1972; Tadria, 1985: cited in Barnett & Blaikie, 1992). This notwithstanding, Barnett & Blaikie (1992:77) still argue that "in so far as most women do not have access to sufficient cash to make their own purchases, their main source is through inheritance. Given this and the widespread male attitude that it is not right for women to own land, it must be concluded that few women actually have independent *de* facto rights in land." A 1995 study on gender perspectives on land ownership and inheritance in Uganda found that 7 percent of the applications for "legal papers" (title) for land in three districts were by women, mostly for urban plots (Sebina-Zziwa, 1995: 20).

Freehold tenure: The third type of land tenure system, freehold tenure was also established by agreement between the Kingdoms and the British Government and was mainly found in the Western part of the country. In Toro, freeholds were granted under the 1900 Agreement. A grantee of land in freehold was given a freehold title. Most of this land was allocated to church missionaries, academic Institutions, Kings, chiefs, notables as well as large scale estate developers (Kabonesa, 2002). However, this type of land is owned by very few people in the population. Freehold tenure is land with full powers of ownership and is held in perpetuity.

Leasehold tenure: Leasehold tenure, has two forms: statutory and private leasehold. Under leasehold, the lessee is granted the right to possession, use or occupation of land for a specified duration and under agreed rental terms, by the lessor. The lessor may be the Uganda Land Commission (or the Crown as in the past) or an owner of freehold. The lease period varied but periods of 3 years or more entitled the grantee to a certificate of title. Today the Uganda Land Commission grants leases of 45 or 99 years over public land in rural areas while urban authorities like Masaka and Kabarole town councils grant leases over land within urban areas. All leases are subject to development conditions and failure to meet them results in forfeiture of the lease (Bikaako & Ssenkumba, 2003).

Land ownership and access

Table 4.6 presents the type of land ownership among survey respondents. The greater majority of the surveyed households cultivate their own land. There was an overwhelming access to land for agriculture (> 95%) with less than three percent being landless and about 85 percent of the land holdings owned. Of the land owned, only 13 percent was legally registered with title the rest being *kibanja.* This implies

Table 4.6 Type of land ownership - main plot (N =539).

Type of ownership	Frequency	Percent
Personal with title (*Mailo* & Lease hold)	69	12.80
Personal without title (*Kibanja*)	389	72.17
Family land (communal tenure)	60	11.13
Hired	9	1.67
Public	10	1.86
Live on friend's land	2	0.37
Total	539	100

Source: Household Survey.

that only 13 percent of household heads could use their land to access credit from financial institutions if need arises. Fifteen percent of household had a second piece of land that that they were using for agricultural production. Most of the second plots of land reported were likely to be either hired (70%) or borrowed (14%).

Clear gender-based distinctions in the rights to land of men and women throughout Uganda still exist today (Ovonji-Odida *et al.*, 2000). While both men and women in the study area had access to land, ownership and control over land is vested in men, regardless of type of tenure. Although there are no formal restrictions on women to acquire land in their own right, buying land is not an option for many women given women's poorer access to resources and associated transaction costs. For both men and women most land is still acquired through inheritance rather than purchase (Kwesiga, 1998). For women living under customary land, marriage remains the primary means through which they obtain access to land on which to live and grow food or cash crops. While the two types of female-headed households had far smaller parcels of land compared to the male-headed ones, single-female-headed households were worse off than widow-headed ones. Considering their lower mean age compared to widows, possibly lower access to land could be related to less time to acquire land. However, the pattern of women's access to land through marriage may be a factor given that the majority of single women are not in relationships that guarantee them access to land.

Almost all (> 90%) the widows interviewed, inherited the land they were cultivating. In the event of death of a spouse the Uganda law allows a widow to retain 15 percent of her late husband's property (Bikaako & Ssenkumba, 2003). However, in practice this share may be withheld partly because some women do not know their rights but more so because of existing socio-cultural factors. It has been documented that inheritance customs, especially the traditional claiming of land and property by the deceased man's male family members and sons, for example, has resulted in some orphans and widows being dispossessed of their parent's or spouse's inheritance (which is mainly land in the rural areas), thus increasing the vulnerability of widows and orphans (Wakhweya *et al.*, 2002; UNDP, 2002). Information obtained from interviews with three widows and two orphans in Masaka indicated that they lost their land to the spouse's or father's male relatives. For one orphan, it was her paternal aunt who was supposed to be care taker who sold some of the land. HIV/AIDS widows reported incidences of losing land and other property to relatives of the late. According to women focus group participants, some local leaders have been helpful in limiting the problem of land grabbing. Furthermore, according to these women, women's limited access to land has been aggravated by land sales to meet HIV/AIDS-related costs and marital conflicts. Some men sell most of their land before they died, thus leaving almost no land for the widow to inherit. Similar results have been reported for Bushenyi and Mubende districts (Bikaako & Ssenkumba, 2003). About half of all female focus group discussions mentioned the increasing incidences of men divorcing their wives before they died, accusing them of either having "bewitched" them or being responsible for their infection with AIDS. In such a case of divorce, it would be very difficult for the widow to even claim any part of the inheritance, let alone land. Thus, while women continue to depend on men for access to land, it predisposes them to increased vulnerability in the face of future shocks.

While almost all households have access to land, there is very unequal distribution. About 60 percent of all households had less than a hectare (less than 2 acres)[34] of land. Maximum land owned was 65 acres (Kabarole) and 75 acres (Masaka) but this was total of several pieces of land holdings. There were, however, no significant differences in the mean land acreage owned between the districts. At household level, however, while there was no significant difference between the two types of female-headed households, male-headed households had bigger land holdings than their female counterparts ($p<0.10$ level). For example, the proportion of women-headed households with smaller acreages, that is, up to 0.75 of an acre, was slightly higher ($p<0.10$) than that for male-headed households (26% for single-female-headed and 15% for widow-headed against 10% for male-headed). Likewise, the proportion of women-headed households with large acreages, that is, five acres or more, was smaller (not more than 5% for each of the two types) than that of male-headed households (18%).

[34] It is noteworthy that this is total household landholding; therefore the actual total cultivated land is likely to be less. This is to some extent compensated for by multiple cropping made possible because of the bi-modal rain seasons.

The variations in the proportions of land across household categories reflect the relative severity of land shortages–particularly among the two types of female-headed households. Therefore, despite the high agricultural potential - good rainfall and volcanic soils (particularly for Kabarole) - farmers with very small land holdings (particularly those with less than 0.2 ha or half an acre) find it difficult to be food sufficient. The problems of limited land holdings are further aggravated by land fragmentation due to increasing population pressure as well as declining soil fertility which is a consequence of continuous cropping with limited or no fertilization. It was apparent from focus group discussions, mostly in Masaka, that farmers are experiencing substantial decline in soil fertility. Soil productivity problems are more pronounced in Masaka than in to Kabarole according to information obtained from group discussions and agricultural extension staff.

4.3.2 Crop production

Introduction: The study districts are located in the Central (for Masaka) and Western (Kabarole) banana and coffee farming systems. Although both districts fall under the banana-coffee farming system, Masaka falls under the intensive banana-coffee system, while Kabarole falls under the montane system (refer to Chapter 1). In the intensive banana-coffee system, bananas are the dominant food crop while coffee is the cash crop (though the importance of these two crops was found to vary at household level). Livestock is not very important. The montane system, although similar to the intensive banana-coffee system in having bananas and coffee as major crops, has cooler temperatures than the former and the relief is steeper. In this system the bananas are planted along the slopes and at the foot hills and *Arabica* coffee which prefers cooler temperatures is dominant. Agriculture is predominantly rain-fed and the rainfall pattern in both districts is bi-modal.

Agriculture is the main form of land use, with livestock production being the second economic activity to crop production. Crop farming is the most important livelihood activity and majority of respondents cultivate their own land. Male-headed households with an average land size of 3.38 acres had significantly bigger land holdings than single female headed (mean =1.76 acres) and widow-headed (mean = 2.16 acres) ($p < 0.1$ level). Given the general small size of land holdings, farmers hire land or engage in sharecropping arrangements, or both, to increase land for cultivation. Table 4.7 presents proportion of households growing different crops in the two districts.

Crops grown: Information obtained from focus group discussions and key informants working with the district agriculture departments indicated that banana is the most important food and cash crop grown, the major reason being that the possibility of continuous harvesting throughout the year means that one is assured of cash as well. It is followed by maize and then beans. The crops were ranked basing on the

Table 4.7. Proportion of agricultural households growing selected crops and number of plots operated by district.

Crop	Masaka		Kabarole	
	HH growing the crop (%)	No. of plots	HH growing the crop (%)	No. of plots
Banana	48.6	85,205	61.2	50,908
Cassava	32.5	59,898	32.2	25,613
S. Potato	22.7	41,139	24.1	17,888
Maize	41.6	76,151	24	20,141
Beans	60.4	114,299	54.3	45,496
Millet	3.2	6,276	10.1	7,645
Groundnuts	10.7	19,073	4.9	3,602
Coffee	18.1	32,927	3.8	2,879

Source: Report on the agricultural module (UBOS, 2004).

proportions of individuals and households that consider them as important sources of household income throughout the year. Focus group participants indicated that while coffee may bring in a lot of money when sold, this is available to the household only at certain periods of the year, whereas one is assured of at least some weekly income (however small) from a banana plantation, which income is very essential in solving day-to-day basic household necessities. However, some FGD participants and key informant respondents in Kabarole said that for some households in the district, maize is replacing banana, both as a food and cash crop. This could partly be due to the government's NTAEs program, which has encouraged farmers to grow maize. There has also been an increased market for the crop, with traders selling maize to World food program for distribution in areas affected by war in the northern part of the country. In both districts, men mainly grow coffee and bananas because of the perennial nature of the crops and land requirement. Apart from banana where it is common to have a "household" plantation, gardens are rarely jointly owned by husband and wife. Even with banana, it was observed that among the rich households with two (or more) plantations, one plantation is used for household provisioning while another one (or others) is (are) owned by the male household head and is (are) for purely commercial purposes (this was mentioned in Masaka). The banana plantation for home consumption is usually located near the homestead. In Table 4.8 the area under banana and different annual crops by household headship is presented.

Table 4.8. Household land ownership and utilization.

	Single-female HH Mean (SE)	Male HH Mean (SE)	Widow HH Mean (SE)
Land owned (acres)*	1.76 (0.21)a	3.37(0.27) b	2.16 (0.19)c
Major crops grown (acres)			
Banana*	1.03 (0.16)ac	1.28(0.05)b	1.07(0.11)c
Maize*	0.80 (0.16)a	1.11(0.05)b	0.79(0.12)a
Beans	0.81 (0.10)	0.76(0.04)	0.72(0.07)
Groundnuts	0.30(0.14)	0.42(0.05)	0.60(0.11)
Irish potatoes	0.25(0.19)	0.42(0.06)	0.38(0.11)
HH owning land	94%	99%	94%
N	50	390	101

Source: Household Survey. * implies significantly difference at 10%.
Superscripts with the same letter across the row are not significantly different.

Cropping calendar: Most farmers cultivate two crops per year, profiting from the two distinct rainy periods (March-May and September-November). The first rain season–March to May- is the main growing season. Land preparation for the first cropping season is expected to take place between January and February. Planting follows mainly in the months of March and April and weeding from about mid-March through April. For those households that can afford pesticides, spraying for pest control in maize is undertaken in April. Harvesting starts in May through July. During the second cropping season, land preparation begins in July through August while planting takes place between September and October. Some early planting in the month of August was mentioned in some focus group discussions. Weeding is expected to start in October through November, spraying in September while harvesting begins in December till January. Off-season production of tomatoes, cabbages, yams, sweet potato and other vegetables is undertaken by farmers who have access to land in wetlands.

Machinery and equipment: None of the households reported machinery and equipment of high value. Ownership of simple hand-held agricultural implements such as the hand hoe (99%), the machete or panga (71%) and the long handled pruning knife used in banana plantations (40%) accounted for over half of all items reported. Ownership of each of the other basic farm implements[35] was very low, at less than 30%. Very few households owned any type of motor vehicle and none reported

[35] Ownership of other farm implements: Axe (29.6%); spade (17%); small pruning knife (14%); post hole digger (13%); slasher (12%); sprayer (9%); and wheel barrow (4%).

ploughs or other animal traction equipment, let alone tractors. Apart from a few cases where equipment was inherited or borrowed, almost all equipment was purchased. Multiple units of the same item were frequently reported for the machete and hand hoe, otherwise, for most other equipment, few households owned more than a single unit. At least 18 percent of respondents reported the lack of basic farm implements as a major constraint to agricultural production.

Additional information was collected on ownership of other household items. The Participatory Poverty Assessment studies in Uganda have shown that a radio and a bicycle are regarded as some of the most important assets for welfare ranking. The bicycle is the commonest and most important mode of transport in rural areas. It is used for human transportation, ferrying goods to the market, carrying water and it can be a source of household income when hired-out at a fee. The proportions of male-headed households owning bicycle (57%) and radio (79%) were significantly higher than those for both types of female-headed ones (30% and 50%, respectively; $p < 0.01$). Apart from two single female household heads that reported ownership of a motorcycle, all the other households (27) owning motorcycles were male-headed. The same applies to the other household items (like beds, mattresses, tables, and chairs) with the proportion of male-headed households owning these items more than that for two types of female-headed households ($p < 0.1$). The importance of highlighting these items is that they are normally used to evaluate the credit worthiness of individuals when such individuals are seeking group or individual credit from microfinance institutions or rotating credit-and-saving associations (ROSCAs). Additionally, these are resources that can be sold in case of a crisis when the members of the household do not have any other source of income.

Input use during the previous main growing season: As noted by Bayliss-Smith (1991), poor farmers often find it difficult to supply the necessary inputs with which to maintain fertility of their limited land with consequences of livelihoods becoming more compromised. Indeed, despite the modernization drive by the government, farming in the study area continues to be subsistence in nature and characterized by very limited use of external inputs/high output technologies, credit facilities, and hired labour. Information on the use of both labour and non-labour inputs on plots cultivated by households during the second growing season – July to December of 2002 (in Masaka) – and the first growing season – January to June of 2003 (in Kabarole) – was obtained. For each household, information was recorded on expenditures on improved seed, chemical fertilizers, pesticides and hired labour. In general, households in the study area made little use of "modern" inputs. That is, less than one percent spent on improved seed, chemical fertilizers, pesticides– all combined and one percent spent on veterinary services and drugs. Improved seed was the most commonly reported purchased input. Despite the importance of banana, the use of inorganic fertilizer in banana plots was almost non-existent and respondents mentioned low profitability (cost higher than benefit) as one of the causes of limited use. As has been documented in literature (Bekunda, 1999; Pender *et al.*, 1999) banana production is dependent on own supplied inputs (mainly manure and crop residues), a method that recycles nutrients within the farming system, but does not add to the stock of nutrients. Lack of ability by farmers to afford inputs has been responsible for declining soil fertility on one hand and declining yields on the other. For the households in which the respondents reported use of fertilizer or pesticides, it was most often applied to maize. Therefore, major improvements in the market conditions facing Ugandan farmers are likely to be a prerequisite for substantial adoption of inorganic fertilizer (and other inputs) to occur (Nkonya *et al.*, 2005).

Family labour is the commonest form of labour used for agricultural production. Of the surveyed households, 45 percent reported using only family labour while 40 percent hire extra labour in addition to family labour. However for the previous growing season only seven percent of surveyed households reported having hired labour. Farmers in Kabarole were more likely to use hired labour for bean and maize production compared to those in Masaka district. Widow headed households were less likely to hire labour for bean and maize production compared to male- and single-female-headed households. No significant difference was observed in the extent of hired labour use between districts or across the three household categories.

Division of labour for agricultural activities: Traditionally, in many parts of Africa, there has been a strict gendered division of labour in agriculture, which is based on crop (Hoddinott & Haddad, 1995), task (Saito, 1994), or both. As Mettrick wrote four decades ago, for most of the traditional tribal societies of Uganda the division of labour between the sexes left almost all the growing of crops to women, although the men would undertake the heavy work of breaking new ground. He observed that it was such activities as cattle keeping, hunting, and fishing that were considered as more proper manly pursuits and later cash crop farming when this was introduced (Mettrick, 1967). According to Mamdani (1992), writing about Uganda, this distinction arose under colonialism, because men were regarded as the undisputed heads of the household and therefore the ones who were liable to pay taxes. Thus the newly introduced export crops of coffee and tea crops which could be sold for cash, became identified as male crops while crops which were traditionally grown to feed the family became more tightly associated with women.

Although tradition has often described some crops or tasks as men's and some as women's, with new opportunities arising the gender division of labour in many places is becoming less rigid (Alwang & Siegel, 1994; Saito, 1994). What seems to be persisting though is that the household food production is left to the women, while the men are responsible for the cash crops. Nonetheless, a number of factors such as household headship, socioeconomic-status, type of crop, and culture may dictate who undertakes what agricultural activity in a household. While participants in group discussions broadly indicated that both men and women are involved in land preparation, planting and weeding, some activities remain fairly gendered. Weeding remains mainly women's work (sometimes men involved when it is paid labour or an important cash crop like coffee, banana and maize), while chemical spraying of pesticides, was said to be almost exclusively a man's activity because of the heavy sprayer that has to be carried on the back and women's inability to mix the chemicals before spraying. In both districts men said they never plant or weed beans. Harvesting is mainly done by women and children with very limited involvement of men.

Table 4.9 presents information obtained from focus group discussions on the magnitude of labour intensity of different agricultural activities. Labour intensity (LI) was evaluated on a scale of 1-5 on the basis of the amount of energy and time required to undertake a given activity. Given the gender division of agricultural activities, women are more engaged in labour intensive activities than men. The most labour-intensive activities included: land preparation for all crops except cassava; planting for banana, maize and beans; weeding and harvesting for maize and beans; and pest control in maize.

Access to labour: Three main causes of reduced household labour supply were identified in the survey and included: firstly, ill health[36] especially due to malaria and HIV/AIDS (50%); secondly death affecting people in their youthful age – again

Table 4.9. Labour intensity for different activities by crop in Masaka and Kabarole.

Crop	Banana LI		Maize LI		Beans LI		S/Potato LI		Cassava LI	
	Mka	Klre	Mka	Klre	Mka	Klre	Mka	Klre	Mka	Klre
Land preparation	5	5	2	5	2	5	4	3	1	1
Planting	5	5	3	4	4	3	3	2	1	1
Weeding	2	2	4	5	5	5	2	2	1	1
Harvesting	1	2	5	5	4	3	1	2	1	2
Pest Control	3	3	5	1	2	2	1	1	1	1

Source: Mixed FGD, Masaka and Kabarole. Mka = Masaka; Klre = Kabarole.
Labour Intensity (LI): 1= not labour intensive; 2=moderately labour intensive; 3= labour intensive; 4= very labour intensive; 5= extremely labour intensive.

[36] Poor health was the most often mentioned cause of poverty during the poverty assessment studies (UPPAP, 1999; MFPED, 2003).

mainly due to HIV/AIDS (41%) and malaria (35%) – and thirdly rural-urban migration (particularly of young men) in search of employment (33%). The other threats to health found among the study population relate to respiratory tract infections, diarrhoea in children and poor water and sanitation (more so among households in Masaka). While health facilities existed in the study areas, focus group participants complained of the lack of medicines in the health facilities and for some, the long distances required to get to these facilities (4-6 miles).

In addition to ill health, death and migration, the low participation of adult males in agricultural activities as well as reduced availability of child[37] labour were identified as other causes of reduced household labour. The overall effect has been that women in both male- and female-headed households now constitute the bulk of the agricultural labour force. The increased care needs associated with HIV/AIDS in affected households has not made things easier in such households given the fact that female labour is already over-burdened with production and domestic household responsibilities. Farming being the most important livelihood activity, respondents identified the effect of declining household labour on agricultural activities as follows; (i) poor farm management (37%); (ii) gardens overgrown with weeds (37%); (iii) reduced crop yields due to untimely farm operations (30%); and (iv) reduction in area under crop production due to inability to cultivate sufficient area (26%). The situation arising from this was described by both male and female focus group participants as one of increasing food insecurity in the study area, reduced agricultural incomes as well as poor feeding and health that have together led to increased vulnerability, mostly of the poor households and those affected by HIV/AIDS.

According to key informant interviews (local extension and NGO staff), besides household demographics there are other factors responsible for household labour shortage. For example, drunkenness among men and delinquent youth and orphans deny their households of what would have been otherwise important productive labour. In addition is the limited access to agricultural extension services by majority of the respondents in the study area (see section 4.3.5). Its noteworthy that this limited access denies the people of critical farming information to increase their productivity, particularly more so for children in child-headed households who lack or have inadequate farming skills and experience. Furthermore, the breakdown of traditional collective farming practices also highlighted by key informants implies that households that used to benefit from such arrangements (for the most part those that lacked male labour) now face the challenges of limited household labour of their own. Finally, the lack of inter-generational transfer of family knowledge, particularly with regard to farming knowledge and skills, apparently presents

[37] Since the introduction of free Universal Primary Education (UPE)in 1997, it is a requirement for parents to send their children to school.

challenges to the local leadership in the study areas of how to make the growing number of orphans and child-headed households productive.

Banana production

Banana production mainly occurs in high rainfall areas and is predominant in the banana-coffee and banana-millet farming systems. The banana (*Musa* species) continues to occupy an important position as a major food and cash crop in Uganda. Though there is a lack of reliable banana production figures, available data indicates that banana occupies between 1.3 and 1.4 million hectares (33 - 38% of all cropped land) in terms of acreage planted (Tushemerirwe *et al.*, 2001; Nowakunda & Tushemerirwe, 2004), making banana the most important food crop in the country. The bananas are grown by about 75 percent of farmers and consumption of banana and plantain has been estimated at 243Kg/capita/year; the highest in the world (Nowakunda & Tushemerirwe, 2004). Table 4.10 presents the number of agricultural households with bananas by number of banana plots operated, by type of stand, and by district. In the study areas, bananas are grown for food security, income and to meet a variety of other socio-cultural needs of the household and community.

Matooke is cooked green, *bogoya* and *Sukari- Ndizi* eaten fresh, while *mbidde* and *kayinja* are fermented to make a local wine *(omubisi)* or a local beer *(*called *mwenge muganda* or *tonto)* or distilled to produce *waragi*, alcoholic beverage. Almost every part of the banana plant is useful and can be sold for cash. Farmers sell food, alcohol, planting materials (young suckers), banana leaves (used in cooking the *matooke).* The banana fibres are also used for making mats. Additionally the crop has a significant role in traditional ceremonies particularly those associated with birth, marriage and death.

Table 4.10. Number of Agricultural households with bananas by number of banana plots operated, by type of stand and by district.

District	Agricultural HH	Banana growing HH		Banana Plots			
	Total	Total	%	Pure stand	Mixed stand	Not specified	Total
Masaka	131,565	63,935	48.6	52,949	32,186	70	85,205
Kabarole	59,524	36,418	61.2	29,063	21,819	26	50,908

Source: Report on the agricultural module (UBOS, 2004).

Traditionally farmers grow multiple varieties distributed at random in the same plantation because the varieties have different characteristics in terms of palatability, resistance to pests and diseases, tolerance to drought, as well as yield and marketability potential. For example, farmers in Masaka grow *Nabusa* because of its fast growth rate, drought resistance and marketability; *Nakitembe* because of its fast maturing characteristics, palatability and ability to grow on a range of soil types; while *Kibuzi* is grown because of its large bunch size and fact that it has a longer shelf life before ripening. Farmers' use of crop biodiversity for livelihood security has also been reported among enset growers in Ethiopia (Negash, 2001).

The most commonly grown cultivars are the green cooking bananas (*matooke*). Others include the types used for brewing (*Mbidde, Kayinja, Kivuvu*), the plantains (e.g. *Gonja*), and dessert bananas (*Sukari-Ndizi* and *Bogoya*)[38]. In addition to multiple cultivars, and particularly among farmers with small land holdings, the usual practice is to grow banana inter-crop banana with different annuals, trees and shrubs. In Masaka, beans, cassava, coffee trees, avocado and *Ficus natalensis*[39] are inter-cropped with banana while in Kabarole it is avocado, coffee trees and beans. Forty percent of the respondents reported having intercropped banana plantations.

Figure 4.1 presents the yield trends of cooking banana over a ten year period–1992 to 2001. Yield data on banana (and other crops) has not been included in the analysis the main reason for this omission being the wide range of crop combinations found on farms in the study area. These include single, double and triple combinations of annual crops, often but not always in association with banana and coffee of different maturities. The result of such diversity is that yield data for different plots are not readily comparable on a per hectare, per year basis. Another reason was that farmer responses were not considered reliable after they had been checked. This could partly be explained by farmers' inability to accurately recall the output of a previous season given the widespread lack of record keeping or the usual reluctance to reveal their output, perhaps due to fear of increased taxation. Without reliable yield data, it has not been possible to compare the differences in agricultural productivity of the sampled households between the districts and household types.

Plantation management: Banana production involves a variety of activities. All farmers in the survey sample had plantations older than three years. Hence, activities regarding land preparation, clearing and planting were not discussed much. Table 4.11 presents the different types of banana management practices undertaken by

[38] There are three categories of bananas found in Uganda (Karamura, 1998): 1. The cultivars of the East African coast and nearby islands (e.g. *Sukari-ndizi, Bogoya, Kayinja, Kivuvu*); 2. The plantains (e.g *Gonja*); and 3. The East African Highland bananas (Matooke and Mbidde).

[39] Farmers obtain bark cloth from the bark of *Ficus natalensis* tree and its leaves improve soil fertility. Other uses of the tree include providing shade and protecting the bananas from strong winds. Pruned branches are also used for fuel wood.

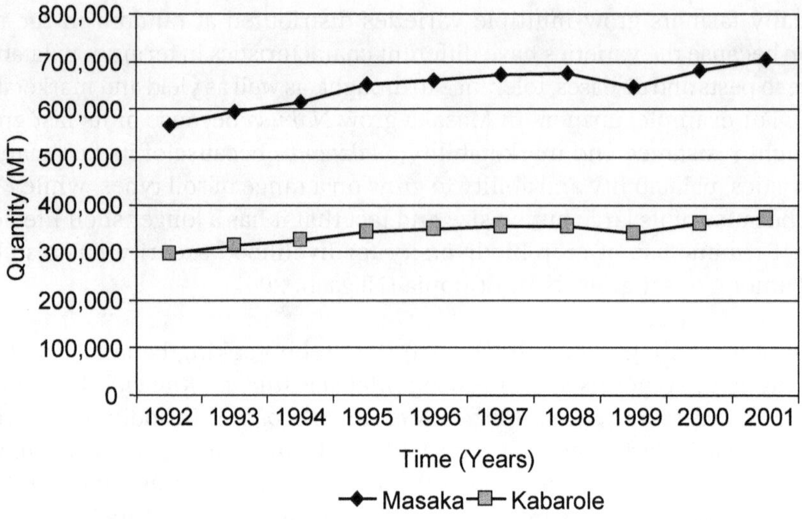

Figure 4.1. Cooking banana production in Masaka and Kabarole districts. Source: Report on the agricultural module (UBOS, 2004).

Table 4.11. Type of banana management practices carried out by household headship.

Banana management practices	SF-HH (%)	Male HH (%)	Widow HH (%)	Row total (%)
De-sheathing/pruning	98.0	97.1	98.0	97.3
Weeding	85.7	90.7	87.8	89.7
Trimming the male part	87.8	78.0	80.6	79.4
De-suckering	73.5	80.9	71.4	78.4
Mulching	73.5	78.8	75.5	77.7
Earthing up (softening soil around plants)	65.3	65.5	69.4	66.2
Removing corms	67.3	63.7	64.3	64.1
Selecting and planting clean materials	48.9	61.0	35.7	55.1
Splitting stems	36.7	52.0	40.8	48.5
Making water trenches	30.6	49.1	37.8	45.2
Removing & replacing sick plants	28.6	40.3	28.6	37.0
Pest and disease control	26.5	32.4	27.6	30.9
Making soil bands	16.3	25.7	17.3	23.3
Applying manure	16.3	19.1	11.2	17.4
N	49	377	98	524
Total (%)	9.2	72.1	18.7	100

Source: Household Survey. SF-HH=Single-female-headed.

household headship. De-sheathing/pruning, weeding, de-suckering, mulching and corm removal, are practices implemented by over than half of the surveyed households. These together with water conservation practices are also regarded by farmers as crucial activities in the management of water for the banana plantation. As Purseglove (1988) notes, bananas require good amounts of water for growth and some cultivars have been found to be severely affected by drought.

Table 4.12 presents the ranking of various banana management practices in terms of their labour requirements. It is noteworthy that activities that have been identified as crucial for good banana growth are also very labour intensive, that is, planting, corms removal and splitting stems , making soil bands and digging water trenches, and de-suckering. The high labour requirements associated with some banana management practices and the lack or limited availability of resources to hire labour by certain households has resulted in the majority of farmers abandoning such practices: 90 percent of all survey respondents reported having abandoned at least one practice and in some cases completely abandoning the production of the crop (32 households).

Table 4.13 presents selected activities for which change in implementation was found significant between the two districts. A significantly higher proportion of Masaka farmers no longer mulch and control pests or implement soil management practices in their banana plantations than that in Kabarole. This may partly be due

Table 4.12. Ranking of labour intensity of various banana management practices.

Banana management activity	Labour intensity*	Rank for all activities (1=most labour-intensive; 9=least labour-intensive)
Planting	5	1
Corms removal & splitting stems	5	2
Making soil bands & digging water trenches	5	3
De-suckering	5	4
Making compost manure	3	5
Weeding	2	6
De-sheathing/pruning	2	7
Applying manure (Fertilizer)	2	8
Pest & diseases control	1	9

Source: Household Survey.
Labour intensity*: 1= not labour intensive; 2=moderately labour intensive; 3= labour intensive; 4= very labour intensive; 5= extremely labour intensive.

Table 4.13. Change in implementation of banana management practices (2003-5) by district.

	Masaka (N= 302)		Kabarole (N=239)		Overall (N= 541)		X^2
	N	%	N	%	N	%	
Used water and soil methods							
Yes	55	18.15	111	46.64	166	30.68	50.859***
No	248	81.85	127	53.36	375	69.32	
Mulching							
Yes	82	64.57	45	35.43	127	23.48	4.935**
No	221	53.38	193	46.62	414	76.52	
Controls pests & disease							
Yes	62	20.46	80	33.61	142	26.25	11.910***
No	241	79.54	158	66.39	399	73.75	

Source: Household Survey.
***, **, implies significant difference at 1% and 5% respectively.

to HIV/AIDS-related labour constraints given the higher HIV-prevalence levels in Masaka.

Survey data and focus group information further reveals that climatic variability and infestation with banana weevil and Sigatoka are the major factors contributing to low banana production.

Gender division of labour in banana production: Table 4.14 gives the gender division of labour in banana production, highlighting common activities. The ticks provide an indication of the level of involvement in a given activity by men and women. The more the ticks the higher the involvement; one tick implies limited involvement; two ticks moderate involvement and three ticks heavy involvement. The gender division of labour shown is typical of a male-headed household, but as the discussion below indicates this may vary depending on different household factors.

Focus group discussions revealed that men and women's roles in banana production are complementary, may overlap or interchange depending on household resources. Therefore household capacity to hire labour, gender of household head, ownership of the banana plantation, whether the work is paid or is part of ordinary household production and also whether banana production is an important food and cash crop for the household were key determinants of household members' involvement in different banana management activities. In an ordinary male-headed household and where the crop contributes significantly to household income, men usually undertake

Table 4.14. Gender division of labour in banana production.

Banana management activity	Men	Women
De-sheathing/pruning	√ √√	√
Weeding	√	√ √√
De-suckering	√√	√√
Corms removal	√ √√	√
Mulching	√ √√	√
Earthing up	√√	√√
Trimming male part of the plant	√√	√√
Pest & diseases control (weevil trapping & other cultural control)	√	√ √√
Chemical control of Pest & diseases	√ √√	√
Soil & water conservation practices	√ √√	√
Digging water trenches	√√	√√
Selecting materials and planting	√√	√√√
Applying manure	√√	√√
Applying Fertilizer	√ √√	√
Marketing	√√	√√

Source: Household survey.

the heavy tasks such as uprooting corms, splitting stems, de-sheathing, making soil conservation structures, and carrying heavy mulch as indicated in Table 4.14. Men were also found to be more engaged in activities that may require some cash outlays such as buying mulch for the banana plantations and transporting it, and buying agricultural inputs like pesticides and fertilizers. Below are quotations on fertilizer use in banana plots from group discussions during the survey in Masaka.

> *Some of us have plantations that were planted by our grandfathers. The land is therefore over cropped and we know that the soil needs to be replenished. The only thing we try to do is use what is available to us: peelings, banana leaves, and other household refuse is what we put in the plantation. But a banana plantation needs manure. Because we lack animals we cannot make compost. As for fertilizers, we left that for the rich who can afford it.* (Women's FGD, Ddegeya village, Masaka).

> *Fertilizer is rarely used but some farmers (men) buy and use it whenever money is available.* (Men's FGD, Mbirizi, Masaka).

Women participate in all activities but to varying degrees. The women in Masaka district were more involved in banana production activities compared to those in

Kabarole district. Additionally, women in female-headed households (widowed and single) do most of the work in their plantations but because of constraints of limited labour and funds to hire labour; their plantations are likely to be poorly managed and overgrown with weeds. However, weeding and use of cultural methods for pest control were described as mainly women's work with older children helping out during weekends and/or holiday periods. In male-headed households men were found to be in control of household labour such that where the household had more than one plantation/garden to work in (something that was common in Masaka) the men determined which garden was worked on first. With regard to marketing of banana, both men and women are involved. Both male and female FGD participants indicated that in male-headed households, men usually control the proceeds from banana sales. However, the women participate in selling of banana at the farm gate. If buyers come when the spouse is not at home, the woman receives the money which she hands over to her spouse on return. It was, however, also revealed during the FGDs that women could make decisions to sale and use the money in case there was an urgent household need that required immediate attention. But male and female FGD participants indicated that the big bunches are reserved for sale while the small ones are harvested for home consumption.

Several male FGD participants in Kabarole said that they sell bananas after their wives have taken care of the food requirements of the household. This could partly explain the better food security status of households in Kabarole compared to those in Masaka (see Chapter 5). Nonetheless, issues of ethnicity seemed to play a significant role in household gender relations in male-headed households. For example, women of Banyarwanda, Banyankole and Bakiga ethnicity were less likely to take decisions regarding banana sales without consulting the spouses than their female counterparts of the Baganda and Batoro ethnic groups. Furthermore, gender relations are also mediated by the interpersonal relations between spouses. A good example is one given by a female FGD participant in Lwera village, Masaka:

> *The way a man treats you or how much control over household resources he gives you depends on how much he loves you. For example, you find that a man with two wives is, for example, overly controlling to his older wife while he allows his younger wife to manage his resources and even cash from the sale of produce. There are also other men who work together with their wives-but these are the minority. Anyway, the fact is that women we are not the same. Some are fine while others are suffering even when their husbands have money!*

In the markets women dominate retail selling of banana while the men are mainly involved in bulk purchases and sales and hiring of big trucks that ferry bananas from mainly upcountry stations to the towns. Young boys and men also work as casual workers in loading and off-loading banana trucks.

Production of other major food crops

Maize: Masaka and Kabarole are among the major maize growing districts in Uganda. In the study areas, the crop was mainly grown as a source of income but is now also ranked high as a major household food security crop. Its long storage life, filling capacity and relatively lower cost compared to other foods have allowed it to be integrated into the diets of people in the study areas as the main staple, banana, has become in short supply due to a variety of causes. Below is a quotation that shows the importance of maize in people's livelihood.

> *We formed a group of twenty HIV/AIDS widows and one of our objectives is to engage in income-generating projects. We have started with maize because there are agents of an international NGO (World Food Program) who want to buy maize. We hired a two acre piece of land and we use it to grow maize as a group. After harvesting we agree on how much to sell and the remainder is shared. We have agreed that the maize that is not sold should be stored and used in times of food shortage. During the last season, each of us received one debe (1 tin of about 15kgs) of grain. The money from the sold maize is kept in our bank account and members can borrow it whenever they are in problems. At the moment the market for maize is good. But we agreed not to hire more land because group things are difficult. Some members do not keep their commitments.* (HIV/AIDS widow, Kabarole).

Maize is grown in both seasons and is planted inter-cropped with beans, cassava or millet or in pure stands. In the study area, almost all cases of external input use (fertilizer and pesticides) were related to maize production. Seed for planting constitutes that retained from the previous harvest or certified seed purchased from local markets. While some farmers plant maize by hand in a chop and plant method, others do row planting, though both the inter- and intra-row spacing was found to vary considerably within and between the districts. Maize is a labour intensive crop requiring clearing of land, at least two weedings, and chemical pest control for one to have good yields. The crop also requires good rainfall which the farmers cannot guarantee. Improved fast maturing and high yielding varieties like *longe1* exist on the market but some farmers need to purchase seeds, chemical pesticides and fertilizer, which becomes a constraint among the poor farmers. The maize cobs are roasted or cooked when still green. Otherwise they are dried and stored in granaries, cribs or in gunny sacs in the houses. Here the maize is stored till there is need for it to be sold or milled for family consumption. Maize may be taken as a porridge or maize bread (*posho* or *akawunga*). Both field and storage pests are a big problem. Maize is grown by both men and women (but more so by men) in Kabarole district and by mainly women and relatively poor men in Masaka district.

Beans: Beans became established as a food crop in Uganda well before the colonial era (see Binns, 1976 and Greenway, 1944: both cited in Mukiibi, 2001). The crop also occupies an important niche in the Uganda's agricultural sector and farm household economy (Opio *et al.*, 2001). Beans are an integral part of traditional diets providing a rich source of protein and carbohydrates, and thus important as a food security crop. The crop is also an important source of cash, being sold locally and exported to external markets. Beans like maize is one of the crops being promoted under the export diversification initiative, and by 1992 beans ranked number three in terms of tonnage exported and number four in terms of monetary export value (Accasio & Barsdorf, 1994: cited in Mukiibi, 2001).

The major cropping systems observed in the study areas included the maize-bean, banana-bean, cassava-bean, sweet potato-bean and cassava-maize-bean intercropping systems. Bean monoculture system was less common and observed more in Masaka among farmers that had more than 3 acres of land. The main source of seed among farmers in the study area was seed retained from previous harvest season. The market, reciprocal exchanges and local NGOs promoting agriculture were other ways through which farmers could obtain seed. The crop is labour-intensive requiring considerable digging and weeding. Manual removal of weeds is the basic method of weed control. Good weed control, particularly the first weeding recommended at about three weeks after planting, is very important for good yields. Additionally, beans require very good weather conditions and farmers can lose a whole crop if the rain is too much or too little. Like maize, beans suffer from field (mainly aphids in Masaka and yellowing of leaves in Kabarole) and storage pests. The quotations below indicate the importance of beans in the study areas.

> *Beans are the main household sauce. A woman has to make sure that she grows enough beans to ensure that she will have sauce for her family. If a woman lacked beans in her home, she was considered lazy. Things have now changed because some people have to sell their food (not only beans) in order to get money to cater for household needs.* (Men's FGD, Kyanyaitembe village, Kabarole).
>
> *Lack of beans in a household is an indicator of food insecurity.* (Women's FGD, Rotooma Ntezi village, Kabarole).
>
> *"Fe nga 'bakyala, ekijanjalo mwetuja akasente"* (Women's FGD, Kapoochi village, Masaka).

Literaly meaning: we as women, the bean is our source of small cash).

In spite of the high commercialization of the crop, information obtained from FGD in both Masaka and Kabarole indicate that beans remain almost entirely produced by women This is in contrast to what has been reported for other parts of the country where men are actively involved in production of the crop for marketing purposes.

Sweetpotato: Like beans, sweet potato was established in Uganda before British administration and the crop is said to have entered the country from both the east and western parts of the Africa (Greenway, 1944: cited in Mukiibi, 2001). It ranks third among the starchy staple crops after cassava and banana nationwide but second after banana in the western and central regions where the study was undertaken (Muwanga *et al.*, 2001). The crop is an important food security crop for both rural and urban households. Sweet potato is widely grown in both districts as a food and cash crop.

> *Lumonde (sweet potato) has always been an important food to us. The problem is that we have limited land and the field rats destroy even the little that we grow. Sweet potato is also an important source of cash. Farmers who have bisenyi (wetland areas) grow the crop in the dry season and get a lot of money from traders who come from Kampala looking for sweet potato.* (Women FGD, Kawoko village, Masaka).

The crop is easily propagated from sections of the vines that they produce so there is no need for seed. The crop is grown as a sole crop or intercropped with beans. After land clearing and preparation, farmers make ridges or mounds on which the vines are planted. Farmers in Masaka preferred making mounds because "piece-meal" harvesting is easier. They also believed that destruction of the crop by vertebrate pests, particularly the root rat, was most severe in ridge potato planting. For Kabarole, ridges were more common (possibly because they help in soil erosion control on slopes). For both districts farmers who grew potatoes in wetlands also preferred using ridges as it facilitates drainage. After planting the next activity is weeding and it is usually undertaken about two months after planting. As with other crops, weeding is done by hand or with the hand hoe.

Cassava: The flexibility of cassava to be integrated in traditional farming systems, its ability to do well in marginal and stressed environments, low labour and skill requirements, capacity for *in situ* storage[40], as well as apparent resistance to pests and diseases (Jameson, 1970; Prudencio & Al-Hassan, 1994) led to its rapid spread and adoption in Uganda. The crop ranks second to bananas in terms of area cultivated, total production and per capita consumption (Otim-Nape, 1990). Below is a statement on cassava captured during a women's FGD in Masaka.

---

[40] Cassava can stay in the field for over two years after reaching maturity, without spoilage.

> *We like cassava very much. It is a crop that you can grow anywhere (in any soil type), you can plant without much land preparation (unlike other crops like maize and sweet potato) and you can keep the food in the soil for up to two years. Cassava is our drought food. Before our cassava started being affected by this disease which leads to wrinkling of leaves, we never knew food insecurity.* (Women's FGD, Bulamazi village, Masaka).

In the study area cassava is mainly cultivated for fresh consumption so its mainly the sweet varieties that are grown. For Kabarole, some cassava is dried, milled and mixed in millet flour ready for preparation into millet bread (*akalo*), while in Masaka during periods of food shortage the cassava flour is made into cassava bread without mixing it with anything. Some farmers also grow the crop for cash (through the sale of tubers or disease resistant planting materials), or use it as animal feed and for making drinks. Cassava is usually grown with other crops, mainly beans, maize, and banana. Farmers plant cassava any time of the year but mainly during the peak rain season; march to June and September to November. Land preparation does not require fine seed bed preparation. The crop is propagated from stem cuttings (stakes) which farmers obtain from harvested stems. The most crucial agronomic activity is weeding which needs to be done within three to four months after planting to ensure good yields.

Information revealed through key informant interviews shows that the Departments of Agriculture in Kabarole and Masaka established seed multiplication centres in some sub-counties. The farmers talked to in Masaka said that most of the varieties obtained from the multiplication centres are bitter and not suitable for fresh consumption. Besides farmers obtaining planting materials from their own gardens, they get materials from fellow farmers for free or at a cost. Clean disease resistant planting materials are in limited supply. Since the severe outbreak of Cassava Mosaic Virus disease (CMD) in Uganda in 1989, the two study districts have experienced severe decline in cassava production. In the mid 1960s, farmers were required, by law, to produce 0.4 acres of cassava as a reserve supply to be used in the case of famine (Hougham & Sturrock, 1973). During the study period, all farmers surveyed lost almost all their crop to CMD.

4.2.3 Animal husbandry

Farmers in the study area rear livestock and poultry for a variety of reasons. Livestock products such as meat, milk and eggs are an important source of animal protein. These products are also an important source of income when sold. Livestock and poultry are important in payment of bride price, enhance social capital, and are a symbol of social status. The animal dung and poultry droppings are an important source of organic manure and are used to improve soil fertility. In almost all cases livestock and poultry is reared in combination with arable farming.

This section provides an inventory of the type of animals kept by households. Livestock are managed very simply and typically kept as a form of savings. The animals are usually individually owned though other household members may have access to the products. The main types of livestock reared included goats (43%), pigs (31%) and cattle (25%). Additionally, the majority of households surveyed (68%) kept local chicken. The maximum number of chicken reported by any one household was 29, and the greater majority of households (80%) kept not more than five chickens. Cattle are mainly kept by the relatively well-off and rich households. While the largest number of cattle owned was 32 (in Kabarole), households with cattle were likely to own an average of two animals. Because of limited land, poor farmers who do not have enough land to rear animals engage in shared livestock-rearing arrangements. Normally it is the female animals that are reared and, depending on the type of animals being reared and the level of contribution to the management of the animal/s by the owner or both, the owner and the person to rear agree on the terms of sharing of the off-spring or products (e.g. milk) or both. Table 4.15 shows the distribution of livestock ownership in Masaka and Kabarole. Farmers in Kabarole were more likely to keep cattle and goats and those in Masaka to rear pigs.

Information obtained in FGDs showed that for those keeping small livestock, activities involve very little or no capital investments (less than 1% of surveyed households reported ever spending on veterinary services or drugs or both). The survey results further show that livestock ownership is one of the socially differentiating characteristics between female and male-headed households. Large livestock are predominantly owned by men, while women mainly own smaller stock and chicken. Some children also own chicken and in rare cases small livestock; usually received as gifts from grand parents. For all livestock types and poultry reared, the proportion of male-headed households rearing these animals is slightly higher ($p < 0.10$) than that for the two types of female-headed households. In addition, the mean number of animals per household, for all livestock types, is higher ($p < 0.10$) in male-headed households than in the two types of female-headed households (Table 4.16).

Table 4.15. Proportion of agricultural households keeping animals & poultry by district: January to June 2002.

District	Local cattle (%)	Exotic cattle (%)	Goats (%)	Pigs (%)	Local chicken (%)	Exotic chicken (%)
Masaka	14	2.3	17.6	24.9	36	1.0
Kabarole	15.7	4.3	38.5	10.7	43.9	0.5

Source: Report on the agricultural module (UBOS, 2004).

Table 4.16. Mean livestock/poultry owned by household headship in 2005 (n=the number of households rearing the animals).

	Single-female HH Mean (SD)	Male HH Mean (SD)	Widow HH Mean (SD)	Total Mean (SD)
Cattle (n=137)	2.00 (0.52)	4.13 (0.55)*	2.55 (0.55)	3.8 (0.45)
Goat (n=232)	2.78 (2.59)	3.01 (4.01)*	1.89 (1.95)	2.79 (3.64)
Pig (n= 170)	1.20 (1.96)	1.56 (2.11)*	0.85 (.945)	1.41 (1.96)
Chicken (n=368)	3.55 (3.47)	4.91 (4.73)*	3.16 (4.47)	4.50 (4.64)
Total livestock unit	0.44 (0.69)	1.22(2.71)*	0.56 (1.09)	1.02 (2.22)
N	50	390	101	541

Source: Household Survey.
* implies significant difference (at the 10% level) from that of the two types of female-headed households.

Access to livestock: While access to and control over land is governed by both formal and informal regulations and is mainly vested in men, as has been observed by Dollan (2002) in other parts of Uganda, access to livestock seems to be directed by more informal processes such as inter- and intra-household relationships and bargaining and as such is likely to vary between communities and households as well as within household. Nonetheless, the individual who owns the livestock benefits directly from rights of use of products, sale of livestock or livestock products and the associated social status attached to livestock ownership in the community, while the other household members usually have access to specific services and products like milk, eggs and manure.

Women's access to and control over livestock or poultry and their products was not a problem in female-headed households. For women in male-headed households information from group discussions revealed that marriage relations play a significant role in access to and control over livestock and livestock products. Depending on these relations, control may range from just access to some products like milk and eggs to full control of income from milk or egg sales. Women in male-headed households also said that they have complete access and control over their own livestock and products. For example, some said they had accessed animals from NGOs and were in charge of activities and money from sale of animal products. However, for livestock belonging to men, the men decide how much milk or eggs can be used for the household and how much should be sold. For households with dairy animals, young children especially those below five years are given priority over older children and adults with regard to milk access. While a girl like her mother has access to milk and other livestock products, a boy has the additional claims on his father's animals with regard to animals for inheritance or for bride price at the time of marriage. Livestock products are also accessed by members of other households. Households with milking animals often take milk to sick friends, relatives or neighbours. Focus group participants also said that when members of a given household slaughter an animal, say on festive days, they normally give some meat to friends and neighbours. Land-poor farmers have been able to own livestock through engagement in various types of shared-livestock rearing arrangements with other farmers or relatives with bigger land.

Data were collected on changes in the numbers of livestock owned between 2002 and 2005. Survey data shows that widow-headed households experienced higher reductions in goats and pigs than male-headed households though the differences were marginal ($p < 0.1$). A similar trend is observed for change in chicken numbers, with differences between widow- and male-headed households being more significant in this case ($p < 0.05$). Its noteworthy that the types of livestock and poultry which poor households normally invest in as savings declined over the study period, with female-headed households experiencing more significant reductions in livestock and poultry numbers than male-headed households. Similarly the same types of livestock declined among HIV/AIDS-affected households. There are no differences observed for change in number of livestock owned between the two types of female-headed households.

4.2.4 Marketing of farm produce

An efficient system of marketing, is essential to agricultural development. There is a variety of marketing arrangements of the crops produced in Uganda. Since the collapse of the cooperatives, most of the marketing channels are less formal. For the marketing of food and minor crops a complex network has grown up. The primary buyer may, if the produce is in short supply, buy off the farm, but most likely it will be brought to him at the local market or, if he is a trader, at his shop. A shop keeper may well be an intermediary buyer with his own transport, who collects produce from primary buyers at a number of convenient points. With Uganda's liberalization policy, there is no setting of a minimum price. However, the farmers are exploited by the middle men when there is a large surplus of produce or one is in desperate need of cash. Also the lack of price information makes those farmers, particularly in distant locations to be paid lower farm gate prices. Development of an efficient marketing system is essential for improved agricultural production. There is lack of marketing information. This has also resulted in the exploitation of farmers by middlemen, particularly farmers in remote rural areas and women farmers who have to sell their produce at the farm gate.

4.2.5 Access to agricultural extension and other services

The quality, quantity and out-reach of rural extension services, have been on the decline in the recent years, mainly because of poor remuneration and incentives to technical staff to work up-country. Hence extension workers have neglected farmers in the marginal parts within districts and the country as a whole with adverse effects on agriculture productivity. It is the richer farmers (the minority) who have access to agricultural and veterinary extension services because they can afford to pay service providers to come to their farms. In this situation, the majority of poor farmers have limited or no access to effective extension services in the rural areas. The proportion of households accessing different types of community services are presented in Tables 4.17 and 4.18.

Results in Table 4.17 shows that farmer's access to community services available in the study area is low. Government agricultural extension services provided by the district agricultural departments (30.5%), private extension service providers under the NAADS (24.3%) and various suppliers of agricultural inputs (12.4%) are the most commonly used services. While the proportion of households accessing government agricultural services was about equally distributed between household types, male-

Table 4.17. Community services commonly used by household headship.

Services	S-F HH (%)	Male HH (%)	Widow HH (%)	Total (%)
Government agricultural extension services	30.0	30.9	29.3	30.5
Private service providers under NAADS	16.0	30.1*	6.1	24.3
Input suppliers	16.0	11.3	15.2	12.4
NGOs/CBOs & projects providing agricultural services	12.0	13.1	10.1	12.4
Savings and credit services	8.0	8.6	2.0	7.3
Marketing associations	2.0	4.5	2.0	3.8
Microfinance institutions	2.0	3.4	1.0	2.8
Agricultural research institutions	0.0	0.8	0.0	0.6
NGOs providing health services	0.0	0.3	3.0	0.8
NONE (no service used)	40.0	32.7*	53.5	37.3
N	50	382	99	531
Total (%)	9.4	71.9	18.6	100

Source: Household Survey.
* implies significant difference between male-headed HH and the two types of female-headed HH at 10% level. S-F HH = Single-female-headed HH.

Table 4.18. Access to hired labour, formal credit and extension services by district.

	Masaka (N= 302)		Kabarole (N=239)		Overall (N= 541)		X^2
	N	%	N	%	N	%	
Used Hired labour							
Yes	114	37.62	109	45.80	223	41.22	3.676*
No	189	62.38	129	54.20	318	58.78	
Access to formal credit							
Yes	22	7.26	31	13.03	53	9.80	5.012**
No	281	92.74	207	86.97	488	90.20	
Access to extension							
Yes	162	53.47	121	50.84	283	52.31	0.368NS
No	141	46.53	117	49.16	258	47.69	

Source: Household Survey.
*, ** implies significant difference at the 10% and 5% level respectively.
NS implies Not significantly different.

headed households were more likely to access private service providers under the NAADS than the female-headed households. This could be partly explained by the requirement by NAADS for farmers to form groups in order to access their services. In these groups farmers are also required to make financial contributions. Farmers who lack money do not join or participate in group activities and hence get excluded from accessing extension services. There was no statistically significant difference in access to agricultural extension services in the two districts. A significantly higher proportion of households in Kabarole ($p<0.05$) had access to formal; credit than that in Masaka.

Furthermore, among household that never used any community service in the area, the proportion of male-headed households was significantly lower (33%) than that of single-female-headed households (40%) and widow-headed ones (53.5%). Access to microfinance institutions was extremely low (less than four percent for all household types) and may partly explain the limited use of agricultural inputs or investment in high output agricultural technologies.

4.3 Constraints to agricultural production

In spite of the central role of agriculture in the national economy and the livelihood of the greater majority of Ugandans, the agricultural sector still faces fundamental constraints (socio-economic and technical) to its continued growth. Among the socio-economic production constraints is land shortage, poor farming methods, limited availability of production inputs, poor marketing information and infrastructure and the effects of HIV/AIDS while the technical constraints constitute pests and diseases, soil nutrient deficiencies and lack of pest and disease tolerant varieties (a consequence of technology generation and dissemination related constraints). For the study area, similar constraints ranging from limited resources, climate variability, pests and diseases, as well as limited access to markets and agricultural services ranked among the top farmer concerns for improved agricultural production and productivity. Table 4.19 presents the three major constraints to banana production and agricultural production in general, reported by the respondents.

Unfavourable weather conditions especially prolonged drought was pointed out as the first major constraint to agricultural production and banana production in particular. Uganda's agriculture being primarily rain fed indeed makes it susceptible to rainfall fluctuations and other adverse weather conditions.

Climate variability has had a significant impact on Uganda. Although less severe compared to the situation in the other East African countries, of late, Uganda's rainfall has been irregular in both amount and distribution within each year (FAO, 2000: cited in NEMA, 1998)[41]. Furthermore, the seasonal anomalies are much wider

Table 4.19. Major constraints to banana production and agricultural production in general.

Constraint	Masaka (% response)	Kabarole (% response)	Over all (%)
Constraints to banana production			
Unfavorable weather	75.0	43.4	51.8
Pest and diseases	81.5	80.4	39.3
Lack of labor	12.0	16.2	8.9
Total no. of responses	708	517	1225
Constraints to agricultural production			
Unfavorable weather	66.9	38.1	45.1
Pest /vermin and diseases	48.7	31.8	42.2
limited land -cultivation	13.9	17.6	12.7
Total no. of responses	754	547	1301

Source: Household Survey.

[41] In the last thirty years, there has been at least one major drought episode each decade: in 1973/74; 1984/85; 1992/94; and 1999/2000; and 2002/03. The rainfall analysis carried out for the years 1943-99, indicate that all regions of the country experience wide seasonal to inter-annual rainfall variations.

and quite often anomalies of consecutive seasons tend to be in opposite directions. This implies that incidence of drought/flood conditions at the seasonal level are more prevalent than on the annual scale.

The amount, incidence and duration of rainfall are of particular concern to Uganda. Farmers in the study areas have experienced years of drought, the most recent prior to the study being the 2002/2003 drought that was particularly severe in Masaka district. Information obtained from agricultural extension workers and focus group participants revealed the major impacts of persistent rainfall deficits to be significant reduction in crop yields or sometimes total crop failure. The fact that drought often extends over several seasons, makes it particularly damaging. In addition to drought, respondents also reported some years that they experienced too much rainfall with the excessive water resulting in destruction of crops, floods, the washing away of roads and bridges, soil erosion, the silting of rivers, and outbreaks of Cholera in parts of Masaka (Kyazanga areas).

While the absolute quantities of the amount of rainfall received are important, of equal concern is the ability of soils to retain moisture. The ability of soils to retain moisture is partly influenced by the potential rate of evapo-transpiration and where this exceeds the amount of rainfall received by an area, the soils experience moisture deficit (NEMA, 1998). According to NEMA (1998), this has been the cause of the high incidence of recurrent drought, which has led to severe impacts, particularly in the area known as the "cattle corridor". Focus group participants in parts of Masaka district that are part of the "cattle corridor" (Kyazanga) expressed this problem as soils drying up very quickly after rains and the ground being very difficult to hard to dig. The impacts of climate variability mean that farmers have to cope with late rains, mid-season cessation of rains or even with hail storms and localized floods.

Pests and diseases of both crops and animals have been a cause of significant losses to farmers in the study area and they were ranked second as constraints for both banana and general agricultural production. Major crop diseases identified included banana wilt, coffee wilt, cassava mosaic and maize streak virus disease while banana weevils and nematodes, maize stalk borer, pests of beans and sweet potato are considered the commonest types of pests reported.

Storage pests for mainly maize and beans (maize and bean weevils) are a significant cause of post harvest losses. Storage of crops is a serious problem in a tropical country like Uganda and there can be no doubt that there are serious losses each year to insects and rodents – Worthington (1955) put it as high as 25 percent sixty years ago. Researchers at Kawanda Agricultural Research Institute, KARI, (personal communication) have made estimates of 30 percent – even higher today.

Respondents from 43 percent of all surveyed households reported loss of animals due to disease. Of these, one third lost livestock, while two thirds lost chicken. Main cause of death was tick-borne diseases and liver-fluke infestation for the livestock and New Castle disease for poultry. However, in many cases farmers said they did not know what was killing their animals.

Limited land for agricultural production ranks third among the three most important constraints to agricultural production. One of the most important trends in African agriculture is the steady increase in the person-to-land ratio. While for a long time Africa was seen as a continent of ample land and scarce labor, this no longer applies to much of Southern and Eastern Africa (Jayne *et al.*, 2006). According to the FAO[42] data, the last 40 years of the twentieth century were characterized by almost a tripling of the population of households engaged in agriculture but with only marginal increases in the amount of arable land under cultivation (including permanent crops). A similar trend is observed for Uganda over the same period with the person-to-land ratio[43] increasing from 1.7 in 1969/1971 to 2.7 in 2001/2003. The problem is aggravated by a decline in soil fertility. Land degradation due to continuous cultivation and low fertilization ranks among the top agriculture-related environmental problems in Uganda (NEMA, 1998). Results from the survey suggest that some farmers (6.6%) likewise perceive a long-term decline in their soil fertility due to over-cropping, declining availability of land, as well as inability to improve soil fertility on the small land holdings.

Lack of labour due to limited capacity to hire labour or due to reduced household labour as a result of sickness was also identified as having significant impact on agricultural production. As has already been indicated in section one of this chapter, the risk of malaria, HIV and other infectious diseases is high. The data reveals that malaria and AIDS are the leading causes of ill health and death. Survey information obtained on the type of illnesses and the days bedridden shows that malaria is the commonest cause of sickness. All households had at least one member having suffered from malaria in the period two months prior to the survey and over 50 percent of the households having an at least one economically active member severely affected to point of being bedridden. Survey results show that at least one week's worth of labour time per month is lost due to malaria. Individuals suffering from AIDS were reported in only nine households (this is likely to be an under estimate given people's fear of being stigmatized) and about twice as much time as that for malaria is said to have been lost due to HIV/AIDS-related sickness. This implies that AIDS is likely to cause a more severe impact on household labour availability than malaria.

[42] Source: http://www.fao.org/faostat/foodsecurity/Files/Agric_Pop_Density_en.xls: (Downloaded May 3, 2007)

[43] Person to land ratio = (Population in agriculture) / (land cultivated to annual and permanent crops)

The most cited effects of ill health on agricultural production included poor management of crop fields due to activities being done late (74.5%); reduced crop yields (30.6%); reduction in area under cultivation (27.8%) and reduced household labour (12.8%). No significant difference in the type of constraints experienced was observed among the different types of households and the first six most cited effects were the same. Table 4.20 presents the effects of illness on banana production by household headship and they are almost similar to those reported for agricultural production. The results imply a likely reduction in the capacity of households to produce enough food.

While differences were not statistically different, major effects of ill health experienced varied slightly. More than one third male-headed households reported mainly experiencing delay in implementation of agricultural practices and lack of money to buy inputs. About half of the widow-headed households that had sick members suffered reduced household labour and yields in banana. And a higher proportion of female- and widow-headed households (about half in each case) experienced reduced household labour as a consequence of illness of members than male-headed households.

Table 4.21 presents constraints limiting access to and use of community services in Masaka and Kabarole districts. The lack of extension services in some areas (reported by 20% of the respondents) is one of the major constraints reported. In addition to this, farmers (25%) said that they lack information on some of the services that exist in their areas as well as the programs being organized by those service providers. About eight percent of the respondents were of the view that some local leaders are partly responsible for the lack of information among farmers since with the government's decentralization policy, all programs operating in any given area have to receive consent from the local leadership. So the argument is that

Table 4.20. Effects of ill health on banana production by household headship.

Effects of sickness	Single-female HH (%)	Male HH (%)	Widow HH (%)	Row total (%)
Agricultural activities delayed	60.0	41.2	25.5	39.9
Reduced household labour	46.6	26.0	51.0	32.8
Lack of capital to buy inputs	17.8	33.9	25.5	30.8
Reduced banana yield	22.2	25.1	45.7	28.9
Increase in pests and disease	20.0	12.6	27.7	16.2
Total cases	45	342	94	481

Source: Household Survey.

Table 4.21. Constraints limiting access to community services in the area.

Constraints	S-F-HH (%)	M-HH (%)	W-HH (%)	Total (%)
Lack of information on services/trainings	18.4	26.1	24.7	25.2
Lack of extension services in area	32.7	19.3	17.5	20.2
Limited time to attend	10.2	14.7	17.5	14.8
Transport costs to training points not affordable	10.2	12.9	18.6	13.7
Bad roads prevent service providers from going to rural areas	12.2	10.7	8.2	10.4
Some leaders do not mobilize farmers to access services	14.3	7.2	9.3	8.3
Late communication	16.3	6.7	6.2	7.5
Sickness hence cannot attend meetings	6.1	4.0	21.6	7.5
Extension workers focus on only banana production	4.1	6.2	5.2	5.8
Lack collateral to access credit	4.0	8.0	4.1	6.9
Lack of funds to pay for services	2.0	4.0	8.2	4.6
Lack of capital to purchase inputs	8.2	3.5	4.1	4.0
Extension agents only target progressive farmers	6.1	3.2	6.2	4.0
Farmers are not cooperative	4.1	3.8	0.0	3.1
Limited land	0.0	1.9	6.2	2.5
Laziness	6.1	1.6	2.1	2.1
Extensionists not practical in their approaches	0.0	1.6	0.0	1.2
Agro-inputs are very expensive	2.0	1.1	0.0	1.0
Others	2	3.5	0	2.8
No constraint	4.1	9.4	6.2	8.3
N	49	373	97	519
Total (%)	9.4	71.9	18.7	100

Source: Household survey.
S-F-HH=Single-female-headed HH; M-HH=Male-headed HH; W-HH=Widow-headed.

leaders need to mobilize their people and encourage them to make use of available opportunities. Poor road infrastructure (mentioned by 10% of the respondents) further aggravates the problems of limited access to extension services.

Though reported to a much lower level, the nature of extension services provided seems to be problematic. For example, some respondents complained about communication about extension programs being late (8%); extension workers providing technical information on only banana and neglecting other crops (6%); targeting of only progressive farmers (4%); and extension workers not being practical in their approaches (1.2%). Other respondents highlighted individual level factors affecting access to services. These include: limited time to attend extension meetings (15%); lack of transport money to go for trainings (14%); sickness (8%) and lack of funds to pay for services (4%).

Some respondents think that participation in extension programs is useless when you don't have money to purchase recommended inputs or land on which to implement extension workers' recommendations. Table 4.22 shows the banana management practices that farmers have abandoned and reasons for no longer applying them. Theses results point to the likely impact of existing constraints on agricultural production and food security.

4.4 Food security status

In Chapter 3 food security was defined as the household's ability to command an adequate amount of required food through anyone of a combination of existing sources. Furthermore, it was shown that food security entails several other

Table 4.22. Banana management practices not applied and reasons for not applying them (n=499).

	HH not applying practice (%)	Reasons (combined) for abandoning the practices	Fre-quency	% responses
Applying fertilizer or manure	69.3	Lack of capital to buy inputs	270	38.5
Making soil bands and water trenches	33.5	High cost of inputs (pesticides & fertilizer)	166	23.7
Pest and disease control	28.5	Lack of technical know how to implement the practices	109	15.6
Mulching	25.7	Activity/practice very labour intensive	43	6.1
Use of clean planting materials	15.6	Limited labour availability for hire	41	5.8
Splitting stems and Uprooting corms	9.0	Hired labour is very expensive	38	5.4
Other (weeding, de-suckering & pruning)	4.6	Sickness	34	4.9
Total	92.2		701	100

Source: Household survey.

things, some of which are intangible, therefore necessitating the need to take into consideration people's perceptions on how they view consumption needs and what they perceive as adequate in the context of other livelihood needs. The main food security crops grown have been discussed in the preceding sections. Information obtained from FGDs reveals that the majority of households depend on own production as the main source of household food. Other sources include the market, social networks and to a limited extent, food aid from NGOs among HIV/AIDS-affected households.

Data was collected on 10 different crops grown and 14 foods consumed. For the foods consumed, the respondents were asked to state the number of times a particular food was consumed and to rank the level of food adequacy with regard to availability and sufficiency through the year. The ranks ranged from 1 to 4, with rank 1 = inadequate and rank 4 = very adequate. From the adequacy ranks recorded per food type, an aggregate food adequacy score for the 14 food types was calculated for each household. The food types were also categorized[44] into proteins, carbohydrates and vitamins and mean adequacy scores per food category type also calculated for each household. Foods that were commonly mentioned as adequate by most respondent (over 60%) included; banana, maize, beans, fruits and vegetables. All household types said that protein foods were in most cases not sufficiently available or adequate. Survey data also reveals that individuals in male-headed households were likely to consume bananas, milk and all types of meats more often than individuals in female-headed households ($p < 0.10$). For example, respondents in male-headed households on average consume bananas 20 days in a month, beef five days per month and milk 20 days per month. Respondents in the other two types of female-headed households said that they consume bananas about 17 days per month, beef three times a month and milk 14 days per month. Fruits and vegetables (vitamins) were the most abundantly available foods. Figures 4.2 and 4.3 present the mean food category adequacy scores by household headship and by district.

District level analysis reveals significant differences in the mean adequacy food scores ($p < 0.1$) for the two districts. Kabarole district had a higher adequacy score of 2.9 than that of Masaka district of 2.2. For households in Masaka, food adequacy mainly ranges between barely adequate and adequate. The difference between the districts can be partly explained by information obtained from FGDs, revealing that farmers in Masaka district had experienced long periods of drought and other weather-related problems between 2004 and 2005 than to those in Kabarole district. However, the higher economic dependency ratio of households in Masaka (2.8),

[44] Protein foods constituted: beans, milk, meat (all types), poultry meat, fish; Carbohydrates constituted: banana (matoke), maize meal, cassava, sweet potato, yams, ground nuts; vitamins: Any leafy vegetables and fruits (cabbage, dodo, pawpaw, mango, jack fruit, passion fruits)

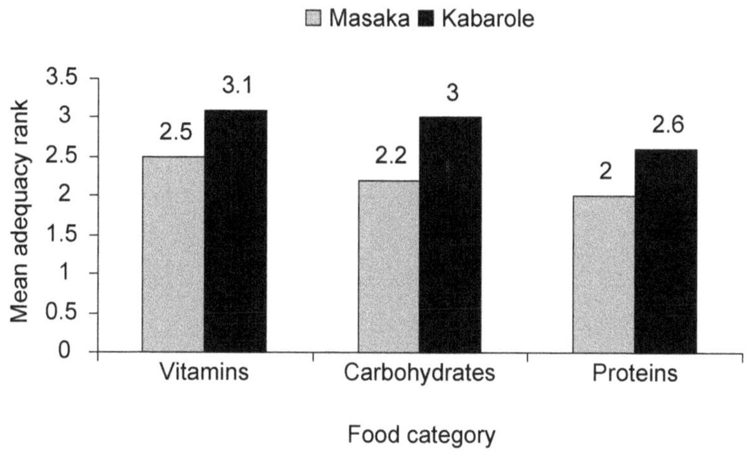

Figure 4.2. Food category adequacy by district. Source: Household survey.

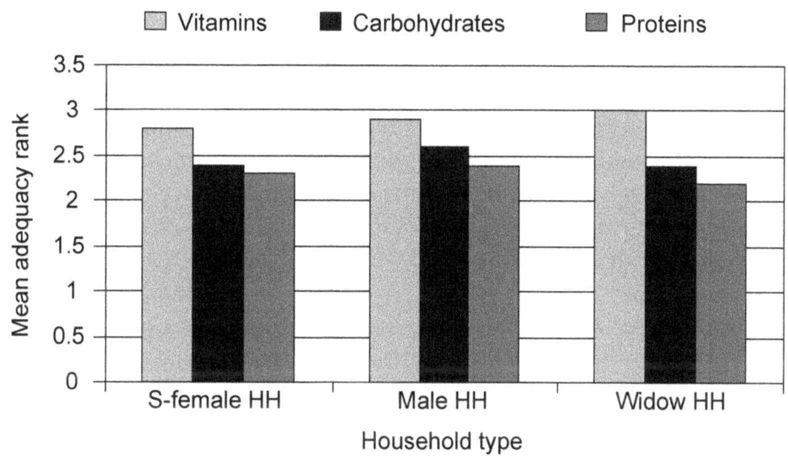

Figure 4.3. Food category adequacy by household headship. Source: Household survey.

compared to that of Kabarole (1.8) can be another contributing factor (cf. Table 4.3). Table 4.23 shows that male-headed households have significantly higher ($p<0.01$) food adequacy scores than the two types of female-headed households. Single-female headed households have the lowest food adequacy score. Aggregate scores for each household were also used to categorize households into three groups indicating their food security status[45]. For the sample as a whole, 24 percent of

[45] Food Insecure had Aggregate scores <21; Barely Food Secure had aggregate scores ≥ 21 but <35; Food Secure had aggregate scores >35.

Table 4.23. Mean adequacy score in the study area by household headship.

Household type	Mean adequacy score	Standard deviation	χ^2	p
Single-female headed	2.325	0.427	9.571	0.008
Male-headed	2.575	0.348		
Widow-headed	2.450	0.389		

Source: Household survey.

the households can be said to be food secure, 43 percent barely food secure, while food adequacy scores for about one third of the households put them in the food insecure category.

Challenges to food security: Information obtained from almost all FGDs revealed that most of the problems of food shortage stem from constraints faced in agricultural production (Table 4.18). Lack of labour due to inability to hire labour or due to reduced household labour as a result of sickness as well as limited land were the other major constraints mentioned by respondents. According to the PEAP (2004) climate changes leading to more frequent droughts, limited alternative income, widespread land degradation, increased population pressure, limited access to basic services and inputs are the major agriculture-sector constraints that underlie food insecurity in Uganda.

Survey data further show that there are some households that are chronically food insecure, experiencing food shortages throughout the year (see Figure 4.4). The months of March and April in the first cropping season and those of October, November and December during the second cropping season were reported by more than one fifth of the households as months of food scarcity. Uganda's agriculture being primarily rain-fed makes household food availability susceptible to rainfall fluctuations and other adverse weather conditions. One of the government's strategies with regard to water supply is the promotion of small-scale irrigation technologies, but these plans remain to be operationalized. Therefore, farmers' dependence on rain-fed agriculture is likely to continue, entailing consequences of increased vulnerability to food insecurity among rural households.

Qualitative and quantitative data evidence reveal reduced capacity of households to rely on own production, which is gradually becoming an important food insecurity risk factor. Therefore, households that have access to off-farm employment or income generating activities are likely to be more food secure compared to households without these opportunities. Survey data also reveals that the two types of female-

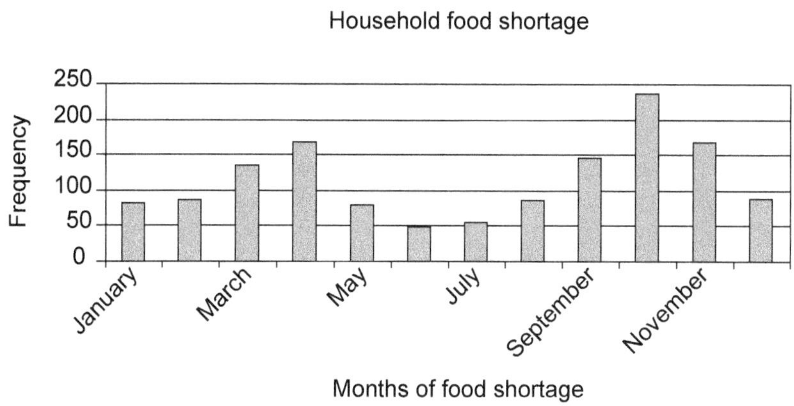

Figure 4.4. Months in which households experience food shortage. Source: Household survey.

headed households in the sample population have mor limited sources of income than their male counterparts. This coupled with women's constrained mobility due heavy work load may partly explain why female-headed households in this study have been identified as vulnerable to food insecurity.

4.6 Conclusion

This chapter has reviewed the structure of sampled households in the two districts. Apart from the economic dependency ratio and the proportion of households fostering orphans, which are higher for Masaka, the other demographic characteristics and farming practices are similar. Household level differences seem to play a more significant role in the type of farming activities undertaken than between district differences. The results reveal that large households have more dependants, thus not a greater labour supply. Furthermore, there are low levels of education among household heads, limited access to agricultural information and credit due to few institutions operating in the area, which make it difficult for farmers to adopt labour or capital-intensive technologies. Timely and relevant information can fundamentally alter people's decision making capacity and is crucial to increasing agricultural productivity. In the same vein, access to finance and credit facilities are equally important. Bagamba (2007) makes similar arguments.

The chapter further demonstrates the importance of land as the primary productive resource of households. There is a diversity of land tenure arrangements with widely ranging degrees of security, access, and use rights, between households and within members of the same household. While mostly men own and control land use and women have usufruct rights, there are subtle differences within these categories. For example, poor men and widows have less access to land than rich men and widows. Furthermore, single-female household heads have less arable land that they own and occupy compared to widowed household heads. Beyond this there are also other important differences among women in terms of land access and security of tenure. However, some women have access to more land than some men, some women are not poor, and landlessness and poverty are not confined to women only. And while inheritance of land is patrilineal, male orphaned children are likely to have less secure tenure after the loss of one or both of their parents than those with parents. For most countries security of tenure has been found to be directly related to investments in land and inputs. As Saito (1992) notes, the greater the security of tenure individuals have, the greater the productivity of the land. Therefore, given the existing problems of land scarcity, land tenure insecurity is likely to have significant constraints on farming.

Besides land scarcity and tenure-related constraints, the agricultural sector still faces fundamental challenges. Farmers' dependence on rain-fed agriculture, pests and diseases, limited land, declining soil fertility, limited household labour, limited access to extension and financial services, limited use of modern inputs as well as limited availability of appropriate technologies, have been identified as limiting households' capacity to increase agricultural production. Declining soil fertility and infestation with the banana weevil significantly contribute to low banana production in Masaka than in Kabarole. Improved access to irrigation technologies and to information on recommended plant and animal management practices, pests and diseases control, new marketing opportunities, and prices of farm inputs and outputs is fundamental to an efficient and productive agricultural economy. As was highlighted by the farmers, improved transport and communications infrastructures as well as availability of functioning markets for agriculture inputs and products are of crucial importance.

While women play an important part in agricultural production, especially the food crops, their role as producers and agents of change in the much-needed rural transformation has been severely constrained by their meagre share in the means of production, land, capital, credit and technology, and by their marginalization in production (Nzioki, 2001). This is not to say that poor men are not disadvantaged. But poor women are worse off because of their subordinate position to men and limited access to productive resources. As the study shows, women's insecure land rights and negative effects on this by HIV/AIDS coupled with the higher number of dependants that further constrain the already limited household labour in their households, and low resource base, are likely to limit their capacity to engage in gainful farming, thus making their livelihoods vulnerable to any future shocks.

The importance of farming to the livelihoods of farmers in the study area cannot be overemphasized. Low productivity due to the challenges mentioned above combined with small land holdings mean that few farmers are able to grow enough food to meet their needs. In the next chapter, I will discuss the different livelihood activities and strategies that banana farmers engage in to sustain their livelihoods.

Chapter 5

Case studies

This chapter presents twenty case studies of households in Masaka and Kabarole districts that illustrate the realities of the ways people generate their livelihood and the ways in which they respond to various shocks, in particular HIV/AIDS. The chapter is organized as follows. In the first section five case studies that illustrate the different strategies people use in livelihood generation are presented. In the second section the cases illustrate the ways in which the different impacts of HIV/ AIDS are experienced and how people respond. The chapter ends with concluding remarks on the cases presented. Table 5.1 gives a summary of the characteristics of all cases presented.

5.1 Livelihood strategies

The six cases in this section provide insights on (i) the type of resources people have access to and use, ((ii) ways people juggle their labour and resources between different activities to sustain their living and (iii) the various decisions and choices made by individuals or households in the process of livelihood generation given existing constraints and available opportunities. In Chapter 6, the processes captured in these cases will be combined with quantitative analysis to provide a clear understanding of the processes and factors determining the pursuit of different livelihood strategies in the study area.

Case 5.1. Perennial crops producer strategy

Akiki is a 47-year old farmer with two wives. He has been married for 22 years to his first wife with whom he has four children; two girls aged 15 and 12, and two boys aged 17 and 13. the first three children are in private boarding schools in Kampala while the last girl is in her primary seven also in a private primary school in Kabarole. He married his second wife in 2003. She is a primary school teacher and has two girls, aged three and one. Akiki's first wife Adyeri lives on their 10-acre piece of land about 25 km from Kabarole town. The young wife Amooti lives in Kabarole town in one of Akiki's new houses. Akiki has three other buildings in the town, two of which are rented out and the other he uses for his businesses. Akiki inherited his 10 acre piece of land from his father who was a chief for the *Mukama* (King) of Toro. Akiki talks about how his interest in farming developed:

> *I developed interest in farming from a very young age. My father who was one of the best banana and coffee farmers in the district, used to have close links with agricultural extension officers and researchers who made different technological trials on our farm. I remember him winning many*

Table 5.1. Characteristics of case studies investigated[1].

Case	District	Sex/age	Characteristics
Case 5.1: Akiiki	Kabarole	Male/47	Perennial crops producer strategy
Case 5.2: Tadeo	Kabarole	Male/30	Diversified small-holder strategy
Case 5.3: Namatovu	Masaka	Female/60	Labourer
Case 5.4: Specioza	Masaka	Female/66	Staples grower strategy
Case 5.5: Jane	Masaka	Female/32	Staples grower and selling services
Case 5.6: Kamurari	Masaka	Male/76	AIDS morbidity-related effects of adult male household head.
Case 5.7: Maria	Masaka	Female/46	AIDS mortality-related effects. AIDS widow (widow also infected).
Case 5.8: Monica	Masaka	Female/80	Grandmother-headed households that has taken in orphans, but the household is child supported.
Case 5.9: Kibita	Masaka	Male/38	HIV/AIDS-related morbidity in a young household and grandmother support
Case 5.10: Veronica	Masaka	Female/58	AIDS-related morbidity of female adult (HIV-infected grandmother) and AIDS orphans.
Case5.11: Mutebi	Masaka	Female/55	Household with non-HIV/AIDS-related spouse death
Case 5.12: Samuel	Masaka	Male/22	Child-headed household
Case 5.13: Agnes	Kabarole	Female/16	Double orphanhood – fostered orphan girl
Case 5.14: Anazia	Kabarole	Female/65	Single-female-headed household fostering AIDS orphans, including an AIDS-orphan.
Case 5.15: Matthew	Kabarole	Male/30	Matthew, young heir in polygamous AIDS household. Clustering effects of AIDS.
Case 5.16: Nathan	Kabarole	Male/22	Orphan-headed household
Case 5.17: Irari	Kabarole	Male/82	Grandfather-headed household with an HIV-infected orphaned child
Case 5.18: Leo	Kabarole	Male/50	AIDS widower
Case 5.19: Esther	Kabarole	Female/66	Orphan & AIDS-morbidity household that is coping
Case 5.20: Nakalembe	Masaka	Female/24	AIDS-related divorce, stigma and exclusion.

[1] All names are pseudonyms.

> *prizes and one time as the best farmer he was taken for a tour in Europe. All these things captivated me. My father used to tell me that the land was the source of wealth. I also used to see people around us who had small gardens being poorer than us. So I got the determination to emulate my father and be a better farmer than him. None of my siblings though developed interest in farming. Our eldest sister is a practicing Doctor in the UK, my elder brother is a business man in Kampala and our last born, a boy didn't get far in his education and died in 2002 from AIDS. After my tertiary education in business accounting I got married and my father gave me land. I partly attribute my success in farming to knowledge and advice sought from extension workers some of whom I have known from childhood as they worked for my father. I think our hard work (My wife and I) is something to contend with as well. I always tell people that my wife is like a tractor! She is a very hard working woman.*

On the 10 acres of land, the household uses about seven and the other three are usually rented out. They have a two-and-a-half acres plantation of banana, three acres of clonal coffee, and three acres of Eucalyptus forest. In addition to this, Adyeri grows beans, maize, irish potato, sweet potato, millet, onions, passion fruits, ovacado, and a variety of leafy vegetables. In the past Akiki used to be in charge of the banana and coffee plantations but Adyeri has now taken over most of the management decisions because her husband is usually away in Kampala engaged in other businesses. She describes what she does in the following way:

> *I make all decisions on the farm these days because Akiki is never here. So I decide on what we should grow where and how much, how much land we will rent out in any given season, the number of casual labourers to take on, and so on. However, I always inform my husband about the decisions I make and when he is around we decide together what needs to be done. We also agreed that all the money from bananas, coffee and sale of Eucalyptus trees be used for children's school fees and other household developments like the buildings he is constructing in Kabarole town. So he is actually in charge of all the money from those enterprises. Money from the other crops I grow and from renting out of land is in my control and is used for paying labourers, buying fertilizer and seeds, and for maintaining the home. So I do not ask my husband for money for salt or sugar or children's clothes, let alone mine! However, I also have a small poultry project of about 200 layers. From this I get personal income which I use to pay school fees for my late sister's and brother's children that live with my mother. We have never lacked food in this household.*

Over the years, Akiki has been able to buy 30 more acres of land because he wanted to increase production and start dairy farming. On these 30 acres, he has established a farm with 25 high-grade (Friesian) dairy cows. Each of the two wives receives five liters of milk from the farm daily. He has put his cousin brother (whom he also pays) in charge of the farm and employs five other permanent workers. The number of casual labourers working on the farm varies depending on need. At this farm, he has also established another two acres of banana, one acre passion fruit, and one acre of pine trees as well as four acres of Cassava Mosaic-resistant varieties. Other crops like maize, beans, irish potato are also grown. Akiki told us that the food from the dairy farm is for his second wife. For Akiki's household(s) income is derived mainly from sale of banana, coffee, maize, beans, timbre/poles, cassava and cassava cuttings (planting materals), milk and land hire. Milk and banana are important sources of income. On average they sell 200 liters of milk daily and 70-100 banana bunches every two weeks. In the first crop season of 2003 (one season previous to interview), Adyeri produced 1000kg of Maize, 400kg of beans and 300kg of irish potato, in addition to other crops. This is in addition to food given in kind by those who rent land. Since 2000, Akiki decided to invest money from the farm into non-farm activities. He describes his decisions:

> *In 2000 I decided to invest in buildings. First I realized that there was a gap in terms of available buildings for rent and business. Additionally, Kabarole district produces a lot of coffee and cereal grains but we do not have adequate storage facilities. So initially my interest was to construct a big store where I could store my produce so that I sell when the prices were good or rent out as a store. In the process, I learnt from those renting my stores and started trading in produce myself. I realized that this business was very profitable. The other factor that pushed me was the fact that agriculture is no longer paying well. We put in a lot and the profits are little. The main problem has been poor road infrastructure, almost alienating us from markets for agricultural products but the cost of inputs and labour are also high. Money from produce has been re-invested into construction of two other buildings in town. I have also started a hardware business because it is now the most profitable given that there is a lot of rehabilitation and construction going on in the district presently. The hardware business entails a lot of movements to Kampala so in 2003 that's why I decided to marry another wife so that she can look after the investments in Kabarole town. Income from property rents and the hardware business has helped me in improving my dairy farm.*

We were told that Amooti teaches in a nearby primary school in the mornings and attends to her husband's hardware shop in the afternoons. Akiki's nephew, Sam, also helps out in the shop.

Case 5.2. Diversified small-holder strategy

Tadeo and Allen are a young couple and have been married for three years. Tadeo is 30 years and Allen 25. They have a one-and-a-half year old daughter. They live in Kyakazini village, Kabarole, where they have a two-acre piece of land that Tadeo acquired from his father. Tadeo's parents have AIDS and are both on ARVs. His mother has been responding well to the treatment but the father is always sickly and very weak. Out of five children, Tadeo is the only one living: all four elder brothers died of AIDS between 2001 and 2004. He has taken on two nephews aged 6 and 8 (children of one of his late brother whose wife also recently died). The other orphans live with his mother. On their two acres, Tadeo and Allen have established a banana plantation on about three quarters of an acre, and grow maize, beans, sweetpotato, cassava and groundnuts on the rest of the land. They also keep two goats and one pig. However, for the two years prior to the interview (2004,2005) the crop yields have been declining. Tadeo thinks that the soils are poor, but fertilizers are expensive. So, Tadeo decided to get involved in a sharecropping arrangement. He explains the arrangement and how it came about.

> *For about two years, crop yields have been going down and it was becoming clear that we could not depend on farming from my limited piece of land alone. In fact we experienced some food shortages in 2003 when my nephews started living with us. Fortunately, two years ago, the NAADS programme organized trainings on income generating activities in our parish and our group (Kyakazini Youth Group) received training in tomato and cabbage production. After the training I approached two of my group members and suggested to them that we start a cabbage project together. They agreed and we decided to undertake the project and one of them proposed that we use a wetland area that is part of some land he had acquired from his father.*
>
> *Since then, we have worked together very well as a team. The first two seasons of 2003 were very good and we got good money. However, the 2004 crop was infested with pests and we almost lost the whole crop. The pesticides on the market seem to have been adulterated because they seem to have had no impact on the pests. After this incident we decided not to put our eggs in one basket. We acquired more land and have also started growing tomatoes. One of us has to travel to Kasese town to buy the pesticides because we are not sure of the local source. The three of us have goats at home so we collect the droppings and use them to fertilize the vegetable gardens. With regard to profits, we share equally, after removing the would be equivalent land hire costs which we give to our friend that provided the land. With the profits obtained from the cabbage and tomato production I have been able to start a retail shop in Mbirizi town. In addition to the usual household essentials we sell, my wife bakes a few food stuffs like pan*

> *cakes and bread that we sell in the shop. I normally wake up early and work in the garden with my wife and then open the shop mid morning. Tuesday and Thursday mornings are my days for working in the cabbage and tomato fields.*

The Tadeos now say that they are not worried about food for the home. The shop helps them generate money that can enable them buy food. Allen told us that she also earns some income with braiding people's hair from home. She says that she would get more money if she had a saloon in a nearby trading center. But this option is not viable given the farm work (particularly now that Tadeo has the cabbage sharecropping arrangements and the shop to look after) and a young baby. Tadeo says that he wants to buy a *boda boda* (motor cycle) with his next savings. If all goes well this may take him like a year. But he says everyone, his nephews, Allen and himself must work hard and make sacrifices to make sure this is achieved. Nonetheless, he thinks that it will be a worthwhile investment because the *Boda Bodas,* which are the main means of transport in the area, are presently few. He said that when hired out, one would expect at least 5,000/- per day. Besides, he is of the view, that the two sources of daily income (shop and *boda boda)* can help him improve farming so that the household can be food sufficient.

Case 5.3. Labourer

Namatovu says she is about 60 years old but does not remember exactly when she was born. She was born in Ekunuka, Kabula Masaka district. She never went to school. She got married in 1967 to Lawrencio, who died in 1987. The couple produced seven children; three boys and four girls, of whom only three children (two girls and one boy) are still alive. The four children who died, died below the age of three years: two died of sudden death, one of measles and the other two days after birth. The two girls living are married, the eldest with four boys and the other with two girls. The son is not married and is a fisherman by trade on the Lake Victoria. Namatovu says he has never sent her any money. Yet he has been away for more than a year. She lives alone and her children rarely come to visit her.

Since her childhood Namatovu says she has lived in a life of scarcity and the situation was made worse when she got married to a man who never had resources. For her whole life they have depended on their labour as a source of livelihood. The half acre of land that they have owned was used for growing a few crops like banana, beans, maize, cassava and sweetpotato. Given land shortage all the other crops are usually intercropped in the banana plantation. The food grown was always not enough to support household consumption even for one season and had to be supplemented through money or food obtained from casual labour. The whole family, children and parents would look for work among the villagers and provide their labour as a source of income. Their son was mainly involved in fetching water, carrying goods to markets and brick making, while the girls and their mother normally looked for planting and weeding opportunities.

The death of her husband affected the family very much because he was a very hard-working man and the main source of income for the household. Everyone in the village knew him because of his hard work and other labourers were jealous because they would never get a job (particularly when casual labour would be limited) before Lawrencio. Because of their small land, the family found it more profitable for Lawrencio to sell his labour and work on other peoples farms while the wife grew the food crops at home and also occasionally participated in casual labour. In the evenings, Lawrencio would work in their small plantation to ensure that it remained productive. Since his death, Namatovu says life became difficult because her husband left her no assets to look after the children. The house that they live in was of mud and wattle and in a very dilapidated condition. The family became chronically short of money, household necessities and school fees for the children. When Lawrencia died, the eldest children were in primary school (Grade two and six). Namatovu ensured that both got to the seventh grade but could not afford to go beyond this level. The small banana plantation also suffered because of loss of Lawrencia's labour. Namatovu had to engage in more casual labour because it brought in relatively more money compared to the little food from her own gardens. From about 12 years, Namatovu would take the girls with her to look for work. The harder she worked, the more the small home gardens suffered and the management of the banana plantation deteriorated. Because of the difficult circumstances at home, Namatovu says that she had to marry off one of her daughters at the early age of 17. As soon as the younger one had completed her Primary seven (that is between 14 and 15 years), she made the decision to get married herself. The son also went to look for employment at the age of 15.

Namatovu now lives alone but she says that provision of casual labour for agriculture remains her sole source of income, even at 60. She still continues to grow a few crops on her small piece of land. Recently her house was about to collapse and the local village authorities organized some youths who helped reconstruct it. Namatovu also said that she lives a very lonely life, something that could even be seen in her eyes. The villagers regard her household as one of the poorest, if not actually the poorest household. She has no relatives, her only friends are women labourers in the same situation, with whom she looks for casual employment.

Case 5.4. Staples grower strategy

Specioza is 66 year-old widow born in Bwasandeku village, Masaka District. She studied up to primary six[46]. She was born in a polygamous family. She has three living siblings. Specioza says that they are very close; her siblings and her two sisters and brother usually come and visit her. She also occasionally sends them food like beans and maize.

Specioza got married at the age of 20 to Tito. They produced seven children: three girls and four boys. Her eldest two daughters – Ane and Teddy – are married. Ane has one girl and two boys. Teddy lives in a nearby Sub-county and has three girls and two boys. Specioza's youngest daughter Macu, after completing her S4 in Nakyenyi Secondary School, started a nursing course in 2006. Initially, Specioza did not have money to pay for Macu's secondary education. However, being a good Christian and her participation in the church prompted the Reverend of the church to introduce her to World Vision, a NGO supporting orphaned children. The World Vision paid half of Veronica's school fees from S1-S4 and Veronica's brother paid the other half. After S4, one of Macu's maternal aunts is paying her tuition for a nursing course. After completing Primary seven, David, Specioza's youngest son, was taken by his maternal uncle as an apprentice in motor vehicle mechanics.

Specioza now lives with three grandsons in the same compound as her son Andrew. Andrew is married and has built his own house next to his mothers house. He is married with four children; three girls and one boy. The boy is one of the three grandsons that Specioza is living with. Specioza's husband died in 1998. However, he used to be a very good banana and coffee farmer. He would work in the plantations in the mornings and go to Kinoni trading centre where he did his welding work. The money from the coffee and banana plus that from his welding work was comfortably sustaining the household needs according to Specioza. Specioza now lives on a four-acre piece of land that the wider family and local leaders decided to give her after her husband's death. Specioza's step children (six) wanted to take away the banana plantation but the husband had left a will and the local authorities intervened. However, the step children were also given four acres. She says the four acres given to her actually belong to her four sons.

About half of the total land acreage is under coffee and banana plantation with these crops providing the main source of income. She also grows beans, maize and

[46] It is important to note that this level of education was good in those days. Many women who reached upper primary demonstrate an increased appreciation of the importance of education for an improved livelihood and you find that they struggle to educate their children – on their own or by identifying potential relatives who can help them educate their children. They go looking, begging, being humiliated trying to get someone kind, be it a brother, sister or an in-law who can secure their child's future.

local vegetables basically for home consumption because of limited labour. In the banana-coffee plantation, Specioza's main activities include weeding and pruning. Her sons live nearby so they normally come in to help with difficult activities like removing and splitting of corms and de-suckering. Justine the eldest son lives about two kilometers away while Yusuf is one kilometer away. Both are married with two boys and two girls each. Apart from the sale of banana and coffee, Specioza gets extra income from the sale of handcrafts – she makes mats and baskets. Her sons and relatives also give her money that she uses to buy medicines and look after the grandsons, particularly paying their school fees. They also occasionally buy for her household necessities like food, paraffin for lighting and clothes. Justine and Yusuf have each purchased more land for cultivation because they say that land their father left them is too small for their families. Specioza does not seem to be utilizing her land maximally. She says old age and labour are her main constraints, explaining:

> *I lack money to hire labour. Although my sons come in to help, they also have their families to look after and therefore must put more time in their own gardens. I do not want to bother them a lot, so I mainly rely on my own strength.* (This is not very much given her age). *My husband used to buy mulch but now the bananas are full of weeds because of lack of mulch. Because of poor management the yields have greatly reduced. I do not have the energy to cut and bring that grass nor the money to pay someone to do it. I do what I can and the rest God takes over. Whatever, I get is what I eat. Besides, if I don't have enough food, my sons will have to bring me food because they cannot leave their children to go hungry.*

Specioza seems to be very good at investing in social networks. The decision to live with her three grandsons may be a strategy; when she grows old and cannot take care of herself, then any of her daughters-in-law may take her in. These boys came from her married sons. Of course, in the process she is also helping her daughters-in-law to take care of their children.

Case 5.5. Staples grower and selling services

Jane is 32 years and was born in 1974 in Mbarara district. At the age of 4 her parents took her to live with her maternal grandmother in Lwengo in Masaka so that she could get an education. Here she went to a nearby primary school where she studied up to Primary five and became pregnant at the age of 13. Her grandmother then arranged and got her married to the man who had made her pregnant. Jane has five children: four girls and a four-year-old boy who has not started school. The eldest daughter is in Senior five, and the others in primary, that is, Grades seven, three and one. Jane's husband died two years ago after a one month's hospitalization at Masaka referral hospital. He had a chronic cough and on and off fever for about six months before he became bed ridden and had to be hospitalized. In the hospital he was diagnosed HIV positive. The news devastated him very much and Jane says that he quickly lost the will to live. He told his wife to return him home so that he dies at home. When they returned home, he died within a week. He died in October 2003. During his last months of life he worked very hard to build a permanent house and used most of his savings. The house was completed just two months before he died.

Like is the case in many families in Lwengo sub-county, Jane's husband was the bread winner. When she moved in to live with him, her father-in-law gave them a two acre piece of land for cultivation. They established a banana plantation and grew other food crops like maize, groundnuts, cassava and beans. However, because the land was small, her husband decided to start saving cash to invest in other activities other than farming. Initial savings came from the banana plantation. The money was invested in trading in banana which is one of the main businesses in this part of the country. So the husband would buy bananas from farmers around, hire a lorry and go and sell them in Kampala. Sometimes he would travel as far as Mbarara (a neighbouring district) if the price of the bananas was better and then take the bananas to Kampala where he had established buyers in the markets there. This business involves a lot of travel and the husband would be away from home most of the time. To increase on the profits, usually the lorries are overloaded and sometimes not in good mechanical condition. So the traders prefer to travel in the late hours of the evening, the banana trucks then make stopovers and stay the night in any of the several towns along the Kampala Masaka highway to enable them make a very early start so that they arrive in Kampala very early in the morning before the police is on the road. The money from the banana business was good and the family did not lack anything, the children were in school and the family was able to take care of three other orphans (children of her two late brother-in-laws). From his business trips, Janes's husband would bring meat, sugar, rice, and bread. To ensure food security, the food crops grown were supplemented by the income her husband was bringing. Since her husband's death life has been difficult. She says:

> *I had to be the man in the household taking care of each and everything. It was difficult for me initially because my husband was the one taking care of children's school fees, clothing and even buying food for the home. Now I have to struggle to make ends meet. He left no land, no property and the savings he had made all went to building this house.*

Her main source of income is through the sale of surplus crops like maize and beans. With money obtained from the sale of her maize, she was able to buy a pig (a cross breed) two years ago. The pig has given her four litters so far and she sells young piglets at 10,000/- each when they are one month old. So far, it has given her a total of 22 piglets. Money from the sale of beans also enabled her to start a small business of selling *tonto*, a local brew. Customers buy or have a drink in her sitting room which is like a small bar. The banana plantation is no longer productive because of the poor management. She can no longer afford to buy mulch or hire labour to work in the plantation. Their land is also infertile and she says that the plantation needed manure which she could not get. Her husband used to hire a labourer to help her with work in the plantation but she cannot afford to hire labour any more. Apart from one brother in law who is helping in paying school fees for her daughter in P7, she has no other outside support. She says that it is becoming more and more difficult to raise school fees for the children. But the children and especially the eldest is interested in her studies and wants to study up to university.

After her husband's death, Jane also started getting fevers and later developed a skin rash. She went to Masaka referral Hospital and tested HIV positive in December 2003. She was then put on ARVs and had to travel to Masaka town every month to get her drugs. Since 2005, the hospital has a mobile unit that delivers the drugs at Mbirizi town (4 km away from her home). Since she started the treatment, the fevers have stopped. She only complains of general body weakness and as a result she can't engage in serious agricultural work. She also finds that small ailments like flue which never used to have a serious impact on her, now make her very weak.

Jane is pregnant. She says that one of her male customer friends is responsible but both have no intension of marriage. She explains why she decided to have another baby despite being aware of the health risks involved:

> *After the death of my husband, I was devastated, scared and very lonely. No one wanted to come near me because of the rumours that were going around. But Habib has been good to me and in the process we have become friends. There is a time I was very sick last year and he would bring us food. He now brings us a kilo of sugar and meat every weekend. I also usually borrow money from him when my tonto business is not doing well or when I need money for school fees. Last year he insisted that I had to bear him a child. Of course I know that this pregnancy will make me weaker given my status. The counselors at the clinic have explained to us everything. But one also has to consider the circumstances. My man died, Iam not educated, Iam sick and therefore cannot do heavy farm work, so how do I survive? Habib has been very supportive and I felt that I could give him a child. Besides, it is very difficult to remain there without a man when you are a young woman like me. Habib has promised to start a small poultry project for me.*

The children said that they miss their father very much. The eldest daughter says that she wants to study so that she can be able to look after her siblings because she is aware that her mother is sick. Jane wanted to marry off her daughter but she is not interested. The children are also not happy with their mother's male friends who sometimes spend the night. The young boy, however, said that when the men come to the house they bring meat, milk and bread. Their three cousins (the orphans talked about above) no longer live with them. Jane said that she could not manage feeding them. They went to live with their grandmother.

5.2 Living with AIDS

In this section, 14 case studies to illustrate how HIV/AIDS is experienced are presented. Another case study describing a household affected by a non-AIDS-related death is also presented to draw similarities and differences on effects of an adult death on a given household. The cases illustrate HIV/AIDS-related effects including reduced household labour availability and re-allocation, increased time needed for reproductive care activities, depletion of household resources and reduced access to and control over these resources, reduced engagement in productive activities, and increased incidence of orphanhood. The cases further show, among other factors, that HIV/AIDS-related effects vary by wealth status and by gender. The insights drawn from cases in this section are also used in the interpretation of quantitative data on HIV/AIDS-related effects in Chapter 7.

Case 5.6. Morbidity-related effects (infected male household head)

Kamurari is 76 years old and was born in Buyikuzi, Rakai district and is a Muganda. He was born in a family of three children: two boys and one girl. His sister got married and lives in another sub-county with her eight children. Apart from knowing that she lost her husband, Kamurari has no information about her or her children. His brother lives next to him on the neighbouring *kibanja*. The brother produced six children of which only two are still living, the others died, three of them from AIDS.

Kamurari studied up to primary five in Buyikuzi before joining a tertiary institution for two years where he studied tailoring. After his education he worked briefly with the Asians where he improved his skills in tailoring. He then migrated, with his brother, from Rakai district and they bought land (15 acres) in Lwengo sub-county Masaka district. Kamurari married his first wife when he was in his mid twenties. They wedded in the Catholic Church. However, his family did not want his wife because she was from a different ethnic background (Munyarwanda). Although he loved his wife, because of family pressures, they had to separate and the woman went back to her natal home. He had three children from his first marriage and they live with their mother. The family then organized and got him a second wife of the same ethnic background. He produced five children (1 girl and 4 boys) in his second marriage but all have died of HIV/AIDS, with the youngest to die being 17 and the eldest 25 years.

Livelihood activities: After settling in Lwengo, Kamurari embarked on ensuring that his family was food secure. He established three acres of coffee plantation and about two acres of banana plantation. This was in addition to the growing of other foods crops like beans, maize and sweet potatoes. He was a model farmer in the area, and extension agents used him as a contact farmer and conducted demonstrations on his farm. After establishing his farm, Kamurari bought a sowing machine, and started tailoring work at a nearby trading center where he had hired some working space. He would work in his gardens in the morning and go for tailoring in the afternoons. Later with money from the coffee and bananas he was able to start a lucrative livestock trading business. This would necessitate him to move in cattle markets all over the district looking for animals to buy and then take them to Kampala for slaughter. Kamurari was a very enterprising man. He hired public land from the local authorities and constructed a market and he would get market dues from the vendors. Kamurari was therefore very well known in the whole Sub-county because of his industriousness and enviable farm.

When HIV came into the picture: Problems stated in 1996 when Kamurari started falling sick. His health deteriorated very rapidly because he had severe diarrhoea, could not eat and was not responding to any medical treatment. Kamurari refused to go to hospital despite his wife's confession that she had tested HIV positive and was on treatment. He became bed ridden for two years and was almost dying until, in 1998, his brother convinced him to be taken for HIV testing to Mbirizi town (4 Km from his home), one of the centers managed by the Kitovu Mobile AIDS Care, Counseling and Orphans Programme (MAHCOP). Results showed he was HIV positive. Immediately MAHCOP enrolled him in their HIV/AIDS support programme under which, for 8 years he was receiving counseling and treatment for opportunistic infections. For four and a half years since 2001, Kamurari has been enrolled in the MAHCOP food programme. He was receiving 45 Kg of corn/soya blend and 3 liters of coking oil per month as food supplement himself and his AIDS orphaned grand son. By the time of the interview, Kamurari had been on ARV treatment for one year. He says he owes his life to MAHCOP which has given him "a life line" as he calls it. That is, treatment and food support for eight years, without which he does not think that he would still be alive. "I was supposed to die eight years ago. I remember hearing neighbours asking my wife every morning whether the patient - implying me-had survived the night. By the time my brother took me for HIV testing, I too had lost the hope and will to live." Kamurari's physical appearance is good but he feels very frail and weak.

Impacts of HIV: He says the disease reduces you to almost sub-human level. "AIDS has taken away all my self esteem and glory." From the time he became sick, he has not been on good relations with his wife. The wife was blaming him for infecting her.

> *Am now a poor man depending on food handouts as if I had no energy to grow my own food. My house is infested with flees and I have jiggers in my feet! All my enterprises are no more. All the bananas in the plantation have died, and the few coffee trees that have survived are in bush. I cannot afford to hire labour any more. I used to be known as the smart and handsome Kamurari. But look at me now; pale, shrunken, skin rashes and hair falling out. Some people who used to know me pass me by on the road; they do not recognize me. Whenever I go to the health centre to collect my medication, people start whispering as they pass me by on the road. I used to represent Mbirizi farmers at district level in the Masaka Farmers Association and also sit on a number of local council committees. I no longer participate in these activities because I have no energy but also because I hate the rumors and whispers behind my back. Besides, when you are poor and sick, no one would regard your contributions as important. Am also a very lonely man. In those days I always got any woman I wanted. But now, no one wants to associate with an old, poor and AIDS infected man! If it were not because of my grandson, I think I would have starved to death.*

All the money that he had saved and also the capital for his cattle business went to medical expenses. He says that the substantial savings he had accumulated enabled him not to sell any part of his land.

Because of the severe debilitating effects of the disease, he could no longer continue with his tailoring work and he sold the sowing machine. The market is no longer functional because organizing of the market days and market venders depended on him. So that source of income was also lost too. The cattle business definitely could not continue as he lost all his contacts the two years he was very sick and bedridden. During this period of sickness, Kamurari has had to deal with the pain of losing all his five children from the second marriage from HIV/AIDS. Kamurari is a strong Catholic and sometimes thinks that God was not happy with his second marriage. "Everyone from this marriage has died or is going to die from AIDS". Two years ago, the Parish Priest advised Kamurari and his wife to separate so that each leaves alone since their marriage was not "holy before God" and therefore not legally recognized by the Church. The Catholic Parish Priest is the one in charge of identifying and recommending HIV/AIDS-affected individuals for support to MAHCOP. So not to jeopardize the support from MAHCOP the couple agreed to live separately with Kamurari's wife having to move to an old house of one of his late sons with three orphaned grandsons. Kamurari now lives with one grandson who helps him with cooking and other household chores. Although he says he feels lonely, Kamurari feels that its better to be right with God, particularly at this time in his life.

Dealing with AIDS: Kamurari says that if it were not for the support received from MAHCOP, he would be long dead. Adding that, although the medication is very important, if you do not have food you cannot survive on the drugs alone because the medication increases your appetite and one also requires a balanced diet. With regard to coping, he actually says that the issue is not coping but just surviving with whatever is there. When he gets energy, he grows some little beans around the house. He also sometimes harvests some coffee beans from the now wildly growing coffee, if thieves or neighbours have not taken all of it. In addition to very small incomes from the beans and coffee, he hires out a weighing scale to one of his nephews at 5,000/- per month. This money enables him to buy sugar, soap, salt and some good sauce like meat when he wants it. The main constraint to agricultural production is farm labour. He is not strong enough to engage in active agricultural work yet he has no money to hire labour. However, Kamurari is very worried because the food support programme is to end in December, 2006. All those in the programme have been given improved maize and bean seeds to grow their own food. He says this will not be practical for people like him who no longer have energy to work.

Case 5.7. AIDS widow

Maria is an AIDS widow, 46 years of age and was born in Buyoga, Kibinge sub-county, Masaka District. Life for Maria has always been difficult. Maria was born in a family of six. Her father died when they were still very young and their mother raised them up single handed. When growing up, they used to first go to "*kupakasa*" (dig for other people for food or cash) together with their mother before going to school. Because of being orphans, Maria and her siblings never went beyond primary seven in their education. In actual fact, Maria studied up to primary six after which she got married at about the age of 19 years. They produced six children. Her husband tested HIV positive in 1997 and died at the end of 1999. Maria relates the experience of losing a spouse due to HIV/AIDS:

> *My husband was a hard working man. He was also good to me. We used to work together in everything. He would cut the grass for mulching the banana plantation and the children and I would go and help him to carry it. The mulch was good for our banana plantation because we used to get big bunches. He also used to do most of the heavy work in the banana plantation like de-suckering and removing of corms. Now this is no longer done, there is no mulch and the banana plantation is no longer productive. Not only did I lose his labour but my sickness does not allow me to do as much work as I used to do. When you have AIDS, you have to be careful not to stress yourself. For example, about one third of the plantation has been completely destroyed by weeds and pests due to poor management. We used to harvest at least ten big bunches of bananas per month for sale and*

leave the rest for food, but this is no longer possible. While the children have been very helpful in doing farm work, some of them are still young and they need my guidance. However, because of my poor health I sometimes find it difficult to wake up early in the cold and work with them. Agricultural activities seem easy but one needs experience. Therefore children need to be taught how to do these things.

Men are usually industrious and have different ways of getting money. It is difficult to depend on farming alone. So in addition to farming, my late husband used to engage in produce trading, particularly banana, maize and beans. That's how he managed to pay the children's school fees. When he died the older children had to stop schooling in Primary six because I could no longer afford to pay for their school fees and other requirements. My disabled daughter of 14 has never attended school because there are no special schools for handicapped-children in the area and we could not afford taking her to a special school elsewhere. The two youngest children are in school under the UPE programme, with the girl of 12 being in Primary 5 and the boy of 8 in P1.

Due to the high expenditure that was associated with my husband's sickness (drugs, hospital charges, and special protein diet) he had to sell a piece of land planted with eucalyptus. During the same period, medical expenses were further increased when our eldest son developed a cancerous condition of the nose. The disease condition was so bad; from the nose you had this highly putrid excretion coming out all the time. The whole house was smelling and neighbours stopped coming to our house. I had to oscillate between conventional medical doctors and traditional healers looking for medicines for both my husband and our son. Transport to collect these medicines was a lot and sometimes I had to walk seven kilometers to get my son's medication. The whole situation of sick people, limited resources, increased workload and worry of when I too would start feeling sick was both physically and emotionally depressing. Eventually we were lucky to get a female traditional healer who took in my son and after four months of intensive treatment the condition was completely cured. I had to sell my husband's bicycle and another piece of land to pay the traditional healer.

Because we do not produce enough food, our feeding has changed. We used to have two hot meals a day but we now take one meal in the evenings and maize porridge during the day. Pests and diseases for banana, soil infertility and luck of money to buy mulch or good seed for planting have contributed to low yields. Am always worried about our food security especially if the rains fail and the little that we normally produce dies. However, AIDS also

> *made us poorer because it killed the main income earner in this household and sickness has reduced how much I can work.*

After the death of her husband, Maria started falling sick more often. In 2001, she went to Masaka referral Hospital where she was tested to be HIV positive. In 2003, she started antiretroviral therapy, which she says has greatly improved her health. She used to go for her medication once a month to TASO offices in Masaka town. Since the beginning of 2005, the organization sends a health worker that delivers the medication to her home. Maria says she owes her life to TASO.

The family has an estimated land acreage of one-and-a-quarter acres on which they grow a variety of crops including banana, beans, maize, and a few coffee trees. The main source of household income is through the sale of beans and coffee. Maria's eldest daughter is doing a tailoring course and the family hopes that when she completes she will be able to help out with some of the financial problems. The eldest son seems to be taking over his late father's responsibilities. He helps Maria to farm, handles the selling of produce that the two of them agree on, and takes care of the siblings.

Maria's sister built her a house because the one that her husband had left, the roof was almost falling on them. Maria's sister is a business woman and she is always on the move. So being a single mother she felt that her children missed on parental care. The two sisters agreed that Maria takes in her sister's children (three) but in return she pays school fees for Maria's two children that are still in school in addition to receiving other support. Maria's sister therefore sends them money at regular intervals, often before the school term opens. The money she sends is used for buying basic household needs like salt, paraffin, and food, when sources from own production are exhausted as well as school uniform, scholastic materials and other school-related expenditures.

Maria has lost two sisters to AIDS and according to her, one brother to witchcraft. Her remaining brother has TB and is likely to be HIV positive though he has refused to go for testing. Maria is also a member of a village group called "Muno Mukabi". The main objective of the group is to help members during times of hardship, say at funerals when a member loses a loved one. The group organizes the funeral and meets major funeral costs. Members contribute five hundred Uganda shillings per month. Members can also access some little credit in case one has problems.

Case 5.8. Grandmother-headed household but child supported

Monica Nabwami says she is over 80 years old and has been a widow for over 20 years. Monica produced 10 children, five permanently migrated to Kampala but do not give her any support, while the other five that she used to receive support from have all died of AIDS. Monica now lives with 10 orphans (aged between 20 and 9): grandchildren from two of her dead sons. Four of these children are total orphans while the other six have their mother but she abandoned them when her husband died. Monica says that her daughter-in-law told her that she could not die in poverty since her husband had left no property to take care of the children. Available information indicates that, Monica's daughter-in-law got married to another man.

A few years back, Monica said that through the sale of farm produce she managed to support the orphans' education. But as of now, she says she is old and frail and the children have to look after themselves. "Their own mother abandoned them. I have nothing to do, I have done my part. Even if I wanted to do more, age cannot allow me." In the mornings, the children divide farm activities amongst each other with some ending up in the banana plantation while others tend other crops: beans, maize, cassava and sweet potato on the 2.5 acre piece of land. After the farm work, the boys normally collect water for the home and the girls cook food and do other household chores. After fetching water, the boys are free to go and do their own business which normally involves looking for casual employment in the village to earn money for clothing and other necessities. Jobs normally looked for include fetching water, transporting produce to markets (on the head) and casual labour. Monica does not stop the girls from seeking employment opportunities like their brothers, but the girls normally do not have time. Besides, there are limited employment opportunities for girls compared to boys. The money that the children earn, in addition to meeting personal needs, also contributes to family welfare through buying household necessities like salt, soap, paraffin and other food items. However, Monica says that contributions were mainly from the older boys. This could be because they have more opportunities for earning income compared to their sisters or they already perceive taking charge of the household affairs as a society role expected of men. Despite, the large household size, the households seemed fairly food secure. Members can still afford to eat two meals a day. Monica acknowledges that she has taught the orphans to be hard-working and they respect what she tells them to do.

Apart from two children, Babirye and Kato, all the others dropped out of school. Babirye and Kato are twins of 15 years. Kato, the boy is in his second year of secondary education while Babirye is in Primary six. The children are more or less paying for their education because they have to raise the biggest bulk of their school fees through casual labour in addition to begging friends and relatives. The reason for the differences in classes is that Kato engages in more paid casual work than the sister so he has been able to raise more money for his school fees. Even when he fails to raise everything, the grandmother said that it is easier to ask friends to support a boy's education. For the girl, people will say that she can get married. The girl was in and out of school on several occasions because there was not enough money for her school fees. Babirye also complains of too much domestic work that in most cases leaves very little time to look for casual work.

Case 5.9. HIV/AIDS-related morbidity in a young household and grandmother support

Kibita is 38 years and a community worker with World Vision. In 2005, him and his wife were diagnosed HIV positive. They have five children the eldest is 11 and the youngest two are 2 and 3 years old. His wife has been very sick and bed ridden for one and a half years, on and off. Kibita almost has no time for concentrating on any productive work because he is either nursing the wife at home or he is taking care of her in hospital because she gets hospitalized almost every month. He has been hiring labour for the banana plantation, but because of lack of supervision, the plantation is not doing well. The other crop fields have been neglected. Apart from his old mother, they have no other relatives who can come to help looking after Kibita's wife. Kibita has lost ten brothers to HIV/AIDS. His wife has also lost her only two siblings to HIV/AIDS. Kibira was one of the farmers that was rearing improved goats but most of these have been sold to meet medical expenses. The previous month, he had to sell the only cow they had, because the wife had to be hospitalized again. Kibira says that he loves his wife very much and will sell anything to make sure she gets good medical care. "I have to take care of her very well. She worked very hard to make these assets."

Kibira's mother, Yayeri, a widow of 80 years, is the only helping hand that the Kibiras have. They share the same compound with about 50 meters of ground separating their two houses. Despite her poor physical condition after years of physical brutality at the hands of her late husband, every morning Yayeri goes to his son's house to take care of the young babies. Yayeri suffered severe injuries to her spine and due to the pain in her back, sometimes she literally has to crawl in order to move. For the year-and-a-half that her daughter-in-law has been sick, she has tirelessly cared for the children. While Yayeri is not aware that her daughter-in-law has AIDS, she is very worried because the sickness has taken a very long time. Her other biggest worry is that she is afraid of what will happen to the children in case their mother dies. "There is no way I can manage to look after these children with my back problems and age if their mother dies", she says in desperation. Yayeri's other four children live in Kampala, but she does not know what kind of work they do, though she has heard that one of her daughters is married.

> *Those who died went and looked for death and brought it back to me, now I don't know whether these ones will also do the same" Yayeri talking about her dead children and those who are still alive. "Why has God punished me like this? Why can't I die and stop seeing such things."*

Yayeri broke down and wept, and, for that day, I had to terminate the interview and request another appointment.

Case 5.10. AIDS morbidity effects (female household head)

Veronica was born in 1948, got married to Kamurari (Case 5.6) when she was 22 and the two produced five children. After separation with her husband, she moved into a late son's dilapidated house. She lives with five orphans, children of her two dead sons. Veronica has this to say about HIV/AIDS:

> *My husband brought the disease. Long before we started falling sick, I knew that he had an affair with a woman who used to sell local beer in the neighbouring village. We had heard rumours that this woman had lost many husbands before she migrated. I tried to talk to him but he could not listen to me. Later, this woman developed all the signs of "slim" (AIDS) and died. After about a year, my husband started falling sick. I advised him to go for HIV testing but again he wouldn't listen to me. In the beginning I was also scared to go for testing but when I started getting funny fevers, I went for the test. AIDS is hear with us to stay, so it is stupid to refuse to go for testing when doctors can give you some pills that can prolong your life! I tested HIV positive in 1997 and was immediately started on prophylactic treatment to control opportunistic infections. MAHCOP started me on anti retro virus therapy in 2003, after my health had started deteriorating again.*
>
> *After the death of his (husband) lover our relationship became strained. It is difficult to stay with someone when you know that they are going to kill you. But what could I do? I had no where to go. However, despite the marriage problems I have nursed him until we were advised to live separately.*
>
> *The disease (AIDS) takes away all your people and in the process impoverishes you. In our culture we have a proverb that says "Oluganda bugaga", literally means that "kinship relations are wealth". All my children have died. The last one of my sons who was very progressive and was helping the orphans of my eldest son was also killed by AIDS three years ago. He is also the one who used to take care of me in everything. Our living conditions had deteriorated so badly before World Vision constructed this house. When it would rain, all our few belongings would get wet. So the children were really not happy. Now we have a roof over our head and we receive some food from MAHCOP. By depending on food hand outs from MAHCOP or being forced to ask neighbours to give you some money to buy paraffin for lighting or an exercise book for your child who has been sent away from school, AIDS reduces you to a beggar and erodes your self esteem.*

> *Furthermore, when you have AIDS, physically the body feels weak all the time and you don't feel good about yourself and any small infection puts you down. Am always worried about my health in case the medication fails to work on me as we see happening to some individuals. Because the children know about my HIV status they get worried every time I fall sick. So there is this feeling of uncertainty and insecurity amongst us. I also worry about what will happen to my grandchildren when I die. These poor orphans have no relatives (uncles or aunties) to help them. We have no relative to turn to apart from well wishers in the community, MAHCOP, World Vision, Uganda CARES and friends.*

Under MAHCOP, Veronica receives 50 Kg of the corn/soya blend and 3 liters of cooking oil per month. She says that the community is very supportive and people sometimes give her food. World Vision has built a good permanent house for her and registered it in one of the names of the orphans. World Vision is also paying school fees for one orphan that has joined secondary school. Three of Veronica's other grandchildren are in primary school under the government UPE programme. The primary school Head teacher has been helpful in that sometimes he allows the children to study without paying the extra school fee requirements because he is aware that the grandmother cannot afford. One child has refused school and looks for casual employment in the village. From Uganda CARES, she has received improved bean seeds and cassava planting materials. Otherwise, her other source of livelihood is the small piece of land on which she grows a few crops. Her husband has a lot of land but he has denied her access to it. Veronica's house is along the main village road, so with money from sale of crops or gifts she buys fuel wood and sugar cane village vendors and sells them in front of her house. She has been able to save and buy a piglet, which she intends to rear into a breeding sow.

However, Veronica is worried about her only still surviving daughter-in-law and her five children. The daughter-in-law has got another partner and she is pregnant a situation that is likely to further compromise her health status. Veronica says she is very frustrated about her daughter-in-law's decision. But what is worse is that she does not want to contemplate the thought of having to take in five more orphans in the event that the daughter-in-law dies.

Case 5.11. Household with non-AIDS-related spouse death

Mrs Mutebi is a widow with 9 children. Her husband an agricultural extension officer working with an international NGO died in 1994 due to a motor accident. However, long before this, Mrs Mutebi a grade 2 teacher by training had decided in 1980 to stop teaching and to concentrate on looking after her children and produce food for them. The five acre piece of land that her husband had purchased was being under utilized and the household did not have enough food. Yet her salary from teaching was not meaningful because almost all household expenditures were being met by her husband. Therefore, using her husband's technical advice and support over the weekends, the Mutebis were able to establish one-and-a-half acres of banana-coffee plantation. In addition, they grew almost all food crops and vegetables but with emphasis on cassava, sweet potato, maize and beans. By the time her husband died they were also rearing goats. Very early on, Mrs Mutebi had taught her children how to farm and the virtue of hard work.

> *The death of my husband was a big blow to the family. It came so fast and nothing could have prepared me for it. Immediately, there was no money for children's school fees (this had been his sole responsibility) and no money for agricultural inputs: seeds, fertilizer or mulch. At the time of his death, the eldest child was in their fourth year of secondary education. However, one thing I was determined about was to keep all my children in school. My mother was illiterate but through her hard work she had managed to educate us and I have found that to be the most important thing that she gave me. So after my husband's death, I told myself that I had to work doubly hard to meet the dream of my children's education. I had no relatives to look to for help. I knew that my two brothers-in-laws were struggling with their families. My only sister is poor and couldn't be of help. For 10 years I have worked hard and tried to use whatever money I earned judiciously. I don't even remember buying myself a new gomasi (traditional Kiganda dress)! The children also had to learn to live with just the basics. Whenever they were not at school, they all helped me in the garden. Though people knew me as a teacher, it did not stop me looking for casual employment from the church to earn extra income. Am now in charge of all the parish crop fields and in addition to being paid for the job, the parish gives me some food after the harvest. Because of this job, I have also been able to help women in my group to access similar paid casual jobs.*
>
> *To deal with the high educational costs, I sold my husband's motorcycle to raise money and children were removed from boarding to day schools. I also joined women's groups and other organizations that support widows. For example, Masaka Diocese Development Organization (MADDO) pays half the school fees for two children while two other children in secondary have received tuition support through the CHAI project.*[47] *When my eldest*

[47] Community HIV/AIDS Initiative (CHAI) is a government project proving grant funds for AIDS orphan's education and income generating activities for widows or people fostering orphans. The requirement is that beneficiaries be in organized groups, have a bank account and prove to have capacity to account for funds received following certain criteria. The last two requirements have obstructed many women's groups from accessing the funds.

two sons finished school and started working, they started helping with school fees and other requirements for their siblings.

Am also one of the beneficiaries of "Send a Cow" project where MADDO gives out in-calf heifers to widows. It produced a female calf and now I have two cows. The cow I received from MADDO, however, is not a good milker because it is of a local breed. But its manure has been useful for my vegetable gardens and making of compost. I intend to sell the local cow and buy an improved cross breed. I have five goats, two of which are of an exotic breed (The Angolan breed) type. These were received from NAADS through our participation in their training programmes but the goats belong to our group (Mbirizi Widow's group). With savings from banana and maize sales I bought two sows. They have furrowed once giving me a total of 10 piglets of which I sold eight each at UGX 10,000 and retained two. Finally I keep two local hens which give me one tray of eggs every two weeks. I mix my own feeds for them (maize bran, small fish and shells). Livestock are a very important source of household income and protein (eggs and milk). During periods of high agricultural activity, money from eggs help me to hire labour. Besides, they are less affected than crops, by weather fluctuations. In fact, one of the main objectives of our widows' group is to facilitate all members start rearing livestock.

Through extreme hard work, Mrs Mutebi has been able to realize her dream of educating all her children. By 2006, her last born was in senior six with the others having graduated in a number of trades; nursing, physiotherapy, technical building, accounting and teaching. She says her next major task is rehabilitating and completing her house which the husband left unfinished. She emphasized the importance of education in these words; "When you are educated, you are able to sniff around in big offices and come to know about existing opportunities and make strategic alliances. You can read documents to know what opportunities exist and how to access them. But most importantly you are confident to approach any office." Despite her success, Mrs Mutebi is quick to emphasize that it has not been easy being a widow. Looking after a large household single-handedly calls for longer hours of hard work, a lot of initiative, and connections. Nonetheless, she believes that her connections with the church and her decision in 1980 to leave teaching for farming have been crutial. Her friends, many of them members of Mbirizi widows group, have also been an important source of free labour whenever she calls on them, possibly as a good turn because she gets them paid work.

Case 5.12. Child-headed household: Samuel's story

Samuel was born in Mukibinge Misanvu village in a family of three. Samuel's father died suddenly when he was a baby of about three-and-a-half years in 1987. Before the father died, sold almost all the land they had and left a very small plot on which the house was located. However, following his death, some people came and took the iron sheets so Samuel and his two sisters had to be taken in by a paternal aunt. They lived with the aunt for four years after which the aunt chased them saying that if they stayed longer then they may make claims over her children's land. So Samuel and sisters went back to live with their mother at the small plot that the father had left them. By the time the aunt chased them away, Samuel was in primary three and his education and that of his sisters ended then because they found that their mother was already suffering from AIDS. The mother died when Samuel was about 8 years. Life became very difficult. The children were on their own, finding it difficult to get food, depending on begging and no health care when one got sick because the nearest government health facility was about six miles away. One of Samuel's sisters left them and got "married" (started cohabiting with a man). Through small casual jobs the remaining two children tried to survive. Because the conditions were so poor, Samuel became very sick up to the point of death. As Sister Ursula the founder of MAHCOP was on one of her visitation rounds to clients in the area, community members asked her to take Samuel to hospital. The community workers say that the boy was so malnourished that no one thought he could survive.

He was taken to Kitovu Hospital where he was treated for over a year before he could be on his feet again. After the long stay in hospital, when health personnel took Samuel back home, his second sister had left to get married and no one knew her whereabouts. MAHCOP enrolled Samuel in the food aid programme and placed him with one of the female community workers where he lived for about two years. After two years he no longer wanted to live with the community worker because he says he was being overworked, not given enough food and sometimes the portion of his food aid was taken away from him. Samuel was moved and taken to live with another community worker, but this time a male one. The same year he was enrolled into the MAHCOP farm school programme where he attended training for one year between 2002/2003. Samuel stayed at the new home for only three months complaining that he was over worked, and the community worker stopped him doing casual jobs because he wanted Samuel to work only in his crop fields.

In 2006 MAHCOP bought for Samuel one acre of land on which they have built him a semi-permanent house with an iron roof so that he can live independently. He uses the skills acquired from the farm school to grow a variety of food crops for home consumption and sale. His main source of livelihood though is agricultural laboring. MAHCOP has identified him as one of the orphans that needs intensive socio-psychological support but Samuel refuses to attend counseling sessions. The programme had also suggested that he joins a farming group through which he can access improved seeds and other planting materials in addition to extension information. While he has accessed seeds once, he does not want to participate in the group meetings. His biggest problem is living alone, not having family, feeling so lonely, and having lost the opportunity for education because of his circumstances.

Case 5.13. Fostered orphan girl

Agnes is a 16 year orphaned girl born in Nyabukara village, Kabarole district. This is her experience after her father's death:

> *When my father died of HIV/AIDS in 2003, I was in senior one and my grandmother took me in and she started paying for my education. She was so good and kind to me and always told me that despite my parents' deaths, if I behaved well and concentrated on my studies I would make it in life. Unfortunately, she also died in 2005 and that was the end of my education. I now live with another "grandmother" a co-wife of my late grandmother. The conditions are not good. Am made to do lot of farm work and though there are other girls (my grandmother's other grandchildren from her son) most of the cooking is left to me. Yet they always tell me that am lazy and just came to eat their food. Sometimes they threaten to send me back to my fathers home (where there is no one) so that I will live there alone. What is so hurting is that several times they have indicated that they will get me a man to marry me. Something that I hate at such a young age. However, my younger sister decided to get married when our father died because she so no other hope to life. It also pains me when I see all the other children going to school and for me am just at home cooking. Sometimes the way am treated also makes me feel like killing myself. I wouldn't have minded even if I were made to work very hard or be mistreated, so long as am given an opportunity to study. However, I do not think I will ever realize that in my life.*

Case 5.14. Affected single-female-headed household

Anazia is a resident of Nyabukara village outside Fort Portal town. She is a single mother, aged 65, who ran away (25 years ago) from an abusive polygamous relationship with her five children.

Anazia became pregnant at the age of 17 when she was in primary four and had to immediately get married to Charles, the man who had made her pregnant. Charles was also young (aged 22) and had acquired two acres of family land from his mother on which he settled with his wife. Initially the couple worked together very well, established a banana plantation in addition to growing other crops. After the birth of their third child, Charles' mother told them to sell the land they were using and go and live with her in Toro where she had a bigger piece of land. The land was sold and the family moved to Toro although Anazia was against the whole idea, especially after all the effort she had put in establishing a good banana plantation. Anazia's mother-in-law had inherited a five-acre piece of land from her father but because she was getting old she wanted her son to start using it.

When they moved to Toro, Anazia worked hard and established many gardens so that she would take opportunity of the available land and also please her mother-in-law. Soon Anazia was to realize that her mother-in-law would be in charge of all crop sales, not even her husband. However, after the sale of produce Anazia's mother-in-law would give most of the money to Charles while she kept some to "cover basic household needs". Anazia had no business with money yet she was the main source of labour for almost everything produced given that in many cases Charles was never at home. Previously, on their former piece of land, even if the husband controlled income from produce sales, it was ok for Anazia to sell, for example, one bunch of banana and use the money to buy any household needs or something personal that she needed. In this new setting she had to completely depend on her husband for money. In addition, the mother-in-law determined what she would grow and where. If Anazia was to sell something, then this would be done secretly without the old woman knowing.

For one whole year, Anazia saved money from stealing and selling the produce she had produced but which she was being denied access to. Meanwhile Charles had married two other women. When she thought she had saved enough money, through friends, she bought an acre of land outside Fort Portal Town. After buying the land, she abandoned the marriage and took all her five children with her. It was difficult looking after all these children and she initially started by selling alcohol. While she said that the business was good and it helped her sustain the family, she has stopped it because she thinks it contributed to her children getting AIDS. She has lost four children to AIDS. Charles died of AIDS but Anazia was lucky to leave him before she could get infected. She now lives with five orphaned grandchildren. The youngest grandson, Simon is HIV positive. Prior to the interview Simon had been sick for one year with a very strange skin disease affecting his scalp. Anazia described that year as the most stressful period that she had ever experienced in her life:

> *The child was sick all the time. I spent most of the time running around from clinic to hospital to traditional healer, wherever they told me that I could get help for my child. Nights were difficult because the boy would get high fevers, and sometimes start convulsing in the middle of the night. Then I would get one of grandsons – the one who is 11 years – to go with me at night to take his brother to the clinic. I would leave my grand daughter to take care of the younger boys. He almost died until some neighbours advised me to take him for HIV testing. He tested HIV-positive and he has*

been on anti-retroviral drugs since October 2004. Simon is coping well and rarely falls sick. During this period I depended on members of our group: The Disables people's group. They would bring me food and I was also able to borrow money from our savings association without interest. I have a woman friend who would come and stay with the children when Simon would be hospitalized and sometimes help with the weeding. All this time I was unable to engage in any serious farming. I don't know what I could have done without their support.

Case 5.15. AIDS in a polygamous household

Mathew is a young man of 30 years, born in a polygamous family of four wives and 13 siblings. He is one of the sons of the late Joseph K. a rich farmer in Kabarole district. The family has a total of 75 acres of land in Kyenjojo district and another 15 acres in Kabarole where most of the family resides. Of the 15 acres in Kabarole, three acres are under eucalyptus forest, four under banana intercropped with avocado, two under annual food crops and a dairy farm on three acres. Joseph died of HIV/AIDS in 1997 followed by Matthew's mother in 2001. In 2002 and 2003, Mathew lost two other stepmothers. For two years, he has been nursing his youngest step mother, bedridden from AIDS. Following the death of Joseph, most of the agricultural enterprises declined due to neglect, poor management and sickness among the wives. There were also a lot of family wrangles as who should be heir, so it was difficult to work on any land because one would be misinterpreted as intending to grab that piece of land. While Joseph had left a will that Matthew should be heir, the stepmothers first refused because he was not the eldest son nor from the first wife. However, through intervention of local leaders and clan members, Mathew was accepted as the rightful heir and given mandate to take charge of his father's estate.

But by this time the family had lost all 10 Friesian dairy animals due to neglect, and the banana plantation had equally suffered mismanagement and was in a poor state. School fees for those in secondary school were becoming a problem and at one point all children never attended school for one term. However, with guidance from one of Mathew's paternal uncles and reduced intrigue and influence among the children, Mathew is slowly taking charge and he is seeing a turn around in production. He is using money from the eucalyptus forest to rehabilitate the farm and banana plantation as well as hire agricultural labour. Currently Mathew has only one animal in the farm but he has taken on five others in a shared rearing arrangements. The milk from all the animals, helps to maintain the farm and pay the workers. The farm is producing about 40 liters of milk per day. Mathew hopes to start restocking the farm with money from the banana plantation when production returns to profitable levels.

Apart from putting the farming in order, Mathew had to ensure that his siblings get education. Through connections with his father's friends he has been able to secure commitment for school fees for two of his brothers. Then through connections to his stepmother's boss, the District Medical Officer, he has secured funding to support his sister's training in nursing. He says that the money from the banana plantation will be able to support the education of the remaining four siblings.

Case 5.16. Affected orphan household

Nathan a resident of Nyamiseke village (Kabarole district), is 22 years old and has been a double orphan since 2003. His father died of AIDS in 2001 and the mother two years later. He has one brother aged 20 and a sister aged 15. After the death of his father, Nathan says he hoped that his mother had not contracted the disease. But when she started showing the typical signs, he became devastated. He narrates part of his experience as follows:

> *A few months after my father's death, my mother's health started to deteriorate. She started developing skin rashes and other signs that my father had. Besides the rumors going around in the village, it became clear to us that she had AIDS. I became frustrated, scared, and desperate because the only parent we had was also going to die. I feared what would happen to us, my education, my life, and many other things, if my mother died. Life was already difficult with my father dead. Since my father's death, for example, my mother had sold his bicycle, radio and other small household items to raise our school fees and get money for her treatment. But money was scarce and sometimes she could not afford public transport to go and seek medical help. It was difficult to see her in severe pain without treatment. There was no happiness at home, only fear and worry when she would die. She eventually passed away in the last week of March, 2003. After her burial, our grandparents and uncles said that I had to look after my sister and brother since I was old enough. Then my grandfather said that the land my father was using belonged to him so we were chased from part of the land that had our permanent house and given a smaller area of about an acre on which we now live. We could no longer live in our fathers house and had to build a temporary house for ourselves. Before my mother died she took me to Hima in Kasese district and showed me a house and a two-and-a-half acre piece of land that my father had left us.*
>
> *My brother and I had to stop school because of lack of school fees. Dropping out of school was the most painful thing in my life. If given opportunity, I can go back to study. Our main source of livelihood is farming. We established a small banana plantation and in addition grow maize and beans. Its mainly my brother and I who do the farming. Our sister mainly does the other*

work of cooking and cleaning the home when she comes back from school. The plot of land in Hima is rented out every season because we cannot use it by ourselves. This is supplemented with money from the house in Hima. The house in Hima needs some repairs but which I have not been able to do. So we are getting about three quarters of what would have been its true rental value. Though the money is not much it helps us to meet the basic household needs. However, we experience problems when one of us falls sick. The nearest government dispensary is about seven miles from where we live. Apart from one maternal uncle who is friendly to us, we are alone in the world. My paternal relatives do not want to have anything to do with us. Our maternal uncle usually visits us and gives us advice on farming and how to avoid being infected with AIDS.

Nathan's greatest desire is to get money to support him and his brother start school again and to ensure that when their sister completes her primary seven, she is able to go to secondary school. He is also interested in starting up poultry farming while his brother wants to do apiary but start up capital is a problem.

Case 5.17. Affected grandfather-headed household

Irari John says he was born on the 27th of February 1923, in a family of ten children (two brothers, one sister and six maternal step brothers). All his siblings are dead. John has been a widower for twenty years after his first wife died of peptic ulcers in 1985. He produced seven children with his first wife, four died of AIDS, one is in Kenya and he does not know where the other two live. The four children he produced with the second wife live with their mother in Kabale but he has spent more than 5 years without seeing them. He now lives with his grandson Paulo who is HIV positive. John says AIDS has brought poverty to his household. He started experiencing AIDS impacts 15 years ago. After the death of his wife, one of his eldest daughters Sanyu who had separated from her husband came to live with him. She came with two girls. In 1990, Sanyu's health started deteriorating. But since she was one of the first cases to contract AIDS in the village it took time before the family knew that she was infected with HIV. In 1993 she was diagnosed HIV positive. John single handedly nursed his daughter because his granddaughters were too young to help. Sanyu's medical expenses were high and in the process John sold the three cows, four goats, one sow and even their three acre piece of land to raise money to take care of her and also "cover other household needs. The two acres of land that John now lives on belong to the parish church. In 1994, Sanyu's health seemed to improve a bit. But when Sanyu became pregnant, her health deteriorated again and she died in 1995 leaving a six month baby-Paulo. Apart from being physically draining, Sanyu's sickness took a great toll on agricultural production too. John says he had no time to look after his banana plantation, part of which is now bush. He also used to earn income through repair of bicycles and stoves but he lost most of his clients because his daughters sickness could not allow him to do the repairs on time. However, because of poor eyesight, John could not continue with the bicycle repair trade after Sanyu's death.

John has also looked after Paulo since he was six months more or less single handed. He says that the two granddaughters were also very supportive during Nathan's first four years of life. However, in 1999 one of the granddaughters died of malaria while the following year the other one run away from home to get married to a trader in Masaka. John says that Paulo has been sickly since he was a toddler. In 2001 he was diagnosed HIV positive and started on prophylactic treatment. In 2004, Paulo was among the first children to be put on anti retro viral treatment (ART). But because of poor nutrition, John says that the drugs made Nathan very weak so he stopped using them. The two mainly depend on matoke and beans, but in most cases they have no sauce. One of the neighbours usually gives them half a liter of milk when Paulo is very sick. The signs of malnourishment are eminent when one looks at Paulo. Paulo now mainly receives treatment for opportunistic infections. He says that the two of them have to walk to Muhanga hospital in Fort Portal town which is about six kilometers away to access health care. When Paulo is too weak to walk they have to miss medical appointments because John has no money to hire a motorcycle. To summarize the impact of the epidemic on his life, John says that "AIDS has killed my children and made me poor and dirty!" John has not received any support from any organizations.

Case 5.18. AIDS widower

Leo is 50 years and lives in Rwangoma villave with four sons, a daughter-in-law and two grandsons. He said that his first wife Adyeri and eldest son Akiiki died of AIDS at the beginning of 2000. He relates his experience as follows:

> *In 1995, my wife suddenly became mentally deranged and run away from our home for a month before we could find her. This was about a year after I had married a second wife so all relatives believed that the second wife had bewitched Adyeri. Her relatives told me to give them money so that they could take her to "well-known" medicine men in the country. For the whole of 1996 and 1997 Adyeri was moved from Masaka, Mukono and Kisoro but her health just deteriorated. During this period I had to sell my mortocycle and a herd of 30 cross-bred goats to meet the witch doctor's costs, maintenance costs of Adyeri and her two sisters while they were away from home as well as those for transport.*
>
> *In 1998 my second wife Amooti died after a short illness. During the burial, my brother was told that rumour had it that Amooti had lost her first husband due to AIDS. He advised that I go to hospital to check my HIV*

status and that of Adyeri. This news was a very big shock to me because I had never suspected that Amooti had AIDS. The fear of knowing that I have AIDS stopped from even taking Adyeri for the check up. But in 1999 when I started falling sick, my brother took Adyeri and me to hospital and both of us were found to have AIDS. Adyeri was also found to have TB. We were started on treatment in August of the same year but Adyeri died a few months later.

Since Adyeri's death I have been haunted by the fact that I infected her with AIDS and refused to take her to hospital early enough. This also made it very difficult to tell the children. In 2003 when I became very sick and had to be hospitalized, I told my sons about my HIV status. Contrary to what I thought, the boys have been very supportive. Since then they do not want to see me overwork, they ensure that I take my medication on time and also feed well. My brother has also been very supportive. He takes care of the banana plantation in next village which Amooti was looking after. With money from that plantation and his own, he pays school fees for the two youngest boys in secondary grades two and four. The two eldest boys couldn't go for tertiary education after their senior six because of lack of school fees. They now take care of the plantation here and grow the food we eat. However, the variety of food crops grown have reduced. The boys mainly grow maize, beans and Irish potato. In addition, my wife used to grow sweet potato, cassava, millet, and a variety of local vegetables. She also used to sell second hand clothes, the money from which contributed significantly to school fees.

While we eat together, my daughter-in-law lives in her own house with four children. Since my son died she has had two other children each with a different father, yet she has AIDS. In fact, her youngest child is sickly and we suspect that it has AIDS. While I find this unacceptable, I have nothing to do. Besides she helps with most of the domestic chores and am not in position to help her take care of my two grandsons.

What key things have helped you to cope? In 2003 I was lucky to be started on ARVs and the improvement in my health has given me hope again. Having a supportive family that accepted my status has been a source of strength and it has encouraged me to live on. The investments I had made also enabled me to meet the increased health-related costs, including those of my wife albeit for wrong remedies. However, apart from the four acres of land most of my other assets have gone to AIDS. Because of improved health, I have started rearing pigs, they have a good local market. If God continues to give me good health, I know the money from the pigs and banana plantation can maintain us.

Case 5.19. Esther Kagoro

Esther, born in November of 1939, has been a widow since 1979 when her husband died of pneumonia. Esther was born in a family of five, three of her siblings died and her only living relative, a sister lives in Kisoro. They have not seen each other since Esther's husband died.

Esther is a Grade two teacher by profession but retired in 1994. She produced two daughters but lost the eldest one Sanyu due to AIDS in 2000, leaving her with six orphans. Sanyu's husband had died earlier in 1998 of the same cause. One year after Sanyu's death, Esther lost her youngest grandson also from AIDS.

Grace is Esther's second daughter. Since 2002, Grace has been living with her mother. Prior to 2002 she had been away from home for about 20 years. She abandoned school when she was in senior two because of lack of interest. When Esther had tried to force her to go back to school, she ran away and went to live with a relative in Kampala. Towards the end of 2002, some friends brought her home when she was very sick almost at the point of death. Esther took her daughter to Virika hospital where she was diagnosed to be HIV positive and started on treatment. Since August 2004 Grace has been on antiretroviral treatment which is said to have improved her health tremendously. In addition Grace also gets local herbal preparations that are said to "treat" AIDS from the traditional medicine man in their village. Besides the medication, Esther believes that good feeding and a supportive home environment has been crucial in the turn around observed in her daughter's health. Grace's diet includes fish, eggs, beef, milk and chicken, Irish potato, rice and fruits. This is in addition to an assortment of local vegetables and other plants that, according to Esther are known to reduce anaemia and boost immunity. Grace also said that her grandchildren have been very supportive in caring for their ailing aunt otherwise, she could not have managed alone. Wondering how she has been managing to maintain Grace's special diet, Esther indicated that apart from the beef and fish, almost all other foods are home produced.

> *All the food we eat at home is produced by my grand children. They grow maize, beans sweet potatoes and vegetables. I have a man who helps me manage the banana plantation. I pay him 20.000 Uganda Shillings a month. He also helps me cut grass for the cows. In 1998 I received an in-calf heifer from the Christian Women Association (CWA), a project started by the Catholic church to support widows. To-date my cow has produced three calves; one was a bull and I sold it. In addition to my pension money, the money from the bull calf was used to start up a poultry unit of one hundred layers. This has helped me to make sure that Grace has eggs all the time. The cow also gives me an average of twelve liters of milk per day.*

Apart from income from the milk and egg sales, Esther owns a private nursery school, she receives a pension of 90,000 UGX per month (this was increased from 70,000 UGX in July 2005) and she receives 10,000 per month for her work as a volunteer in a children's local NGO. Esther's major expenditures include school fees (four of the orphans are in secondary schools) and Grace's health-related costs. With the latter, besides food and medicines, Esther has to spend 6,000 UGX (1000 for hospital registration, and 5,000 for transport) for Grace's monthly visit to the hospital. Grace's improved health has helped reduce the transport costs because she now takes herself to hospital unlike in the past when her mother had to go with her. When asked about the impact of HIV/AIDS, Grace had this to say:

> *AIDS has killed my people. Taking care of orphans has meant that I have to work hard at an old age and single handed. I have lost my people through AIDS. Taking care of an AIDS patient is physically and emotionally very demanding. When I started nursing Grace, I stopped working at the CWA bakery. While I can say that am somehow managing, expenditure on Grace's care and school fees do not allow me to save money. For example I have failed to construct another classroom for my nursery school. I have also failed to pay for my grandson to go to a technical Institute after he completed senior six, all because of AIDS-related sickness, death and orphans. Nonetheless, hard work, participation in women's groups and church activities and having well-behaved grandchildren has kept me going.*

Case 5.20. A divorced AIDS-affected woman

Nakalembe aged 24 is a terminally ill AIDS woman. She lives with her grandmother Jane of 80 years. At the time of the interview, Nakalembe was too sick and I talked to Jane. Grandmother Jane relates the following story.

> *Nakalembe has been living with me for two years. She got herself a man at 19 years when her father could no longer pay for her school fees. Nakalembe's first child died when it was six months. Then she lost the next three subsequent pregnancies. After her third miscarriage, Nakalembe became very sick and her younger sister moved in to take care of her. The whole of 2003, Nakalembe was sickly and towards the end of the year, her husband married another woman and told her to return to her father's place. But Nakalembe's father could not accept her back because he said that she never got married in the right way and was just a prostitute. That's how Nakalembe ended up here. Am poor and I can only offer her a place to sleep. I have no money to buy her medicines at the local drug shop. Twice, Nakalembe's husband has sent her a little money that we have used to buy for her some fish. Her friends would also take her to church and pray for her. They have been very supportive. For the last four months she has not*

> *got out of her bed and since 10 days ago she has refused to eat anything. Anytime she will die.*

The family lives in a remote village Kappoochi in Masaka which has no access to health services or NGOs providing HIV/AIDS-support. The nearest health facility was about five kilometers away and reportedly with no medication. For all the time Nakalembe has been with her grandmother, she has depended on local herbs and prayers to relieve her physical and psychological pain. Although Nakalembe was never medically diagnosed as having AIDS, Jane said that all signs that people who have died of AIDS in the community present, Nakalembe has had them. It is difficult to imagine that some people have to experience a disease like AIDS without any form of palliative treatment. Jane also lost her two daughters due to AIDS and one of them left her a grandchild Sanyu of six years. Simeon, the other member of the household is mentally retarded. He is 44 and Jane's only living child. Despite her old age, the household depends on what Jane grows, local vegetables and beans intercropped in banana. Jane had two local hens. The eggs from the chicken help in buying salt and paraffin oil for lighting. When asked her biggest constraint, Jane simply said "Poverty! Its poverty that is going to kill Nakalembe because I cannot take her to hospital. She would have lived longer and had a more decent death if we had money. Yes, poverty will finish us."

5.3 Conclusion

The cases discussed in this chapter show similarities and differences between different households with regard to processes of livelihood generation and the dynamics of HIV/AIDS effects. The differential access to and control over resources as well as differences in human capabilities to make use of available opportunities results in the pursuit of different livelihoods with different outcomes. It is also shown that the pursuit of different livelihood strategies does not necessarily translate into secure livelihoods. Farming is the main source of livelihood, after which individuals engage in other activities to supplement incomes and food from agriculture.

AIDS effects cut across individuals of different ages and wealth status. All cases in section two show that HIV/AIDS affects households and individuals through its erosive effects on household resources. AIDS depletes household resources and diverts them from production activities to AIDS related treatment and care. It is shown that the labour of those affected declines as the disease progresses and is lost completely when an individual dies. The reduced household labour is associated with reallocation of labour of other household members and an increase in HIV/AIDS-related care. Furthermore, there is inefficient and unsustainable use of resources among affected households (less land being cultivated or land completely abandoned). Taking into consideration overall food and livelihood security of affected households, similar trends are observed. While it is undeniable that the individuals presented in the case studies have different levels of food insecurity, it is clear that the affected households are food insecure and just surviving. Even where the market would have been an alternative source of food for these households, HIV/AIDS-related resource depletion reduces their purchasing power.

Differences in impacts were also observed. While in most cases, AIDS triggers a downward spiral, a few households, particularly those with a stronger resource base, show resilience to the effects of AIDS. The type of resources depleted and the extent to which they are depleted also differs by household. Some case studies also show that the epidemic produces mixed impacts in different households. For example, the gender and age of orphans and whether an orphan is HIV/AIDS affected or not influence the type and magnitude of the effects experienced by an orphan household. In addition, the chronic illness or death of an adult household member may result in a mixed set of effects depending on whether the lost adult was employed or productive and whether he or she was contributing to the household in the first place.

HIV/AIDS-related effects prove to vary according to, (i) the resources a household has, (ii) its size and composition, (iii) the person who gets affected, (iv) and whether the household is affected by the chronic illness of a member, a recent death of a member, or whether they are supporting orphans. Given that most households in the study areas depend on household labour for agriculture and other economic activities, and the fact that household labour has always been limited, the impacts of HIV/AIDS-related sickness and mortality (while variable) is likely to further constrain AIDS-affected households and individuals' capabilities to pursue meaningful livelihood strategies.

It is noteworthy that households experience other shocks (for example, crop pests and diseases, drought, death or sickness of relatives due to other causes) concurrently with AIDS. Hence, what is observed among affected households is not a direct effect of AIDS alone, but rather livelihood outcomes as a consequence of the interaction between different combinations of vulnerability factors (at different points in time) including AIDS. Nonetheless, a strong asset base, viable kinship networks, and opportunities to diversify activities are likely to assist in protecting a household against external shocks, such as HIV/AIDS.

Chapter 6

Livelihood activities and strategies

This chapter describes contemporary livelihoods in Masaka and Kabarole districts. Besides farming, other activities and resources that people use in the process of livelihood generation are considered. Furthermore, the chapter analyzes livelihoods at a higher level of aggregation than in Chapter 4 where much of the focus was on differences between male- and female-headed households in the two districts. As I also argued in Chapter 2, society is not homogeneous but differences between particular groups or categories of households and individuals exist. This social differentiation influences access to, as well as the allocation of, resources and use of opportunities and, consequently, life chances of individuals.

It can be argued that the approach of disaggregating households in different social categories will facilitate understanding of the different livelihood activities and strategies used, as well as constraints faced in the process of livelihood generation. In Chapter 7, this line of reasoning is also applied to identify livelihoods that are likely to be more vulnerable to HIV/AIDS than others.

Based on farmers' perceptions of well-being and social status, as well as analysis of survey data, sample households were clustered into relatively homogeneous groups. This is discussed in Section 6.1. Subsequently, a synopsis of the livelihood activities and strategies pursued in the study area is provided, summarizing the different ways in which households have diversified their activities and incomes, and analyzing the linkages between diversification and access to household resources. Section 6.3 describes determinants of livelihood strategies both at the micro (household) and macro level. The chapter concludes with remarks on livelihoods as experienced in the districts of Masaka and Kabarole.

6.1 Characterization of households

6.1.1 Farmers' categorization

Livelihoods can be thought of as the different ways and means through which people make a living or continue to exist over time. People's livelihoods are based on the resources and activities employed in more or less strategic ways to enhance the resource base or manage risk and vulnerability (cf. Chapter 2). In order to understand and gain insight into people's livelihoods, we must identify people's local definitions of livelihood, perceptions regarding wealth and social status and how differences in these influence the type of livelihood generated. Farmers' perceptions and interpretations of "livelihood" were therefore sought through focus group discussions conducted in the two districts

Based on this, the participants' livelihoods were ranked. The ranking criteria used were: the level of resource endowment and access, occupation of members, access to basic services and social support as well as decent clothing and shelter. A key feature for farmers is people's wealth status. Table 6.1 summarizes the main findings of exercises conducted with farmers on social status categorization in the study areas. Categorization was based on wealth status in terms of access and ownership of a variety of resources. There was considerable overlap between the social groups identified by farmers. This indicates farmers' varying perceptions of wealth as well as the actual difficulty of drawing demarcation lines between different social categories. It also shows that boundaries between social categories are not static and borderline households may fall in more than one category. The ranges attached to some resources are indicative of the variations encountered both within and between the districts as well as between households.

Summarizing farmers' perceptions

Due to the many similarities and overlaps, groups 1 and 2 were taken together in the category of "poor" households. In terms of definition, poor households tend to possess little or no land, no cattle but a few small stock, lack any means of transport, with agricultural production below or at subsistence level, have individuals relying on farm labouring or begging and are chronically food insecure. In addition, individuals in poor households are unable to pay school fees or are likely to experience problems with keeping children in school, have few non-farm self employment options, produce-vending and beer-brewing being the most commonly cited ones.

The middle wealth category (group 3) has a comparatively stronger asset base, uses external inputs and utilize extension service providers to improve production, own at least a bicycle and is likely to engage in micro and small scale enterprises. Those in the average wealth category were also identified as having access to credit facilities and sufficient financial resources to access basic services (health and education). They have resources to purchase non-food commodities such as clothes, and beddings, and for some, bicycles and radios, that are relatively inaccessible to those in the poorer category.

Households considered to have the best livelihoods are categorized under group 4 (well-off or rich). Generally notable for the rich category is ownership of land holdings above 10 acres, 10 or more heads of cattle, two or more acres of banana and an acre of coffee plantations, at least an acre of commercial woodlot, and a *boda boda* or even a car as a means of transport. Additionally, the rich category was distinguished by ability to: employ non-family labour seasonally, offer their children good primary and secondary education, have a daily income from milk or beer and regular incomes from coffee and banana, and own multiple sources of non-farm income generating activities (shops, rent from buildings). Some of

Table 6.1. Characteristics of wealth groups: farmer's categorization.

	Group 1 (very poor)	Group 2 (poor)	Group 3 (average)	Group 4 (well-off/rich)
Land ownership	Less than 1 acre of land or landless.	1-3 acres.	At least 5 acres (3-5).	15 acres or more (10-30).
Land rent	May borrow land to grow more food.	Borrow or hire land to increase production	Rent out land not used	Rent out land not used.
Livestock ownership	May own 2-3 local chicken. Don't own livestock.	Goats: 3; Pigs: 2-3 pigs, 3-4 chicken. Majority do not own cattle.	Cattle: 2-3; Goats: 5; Pigs: 2-5; Local chicken: up to 5 local birds.	10 cattle (10-40); none or few for home consumption-3 goats, 7 chickens.
Banana plantation	Grow a few banana plants intercropped with beans, maize, sweet potato & yams.	0.5 acres or less.	Average 1 acre; But grow a variety of other crops.	At least 2 acres (2-5).
Coffee plantation	Do not grow coffee.	None or grow a few coffee trees in banana plantation.	0.5 acre.	At least 1 acre; But grow annuals
Average production levels	Extremely little	Little: 200-300kg maize; 60-100kg beans.	At least 500kg of maize, 200kg of beans per season.	1,000Kg of maize, 400kg of beans per season.
Input use	None	Do not use improved seed or fertilizers.	Use improved seed but fertilizers use very limited.	Use recommended farming methods, improved seed & fertilizers for maize production.
Use of extension services	None	Generally do not seek extension advice.	Seek advice from extension advisors.	Seek advice from extension advisors.
Labour market	Sell their labour.	Only use family labour.	Uses both family & limited hired labour.	Use both family & hired labour.

Table 6.1. Continued.

	Group 1 (very poor)	Group 2 (poor)	Group 3 (average)	Group 4 (well-off/rich)
Income	Selling casual agricultural labour; begging.	Earn income as agricultural labourers; sometimes begging.	Income from seasonal crops, coffee & animals	Daily income from milk or beer; Regular incomes from coffee and banana.
Other sources of income from farming	For men: other casual work such as split fire wood, fetch water, carry goods to markets, make bricks or charcoal, construct shades at weddings or funerals.	Petty trade; brewing; other casual labour.	Trading in produce; shops. Can access credit from saving and credit schemes.	Commercial woodlots (1 acre). Rent from buildings.
Food security	Chronically food insecure. Do not feed well. Typically take two meals a day but sometimes with no sauce. Main sauce beans and green vegetables. (Children stunted – researcher's own observation).	Production very low cannot sustain household food requirements. Food insecure households. Do not feed well – sometimes food with no sauce. (Children stunted – researcher's own observation).	Food secure – usually just have enough. Sometimes supplements through market purchases with income from other sources; three "balanced" meals a day; children healthy.	Food secure (Normally produces enough food for HH but also has capacity to purchase from market; Feed well -eat fish or meat or both at least every weekend. Have three "balanced" meals a day; children healthy
Education costs	Normally children drop out of school in lower primary to look for petty jobs and contribute to household food or income.	Normally have children in primary school – but children are ever sent away from school due to lack of school materials (books, pencils, pens).	Have children in primary and low status government secondary schools; usually pay school fees on time.	Children in government aided schools of high standard or good private boarding schools (primary and secondary) within and outside the district.

Table 6.1. Continued.

	Group 1 (very poor)	Group 2 (poor)	Group 3 (average)	Group 4 (well-off/rich)
Other assets	No means of transport owned.	A few own bicycles otherwise majority do not own any.	Mainly Bicycle.	Own " motorcycle *boda boda*" or car.
House construction	Temporary housing- grass thatched; walls mud & wattle. Poor sanitation facilities. No kitchen. (House often in poor condition – researcher's observation).	House- grass thatched wall: brick or mud and wattle. Usually lack a kitchen or if available in poor condition. Poor sanitation facilities.	A semi-permanent house: brick or concrete walls, corrugated iron sheet (CIS) or grass thatched roof. Have a kitchen.	A permanent house: brick or concrete walls, permanent floor, with a CIS roof, may have more than one house. Well-built kitchen.
Social characteristics of category	Single, divorced or widowed women with children; unmarried, very old, weak and sick men and men depending on women. Children poorly dressed, don't sleep well. Cannot afford treatment when sick. Lack relatives who can provide social support.	Single or divorced or widowed women with children; unmarried men. Children dress poorly. Have few or no relatives from whom to seek support. Cannot afford treatment when sick.	Some are old men who have accumulated assets others are hard working youth, also usually married with children or salaried employment. Pay for medical services.	Old men who have accumulated assets; others women or youth who have inherited wealth from spouse's or parents; or young men in skilled salaried employment. Wives and children dress well. Can afford treatment in good private clinics or health centres. Help the poor.

Source: Mixed FGDs (Phase 4).

the people in this category were in salaried employment (teachers, policeman). Another category (not indicated in Table 5.1) of the very rich was also mentioned in some focus group discussions but only differed from category 4 with regard to the number of cattle owned which ranged between 40-90, the ownership of several large buildings and whole sale shops in urban centres and tea estates (for the case of Kabarole).

According to farmers' perceptions, the wealth ranking results show that improved livelihood (from "poor" through "average" to "rich") is paralleled with increased access to resources and services (i.e. land, information for agriculture, credit, and additional labour). Additionally, they think that better health status and higher education are indicative of better livelihood.

6.1.2 Characterization of households using survey data

Methods of characterizing household strategies

The literature presents several methods to characterize household livelihood strategies, with data on realized incomes underlying most classifications. For example, Reardon *et al.* (1992) examined the potential determinants of diversified income portfolios amongst smallholder farmers in rural Burkina Faso. Barrett *et al.* (2005) used data from several African countries analyze the relationship between overall household income and the proportion of income earned in on-farm and off-farm activities, noting differences in these proportions across different income quartiles. In the two South African villages of Guquka and Koloni, livelihoods of members of homesteads are categorized according to the main source of income, i.e.: remittances, wages and salaries, social grants, petty trade, agriculture and self employment (Averbeke & Hebinck, 2007).

The limitation associated with classifications based on realized incomes is that they do not capture people's decisions or choices that are crucial for understanding livelihood strategies. Other authors have argued that sustainable livelihood approaches usually focus on asset allocations across distinct activities rather than on income outcomes, because these are heavily impacted by exogenous factors (Bebbington, 1999; Ellis 1998). Carter and Barrett (2006) suggest the asset-based approach as an alternative method of analyzing livelihood strategies, arguing that by directly focusing on the examination of a given household's asset endowment, it is possible to map this into its livelihood strategies and subsequently into its stochastic income realization. Using cluster analysis, Brown *et al.* (2006) applied the asset-based approach to data collected from two villages in the Kenyan highland to identify distinct livelihood strategies. In this study, an approach similar to that of Brown *et al.* (2006) is used to classify farming households in the Masaka and Kabarole districts. Variables found to be important in the farmers' categorization were used in cluster analysis of survey data to characterize household livelihood strategies and attach livelihood labels.

Cluster analysis

Classification of farming households involved two steps: (i) factor analysis and (ii) cluster analysis. Factor analysis is a statistical technique for identifying groups or clusters of variables with the objective of, among other things, reducing a data set to a more manageable size while retaining as much of the original information as possible. Original information is summarized into a smaller set of composite dimensions or factors. Cluster analysis is also a statistical data reduction method. It partitions data into a predetermined number of groups or clusters, thereby minimizing within-cluster variance and maximizing between-cluster variance. The idea is that there will be latent similarities between the variables that allow one to group them together with respect to predetermined criteria (Jansen *et al.*, 2003). Non-hierarchical cluster analysis was used.

For this study, a factor analysis was done on variables such as household demographic characteristics and asset status and farming activities. Three factors that had Eigen values greater than one were then selected and labelled (i) farming activities and assets (ii) indicators for household income status and (iii) household demographics. For each factor, variables that had a high factor loading of over 0.50 were selected and are presented in Table 6.2. The variables identified, compared well with some of the factors that farmers had used in their categorization. In the subsequent step, a K-median cluster analysis (Jansen *et al.*, 2003), was performed on these variables in order to come up with distinct groups to which each household could be assigned. Based on statistical results and checks of the resulting groupings the analysis of the survey data yielded three distinct livelihood strategy clusters in the survey data (i.e. $k=3$). Three clusters were considered appropriate instead of four because the fourth cluster was very small and would not yield any meaningful if used. The clusters were then tested for statistical differences. The number of adult equivalents (AE) in a household used as one of the clustering variables was calculated using Equation 6.1 (Carter & May, 1999).

$$\text{No. of AE} = (\text{no. of adults} + \tfrac{1}{2}\,\text{no. of children})^{0.9} \qquad \text{Equation 6.1}$$

Whereby;
no. of AE = total number of adult equivalents in a household
no. of adults = number of household members aged 15 years or older
no. of children = number of household members younger than 15 years

Table 6.2. Factors and variables that were used in cluster analysis.

Factor	Variable
Farming activities and assets	Acreage under banana Acreage under annual crops Total workers Land/labour ratio
Household income status (proxies)	Daily food expenditure per adult equivalent[1] Per capita household expenditure[2] Total workers (besides the household head, total number of other household members working) Number of other household members working on the farm
Household demographic characteristics	Labour Units[3] (number of economically active household members- standardized for age) Consumer units – CU[4] The number of adult equivalents (AE)

Source: Household survey.

[1] *Daily food expenditure* = $\dfrac{\textit{Annual household food expenditure}}{(\text{No. AE}) \times 365}$

[2] Per capita household expenditure = $\dfrac{\text{total annual household consumption expenditure}}{(\text{No. AE}) \times 365}$

[3] Labour Units: Active household members' labour contribution was calculated as follows: up to 14 years (x 0.6); 15 years (x 0.7);16 years (x 0.8);17 years & >65 years (x 0.9); 18-64 years (x 1).

[4] CU = Household size/ LU

Defining livelihood strategy labels

From the results of the cluster analysis (Table 6.3), it is clear that farming is the main livelihood strategy with farmers in all the three clusters growing the same types of crops and raring the same types of animals. The variations in livelihood strategy and differences in outputs from the activities pursued seem to arise from the scope of these activities as well as the productivity of farmers depending on their access to various resources for agricultural production. For example, the data shows no significant difference between the clusters with regard to household members' engagement in off-farm income generating activities, be it skilled or un-skilled (Table 6.3). One-way analysis of variance and the Chi Square test were used to determine

Table 6.3. Livelihood strategy categories estimated via K-median cluster analysis.

Clustering variables	Cluster 1 (N= 132) Mean (SD)	Cluster 2 (N=215) Mean (SD)	Cluster 3 (N= 194) Mean (SD)	Overall (N= 541) Mean (SD)	F-Statistic
HH size	5.46(2.28)^{a}	6.65(2.57)^{b}	6.43(2.87)^{b}	6.28(2.65)	8.96***
CU	0.65(0.10)^{ab}	0.64(0.09)^{b}	0.66(0.11)^{ac}	0.65(0.10)	2.84*
Land/labour ratio	1.79(2.56)^{ab}	1.87(2.09)^{b}	1.32(2.01)^{ac}	1.66(2.20)	3.56**
Total Workers	1.034(0.81)	1.38(1.02)	1.31(1.27)	1.27(1.08)	4.29**
No. Working on farm	0.86(0.74)^{a}	1.12(0.88)^{b}	1.11(1.18)^{b}	1.06(0.98)	3.42**
Annual crops area(^)	1.93 (1.71)^{a}	1.78(1.71)^{a}	1.34(1.17)^{b}	1.66(1.56)	6.98***
Ruminants	2.48(2.83)^{ac}	3.12(5.25)^{ab}	2.19(3.05)^{c}	2.63(4.05)	2.81*
Daily food expenditure	970.27(1228.89)^{a}	268.32(145.62)^{b}	133.35(133.35)^{b}	391.19(699.62)	79.69***
Per capita expenditure	1851.67(911.48)^{a}	724.02(155.05)^{b}	299.70(126.72)^{c}	847.00(827.98)	298.10***
Age HH head	36.64(11.44)^{a}	43.42(14.09)^{b}	47.61(13.62)^{c}	43.27(13.94)	26.67***
$^{(b)}$Banana (^ ^)	1.24(1.28)	1.19(1.01)	1.05(0.97)	1.15(1.07)	1.47^{NS}
Land owned (acres)	2.85(3.27)^{ab}	3.16(4.27)^{b}	2.27(5.80)^{ac}	3.00(4.71)	0.4 ^{NS}
$^{(c)}$Crop sales (^ ^ ^)	94,130(140,053)^{a}	73,093(153,290)^{b}	33,152(68,241)^{c}	63,903(127,795)	3.99**
Cattle number	0.83(2.77)	1.23(3.89)	0.76(2.33)	0.96(3.14)	1.30^{NS}
Off-farm – unskilled #)	0.08(0.35)	0.11(0.41)	0.11(0.40)	0.10(0.39)	0.19^{NS}
Off-farm – skilled (##)	0.09(0.36)	0.14(0.39)	0.09(0.37)	0.11(0.38)	1.25^{NS}
Livelihood strategy label	Perennial crop producer	Diversified small-holder farmer	Staples grower		

Source: Household survey.

*, **, *** implies significantly different at 10%, 5% and 1% level, respectively. Superscripts with the same letter across the row are not significantly different from each other.

(^) area planted with maize, beans, ground nuts and Irish potatoes.

(^ ^) area under banana.

(^^^) sales from maize and beans in UGX.

(#) number of household members in unskilled off-farm work (agricultural labour and porter work, brick maker).

(##) number of household members in skilled off-farm work (driver, mechanic, carpenter, builder, hair dresser, butcher, trader, teacher, accountant, policeman).

the statistical significance of different variables between the clusters. For purposes of brevity, only variables that were found to differ significantly between the clusters as well as a few that helped in defining the household livelihood strategy categories are presented. Tables 6.3 and 6.4 summarize the mean values of the variables in each livelihood strategy cluster.

A striking result from the cluster analysis is the mean expenditure differences between the three livelihood strategy clusters, ranging from UGX 299 in Cluster 3 to UGX 1,851 in Cluster 1, showing that the three clusters present some kind of wealth

Table 6.4. Other household characteristics by livelihood strategy type.

Clustering variables	Cluster 1 (N= 132)		Cluster 2 (N=215)		Cluster 3 (N= 194)		Overall (N= 541)		X^2
	N	%	N	%	N	%	N	%	
Gender of household head									
Male	104	78.8	166	77.2	122	62.9	392	72.5	13.988***
Female	28	21.2	49	22.8	72	37.1	149	27.5	
HH head education (^)									
Educated	82	62.1	105	48.8	77	39.7	264	48.8	15.818***
Not educated	50	37.9	110	51.2	117	60.3	277	51.2	
Saves with ROSCA									
Yes	23	17.4	39	18.1	19	9.8	81	15.0	6.404**
No	109	82.6	176	81.9	175	90.2	460	85.0	
Used hired labour									
Yes	75	56.8	98	45.6	50	25.8	223	41.2	34.048***
No	57	43.2	117	54.4	144	74.2	318	58.8	
Access to formal credit									
Yes	11	8.3	26	12.1	16	8.3	53	9.8	2.130^{NS}
No	121	91.7	189	87.9	178	91.8	488	90.2	
Access to extension									
Yes	73	55.3	125	58.1	85	43.8	283	52.3	9.016**
No	59	44.7	90	41.9	109	56.2	258	47.7	
Affected									
HIV/AIDS-affected	18	14.4	37	17.2	60	30.9	116	21.4	16.543***
Non-affected	113	85.6	178	82.8	134	69.1	425	78.6	

Source: Household survey.
, * implies significantly different at 5% and 1% level, respectively.
(^) educated implies having at least 5 years of education.

categorization similar to the farmers' perceptions of the association of livelihood strategies and wealth status. The reason that three categories are obtained with the quantitative analysis and not four as the farmers indicated (Table 6.1) may be due to the small differences between the farmers' categories of very poor and poor.

From the cluster analysis, the livelihood strategies identified were labelled as follows:

- Cluster 1: Perennial crop producer (more perennial crops, less food crops, few animals)
- Cluster 2: Diversified small-holder farmer (less perennial crops, more food crops, more livestock production)
- Cluster 3: Staples grower (less food crops, few small livestock)

Livelihood strategy I: perennial crop producer

These farmers represent about one quarter of the sample. Their distinguishing feature is that they tend to specialize in production of perennial cash crops (banana and coffee) and a few annuals such as maize (information on coffee obtained from FGDs). They also keep a few livestock, dairy cattle. They undertake agriculture as a business. Farmers in this group have a relatively high propensity to seek extension advice, use recommended agricultural practices, use hired labour, have more access to credit facilities, and undertake agriculture as a business. They also have a higher expenditure potential compared to the other two clusters. For example, daily food expenditure per adult equivalent was about three-and-a-half times that for the second cluster and about seven times that for Cluster 3. Total per capita expenditure was two-and-a-half times that for Cluster 2 and about 6 times that for Cluster 3. Another distinguishing feature was that the heads of households are significantly younger, with the heads in this cluster on average being more than ten years younger than those in Cluster 3 and seven years younger than those in Cluster 2. Incomes realized from the sale of maize and beans were also significantly higher than for the other two clusters implying more area under annual crops. Apart from a larger acreage under perennial crops, these farmers are engaged in the production of similar food crops and raring of more or less the same types of livestock like farmers in the other two clusters. If per capita household expenditure is used as an indicator for household income, then the difference between Cluster 1 and 2 households is the higher capacity of households in Cluster 1 to access factors of production and hence increase their productivity compared to those in Cluster 2. In the sample, perennial crop producers are largely young and educated males, who are less likely to be HIV/AIDS-affected.

Livelihood strategy 2: diversified small-holder farmer

This is the biggest cluster, slightly larger than Cluster 3 and constituting 40 percent of the households in the sample. The most distinguishing factor of farmers in Cluster 2 is their higher involvement in animal production in addition to crops (multiple crops and livestock combinations) than farmers in the other two clusters. On average they keep three small pigs or goats or both. With about one third owning cattle, this cluster had the largest number of households owning cattle and the biggest cattle population (range = 32). The proportion of households rearing more than five heads of cattle is highest in Cluster 2, with the mean number of cattle kept being 4.5 for those owning cattle. For Cluster 2 this mean is 1.2). On average Cluster 2 households own about three acres of land which is not significantly different from that of households in Cluster 1. Notable for this cluster, as well as for Cluster 1, is the significantly higher ($p<0.05$) proportion of male-headed households with large acreages (i.e. five acres or more) than that for female-headed households in Cluster 3.

Daily food expenditure per adult equivalent and overall per capita household expenditure are significantly lower ($p<0.01$) than for households in Cluster 1, but there is no difference between daily food expenditures for Clusters 2 and 3. Furthermore, there is no difference observed in the area under banana or that planted with annual food crops as well as in per capita land, for Clusters 1 and 2. With regard to labour for agriculture, while the proportion of households in Cluster 2 using family labour is slightly different from that for Cluster 1 households ($p< 0.1$); for hired labour differences are very significant ($p< 0.01$), with Cluster 2 households less likely to afford hired labour than those in Cluster 1. Diversified small-holder farmers are largely middle-age males, with almost equal proportions of heads of households that are educated and non-educated and with a lower incidence of being HIV/AIDS-affected similar to that observed for heads of household in Cluster 1.

Livelihood strategy 3: staples growers

This cluster consisted of 36 percent of the households in the sample. Of the three clusters, these households have the lowest land/labour ratio (1.3) and, with average land holdings of about 2 acres, they also had the smallest area under annual food crops. Though the mean land acreage per cluster is not very different, household level analysis reveals that the proportion of female-headed households with 0.3 ha (0.75 acres) or less is significantly higher than that for male-headed households ($p< 0.05$). With regard to livestock, households in this cluster, have on average two small animals (goat or pig or both) and a cluster mean of 0.76 heads of cattle owned; the majority does not own any cattle. Households in this group are also significantly different ($p<0.01$) from the other two categories by their extremely low total per capita and daily food expenditures. Similarly, incomes from the commonest source of produce sales (maize and beans from the season prior to the survey) were also lowest in this cluster (Table 6.3). In the sample, Cluster 3 households were predominantly headed by elderly women. The majority of these women had no education (only 40 percent of the heads of households in Cluster 3 ever attended school) and had the highest incidence of HIV/AIDS. The limited access to productive resources (credit, information, labour), poor health and large household sizes (consumer units (CU) significantly higher than for Cluster 2, see Table 6.3) may partly explain the low production and productivity levels observed in this category.

6.2 Livelihood activities and income

6.2.1 Diversification of the portfolio

Livelihood strategies comprise the livelihood activities, decisions or choices people employ in pursuit of income, security, improved well-being and a strengthened resource base or for survival (cf. Chapter 2). The nature, scope and effectiveness of these activities depends on a variety of factors including availability of resources, the type and status of these resources, people's capability to create or access them and the contextual risks and uncertainties that they have to deal with. The importance of different resources to any given household varies between households, but also for any given household, the relevance and importance of a particular resource will vary with time, depending on other factors both internal and external to the household. Therefore, while sample households had access to various resources, emphasis will be on those that seemed most important according to the data obtained.

Smallholder farmers generally do not produce adequate amounts of food and generate sufficient income to sustain their household members from farming alone (Ellis, 1998; Reardon, 1997; also see Chapter 4). Indeed, literature on the rural non-farm economy and livelihood diversification in Uganda, illustrates the current reality that many rural households are engaged in a diverse set of livelihood activities (Bigstein & Kayizzi-Mugerwa, 1995; Deininger & Okidi, 2000; Dolan, 2002; Newman & Canagarajah, 1999; UPPAP, 1999). This is called diversification, and defined by Ellis (2000:15) as "The process by which rural households construct an increasingly diverse portfolio of activities and assets in order to survive and to improve their standard of living"). While to a large extent literature defines "diversification" in terms of productive activities or income, individuals also engage in activities that do not necessarily yield direct income but are important in the enhancement of other valued cultural and social aspects of life (Ellis, 1998; Niehof, 2004). Ellis' (1998:4) earlier definition gives a broader view of diversification (my italics) as "the process by which rural families construct a diverse portfolio of activities and *social support capabilities* in their struggle for survival and in order to improve their standard of living". The importance of some of these activities will be discussed later on in the chapter.

In the remaining part of this section, drawing on both qualitative and quantitative household level data, the three types of livelihood strategy categories identified in the previous section are analyzed with regard to the nature of activities undertaken, resources used as well as the decisions underlying these choices according to the farmers.

6.2.2 Main sources of household income

Farmers in Masaka and Kabarole undertake multiple activities to maintain their livelihood. While different household members engage in different activities, usually in accordance with socially defined gender roles, men and women's roles in a household tended to be complementary, sometimes overlapping or even interchanging, depending on a variety of factors. These factors include, but are not limited to, the stage in life cycle, gender of the household head, household composition, whether the household has experienced an adult death in the past, the nature of the activity, as well as the resources available to the household.

In the majority of cases, however, the survey data show that the income of the household head reflects the economic status of the household. This is seen in the number of other household members that were likely to be engaged in productive work, which on average was just one individual in addition to the household head (cf. Table 6.3). Female focus group participants overwhelmingly talked about their limited capacity to contribute income to the household and the dependence of married women on their spouses. This is partly due to the low levels of literacy

Table 6.5. Main source of income of household head.

Occupation	Frequency	Percent
Farming	510	94.3
Self-employed – skilled[1]	10	1.8
Small business[2]	9	1.7
Salaried employment[3]	6	1.1
Do not work	6	1.1
Total	541	100.0

Source: Household survey.

[1] Driver, mechanic, carpenter, builder; [2] Tailor, dry cleaner, hair dresser, butcher, and produce trader; [3] Teacher, accountant, policeman, and pastor.

among women that limit them to unskilled agricultural labour. In Table 6.5 the distribution of household heads across different occupations is presented.

The low involvement of heads of households in off-farm activities (5%) partly explains the lack of significant difference observed between the three household strategies with regard to the number of household members engaged in off-farm activities (Table 6.3).

Respondents were asked to mention the three most important sources of household incomes and rank them accordingly. The sources mentioned included: agriculture, livestock production, self-employed non-agriculture, agricultural casual labour, non-agricultural casual labour, salaried employment, remittances, donations and pensions. Each income source mentioned was ranked, with rank 1 standing for the most important income source and rank 3 the least important one. To calculate the overall rank for each income source, weights were assigned to each rank in declining order such that rank 1 had the greates weight and rank 3 the least. Then Equation 6.2 was used to calculate the overall score for any given income source.

Farming in crop production (59.6%) ranks number one as the most important source of household income, which is similar to the national picture. Results from the Uganda National Housing Survey (UNHS) for 2005/06 showed that about half of the households in Uganda depend on subsistence farming as their major source of earnings with the proportion in rural area being 58 percent (UBOS, 2006).[48]

$$IS_1 = \Sigma \text{ Freq. } (1_i) * (4\text{-}i) \qquad \text{Equation 6.2}$$

Whereby,
IS = overall score for Income Source 1
i = rank position (1, 2, 3)
Freq. (1_i) = number of times Income Source was mentioned in rank i

Overall, non-agricultural self-employment (11.4%) ranked second and farming in livestock (10.2%) third in importance household income. Income from non-agricultural casual labour, at about seven percent, was ranked in fourth position, ahead of income from agricultural labour (4.4%). To a lesser extent, remittances (2.2%), regular salaried employment (1.8%), property rents (1.5%), donations (0.9%), and pensions (0.7%) were considered to be among the three most important sources of household income by some households.

Figure 6.1 shows the distribution of household income sources per livelihood cluster. In addition to farming, perennial crop producers were more likely to be engaged in

[48] http://www.ubos.org/UNHSReport20052006.pdf

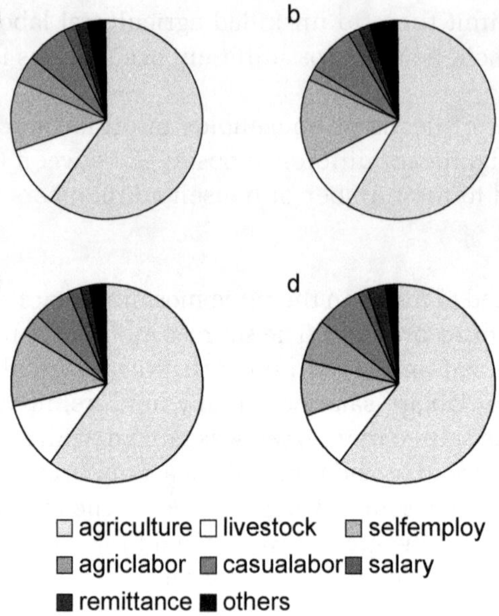

Figure 6.1. Distribution of household income sources: a. all clusters; b. cluster 1; c. cluster 2; d. cluster 3.

other off-farm income generating activities than farmers in the other two clusters ($p < 0.1$). The proportion of households that sell their labour for agricultural activities (7%) is highest in Cluster 3 of staples growers while that for Cluster 2 is about four percent and for Cluster 1 two percent. Another difference in income source, though minimal, is that a higher proportion of households in Cluster 2 (11%) reported livestock as an important income source.

From the ranking and high proportion of households that earned income from agriculture (Figure 6.2), the importance of farming as a key livelihood strategy cannot be overemphasized. Therefore, any stresses or shocks that impact on agricultural production or factors of production are likely to have significant consequences for people's livelihoods.

6.2.3 Income earned

Respondents were asked to give information on income in cash generated from the three most important sources in the three months prior to the survey. Table 6.6 and Figure 6.3 presents the mean income for three months earned from various sources. The data show the very low levels of household incomes in the study areas. Notable are the low mean values for all the income sources ranked one to four, identified as important by the majority of the respondents and which also comprise

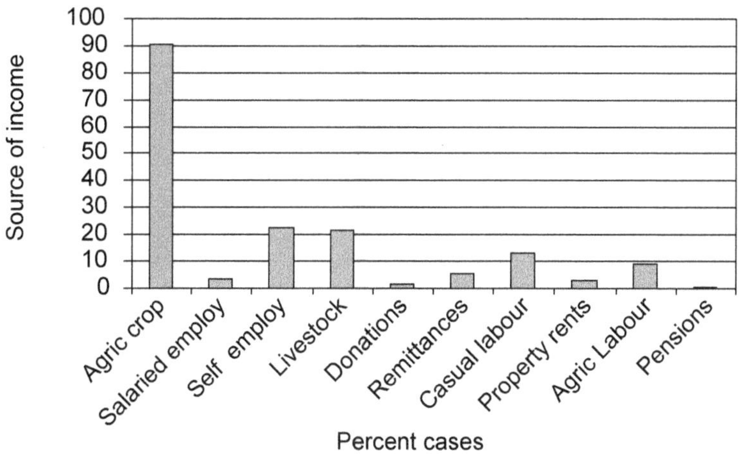

Figure 6.2. Proportion of households accessing different sources of income. Source: Household survey.

Table 6.6. Household income earned in the previous three months before the survey (X 1,000 UGX).

Source of income	Mean	Median	SD	Minimum	Maximum	N
Agriculture crop production	107	50	0	2520	490	107
Salaried employment	238	70	0	1800	20	238
Self employment	112	60	0	1500	121	112
Livestock production	536	16	0	800	118	536
Donations	138	20	0	700	9	138
Remittances	50	20	0	400	30	50
Other casual labour	64	40	0	310	71	64
Property rents	68	30	5	270	15	68
Agricultural Labour	28	10	0	160	49	28
Pensions	37	20	0	90	3	37

Source: Household survey.

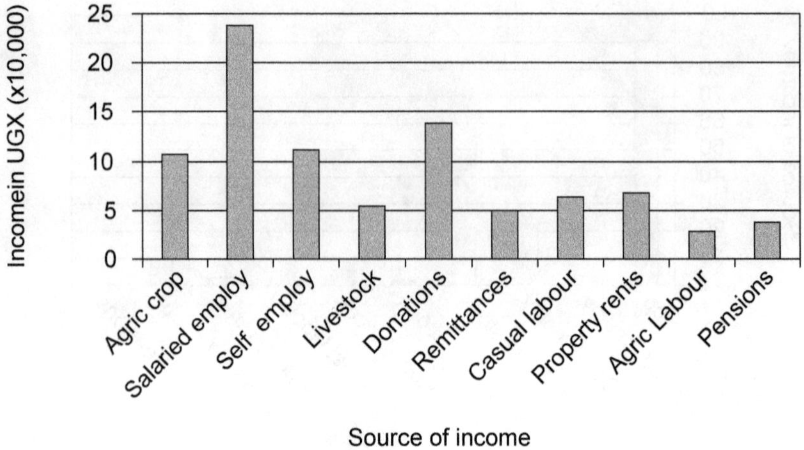

Figure 6.3. Mean income earned in three months. Source: Household survey.

income sources for the poor. Casual agricultural labour had the least mean incomes at Uganda Shillings 28,265 (US $ 15).

Additionally, for all income sources, 50 to 90 percent of the respondents reported receiving at most Uganda Shillings 50,000 (US $ 27) for the three months prior to the survey which is less than ten US dollars per month. This figure may be an underestimation because only the three most important income sources were considered. Furthermore, the fact that most households derive their income from agriculture and agriculture-related activities, and that the survey was conducted in the middle of the growing season, could also partly explain the low incomes reported. Nonetheless, the findings do not differ significantly from those obtained by the UNHS in 2005/06. In the latter survey, the percentage distribution of households by income class and residence indicate that in rural areas about 45 percent of households earn monthly incomes of between 0 and 50,000 Uganda Shillings and 22 percent between 50,000 and 100,000 Uganda Shillings (UBOS, 2006:74).

The findings also highlight the irregularity and seasonality of rural incomes and the low levels of remuneration from agricultural activities. Regular salaried employment (teachers, nurses, policemen) generated the highest mean income (Uganda Shillings 237,800 or US $ 129 for the three months or US$ 43 per month). This confirms the literature about the association of skilled employment with higher incomes (Schultz, 1975).

Despite the expected higher income from skilled employment, 13 out of the 20 salaried respondents reported income of below Uganda Shillings 100,000 (US $ 54) for the period and irregular payments due to government inefficiencies (in Table

6.6 the column for minimum indicates zero for salaried employment as well). Remittances appeared to be of little importance in the study area. Even those who received remittances said that they were irregular in frequency and amount. Only 30 respondents (6%) mentioned remittances as one of the three important sources of household income.

6.3 Income-raising livelihood strategies

6.3.1 On-farm diversification and expansion

Apart from a few landless households (less than 5%), all identified farming as a key livelihood activity, and, consequently, employ a number of strategies to improve their livelihood through farming. These strategies ranged from intensification and extensification (increased production and productivity) to on-farm diversification of farming activities (in terms of crops grown and farm enterprises undertaken).

Mixed cropping

All households, whatever livelihood strategy, engaged in farming and grew a variety of similar crops regardless of the size of land. Almost all households cultivated a combination of at least four crops out of banana, maize, beans, cassava, sweet potato, groundnuts, yams and Irish potato as intercrop due to limited land. (cf. Chapter 4). A limited degree of specialization was observed among the perennial crop growers who had a more business-like orientation to farming. These farmers, given their larger land acreages, were also more likely to have banana, maize and coffee plantations in pure stand than the staples growers. Focus group participants said that the diversification into different crops had the advantage of guarding against crop failure of any given crop. If one type of crop became attacked by pests or diseases, then the farmer would be assured of some food from the other crops. The other reason for growing a variety of crops was for food security. The differences in harvesting time (annual or perennial), the ability to be stored (the grains and root crops) and length of storage allow for consumption smoothing. For example, farmers said they liked banana because it could be harvested throughout the year. Cassava and yams were considered important food crops during periods of drought. Also when other food crops were abundant, some varieties of cassava and yams could stay in soil for up to two years without spoilage. For the country as a whole, Tenkir (2000) noted that the poor and non-poor alike engaged in the cultivation of the same types of food and cash crops.

Table 6.7 presents changes in land use by livelihood strategy type. It appears that the perennial crop producers and the diversified small-holder farmers significantly increased the number and types of crops grown compared to the staples growers ($p<0.05$). The 148 households that increased the type of crops grown gave the

Table 6.7. Change in land use by livelihood strategy type.

	Cluster 1 (N= 132)		Cluster 2 (N=215)		Cluster 3 (N= 194)		Overall (N= 541)		X^2
	N	%	N	%	N	%	N	%	
Change in crops grown									
Increased crops	42	31.8	66	30.7	40	20.6	146	27.4	6.962**
Reduced crops	90	68.2	149	69.3	154	79.4	393	72.6	
Control pests & disease									
Yes	87	65.9	167	77.7	145	74.7	399	73.7	6.001**
No	45	31.7	48	33.8	49	34.5	142	26.3	
Change in area for production									
Increased	49	60.5	67	63.8	39	39.8	155	54.6	13.391***
Other	32	39.5	38	36.2	59	60.2	129	45.4	
Change in crop yields									
Yields increased	56	42.4	79	36.7	57	29.4	192	35.5	
Other	76	57.6	136	63.3	137	70.6	349	64.5	6.082**
Sold maize & beans									
Sold	100	75.8	142	66.1	118	60.8	360	66.5	7.907**
Did not sale	32	24.2	73	34.0	76	39.2	181	33.5	
Change in agricultural incomes									
Increased	37	30.6	59	30.7	32	18.8	128	26.5	7.940**
Other	84	69.4	133	69.3	138	81.1	355	73.5	

Source: Household survey. [NS] implies not significant.
*, **, *** implies significantly different at 10%, 5% and 1% level, respectively.

following reasons: (i) 58 percent wanted to take advantage of the good market prices for maize, groundnuts, vanilla and beans at the time, (ii) 45 percent had the objective of being self-reliant in food by increasing food production and incomes from crop sales and (iii) 25 percent took on new crop varieties (maize, bean, cassava, Irish and sweet potato) that are either high yielding, have shorter maturity periods, longer shelf life or are more tolerant to drought and common pests and diseases. In one household, the respondent said that she had started growing a new plant because of its medicinal value (asthma reducing effects). In Chapter 4, some banana varieties that are grown for their medicinal values were discussed.

Use of genetic biodiversity

In addition to growing a variety of crops, farmers reported growing different varieties (local and improved) of the same crop. Again the rationale was that different varieties have different resistance to pests and diseases, drought conditions, differ in maturation period and palatability. Focus group participants revealed that this strategy was used across all household types. For the perennial producers, however, the use of genetic biodiversity seemed to be limited to crop fields that were for home production. For example, farmers with maize gardens and banana plantations where the production was basically for the market, were specializing in varieties that had better market prices. Negash and Niehof (2004) also reported the use of enset biodiversity by both poor and rich households as an on-farm diversification strategy. While their data showed that on-farm biodiversity depended on household socio-economic status, the poor were also found to maintain as many clones as possible, but selecting the disease resistant ones first.

Crop and livestock integration

The survey results show that about half of the farming households keep livestock. Farmers keep different types of animals at the same time. Generally, a combination of small animals (goats and pigs) was kept because the majority of farmers cannot afford to purchase cattle and, does not have enough land to rear cattle. Focus group participants indicated that households with animals were likely to have better yields because they used the manure to improve soil fertility, either by direct application or through compost-making.

Farmers further indicated that they see keeping livestock as a form of saving. Farmers who had dairy animals, income from milk sales is used to support crop-farming activities (purchasing inputs and hiring labour). Information from group discussions revealed that for some ethnic groups (for example, the Banyankole, Bakiga, Batoro and Banyarwanda) ownership of livestock is a status and livelihood security issue. The lack of ownership of any form of livestock in such ethnic groups is considered as an indicator of poverty. Unlike crop production, livestock production plays a minor role as an income-generating activity among the sample households. Keeping livestock, as an income-earning strategy, is even less observed among the two types of female-headed households than among the male-headed ones.

Increasing production and productivity

During the three years prior to the study, some households engaged in activities that resulted in increases in agricultural production, agricultural income and total income. For example, about 30 percent of the surveyed households increased the area under agricultural production and 24 percent reported increased income from agricultural production between 2002 and 2005. The percentage reporting increased total household income is the same as that with increased income from agriculture over the same period. This further shows the importance of agriculture as a key source of household income.

The results presented in Table 6.7 show that the proportion of households in Clusters 1 and 2 that increased area for agricultural production is about one-and-a-half times in each case that of households in Cluster 3 ($p < 0.01$). The majority (76%) expanded the area under production to increase food production, 13 percent to increase grazing area and grow new crop varieties, while seven percent said it was to increase household income. These results confirm the observation that in Uganda, farmers' key strategy to improve food security is through own production (Bahiigwa, 2002).

The staples growers lagged behind in these strategies partly because of lack of labour. For example, in Table 6.7, the proportion of households in Cluster 1 that hired labour is significantly higher than that for households in Cluster 2 and 3 ($p < 0.01$). Households in Cluster 3 are also less likely to use hired labour than those in Cluster 2 ($p < 0.01$).

One of the outcomes of increased area under agriculture is increased output in terms of yields. Table 6.7 shows inter-cluster differences among the 192 households that had increased yields over the study period. The proportion of perennial producers reporting increased yields is about one-a-half times that of staples growers ($p < 0.05$). However, no significant difference is found in the proportions of farmers that had increased yields between the perennial producers and the diversified small-holder farmers or between diversified small-holders and staples growers. The main reason for increased yields mentioned by 68 percent of the farmers was improved management, particularly, better management of crop pests and diseases, use of fertilizers, and use of improved seeds. The proportion of households that controlled pests and diseases is significantly higher in Cluster 1 than in Cluster 2. It is therefore not surprising that more Cluster 1 households, who are relatively better off than the others and had the capacity to purchase inputs, reported higher yields. Other reasons for increased yields include favourable weather (21%), hard work to ensure good management and timely implementation of agricultural activities (4%) and specialization into specific crops (3.5%).

Increased agricultural incomes

All the above strategies paid off for households that employed them because they increased agricultural incomes. For example, of those who mentioned increased agricultural incomes, 25 percent said it was due to increased crop yields and consequent sales, 20 percent attributed it to their use of recommended agronomic practices that also resulted in increased yields, while 14 percent said it was due to increased production because of expanding area under crops and livestock. Nine percent attributed the agricultural incomes realized to their hard work. These are unlikely to be in Cluster 3 that had a large number of HIV/AIDS affected households, as case study data show. For example, in Case 5.12 Mrs Mutebi's good health enables her to work harder and longer hours to cater her household, something that Maria or Veronica (Cases 1.1 and 5.10 respectively) cannot manage, due to the debilitating effects of HIV/AIDS. Other factors external to the households such as increase in prices of agricultural products (mentioned by 14%) and availability of markets (mentioned by 10%) at the time, were also said to have contributed to increase in household incomes earned from agricultural activities. It cannot be assumed that all farmers benefit from higher produce prices and, therefore, increase production to tap into such opportunities. In this case we see that few farmers, mainly in the relatively well-off Cluster 1 benefited from the good prices and available markets. Farmers in Cluster 3 are structurally limited by resources and cannot fully respond to price increases. Indeed, the proportion of households with increased incomes from agriculture is significantly higher among Clusters 1 and 2 households than in Cluster 3 ($p<0.05$, Table 6.7).

When asked how incomes are invested, the responses from focus group participants varied, but the main allocation given was improving and intensifying agricultural activities. Common responses included: buy improved seed, fertilizer for maize, a goat or pig or cow, improved breed of cows, hire or buy more land for agriculture and increase the number of animals. Only when individuals were fairly comfortable with farming they would think of investing in small businesses like stocking up a retail shop, buying a *boda boda*, or constructing buildings (with the latter mainly seen for Cluster 1).

6.3.2 Responding to a changing household resource base

Responding to changes in land access and availability

Land for farming and grazing is central to the agriculture-based livelihood strategies pursued by the majority of the population in the study areas. Nearly all (over 90%) of the respondents in the study identified land as the primary resource by which individuals produce food and generate cash through a variety of activities.

Despite its importance, access to land remains problematic for the majority of poor farmers. Land is typically acquired through patrilineal inheritance. Social or kinships relations with the land owners and ability to hire land are also ways through which individuals are able to access extra parcels of land for cultivation. However, increasing population pressure and land fragmentation has reduced accessibility by these means. Rich farmers with plenty of idle land rent out their land at a fee or are paid in kind with part of the produce. Depending on the size of the plot and its location, farmers pay land rents ranging from 10,000 to 40,000 Uganda Shillings (US$ 6 to 22) per season. The amount of produce paid in kind also depends on the amount of land rented.

However, land for rent is not readily available, as was revealed in more than half of all the focus group discussions conducted. As a consequence of land scarcity, rental prices have also been on the increase. While additional information indicated that the land rental costs are reasonable, some poor farmers cannot afford them. For example, of the 124 households whose area under agricultural production declined during the period 2002-5, 11 percent said that the main reason was that they could no longer afford to hire land for production. Furthermore, unpredictable weather, particularly drought, and the reported increase in crop pests and diseases make renting land a non-viable option. As was revealed in about half the group discussions, even farmers with money to hire land said that there was no guarantee that they could access the same plot of land the following season. The owner may want to use it or leave it fallow. As scarcity of land increases, even those households that rely on borrowing land from friends or relatives find it difficult to access land; only two percent of the sample households were able to access land in this way.

Other reasons for reduced land under agricultural production included sale of land to cover medical expenses and other household needs (12%), loss of soil fertility (17%) forcing farmers to leave the land fallow. Another 17 percent had to be evicted from land that had been gazetted as wetland by the National Environment Management Authority. Fifteen percent of the households had to reduce the land under crop production because of household members' ill health.

Dealing with land shortage is a challenge for households in the study area. Apart from the crop-sharing arrangements discussed above, the majority just have to do with the land they have. Only 20 percent of the sampled households reported ever buying additional land. Of those who purchased land, the proportion of male-headed households that purchased land (78%) was significantly higher than that for the two types of female-headed households: 15 percent for widow-headed and seven percent single-female-headed ($p < 0.05$). Where land renting was possible, some women's groups in Kabarole had resorted to renting land as a group and grew maize jointly in order to share costs and spread risks. But even then, the group leaders said that the lack of commitment among members to participate in group activities limited the amount of land they could hire.

Those with no other access to land combined casual labouring and other income-generating strategies with the limited farming on their small pieces of land in order to supplement own food production. Case study data also show that some widows whose late spouses left them very little or no land or who lost their land to the late spouse's relatives migrated to other areas and got married or got new partners to support them (Cases 5.5 and 5.9).

For the majority of rural households, access to adequate land is critical to achieving a reasonable degree of self-sufficiency. However, seasonal variation in access to land (particularly the rented or borrowed plots) and the processes associated with women's access to land (i.e. occupying a status *vis-à-vis* men, cf. Chapter 4) increases tenure insecurity of individuals in poor households and more so for women. Considering other factors , households that could access adequate land were likely to increase their agricultural production and improve their food security status, as exemplified by the discussion in the preceding section. In contrast, individuals in households that were unable to access adequate land were not likely to produce sufficient food for their household members. Arguably, such individuals had a high likelihood of being chronically food insecure, given that they were normally engaged in non-skilled labour that were not only poorly remunerated but seasonal or unreliable.

Responding to changes in financial resources

Financial resources comprise (i) available stocks of cash, bank deposits or liquid assets such as livestock, food and jewelry and not having liabilities (ii) regular inflow of money comprising labour income, pensions or other transfers from the state, and remittances, which are mostly dependent on others and need to be reliable (Kollmair & Gamper, 2002). However, as the survey data reveal, very few households had adequate financial resources to enable them smooth consumption when faced with shocks such as drought, famine, illness or death in the family.

Changes in household incomes over the study period could be observed. Thirteen percent of the respondents reported no change in household income in the period between 2002-5. Of the 87 percent that reported change, two-thirds had their incomes reduced while the other one-third reported increased household incomes over the same period. Increase in off-farm income (23.4%), increased agricultural production (21.5%) and good market prices at the time of sale (18.8%) were highlighted as some of the main factors that led to increased household income in the period. For those households that experienced reduced income, the three most commonly reported contributing factors were low yields due to prolonged drought (53%), reduced household labour due to sickness (18.9%) and, to a lesser extent, animal and crop pests and diseases (8.5%).

Despite the limited income flows for the greater majority of the study population, people tried to exercise discipline and invest whatever they could to guard against future periods of unforeseen hardship. The main ways in which farmers save money included having bank accounts, participating in rotating credit-and-savings associations (ROSCAs), investing in livestock and small household assets or keeping their money with trusted friends and relatives. For the sample as a whole, at least seven percent of the respondents mentioned having an individual or group bank account with a rural bank while 15 percent belonged to a ROSCA. The proportion of households in the diversified small-holder cluster that belonged to a ROSCA was significantly higher ($p< 0.05$) than that of households in the staples grower cluster (Table 6.3). The relatively high involvement in ROSCAs of the diversified small-holders gave them an advantage with regard to access to financial resources compared to the staples growers.

Access to institutions providing credit and savings was found to be limited and was reported to be costly. The high cost of credit limits its use in farming. For the sample as a whole, only ten percent of the respondents reported ever accessing credit. The greater majority of rural people in the study area, seemed to live from hand to mouth, considering that in 80 percent of the households people kept their own cash or do not save at all (5%). Information gathered through focus group discussions revealed that this was because the income earned was considered to be too little to be saved, and when received was often used immediately to cover pending household needs or overdue debts.

Lending to others or asking a trusted friend or relative to keep one's money or investing it in self-help groups were other ways in which respondents saved money. Additional information from group discussions revealed that such ways of saving helped individuals to keep their savings where they were not easily accessible to avoid them being spent on more immediate consumption needs or on friends and relatives that may need help.

Apart from cash, liquid assets particularly small livestock and poultry and their products were also important sources of income when sold. With regard to changes in livestock between the two years, there was no significant change in the mean cattle herd size across all household types ($p<0.10$). There was, however, a decrease in the mean number of chicken for all household types; goats among widow- and male-headed households as well as pigs among male-headed households ($p<0.1$). The main reasons given for decrease in livestock included: death due to disease (for chicken, pigs and goats), sold to get money to buy food (chicken and pigs) and other basic household needs (goats), sold to pay for school fees (pigs and goats), sold to pay for medical fees (pigs and goats) and stolen and/or consumed at home (chicken). It is noteworthy that the assets which were likely to be owned by female-headed households (those in Cluster 3) i.e. chicken and goats, decreased significantly in the period under consideration. The limited use of veterinary staff implies that farmers do little to control animal and poultry diseases. Furthermore, limited household incomes and sources to generate income coupled with HIV/AIDS-related livestock sales, make it difficult for farmers to improve management of their animals or restock. Nonetheless, a few households, mainly in the diversified small-holder cluster, were able to invest in small livestock.

While the majority had to respond to reduced household income, those who had realized increase in household income spent it on education and clothing for children as well as other household needs. A number of investments were reported. The commonest form of investment was to expand and improve agriculture production through hire of more land or purchase of land and agricultural inputs, as well as increase in the number or variety of crops grown. Others were able to buy livestock, purchase other household items like bicycle, radio, motorcycle, start new income-generating activities or boost existing ones. Households engaging in these activities were mainly in the perennial crop producers cluster (Cluster 1), and to a lesser extent also in the diversified small-holder farmer cluster (Cluster 2).

Overall, the greater majority of the study population lack adequate financial resources in form of hard cash and/or livestock to use or convert into cash in times of need. The absence of these resources implies that the majority of the respondents lack safety nets to fall back on in case of hardship, which increases their vulnerability. The limited availability of credit institutions in the area further aggravates the situation. The option left to the poor in case of a crisis is to borrow from friends or close kin, but as information generated from almost all focus group discussions shows, most of their friends are in the same circumstances. Therefore, friends are unable to help or if they are able, what they can spare is limited. The last available option to deal with a pressing crisis is the sale of land, which implies depletion of the most important productive resource, entailing consequences of increased impoverishment and vulnerability.

Responding to reduced household labour

Humans are the principal source of power for all farm operations among surveyed households in the two districts, with family labour almost exclusively being the main source of labour for agricultural activities. The general impression provided by focus group participants was one of decreasing labour availability for both farming and non-farming activities.

Individuals and households reported a number of strategies to deal with reduced household labour. About 43 percent of the survey households employ or hire labour to assist with key farm operations. This option was more common among the perennial producers given their higher incomes from agriculture and access to non-farm income sources. Further information obtained from the focus group discussions, particularly those with female participants, revealed that poorer households also hire labour for a few specific operations on a temporary basis. To avoid cash payments, many such households paid in kind or worked together in informal groups under various labour sharing arrangements. In addition, reducing the area under cultivation to suit the available labour, abandoning agricultural activities-particularly those that are labour intensive, reducing the number of crops grown and withdrawing children from school so that they can help out with farm work, were mentioned as ways to deal with the problems of reduced household labour. While these last four responses may be the only available options to the affected households, they are likely to compromise future production prospects and more importantly future human resource capacity of the household. The focus group discussions revealed that free labour from relatives and friends is very limited and cannot be relied upon as a long term strategy.

The availability, quantity and quality of household labour have a direct effect on the type of activities undertaken by household members and the nature of the strategies pursued. There are notable differences in availability and access to labour for production across the three clusters. A higher proportion of the perennial producers have access to hired labour compared to the households in the other two clusters ($p<0.01$, Table 5.3). On the other hand, the staples growers mainly depend on family labour for farming activities ($p<0.01$). Due to higher incomes, perennial producers also have the capacity to access better health services. Focus group participants emphasized the importance of good health among household members as key to survival. Good health and access to health services is fundamental to people's ability to earn their living. However, the low incomes among the staples growers limits access to health services as well as low education levels limits the availability and quality of labour in these households.

6.3.3 Diversification into non-farm income generating activities

Despite the persistent image of Africa as a continent of "subsistence farmers," non-farm sources are increasingly becoming an important part of rural people's livelihood portfolio and may already account for at least 40 percent of average household income in some areas (Bryceson and Jamal, 1997; Reardon, 1997; Little *et al.*, 2001). Information obtained from focus group discussions indicated that limited land, degraded soils, prolonged periods of drought as well as imperfect markets work in synergy to make returns from farming low, particularly for poor households with small landholdings. Individuals therefore diversify activities to mainly take up different non-farm activities to earn income needed to finance farming activities and inputs, deal with poor harvests as well as manage both crop and overall income risk. Survey data indicate that in addition to agriculture (crop and livestock combined) as the primary source of income, 35 percent of the respondents had a second source of income, such as from non-agricultural self-employment, casual labour, remittances, salaried employment, property rents, donations or pensions. These sources of income have the potential to bolster households and individuals against shocks.

The opportunity to develop farm incomes or diversify into non-farm enterprises has been attributed to either a reasonably profitable farming system or access to gifts and/or loans from friends and relatives (Reardon, 1997). Both male and female focus group participants said that profit from agriculture was the main source of income used to start other income-generating activities, followed by gifts and loans. From survey data the perennial producers (Cluster 1), are more likely to have resources to invest in non-farm enterprises given their higher incomes from agriculture and ability to hire labour. This facilitates release of family labour to non-farm activities. However, this can be considered to disadvantage female-headed households who constitute the bulk of Cluster 3 households. They typically have less productive members in the household, generate low incomes from the sale of agricultural products and thus have less opportunity for engaging in own- farm and non-farm activities.

Wage labour

Selling of casual labour is the commonest source of non-farm income accessible to the majority of poor rural households because of the limited inputs requirements. The study area is characterized by few off-farm employment opportunities. Where non-farm employment exists, casual labour for such activities seems to offer better returns than casual labour in agriculture. Non-farm activities requiring casual labour include fetching water, splitting logs for fuel wood, constructing shades during weddings or funerals and brick making. Individuals in households with very small land holdings sell their labour on their neighbours' farms in addition to working on their own land. However, the income from casual labour is reportedly irregular and fluctuates with seasons and rates depend on the number of other labourers available. Frequent periods of prolonged drought make households that depend on casual agricultural labour very vulnerable.

Casual labour, particularly in agriculture is seen as work for the very poor. The Baganda (in Masaka) and the Batoro (in Kabarole) see agricultural labour as work for the migrant ethnic groups that came and settled there. Information obtained from focus group discussions indicates that the Baganda and Batoro would rather migrate and do manual labour outside their village than be seen working on their neighbour's farm. Sometimes casual labour employment opportunities are available, but people prefer remaining poor rather than engaging in activities and being looked down upon. The term used for a manual labourer is "*mupakasi*" and seeking or doing manual agricultural labour is called "*kupakasa*". It is therefore women and men from poor households and of mainly non-Baganda and non-Batoro ethinic backgrounds that usually *kupakasa* to earn the much needed cash to sustain their livelihoods. Payment for casual labour is in cash or in kind (beer and food).

Information provided from focus group participants indicates that men and women can get casual employment to undertake any agricultural task. However, women and children are more likely to engage in the labour-intensive tasks of planting, weeding and harvesting while men engaged in land clearing and ploughing. Available non-agricultural employment is predominantly work that requires significant physical strength, such as brick making, logging, transport (head portage), fetching water (mainly in Masaka), construction, and digging graves, which is mainly men's work. There is no significant difference in the share of engagement in regular wage employment between male-household heads and female heads, possibly because of the small numbers recorded (only ten household heads mentioned being in formal salaried employment).

Self-employment (non-agriculture) and rural trade

Self-employment: Non-agricultural self-employment ranks as the second most important source of household income next to farming in crop production. These activities involve small firms managed by one to two people, and included retail shops, charcoal burning or selling, and running a salon (hair dresser), drug store or health clinic. Other rural non-farm labour activities include provision of the following services: making furniture, building, welding, transport, brewing and selling of alcohol. Information obtained from the mixed focus group discussions indicates that many of the households that engage in these activities have members with certain special skills or own cash resources that enable them set up such businesses. They were thus likely to be farmers in Clusters 1 and 2. It was also noted that some of these households either have the capacity to hire additional labour or have large families or multiple conjugal units (several wives) that provide them with the possibility of allocating some household labour to non-farm activities without compromising farm labour. To illustrate this, two examples are given: (i) of a man who had two wives, puts one in charge of the agricultural activities at his village home while he sets up a retail shop in the local trading centre for the second wife to manage (Case 5.1); and (ii) of a rich man who buys a *boda boda* (motorcycle) from savings made from his banana and coffee sales, which he then gives to his eldest unemployed son to drive as a taxi (Men's focus group discussion, Kyazanga).

Rural trade: Two key factors have been identified as contributing to a growing rural trade in Uganda: (i) the relatively stable economic environment that has allowed those with money to invest in non-farm enterprises, and (ii) the improved communication infrastructure facilitating creation of business contacts between traders in the city and those in the rural areas (Bevan & Ssewaya, 1995). Rural areas are the main source of food for the highly populated urban centres. From colonial times Masaka has been a food basket for the capital city of Kampala. Improvements in the road infrastructure in the late 1980s, particularly rehabilitating the Kampala-Mbarara highway which runs through the district and other feeder roads, stimulated development of commerce in the surrounding rural areas. In addition, there has been road construction and maintenance throughout the district. Kabarole district has great potential as a food basket in the western region. It is the leading producer of cassava and onions, third producer of banana, fourth producer of maize and fifth producer of beans in the region. However, limited road infrastructure development has limited farmers' increased benefit from Kabarole's agricultural potential.

Considerable rural trade in produce (maize, beans), bananas, cabbages, tomatoes, fish and meat as well as in local beer was found to exist in the study area, though it was in the hands of a few relatively well-off individuals. Business men (middlemen) from nearby urban centres or from as far as Kampala as well as local traders and some farmers engage in produce trade. Most traders buy the produce soon after harvest at low prices from the farmers in villages. Following harvest, trucks go to the villages and load sacks of beans, maize, and banana and other produce (although trade in banana is almost throughout the year). Most of it is then transported to the big urban centres where it is sold or prepared for export. Some of it is stored and sold back to the same farmers at higher prices during periods of food shortages.

The majority of the farmers, particularly staples growers, do not earn much money from the farm produce as they sell off most of their produce immediately after harvest, when prices are at their lowest, because of the need for cash for household requirements. Some said to have accumulated debts of school fees or sickness in the pre-harvest period that needed to be paid off. Furthermore, over 95 percent of the farmers did not have storage facilities. Even after a bumper harvest when farmers would have wanted to wait for good prices, the lack of storage facilities becomes a constraint. As Makokha (2001) noted, the lack of food storage facilities not only undermines food security and production (no saving of food or seed), but also leads to the exploitation of poor farmers by their rich counterparts and traders in a liberalized market. Consequently, inequality and class divisions in agricultural production are reproduced. It is important to note that even if producer prices are good, still very few would significantly benefit from this form of rural trade given the low levels of agricultural production that characterize farming in the area. Nevertheless, the existence of rural trade presents income-generating opportunities, however small, for some rural households.

A few households trade in other consumer goods such as clothes, sugar, salt, paraffin oil, bread, cooked food, drugs, agricultural inputs, stationery, and so on. Most of the capital used to finance these enterprises is from the sale of crops and livestock. However, some individuals have been able to access credit to set up off-farm enterprises. Similar to what has been observed by Katwijukye and Doppler (2004), those farmers who decide to take credit, prefer to invest it in off-farm activities (e.g. trading) rather than in farming activities. Women, youth and children (particularly boys) are also engaged in sallling roasted plantain, cassava, sweet potato and other cooked foods at road side markets. Road side markets are more common in Masaka than in Kabarole. In-depth discussions with female case study subjects, revealed that handicrafts (mats and baskets) are an important source of income to women. However, being a traditional activity, women do not consider it as a form of business.

Information obtained in focus group discussions showed that both men and women actively participate in rural trade activities. While participation in petty trade enables both men and women to have increased access to non-farm income, gender segregation in the type of activities is apparent amongst the study population. For example, female respondents mainly participate in low-wage activities such as selling of cooked food, alcohol, small fish, charcoal, fuel wood, home grown fruits and vegetables. The selling of alcohol by women is almost always accompanied by selling of sexual favours. Though both men and women participate in trading of agricultural produce, due to lack of capital women trade in smaller amounts than their male counterparts. They are also more likely to sell at farm-gate prices that are usually less than those in the market. Therefore, women predominantly participate in low entry-barrier activities and income from such activities is also much less than that earned by men's trading activities. The literature shows similar patterns in other parts of sub-Saharan Africa In Burkina Faso, for example, women's main off-farm income earning strategy (selling beer) was found to be less profitable than men's strategy of selling grain (Hussein & Nelson, 1998). Such gender segregation may in part explain the low income levels observed among the staples growers (dominated by female-headed households), despite their involvement in non-farm income-generating activities.

Access to financial services

Although there has been a steady increase in institutions involved in micro-finance provision (MFPED, 2000), limited access to financial services remains a key problem in Uganda (Beijuka, 1999; MFPED, 2000). And gender-based institutional barriers that exclude women from formal credit have been widely documented (Goetz, 1995)[49]. Yet the lack of capital to buy agricultural inputs, hire more land for production and start up an off-farm income-generating activity mentioned by over half of the respondents, is the commonest obstacle to improving livelihood. According to Beijuka (1999), poor physical and communication infrastructure as well as lack of a strong legal system to penalize defaulters have constrained financial service provision in Uganda. Lack of access to financial institutions is worse in rural areas than in urban ones. For both Kabarole and Masaka, access to formal sources of

[49] According to Elson & Evers (1997), Ugandan women's share of formal credit is only one per cent. Gender-based inequalities in obtaining credit stem from several factors, including women's lack of mobility, time and collateral.

credit was found to be very inadequate. The lack of collateral and knowledge about existing credit providers, unfamiliarity with the procedures involved, high initial capita requirements and fear of default, were mentioned as factors limiting access at individual level.

In the study area ROSCAs provide an important source of savings and credit that, among other things, enables members to cope with financial constraints in trade-related activities. However, only a small proportion of households in the staples growers cluster belonged to a ROSCA. A higher proportion of households in the diversified small-holder cluster followed by the perennial crop producers have access to this source of informal credit. The lower participation of household in the staples growers cluster can be attributed to the inability to meet regular payments. Other studies have shown that "the majority of individuals who initiated successful non-farm enterprises used income from farming as base capital", suggesting that without a firm basis in the farm economy effective entry into the non-farm activities is difficult to achieve (Smith, 2001:17). Improved access to formal credit and at terms that are favourable for small trade and agriculture, has the potential not only to increase agricultural production, but also non-farm activities, because of the strong linkage between these activities in the rural areas. While they continue to be an important source of immediate cash for participating members, given their small capital base the potential of ROSCAs as a way to secure significant investment capital remains limited. Therefore, access to formal credit will be a necessary condition for improved livelihoods.

Migration

Migration in search of employment opportunities has been ongoing in the study area. In the 1950s, people migrated from Kisoro, Kabale, Mbarara and Bushenyi to Masaka (due to high labour demand for work in coffee and banana plantations) and to Kabarole (due to availability of vacant land). The majority of the migrants that came to Masaka were seasonal migrants coming during periods of peak agricultural activities like weeding and harvesting. The majority of those who came to Kabarole, came as new settlers seeking employment in the tea estates and on the farms of the host communities, starting off under very difficult conditions of poor housing, feeding and general wellbeing. Over time, some have worked hard and have been able to acquire enough land to improve their situation but many others have not been able to acquire enough to meet basic family needs. Out-migration has become an important livelihood strategy among the latter.

Survey respondents indicated that a number of individuals in the study population have migrated to either a nearby rural town or urban center or the capital Kampala to seek employment or education. People are said to migrate to such towns as Kinoni, Mbirizi, Masaka, Mbarara, Mubende, Kabarole, and Kasese. Information from focus group discussions revealed that migration was important across all household types regardless of wealth status. The rich mainly migrate to engage in more lucrative commerce in urban centers, in search of better schools for their children as well as to look for better-paid jobs. Conversely, individuals from poor households migrate to look for any form of employment. Seasonal and overseas migration does not play a significant role in people's livelihoods in the two districts. Cyclical migration to coffee growing sub-counties, particularly during the coffee harvest season, was reported in Masaka.

About one third of all survey households reported had at least one member migrating to look for employment. The percentage of households reporting migration is higher in Masaka (39%) than Kabarole (24%). No differences were observed between the clusters with regard to the proportion of households with migrating members. However, household level analysis revealed that male-headed households (37%) are more likely to have members migrating to urban areas compared to single-female-headed (23%) and widow-headed households (28%). Focus group participants had mixed views with regard to the importance of migration to rural households. The major positive effects of migration were identified as remittances and gifts from the migrant and the establishment of urban-rural linkages; the migrant would be a source of contact for other relatives or friends who wanted to migrate in the future. Reduced household labour for agricultural activities was mentioned as one of the negative effects of migration. Female group participants further said that migration of male household members for employment increases the work burden of the remaining household members, particularly the female members, as they must take over all the responsibilities of the migrating member. It is noteworthy, that the income-generating options for those left behind become limited due to labour shortages. Besides, sometimes the migrants never send remittances or only irregularly and in small amounts. Another negative impact of migration is that the long periods of separation normally result in men marrying other wives or getting other sexual partners, a situation that increases risk of HIV infection among the migrants and the spouses left behind.

Migration was found to be both a household and individual strategy. It was a household strategy in that the household, as a unit, decides to provide support to an individual to migrate to an urban area, considering that when the migrating member gets employment, he/she will be able to support the remaining household members. However, teenage boys and girls, particularly from poor households, who had dropped out of school, would also decide on their own to migrate to look for employment, or in the case of girls, to get married without the parents' consent. From the limited significance of remittances as a source of household income it can be concluded that the importance of migration as a livelihood strategy, particularly to poor households, is questionable. Factors such as the limited skills of the migrants, causing them to engage in low-paying casual work, and the high cost of living, constrain their ability to regularly or meaningfully remit relatives left in the rural areas.

6.4 Food security strategies and responses

In Chapter 2 food security was defined as the household's ability to have access to an adequate amount of required food at all times and that this is achieved through a combination of strategies. Food security strategies can be broadly categorized into strategies aimed at obtaining food (access to food) and those regarding the use of food (consumption strategies). Almost all sample households depended on own production as the main source of food (cf. Chapter 4). However, Bahiigwa (2002) showed that the market is increasingly becoming an important second source of food for rural households in Uganda. There is evidence of this at the national level. According to MFPED (2004) there has been a major shift out of crop agriculture by household heads during the period 1992-2003, which was accompanied by a drop in consumption of home-produced food and an increase in consumption of purchased foods. In this study also, survey data showed that the main response to reductions in own production is to turn to the market. A higher proportion of households in Masaka ($p < 0.05$) depended on the market in times of food shortage than in Kabarole (Table 6.9). Household level analysis also reveals that a higher proportion of widow-headed households ($p < 0.05$) depend on the market in times of food shortage than male-headed households (Table 6.10). Tables 6.8 - 6.10 present some of the strategies mentioned by respondents that are used to deal with reduced

Table 6.8. Household strategies in times of food scarcity (N=432).

Strategy	Frequency	Responses (%)
Buying maize to supplement other foods	289	40.3
Reduce number of meals eaten per day	90	12.5
Working for others for food (*Okusaka*)	73	10.2
Draw on stored food stocks	62	8.6
Prudent measuring and cooking	54	7.5
Generate money for food through sell of assets	43	6.0
Generate money for food through doing casual work	42	5.8
Substitute lunch with maize porridge or fruits	26	3.6
Borrow food from relatives	22	3.1
Reduce types of foods consumed per meal	10	1.4
Donations from some NGOs	7	1.0
Total	718	100.0

Source: Household survey.

Table 6.9. Strategies employed during food scarcity by district (N=432).

Strategy	Masaka (%)	Kabarole (%)
Buying food e.g. maize**	66	38
Reduce number of meals**	21	12
Reducing wastage by cooking enough**	16	2
Working for others for food	12	16
Storage in preparation for shortages	11	12
Work for others (cash)*	6	10
Sell produce and buy food	5	4

Source: Household survey. *, ** imply significantly different at 10% and 5% level respectively.

Table 6.10. Strategies employed during food scarcity by gender of household head (N=432).

Strategy	Single-female HH (%)	Male HH (%)	Widow HH (%)
Buying food eg maize	60[a]	50.3[ab]	62.4[ac]
Reduce number of meals	18	15.1	21.8
Reducing wastage by cooking enough	12[a]	7.9[ab]	16.8[ac]
Working for others for food	16	12	19.8
Storage in preparation for shortages	12	1.6	7.9
Work for others (cash)	14	6.6	8.9
Sell produce and buy food	4.0	4.0	4.0

Source: Household survey.
Superscripts with the same letter across the row are not significantly different at the 10% level.

household food reserves. It is shown that over two-thirds of the households resort to buying maize to supplement household food supplies. Strategies relating to agricultural and economic production have already been discussed in the foregoing sections. The focus in this section will be on food security strategies related to social relations and consumption. There are no significant differences in the type of strategy employed between the three types of livelihood strategy clusters.

6.4.1 Food security strategies related to social relations

Calling on kinship relations

In addition to own production and purchase from the market, inter-household support plays an important role in facilitating households' access to food in times of scarcity. Survey data and information generated from focus group discussions revealed that members from different households exchange money, food and a variety of other items[50] to support close kin in need. These exchanges seem to go on all the time, though they are particularly important to the survival of individuals during periods of food shortage, as was confirmed by information generated from focus group discussions. It is worth noting that inter-household support is among very close kin, probably one of the reasons why focus group participants characterized the very poor as people not having relatives.

Households that receive support said it was from a son, daughter, daughter-in-law, mother, sister or grandfather, with each of these responses occurring in over 20 percent of the cases. In over half of the surveyed households, respondents indicated giving help of some kind to at least one individual outside their household. On average respondents indicated providing support to two people outside their household. Food was mentioned by over 70 percent of the respondents as the commonest form of support. Focus group participants mentioned a variety of food stuffs, both fresh and dry (in case of grains) that they send to relatives who they think are in need or to return a similar gesture in the past. Some male focus group participants, however, said that one could also send money for food. Survey data further show that 50 percent of households receive support, in the form of food and money. Additionally, the same number of respondents mentioned also receiving basic items like sugar, salt, paraffin, soap, and sauce. The proportion of Masaka households (60%) providing extra-household support was higher ($p<0.10$) than that in Kabarole (48%). Additional strategies indicated by focus group participants, though mentioned to a lesser extent, include borrowing food from relatives and sending children to other relatives who could look after them.

Charity

About 400 households in Masaka district receive food donations from NGOs. Information collected from key informants and through group discussions in Masaka revealed that NGOs like The AIDS Support Organization (TASO) and the Kitovu Mobile AIDS Homecare Counselling and Orphan Programme (MAHCOP)

[50] Apart from food and financial support, school fees (mentioned by over 70%), clothing and medical care (or money for drugs), each by over 50% constituted the other major types of support that households give.

provide AIDS-related treatment and care, planting materials and seed, as well as food supplements to HIV/AIDS-affected households. World Vision (working in both Masaka and Kabarole) is another NGO, targeting households with orphan and vulnerable children (OVCs). Some of their programmes included providing agricultural extension training, information and improved seed varieties to farmers. A very small proportion of respondents (< 1%) mentioned receiving support from the government[51].

Engaging in sexual relations

One strategy specific to poor women, particularly widows and single ones, is selling sexual favours. This information was sensitive and was obtained only through in-depth discussions with some of the case study subjects. Due to limited income and small land holdings, these women had no choice but to get one or even more "male friends" who provide money for food and other basic needs. To obtain more commitment and support from the "male friends" some women decide to bear the man a child so that the child (Case 5.5). Some of these relationships had been fruitful, allowing some women to start up businesses such as a small poultry project, restaurant or a saloon or boost an existing activity like alcohol selling. Some even had their children's school fees paid. However, as one woman indicated, "the man tells you that he will start you a small business but keeps saying that he has not got money yet...in the end you are just used and left there". So not all of these relationships were beneficial. From the discussions it was clear that these women's economic situation left them no other option than engaging in such relationships for survival, risking increasing exposure to HIV/AIDS.

Focus group information further revealed how young girls from poor families are married off early as a strategy to get in-laws to look after the girls and provide support to the family. It is important to note that for women, these relationships are a survival strategy and therefore accept whoever presented themselves as interested and capable of addressing their needs. But for the men, sexual pleasure was the motivating factor and they could take their pick.

6.4.2 Consumption strategies

The strategy ranking second is change in consumption. About 21 percent of the respondents said that they reduced the meals eaten per day. Information obtained from focus group discussion indicated that the meals were normally reduced from

[51] The government through the Community HIV/AIDS Initiative (CHAI) Program provides financial support to women groups caring for HIV/AIDS orphans. The CHAI program was operational in both districts. To access the funds, women must be in an organized group, with a savings bank account and demonstrate ability to manage and account for the money according to stipulated guidelines.

three to two or even one in severe cases. The missed meals were then substituted by porridge for those who could afford it or by fruits such as bananas, jack fruit, sugar cane or any other fruit that may be available. Female group participants, however, emphasized that mothers try to ensure that children, particularly those below ten years, are given some extra meal or maize porridge. This strategy is likely to be employed by widow-headed households in Masaka (Tables 6.9 and 6.10). In addition to reducing the number of meals eaten per day, changes in the type of foods consumed were observed. Female focus group participants, for example, mentioned that they prefer maize over other types of foods, particularly, during times of food shortage because it is relatively cheaper and more filling. In fact, the common practice was for individuals to sell a bunch of banana or some other high-value crops and then buy maize flour for food which can be consumed as a porridge or eaten as maize bread (*posho/ugali*).

Female focus group participants said that recurrent food shortages have taught them to be more prudent with the amounts cooked, to ensure that food is not wasted. Twelve percent of the respondents also gave this as one of the food security strategies. They said that in the past people never minded whether they cooked more food than could be consumed because there was plenty. According to these women, presently one has to properly plan for the little food available, given the decline in production and the increase in the number of mouths to feed because of the rampant orphan problem and the large extended family. Twelve percent of the respondents mentioned this as one of the food security strategies (Table 6.8). Again this strategy is likely to be employed by widow-headed households in Masaka (Tables 6.9 and 6.10). Reducing the number of food types consumed was reported to a lesser extent.

Though the levels of production during the study period were generally very low, it is important to note that at least 14 percent of households managed to store some food that could be consumed during times of food shortage. The most common foods stored were maize and beans. Farmers also used to plant a field of cassava or yams, to be harvested only during periods of food shortage. At the time of the survey, the majority of the farmers had lost almost all their cassava and sweet potato crop to pests.

6.4.3 Other responses and strategies

Engaging in activities that can quickly earn money or food such as casual labour or the sale of household assets are strategies more common among households in the diversified small-holder and staples growers clusters. Items sold included baskets, mats, small animals and chicken. The proportion of persons engaging in casual labour for food is about twice that who work for cash, implying that in times of food shortage, farmers preferred to work for food rather than money.

6.4.4 Food security status among the three livelihood clusters

Figure 6.4 presents the mean food adequacy scores by livelihood strategy. Comparing differences between livelihood strategies, households in the Cluster 1 have slightly higher scores than those in the other two clusters, although the differences were not statistically significant. In Cluster 1 all scores for the various food categories were equal to or above the sample aggregate food score of 2.5. Cluster 1 also has the largest proportion of food secure households (29%) and the least proportion of food insecure households (20%). The staples growers cluster has the lowest proportion of food secure households (19%), with the remaining households either being barely food secure or completely insecure. About one quarter of the households in Cluster 2 are food secure while one third is food insecure. These results imply that households pursuing the staples growers strategy are likely to be more vulnerable to food insecurity.

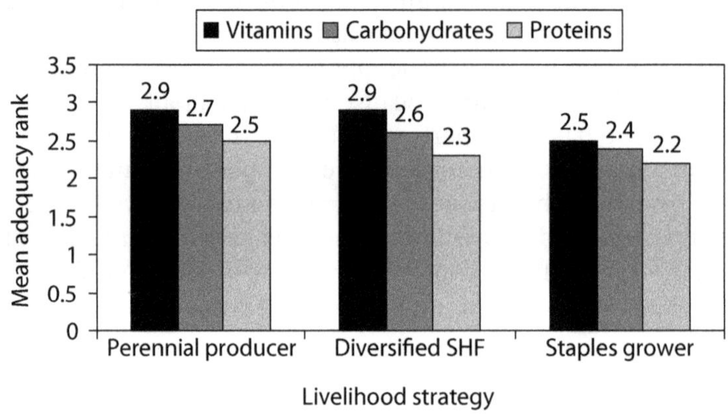

Figure 6.4. Food category adequacy by livelihood strategy. Source: Household survey.

6.5 Determinants of livelihood strategies pursued

There are various internal and external factors that determine rural households' ability to diversify their assets, incomes and activities. The internal factors relate to the composition and internal dynamics of households while the external factors, include among things, the prevailing historical, social, economic, institutional, policy and physical environment.

Barret *et al.* (2001) classified the factors into two sets: the "pull factors" and "push factors". The pull factors motivate individuals to diversify because of new opportunities for income diversification. Examples of these at the household level are: realization of strategic complementarities between activities such as crop-livestock integration, poultry production and vegetable gardening; specializing in specific crops because of comparative advantage or making use of new technologies that offer comparative advantage. At a higher level, proximity to an urban centre or policies promoting commercial agriculture may also act as pull factors. In contrast, push factors are associated with risk reduction or response to diminishing factor returns. Factors such as land fragmentation, declining soil fertility which reduce returns to family labour, and risk in farming due to unreliable rainfall are examples of factors that may cause farmers to diversify. Examples of push factors at higher levels include: incomplete or weak financial systems, climatic uncertainty, and constraints in labor, inputs and land markets.

6.5.1 Econometric model specification of household determinants

In order to identify the factors that influence the choice of a particular livelihood strategy, a multinomial logit (mlogit) regression was used in the study. The choice of the mlogit model was based on its ability to perform better with discrete choice studies (McFadden, 1973; Judge *et al.*, 1985). The probability that a household chooses a given livelihood strategy, lies between zero and one. The model assumes that a household makes a choice that maximizes its utility (McFadden, 1973) and that the random disturbance terms are independently and identically distributed (McFadden, 1973), which is popularly known as the Independency of Irrelevant alternatives assumption (iia). I failed to reject this assumption indicating that the mlogit is the appropriate statistical model for the data. The equation[52] used to estimate the coefficients (by maximum likelihood) is:

$$\ln \frac{P_i}{1-P_i} = b_0 + b_1 x_1 + \ldots + b_n x_n \qquad \text{Equation 6.3}$$

where $\frac{P_i}{1-P_i}$ is the odds ratio; the log odds are expressed as a linear function of the independent factors (x_j and $j = 1 \ldots 25$). $i = 1$ = Perennial crop producer and $i = 3$ = Staples grower strategy. $i = 2$ = diversified small-holder strategy is the reference group. There are two sets of coefficients because strategy 1 and 3 each have to be compared with the reference group. Estimated coefficients measure the estimated change in the logit for a one-unit change in a given variable while the other variables are held constant. A positive estimated coefficient indicates an increase in the likelihood that a household will choose to be in an alternative livelihood strategy. A negative coefficient indicates that there is less likelihood that a household will change to an alternative livelihood strategy.

The definition of the variables used in the mlogit equation are presented in Table 6.11 and the summary statistics of the explanatory variables used in the model are shown in Appendix 2. The parameter estimates are presented in Tables 6.12 and 6.13.

[52] Refer to Appendix 1 for more notes on the derivation of the equation.

The results show that the type of livelihood strategy pursued is highly influenced by characteristics of the household head, household size, household income and expenditure status, and whether a household is affected by HIV/AIDS or not.

Table 6.11. Definition of variables used in the mlogit model[1].

Variable		Definition
X_1	Household size	Total number of household members in 2005
X_2	Cattle number	Number of cattle owned in 2005
X_3	Ruminant number	Number of goats and pigs owned in 2005
X_4	HH head occup 2	Household head engaged in off-farm unskilled work: Yes = 1.
X_5	HH head occup 3	Household head engaged off-farm skilled work: Yes = 1.
X_6	land-labour ratio	Land owned in 2005/ (No. of adult equivalents)
X_7	HH head age	Age of household head in years
	Education*	
X_8	HH head educ 4	Household education level is primary 5-7: Yes =1.
X_9	HH head educ 5	Household education level is secondary 1 through 4: Yes =1.
X_{10}	HH head educ 6	Household education level higher secondary (i.e. 5/6): Yes= 1.
X_{11}	HH head educ 7	Household education level is technical (college): Yes=1.
X_{12}	HH head educ 8	Household education level is university degree: Yes = 1.
X_{13}	HH head educ 9	Household head never attended school: Yes = 1.
X_{14}	Gender	Gender of household head (1 = male; 0 = female)
X_{15}	Hired labour	Hired labour in previous season to survey: Yes = 1.
X_{16}	AIDS-affected HH	Lost adult due to AIDS or reported having a sick individual with HIV/AIDS: Yes =1.
X_{17}	Sold maize	Sold some maize in previous season to survey: Yes =1.
X_{18}	Used clean plantlets	Use clean banana planting material: Yes = 1.
X_{19}	Pest/disease control	Controls banana pests and diseases: Yes =1.
X_{20}	Fertilizer use	Uses fertilizer or manure in banana plantation: Yes = 1.
X_{21}	Soil conservation	Implements soil and water conservation practices: Yes= 1.
X_{22}	Access credit	Has accessed formal credit: Yes =1.
X_{23}	Dependency ratio	Proportion of dependants in household
X_{24}	land owned (2005)	Land owned in 2005 (acres)
X_{25}	District	1 = Masaka; 0 = Kabarole
	ε_i	error term

* Primary education level 1 to 3 was grouped as "Not Educated" under HH head educ 9.
[1] The same variables are used in the ordered logit model in Chapter 7.

Table 6.12. Determinants of livelihood strategy in Masaka and Kabarole districts using mlogit.

Variable	Masaka				Kabarole			
	Perennial crop producer		Staples grower		Perennial crop producer		Staples grower	
	Coefficient	SE	Coefficient	SE	Coefficient	SE	Coefficient	SE
Cattle number	0.024	0.057	-0.055	0.054	-0.129	0.133	-0.036	0.081
Ruminant number	-0.080	0.058	0.026	0.042	-0.013	0.043	-0.227***	0.085
HH head occup 2	22.713***	1.678	21.565	.	0.772	1.118	-0.648	1.410
HH head occup 3	-1.118	1.155	0.871	0.656	-1.745	1.132	-1.768	1.271
HH head age	-0.045***	0.014	0.022**	0.011	-0.049***	0.018	0.033**	0.016
HH head educ 4	1.087**	0.479	0.192	0.370	0.243	0.467	0.738	0.491
HH head educ 5	0.694	0.592	-0.191	0.473	0.135	0.630	0.345	0.693
HH head educ 6	-31.817	1.67E+07	-31.939	1.3E+07	36.390	3.03E+07	2.278	4.49E+07
HH head educ 7	1.389	1.361	-0.745	1.307	-33.023	2.54E+07	-34.103	2.25E+07
HH head educ 8	.	.	.	.	-28.161	1.44E+07	5.491**	2.667
HH head educ 9	0.595	0.561	0.520	0.383	-0.124	0.517	0.929*	0.479
Gender	-0.329	0.392	0.031	0.311	0.243	0.650	-0.449	0.539
Hired labour	0.966***	0.358	-0.501	0.318	0.136	0.369	-1.575***	0.402
AIDS-affected HH	-0.066	0.519	0.416	0.378	0.508	0.516	0.756	0.484
Sold maize	0.207	0.427	0.215	0.347	-0.239	0.515	-0.563	0.461
Used clean plantlets	0.662	0.570	0.239	0.536	0.244	0.430	-0.037	0.457
Pest/disease control	0.804*	0.414	0.071	0.368	0.612	0.387	0.296	0.392
Fertilizer use	0.040	0.340	-0.338	0.287	0.302	0.424	-0.533	0.403
Soil conservation	0.005	0.434	-0.213	0.372	-0.004	0.380	0.061	0.387
Access credit	-0.388	0.597	-0.951	0.592	-0.339	0.584	0.508	0.561
Dependency ratio	-0.109	0.112	0.028	0.078	0.097*	0.161	0.085	0.168
land owned (2005)	-0.020	0.070	-0.021	0.027	0.124	0.072	0.003	0.077
Constant	0.336	0.869	-1.104	0.673	0.522	1.145	-0.328	1.076
Log likelihood	-282.20				-205.88			
Prob> Chi-square	0.0000				0.0000			
Pseudo R^2	0.1308				0.2026			
No. of Observations	303				238			

Source: Household survey.

***,**,* implies significance at 1% , 5%, and at 10% respectively.

Diversified small-holder farmer strategy is the reference category.

Table 6.13. Determinants of livelihood strategy in Kabarole and Masaka districts (overall) using mlogit.

Variable	Perennial crops producer		Staples grower	
	Coefficients	SE	Coefficients	SE
Cattle number	-0.016	0.046	-0.050	0.047
Ruminant number	-0.055*	0.033	-0.037	0.032
HH head occup 2	1.164	1.040	-0.103	0.977
HH head occup 3	-1.193*	0.670	0.138	0.520
HH head age	-0.045***	0.010	0.026***	0.009
HH head educ 4	0.680**	0.309	0.372	0.283
HH head educ 5	0.369	0.394	0.024	0.381
HH head educ 6	1.756	1.687	-34.024***	1.023
HH head educ 7	0.727	1.201	-0.633	1.359
HH head educ 8	-31.811***	1.727	1.860	1.569
HH head educ 9	0.230	0.368	0.620**	0.284
Gender	-0.194	0.331	-0.102	0.251
Hired labour	0.635**	0.250	-0.880***	0.234
AIDS-affected HH	0.063	0.349	0.596**	0.279
Sold maize	0.139	0.316	-0.100	0.260
Used clean plantlets	0.418	0.342	-0.048	0.323
Pest/disease control	0.722**	0.283	0.140	0.252
Fertilizer use	0.106	0.254	-0.385*	0.222
Soil conservation	0.002	0.271	-0.003	0.250
Access credit	-0.387	0.392	-0.228	0.348
Dependency ratio	-0.028	0.085	0.066	0.070
land owned (2005)	0.027	0.030	-0.007	0.021
District	0.045	0.278	0.019	0.245
constant	0.449	0.740	-0.943	0.585
Log likelihood	-510.89237			
Prob> Chi-square	0.0000			
Pseudo R^2	0.1245			
No. of observations	541			

Source: Household survey.
***,**,* implies significance at 1% , 5%, and at 10% respectively.
Diversified small-holder farmer strategy is the base category.

Discussion of results

The pseudo R squared values show that the estimation results are good. Regardless of district and type of livelihood strategy pursued, the age of the household head significantly influences the type of livelihood pursued. Young household heads have a higher likelihood ($p<0.05$) of pursuing the perennial crop producer strategy than the diversified small-holder one, while older household heads have a higher likelihood ($p<0.01$) of pursuing the staples growers livelihood strategy (Table 6.13). The results further show that in each district, different factors influence the pursuit of a given livelihood strategy (Table 6.12).

In Kabarole district, the number of small ruminants owned, ability to hire labour, education of the household head and to a less extent the size of land influence the type of livelihood strategy pursued. The number of small ruminants owned and ability to use hired labour are both negative and significant ($p<0.01$) among households in the staples growers strategy. This implies that in Kabarole households with few small ruminants and mainly using family labour for production are likely to pursue the staples growers strategy than the diversified small-holder strategy. The education level of the household head is positive and significant ($p<0.10$) among the staples growers while size of land owned is also positive and among the perennial crop producers. This implies that uneducated households heads are more likely to pursue the staples grower strategy than the diversified small-holder strategy. At the same time, households with more land are likely to pursue the perennial crop producer strategy than the diversified small-holder one.

For Masaka the results show that households that use hired labour ($p<0.01$), engage in off-farm un-skilled employment ($p<0.01$), are headed by individuals with at least an upper primary education ($p<0.05$) and control banana pests and diseases ($p<0.10$) are more likely to pursue the perennial crop producers strategy than the diversified small-holder strategy.

From the results in Table 6.13, the factors that significantly influence choice of livelihood include age, education, livestock ownership, use of hired labour, HIV/AIDS, and inputs use. Older farmers are less likely to pursue perennial crops but more likely to be engaged in staple food crop production. This might be because at that advanced age they might be only focusing on food security needs more than cash needs. Farmers with less ruminants are less likely to be engaged in perennial production , this might be suggestive that there is a complimentarity between livestock and perennial crop production as the livestock provide in-situ sources of manure that can be used in perennial production.

Use of hired labour is associated with more perennial crop production and less staple crop production, indicating that labour is a big constraint limiting farmers participation in perennial crop production. The results also show that farmers using fertilizers and pesticides are more likely to be engaged in perennial crops than in staple crops production. It seems that inability to use purchased inputs (fertilizers and pesticides) and hire labour are key constraints to the development of agricultural production, which is consistent with previous research findings in Uganda (Nkonya *et al.*, 2004; Pender *et al.*, 2001; 2004; Zake *et al.*, 1997).

Regardless of the type of livelihood strategy, being infected with HIV/AIDS does not have any significant influence on livelihood strategy at district level (Table 6.12). This implies that in the given context, the factors discussed above may be more important livelihood determinants than being affected by HIV/AIDS. However, HIV inflected households are more likely to be in staple food crop production (Table 6.13) possibly because they need nutritious food to complement the HIV chemotherapy and also to meet the household food security needs in case the bread winner is the one infected or sick. This provides evidence in support of our hypothesis that HIV influences livelihood choices, when even other factors have been accounted for. Nonetheless, the finding also seems to suggest the existence of HIV/AIDS-related poverty and the gendered impacts of HIV/AIDS in the study area. The significant coefficient of HIV in the staples growers model ($p < 0.05$) illuminates that when HIV is superimposed on already vulnerable livelihoods it further impairs the capacity of agriculture-based livelihoods and agricultural development in general.

Education has mixed impacts on livelihood strategies. Farmers with university education are more likely to be engaged in staple crop production and less in perennial crop production, while those with secondary education are more likely to be in perennial than in staple crop production. The possible explanation for this mixed finding might be that farmers with higher education have higher non-farm income so they do not have to engage in the perennial cash crop production as the respondents with secondary education. It is noted that large error terms are obtained for education levels of higher secondary and above because there were very few respondents with the corresponding education levels. Other factors where not significant including the district dummy after controlling for other factors.

6.5.2 External determinants of livelihood strategies

History: The political and economic climate during the time of Amin through to the mid 1980s seems to have contributed to triggering a process of diversification. The economic mismanagement during this era necessitated almost everyone in Uganda to participate in a range of activities in order to survive. For those in rural areas, farmers got into trade and diversified their crops (Bevan & Ssewaya, 1995). However, the slow and sometimes declining growth rates in the agricultural sector, an expanding cash economy and the rampant poverty, seemed to have sustained the need for diversification as individuals and households tried to expand their options for survival.

Recent histories of Masaka and Kabarole have in different ways influenced the livelihood opportunities for people in these districts and consequently the nature and extent of livelihood diversification. While both districts were affected by the economic decline of the 1970s and 1980s, they have also been affected by more recent region-specific events. Fort Portal's (capital of Kabarole) infrastructure was devastated during the two liberation wars of 1979 and 1985. Like other districts in the western region of the country Kabarole is vulnerable to earthquakes. The epicentre of the latest to hit (6th February, 1994) was at Kizomoro in Kabarole and caused a lot of damage to property in addition to human deaths. In all affected districts, 500 dwellings were destroyed and damage to public buildings and private property was estimated at US$19 million (The New Vision, 28 February 1994, cited in Bevan & Ssewaya, 1995). Furthermore, since 1996 the district has experienced rebel attacks from the Allied Democratic Forces (ADF). By late 1998, the ADF was launching regular attacks on civilians in Bundibuyo, Kasese and Kabarole districts which caused massive displacements of the civilian population in the three affected districts. The number of people that have been displaced is these districts have been estimated to be between 150,000 to 180,000 (Garbus & Marseille, 2003). All this, coupled with many years of prolonged government neglect, have contributed to widespread poverty and limited development in the district.

While Masaka also suffered from the civil conflict during the 1970s and 1980s, the HIV epidemic constituted its most severe shock. Like in Rakai, the impacts of the epidemic are clearly visible in increased dependency ratios, increased numbers of child-headed households, reduced agricultural productivity, and disproportionate deaths of successful entrepreneurs (Smith *et al.*, 2001). Data in this study also confirm the increased dependency ratios and reduced agricultural activity in Masaka. This differential historical context together with differences in spatial location and agro-ecology (declining soil fertility and recurrent droughts in Masaka as opposed to a higher agro-ecological potential but with a proneness to floods, land slides and earthquakes in Kabarole) produce environments with different opportunities and risks for livelihood generation. This underscores the importance of understanding livelihoods in their local context.

Financial services: The lack of investment capital continues to be the single most constraining factor to increasing investments in agriculture and expansion of non-farm income enterprises. Despite a wide proliferation of micro-finance institutions, limited access to financial services remains a key problem in Uganda (Beijuka, 1999; MFPED, 2000). Furthermore, there are gender-based institutional barriers that exclude women from formal credit (Goetz, 1995)[53]. Constraints associated with access to financial services have already been discussed in section 6.3.3. For households that reported access to formal credit, the proportion in Kabarole is significantly higher ($p < 0.05$) than in Masaka.

Extension services: Knowledge and information are important factors of production. Having timely and relevant information, on, for example , new pest and disease management regimes, new marketing opportunities, or the market prices of farm inputs and produce can influence people's decision making and is important for increased productivity. However, access to agriculture extension services remains very limited, with uneven distribution of the services across the country. Most rural areas, including those in the study area, do not have it. The agricultural extension service in Uganda has also been chronically under-funded and the staff underpaid, with staff lacking funds and transport to reach farmers. Twenty percent of respondents said that they do not have extension services in their areas. While there is no significant difference in the proportion of households accessing extension services between the two districts, the proportions of the two types of female-headed households that had never accessed any extension services is higher than that of male-headed households (cf. Chapter 4).

Physical infrastructure: While both Masaka and Kabarole have received both government and donor support for physical infrastructure, particularly roads, schools and health posts, some rural areas still lack these services, with Kabarole being worse off in terms of coverage. Key informant information from agricultural extension staff and district local leaders in Kabarole indicated that inadequate road infrastructure development has limited farmers' increased benefit from Kabarole's agricultural potential. However, as already discussed, the rehabilitation of the Kampala-Mbarara highway which runs through Masaka district stimulated development of commerce in the surrounding rural areas, particularly for those who had money to start up income-generating activities. In addition, in both districts there are few HIV/AIDS testing and counselling facilities. They are mainly found at district headquarters and thus are out of easy reach for many rural dwellers.

Macroeconomic policies: In the study areas, policies such as liberalization and the Plan to Modernize Agriculture (PMA) are likely to affect the rate of resource accumulation, given, among other things, their effects on input and output prices as well as the type of available investment opportunities and their profitability or risk involved. The National Agricultural Advisory Services (NAADS) programme

[53] According to Elson & Evers (1997), Ugandan women's share of formal credit is only one per cent. Gender-based inequalities in obtaining credit stem from several factors, including women's lack of mobility, time and collateral.

may also determine which agricultural enterprises are prioritized and therefore which farmers will have access to the associated services.

NGOs and social institutions: NGOs like MAHCOP and World Vision also play a role in determining people's livelihood strategies, because through their activities they influence which individuals or groups of individuals will access their resources. The closeness of Masaka to Kampala enables it to have higher access to NGO-supplied support than Kabarole. Finally, social relations between kin and institutions like the church, social norms and regulations, also influence the kind of activities and strategies that certain individuals or groups pursue in Masaka and Kabarole. Based on survey data and focus group discussions, households in Masaka are more likely to have this kind of support (kinship, CBO, NGO, government) than those in Kabarole.

6.6 Conclusions

Using cluster analysis, the sample was categorized into three livelihood strategy clusters, namely the perennial crop producers, diversified smallholder and staples growers livelihood strategy clusters. The proportions of farmers pursuing the various livelihood strategies did not vary by district. Perennial crop producers are largely better-off young and educated males, and less likely to be HIV/AIDS-affected. Diversified smallholder farmers are largely middle-age males, with almost equal proportions of educated and non-educated household heads, and have almost the same incidence of HIV/AIDS but fewer resources than household heads in the perennial crop producers cluster. Households in the staples growers cluster are predominantly female households headed by elderly women, the majority of whom have no education, limited access to productive resources, large household sizes and the highest incidence of being HIV/AIDS-affected.

The low levels of HIV/AIDS among the perennial crop producers contradicts AIDS literature on Uganda that shows that HIV prevalence levels among the rich is higher than that among the poor (Ministry of Health and ORC Macro, 2006; UBOS, 2006). This could be partly explained by HIV/AIDS-asset eroding effects such that those well-off households that get affected become poorer and move from the perennial producer to the staples growers famer cluster. There is evidence of this in the case studies. This further shows the likely effects of HIV/AIDS on social differentiation.

Agriculture is the most important livelihood activity and the economy of both districts depends on it. The sale of crops followed by livestock remains the most important source of income and the involvement in non-farm income activities is strongly linked to farming. The small share of employment in non-agriculture signifies that there are very few employment opportunities. This may be aggravated by people's very low purchasing power which hardly creates demand for labour and services. Nonetheless, across both districts and household types there is evidence that households have diversified activities and incomes both in farming and away from agriculture. The engagement in off-farm diversification largely arose from the crisis in agriculture and constraints experienced by farmers. The picture presented is one of households and individuals straddling different types of activities and earning income from various sources to sustain their livelihood. A gender desegregation of activities is also apparent with the two types of female-headed households specializing in activities and services that relate to gender-prescribed roles and male-headed households in more profitable occupations. This type of labour segregation may in part be explained by women's culturally defined reproductive roles in the home, particularly food and care provision, but also by barrier to entry into the non-farm sector as discussed below.

It is important to distinguish between livelihood activities and strategies that are adopted to reduce risk and avert crisis from those that are part of wider household accumulation strategies (Reardon, 1997). For most female-headed households, livelihood strategies reflect a lack of alternative options rather than opportunity to capitalize on investment opportunities. While these households would have been compelled to diversify, as a response to reduced returns on their labour in farming as well as deteriorating economic options, this does not seem to be the case. They actually seem to be trapped in a type of farming that does not pay. However, not all activities are coping or reactive. The results show evidence of some activities, particularly those pursued by some households in the perennial crop producer and diversified small-holder clusters, to be risk averting or proactive, in the sense that individuals have a conscious plan to avoid environmental, social or economic barriers. For example, because of increased food prices and general cost of living some households worked hard to increase food production in an effort to be self reliant in food. Even as people diversify, the primary interest is to get more income to improve and expand agriculture. The positive effects of diversification are therefore more apparent among male-headed households.

Furthermore, its noteworthy that no significant difference is observed in the proportion of households members participating in off-farm employment across the livelihood strategy clusters. However, the fact that female-headed households constituted the majority (over 70%) of the staples growers cluster with the lowest per capita expenditures, suggests that gender and occupation of the household head are strong indicators of poverty. Furthermore, while studies on whether female-headed households are disproportionately represented among the poor have yielded mixed results, in this study it is clear that the largest proportion of poor households is female-headed. For all types of household resources investigated, female-headed households have the weakest asset base. The small number of adult equivalents in female-headed households not only influences their production and investment decisions, but leaves them also less equipped to cope with seasonal stresses and other livelihood shocks.

Differences in the nature of household level factors influencing livelihood strategy by district is observed. However overall, households in the staples growers cluster are less likely to use fertilisers and hired labour, have lower land labour ratios, and the heads of these households have lower levels of education. It is also shown that the perennial crop producers are more likely to use hired labour, pesticides and have smaller household sizes. Improvement of agriculture-based livelihoods is likely to depend on farmers increased access to formal credit and other factors of production. The results further show that when each district is considered separately, HIV/AIDS is not a significant determinant of livelihood strategy. The significance of HIV/AIDS when the sample is analyzed as a whole implies that HIV/AIDS is just one of the vulnerability-causing factors and that its effects are likely to be significant among households that are already vulnerable, in this case female-headed households pursuing the staples growers strategy.

Higher level determinants of livelihood strategy include: history of the area, access to services, macroeconomic policies and access to services of organizations supporting people with HIV/AIDS. Household level analysis of livelihood determinants seems to show that being old and not educated is associated with being a staples grower. So it is not being a woman per se that is important in determining the type of livelihood pursued, but rather age and skills. Nonetheless, the female heads of households are characterized by lower education and old age. Therefore, one could argue that female headship plays a significant role in inhibiting the pursuit of more remunerative livelihood strategies.

Chapter 7

HIV/AIDS impact and vulnerability

7.1 Introduction

This chapter explores the impact HIV/AIDS has on daily life in Masaka and Kabarole, while zooming in on some of the salient details of social and economic impacts of HIV/AIDS. Aspects of labour and social relationships between and among households draw a picture of how HIV/AIDS shapes the dynamics involved in agricultural development. To highlight the differentiated nature of the impact of HIV/AIDS, a distinction is made between households that are considered to be well-off and those that are considered to be poor. Towards the end of the chapter, I examine the key determinants of livelihood vulnerability in Masaka and Kabarole and work towards an identification of household types and individuals that are likely to be relatively more vulnerable in a situation of AIDS. It is important to point out that the way HIV/AIDS affects people and the ways in which they respond occur within a broader context.

7.2 Analyzing HIV/AIDS-related effects on surveyed households

In Chapter 6, sample households were classified into three clusters in order to obtain fairly homogeneous categories to which livelihood labels were then attached. Analysis of the three clusters with regard to the extent to which households within each cluster are HIV/AIDS-affected indicates that, overall, the proportion of HIV/AIDS-affected households varies significantly ($p < 0.01$) between the three clusters. However, investigation of differences between two clusters at a time, reveals that there is no significant difference between the households in Clusters 1 and 2 (the perennial producers and the diversified small-holder farmer strategies) with regard to being HIV/AIDS-affected or not. Significant differences in the proportions of affected households ($p < 0.01$) were, however, observed between each of these two clusters with Cluster 3 (the staples growers strategy). Given the significant difference in household expenditures between the first two clusters (relatively well-off) and the third (poor), differences in HIV/AIDS status may be linked to household resource base and social status.

For further analysis the sample was re-clustered to obtain meaningful groups with which to further investigate the effects of HIV/AIDS in the study population. A number of variables that showed high levels of significance during the clustering of sample households in Chapter 6 were used. These included: household size, total per capita household expenditure, total per capita daily food expenditure, as well as the total acreage under banana and selected annual crops. To further describe the two clusters, age, sex and education of the household head and the proportion of HIV/AIDS-affected households were included. The two clusters obtained showed differences in wealth status. The new Cluster 1, comprising of the relatively well-off, was labeled "Well-off HH", the other, new Cluster 2, which included the relatively poor households, "Poor HH". The results of the analysis are presented in Tables 7.1 and 7.2. No difference is found in the distribution of the categories of Well-off HH and Poor HH between Masaka and Kabarole.

Households in Cluster 1 (well-off) have fewer household members with the mean household size and mean number of adult equivalents (5.7 and 3.6) being less than the overall sample means (6.3 and 4.0). Household heads in this cluster are about seven years younger than those in Cluster 2(poor) and have higher literacy levels. When using household expenditure as a proxy for household incomes, the relatively well-off households have higher mean values for all household expenditure variables used.

Total per capita household expenditure is about three-and-a-half times, total per capita daily food expenditure ten times and the total annual household expenditure three times that of poor households. Well-off HH have larger land acreages with

Table 7.1. Characteristics of the new household clusters: well-off HH and poor HH.

Variables	Cluster 1 (Well-off HH) (N= 167) Mean (SD)	Cluster 2 (Poor HH) (N=374) Mean (SD)	Overall (N= 541) Mean (SD)	T-statistic
Age HH head(years)	38.1(12.4)	45.6 (14.0)	43.3 (13.9)	-5.983***
HH size	5.7 (2.4)	6.6 (2.7)	6.3 (2.7)	-3.554***
Number of adult equivalents	3.6 (1.4)	4.1 (1.6)	4.0 (1.5)	-3.693***
Per capita food expenditure (UGX)	846.96 (1120.63)	86.72 (6.37)	391.19 (699.62)	11.283***
Total per capita HH expenditure	1666.25(1067.81)	481.19 (224.43)	847.00 (827.98)	20.494***
Annual HH expenditure (x100,000 UGX)	20.87 (14.47)	7.28 (4.52)	11.48 (10.86)	177.61***
Acreage under banana	1.29 (1.29)	1.09 (0.96)	1.15 (1.07)	1.973**
Annual crops acreage	1.93 (1.76)	1.53 (1.45)	1.66 (1.56)	2.742***

Source: Household survey.
UGX=Uganda Shillings.
*, **, *** implies significantly different at 10%, 5% and 1% level, respectively.

Tables 7.2. Demographic characteristics and HIV/AIDS affectedness of new clusters.

Variable	Cluster 1 (Well-off HH)		Cluster 2 (Poor HH)		Overall		X^2
	N	%	N	%	N	%	
Education of HH head							
Educated	99	59.3	165	44.1	264	48.8	10.625***
Not educated	68	40.7	209	55.9	277	51.2	
Gender of HH head							
Male	130	77.8	260	69.5	390	72.1	4.336**
Female	37	22.2	114	30.5	151	27.9	
Use of hired labour							
Yes	91	54.5	132	35.3	223	58.8	17.560***
No	76	45.5	242	64.7	318	41.2	
HIV/AIDS status							
Affected	26	15.6	90	24.1	116	21.4	4.947**
Non-affected	141	84.4	284	75.9	425	78.6	

Source: Household survey.
*, **, *** implies significantly different at 10%, 5% and 1% level, respectively.

the mean acreage under banana (1.29 as against 1.09) and selected annuals (1.93 as against 1.53) being higher in Cluster 1 households. This is in addition to having about one-and-a-half times more households using hired agricultural labour. The majority of Cluster 1 households are likely to be male-headed and have a significantly lower likelihood of being HIV/AIDS-affected. Apart from the area under banana production ($p < 0.05$), all other differences are highly significant ($p < 0.01$). Cluster 2 has a higher proportion of HIV/AIDS-affected households, and households in this cluster are poor, and likely to eat and spend less. Despite being poor, they have more mouths to feed. They are more vulnerable than households in Cluster 1.The majority of households in Cluster 2 are headed by people that did not go to school or did not finish. The implication of this is that they are likely to experience more difficulties in responding to stressful circumstances that their households may face. Thus, with or without HIV/AIDS, these are more vulnerable than those in Cluster 1. This preliminary analysis also shows that vulnerability is socially differentiated. A larger proportion of female-headed households belong to Cluster 2.

7.3 Comparison of HIV/AIDS-affected and non-affected households

To analyze HIV/AIDS-related effects on livelihoods in Masaka and Kabarole districts, survey data were analysed to compare HIV/AIDS-affected and non-affected households, both within and between the two clusters, emphasizing the distribution of the three main household resources: labour, income and land. Selected household characteristics among affected and non-affected households are presented in Tables 7.3 and 7.4. Information obtained from group discussions, key informants as well as case studies is then used to further illustrate the epidemic's effects, drawing from people's actual experiences.

7.3.1 Household labour reduction and re-allocation

HIV/AIDS-related labour loss is one of the most important economic impacts of the epidemic. This labour loss strikes the most productive who often are the bread winners (Barnett and Blaike, 1992; FAO, 2002; Gillespie, 2001). While the duration of the time between HIV infection and the onset of full-blown AIDS varies between individuals, eventually the affected individual's labour input gradually diminishes as the person succumbs to illness and finally dies. Thus the effects of HIV/AIDS-

Table 7.3. Selected household characteristics by whether AIDS-affected and by wealth cluster.

HH characteristic	AIDS-affected Mean (SD)	Non-affected Mean (SD)	Overall (n=541) Mean (SD)	T - statistic
Age of HH head (Years)				
Cluster 1(n=167)	41.3 (13.8)	37.5 (12.1)	38.0 (12.5)	-1.447^{NS}
Cluster 2(n=374)	50.1(14.1)	44.1(13.6)	45.6 (14.0)	-3.607***
Household size				
Cluster 1	5.3 (1.7)	5.7 (2.5)	5.7 (2.4)	0.771^{NS}
Cluster 2	6.7 (2.9)	6.5 (2.6)	6.6 (2.7)	-0.554^{NS}
Days bedridden (in two months)				
Cluster 1	26.3 (23.0)	15.2 (15.7)	17.0 (17.4)	-2.672***
Cluster 2	22.6 (22.9)	14.0 (14.9)	16.3 (17.7)	-3.459***
Area planted with banana				
Cluster 1	0.84(0.8)	1.37(1.4)	1.29(1.3)	1.953*
Cluster 2	1.05(0.8)	1.10(1.0)	1.09(1.0)	0.428^{NS}

Source: Household survey.
***,* implies significantly different at 1% and 10% level respectively.
^{NS} implies not significant.

Table 7.4. Selected household characteristics among AIDS-affected and non-affected households.

HH characteristic	AIDS-affected (N=116)		Non-affected (N=425)		Overall (N=541)		X^2
	N	%	N	%	N	%	
Cluster							
Well-off HH	26	22.4	141	33.2	167	30.9	4.946**
Poor HH	90	77.6	284	66.8	374	69.1	
Education of HH Head							
Educated	37	31.9	227	53.4	264	48.8	16.883***
Not educated	79	68.1	198	46.6	277	51.2	
Gender of HH head							
Male	54	46.6	336	79.1	390	72.1	46.412***
Female	62	53.4	89	20.9	151	27.9	
HH reporting an adult death							
Yes	46	39.7	29	6.8	75	13.9	82.259***
No	70	60.3	396	93.2	466	86.1	
District							
Masaka	49	42.2	254	59.8	303	56.0	11.357***
Kabarole	67	57.8	171	40.2	238	44.0	

Source: Household survey.
, * implies significantly different at 5% and 1% level, respectively.

related labour loss are likely to vary depending on whether a household is caring for an HIV-infected member or is coping with the loss of a dead member.

Composition and size of the household are good indicators of household labour availability and productivity. Composition and size of households, therefore, need to be taken into account in the context of HIV/AIDS.

Age of household head

While the relatively well-off households have significantly ($p<0.01$) younger household heads than poor households, differences within each cluster can be observed (Table 7.3). For example, there is no significant difference according to HIV/AIDS status in the mean age of household heads among the relatively well-off households. However, among poor households the mean age of the household head in HIV/AIDS-affected households is significantly higher ($p< 0.01$) than for household heads in non-affected households. This may be explained by the fact that female-headed households constitute the majority of the poor households. And the majority of these women are widows with a higher proportion being HIV/AIDS-affected. This is corroborated by additional information from group discussions in which participants indicated that HIV/AIDS-affected households are headed by older women and grandmothers. The Cases 1.1, 5.8, 5.10 and 5.14 clearly illustrate this.

Whether households headed by older women are affected by HIV/AIDS or not has implications for agricultural production and the livelihood of members in such households given that with advancing age, one's capacity to produce gradually declines. Therefore, the superimposition of HIV/AIDS-related illness on individuals that are already less productive because of old age is likely to further reduce their productivity. Indeed, one of the main reasons for reduced agricultural production mentioned in the focus group discussions held with HIV/AIDS-widows was lack of energy to work because of old age and having no resources to hire labour. Furthermore, survey data show that the proportion of households that reduced the area under agricultural production because of old age is higher among widow-headed (13%) than male-headed (3%) and single-female-headed (8%) households with the difference between widow- and male-headed households being significant ($p < 0.05$).

Household size and composition

Statistical analysis indicates that there is a significant difference ($p < 0.01$) in household size between the well-off and poor households (Table 7.1). However, there are no significant differences in household size between affected and non-affected households among the two groups (Table 7.3). This is contrary to expections, because for both wealth categories the proportion of HIV/AIDS-affected households reporting an adult death is significantly higher ($p < 0.01$) than for non-affected households. Factors such as the stage of life cycle, fertility, mortality, and migration may influence the size of a given household. Empirical evidence shows that the effects of HIV/AIDS on household size may produce several outcomes. Households may become smaller or larger or even dissolve entirely as is described in the literature (Haddad & Gillespie, 2001; Nguthi, 2007; Urassa *et al.*, 2001; Yamano & Jayne, 2004). For this study, the absence of difference in household size between HIV/AIDS-affected and non-affected households may be attributed to the high fertility rates in the study population as well as other people joining the household. Respondents indicate that over 90 percent of new members that joined the sample households between 2002 and 2005 constituted newborn children. This could imply that the net leavers and joiners of households balanced out. Similar to what has been reported elsewhere (World Bank, 1997), the survey results reveal no significant difference in the dependency ratio between HIV/AIDS-affected households and those not affected.

Using the land/labour ratio[54] as an indicator of household labour, no statistically significant differences between HIV/AIDS-affected and non-affected households were found. While this is also unexpected due to higher death rates among affected households, the same reasons as above can be used to explain this finding. However, again differences in land-labour ratios are found to exist between male- and female-headed households with the two types of female-headed households having a significantly lower ($p < 0.01$) land/labour ratio of 1.8 compared to that in male-headed households of 1.2. The changing demographic structure of households because of death affects access to resources and the capacity to respond to different shocks over time. White and Robinson (2000) argued that such households become more vulnerable. The lower land/labour ratios observed among female-headed households show the difficult situations these households are likely to face in providing for their dependants. These constraints coupled with other problems such as disinheritance has made some HIV/AIDS widows and orphans in Uganda to rely more on their extended family or support in the community, a situation that increases their vulnerability since such support is not always guaranteed (Wakhweya *et al.*, 2002).

Effects of sickness of an adult household member

The effect of chronic illness of an adult often results in the ill person's inability to work and this often leads to a shift of other household members labour and time to care for the ill person. Focus group discussions as well as survey data reveal that some of the AIDS-affected adult patients could be bedridden from several months to as long as three years. Rugalema (1999a) estimated that an HIV/AIDS-affected household may have lost about two person-years by the time of death of the patient. In this study, however, it is difficult to make such generalizations because affected individuals experience different syndromes that are likely to cause different levels of incapacitation and hence result in different levels of household labour availability. Besides, with increased knowledge about the disease over the years, particularly improvements in the control of opportunistic infections using both local and conventional western medicine as well as ARVs, there are less cases of prolonged recumbence among affected individuals as used to be the case. As discussed below, a multiplicity of socio-economic and cultural factors determine the progression of the disease when an individual gets infected and, consequently, the extent to which HIV/AIDS-labour-related constraints is experienced across households.

[54] The land-labour ratio can be used as an indicator of household labour. It is calculated as the agricultural area operated to the number of household members that are engaged in farming on a full time basis. The number of adult equivalents engaged in farming was used to correct for age differences in contribution to labour.

Disease intensity in the study area is reported to be high (Appendix 2). Eighty four percent of the respondents reported having at least one sick individual in the two months prior to the survey. Overall, for individuals reported to be sick, duration of sickness was on average three days while in 70 percent of the cases it resulted in a productive household member becoming bedridden. Differences are also observed in the proportions of individuals bedridden, with a higher proportion of HIV/AIDS-affected households (four-fifths) reporting bedridden productive household members than non-affected ones[55] (one-third). There are significant differences ($p < 0.01$) in both poor and well-off households, in the duration of adults reportedly being bedridden. Individuals in non-affected households reported about one week in a month while those in affected households reported about twice as many days of being bedridden. The effects of disease severity due to HIV/AIDS were compared with those of malaria. While malaria (71%) is reported to be the commonest cause of illness, the number of days adult individuals suffering from malaria are bedridden (seven days per month) are significantly less ($p < 0.05$) than those for individuals suffering from HIV/AIDS (ten days per month). The more days an otherwise active adult individual is bedridden by disease, the more household production is affected. Therefore, days lost to sickness are likely to undermine the livelihoods of those affected and their households. The group discussions as well as survey data further show that individuals in AIDS-affected households who reported to be sick were more likely to suffer from additional ailments than those suffering from other diseases in non-affected households. This is because the reduced immunity associated with HIV infections, makes affected individuals more susceptible to opportunistic infections like malaria (Drimie & Gandure, 2005; Stillwaggon, 2006). AIDS-affected women FGD participants also indicated that HIV increases their susceptibility to "fever". These results imply that AIDS is likely to have more severe consequences for household labour availability and productivity than other diseases. The following statements by women focus group participants illustrates the difference in labour-related impacts of AIDS compared to malaria.

> *AIDS is unlike any other disease. At least for other diseases one experiences specific signs. With AIDS, this week it is diarrhoea, the following week, you get pneumonia or a bad cough, then the rushes, joint pains, chronic fevers and general body weakness – the list is unending – it's a life of frustration and suffering. Sometimes the medication fails to control opportunistic infections. (HIV/AIDS-affected woman, Kabarole).*

> *Of course malaria is also problematic, but with it, we walk and continue with our daily business. When you feel unwell, you send a child to buy some*

[55] Comparison is made with non-affected household but which had reported illness due to malaria of at least one household member.

malaraquin or fansida[56] *tablets from the shops and once you take them, then you are o.k. For instance you cannot say that you will not weed your garden because you are suffering from malaria. (Women FGD, Masaka).*

The effects of HIV/AIDS-related labour re-allocation are presented in Table 7.5. The most important effect is the diversion of household labour from productive activities (reported by about half of the respondents). For example, with regard to specific effects on other household members' time, the survey data show that members could lose up to two months away from school or engagement in a productive activity to take care of a sick relative. While for most of the other diseases reported, one's time for caring for a sick member is often limited, with HIV/AIDS one is not sure for how long it will take. Focus group participants also pointed to foregone labour as a result of labour lost because of care as one of the major effects of HIV/AIDS-related morbidity on household labour.

Effects of disease or death on other household members' time were reported by one third of the respondents. Of the households affected in this manner, the following proportions of respondents mentioned spending their time on caring for a sick household member. In 60 percent at least one week was spent on care, 20 percent spent between one-to-two weeks, 10 percent spent between two-to-four weeks, while six percent said they spent one-to-two months away from school or work looking

Table 7.5. Effects of illness on household labour re-allocation (N=510).

	Frequency	Responses (%)
Reduced work time to help family	262	37.3
No change	126	17.9
Worked harder to substitute for lost income	118	16.8
Left job to take care of the sick person	108	15.4
Left school to take care of the sick person	31	4.4
Less attention given to children	20	2.8
Found supplementary job to raise income	15	2.1
Left school to look for work	11	1.6
Helped with family business	8	1.1
No longer goes to garden	3	0.4
Total responses	702	100.0

Source: Household survey.

[56] Malaraquin and fansida are common anti-malarial drugs that are sold in drug shops/stores.

after a sick household member. Withdrawal of labour of other household members from productive activities and children from school is likely to have significant implications for the household's current and future income-generating capacity and food security status. It also compromises children's rights and the overall future human resource capacity of that household.

Effects of a death of an adult household member

An adult death leads to the permanent loss of that member's contribution to production or income. HIV/AIDS is the leading cause of death among the sampled households. The survey data reveal that of the 22 percent of the sample households reporting death of a member, 29 percent reported death due to HIV/AIDS, followed by death due to malaria (23%). With 41.5 percent of all reported spouse deaths due to HIV/AIDS, the disease is also the leading cause of spousal death in the study area.

In addition, AIDS mainly affects people in prime age. For example, comparing households reporting death of a household member, 90 percent of all individuals who died from AIDS or AIDS-related illness were adults (18-45 years of age)[57], while the greater majority (63%) of all individuals who died from malaria (the second commonest cause of death, see Appendix 3) were children below 17. Jayne and Chapoto (2005) note that AIDS differs from other diseases such as malaria, as it appreciably raises the likelihood of subsequent death in the household after one member contracts the disease. Regardless of social status, the proportion of households reporting an adult death (in the period three years prior to the survey) was significantly higher among HIV/AIDS-affected than non-affected households ($p < 0.01$). Effect of spousal death on household well-being is presented in Table 7.6. The challenge of securing a livelihood for one's household because of increased workload (reported by about 40%), feeling of insecurity due to limited survival options (reported by about one third of the widows) and lost education opportunities for children (reported by one-quarter of affected widows) were the commonly mentioned effects of a household head's death. These and the other effects mentioned are indicators of increased impoverishment and vulnerability.

The case studies show mixed effects with regard to AIDS-related death and the well-being of the household. Death releases the time and energy that had been used for caring for the sick household member or looking for medicines as illustrated by Case 5.7. Cases 5.7 and 1.1 illustrate labour reallocation as surviving household members take over the roles and responsibilities of the dead member. Additionally, an AIDS-related death causes changes in household composition. This can be seen in Cases

[57] 50 respondents reported AIDS-related death, other age categories in which death occurred are: less than 17 (4%); 55 to 58 (6%).

Table 7.6. Effects of spousal death on household well-being according to HIV/AIDS-widows(n=36).

Effects on household members	Frequency	Percent responses
Increased workload – looking after household single handed	14	30.4
Limited means of survival – feeling of insecurity and hopelessness	11	23.9
Children dropped out of school	9	19.6
Daughter had to be married off at very early age	4	8.7
Reduced quality of living –poor feeding, clothing, housing	3	6.5
No impact	3	6.5
Loneliness	2	4.3
Total responses	46	100.0

Source: Household survey.

1.1 and 5.8. Therefore, the overall changes in household labour availability and well-being of surviving members depends on how much labour newly joining members can contribute and the loss of labour of those who leave the household.

Focus group participants associated the impact of a woman's death more with reduced household food security and reduced care of the children, particularly those below five years of age. But again, this seems to depend on a variety of factors. This is illustrated by information from interviews with two Kabarole widowers (who never remarried). The one who had young children (5 and 7) indicated that he was not giving the children enough care like his spouse used to do. However, the other widower's children were all above 17 (Case 5.18), so care for the orphans was not a problem. Instead, the children were looking after their father in ensuring that he had a good diet and that he took his daily intake of ARV medication. Information from all discussion groups (men, women and orphaned children) indicated that when men who lose their wives remarry, the new wives usually mistreat their stepchildren. Therefore, factors such as whether a man remarries following his wife's death, the late woman's level of involvement in household food provision, and gender and age of orphaned children are likely to determine the nature and extent of impacts experienced following an adult female death. With regard to effects due the death of a male head, the general conclusion from group discussions (for both men and women) was that it would result in reduced household labour and incomes.

While it is undeniable that infection of an adult is likely to result in more significant household labour shortages compared to when a child is infected, the diversion of labour to the care of affected children also warrants attention. Anazia's experience in

Case 5.14 shows that HIV/AIDS-related child morbidity may equally have significant effects on household labour availability. Women like Anazia are unlikely to work at their full potential when taking care of a sickly child. Tiredness and associated psychological stress further suppress labour output.

Effects of taking on orphans

Orphan households are originally "normal" households that, following the death of one or both parents, transform into single parent-headed or child-headed households. In some cases households were found to take in orphans, while in others a given household provides support to an orphan or a number of orphans who live in another household. The first scenario is more common because it ensures that the key resource, land is not lost.

The proportion of households fostering one or more orphans is about twice as many among HIV/AIDS-affected households than in non-affected ones ($p<0.01$). Furthermore, the mean number of orphans fostered in HIV/AIDS-affected households is about one-and-a half times more than those fostered in non-affected households, ($p<0.01$). Survey data further show that the proportion of households with children below the age of 14 as well as the actual proportions of school-age-going children is slightly higher ($p<0.1$) among widow-headed households than male-headed households.

While the increased burden of care and stretching of household resources associated with taking in orphans has been quoted in much of the AIDS literature, the cases presented in Chapter 5 show that the results are mixed. Factors such as the status, gender, and age of the orphans (Cases 5.8, 5.9 and 5.14), the number of orphans being taken in as well as the resource status of the host household (Case 5.5) influence the nature and magnitude of orphan-related effects. Information obtained from all focus group discussions also revealed that older orphans help with cooking, collecting water, farming and baby sitting, while taking in younger children is associated with increased care requirements. Cases 5.6 and 5.10 show households that have benefited from fostering HIV/AIDS orphans. NGOs in Masaka such as MAHCOP and World Vision provide orphan support in form of secondary and vocational education, food aid, shelter and income generating activities. However, information by key informants (local leaders in Masaka) and mixed group discussions conducted in Masaka revealed that some households access orphan support without the orphans under their care benefiting. In poor households, the existence of NGOs providing orphan-related support may be an incentive to take in orphans and benefit from such support.

Increased burden of care

The foregoing sections clearly show that HIV/AIDS-associated labour reduction and reallocation leads to increased burden of care on other household members. The increased burden of care falls disproportionately on women. Ninety five percent of the respondents indicated that provision of physical nursing care was a woman's (mother, female spouse, or grandmother) job. An earlier study conducted in selected districts in Uganda by Wakweya *et al.* (2002) revealed that 85 percent of single parent-orphan households were headed by females. Nonetheless, 45 percent of the respondents also indicated that men, often the male household heads, provide the money to buy the medication and other things necessary to take care of the patients. Focus group participants indicated that children also help a lot in HIV/AIDS-related care, depending on their age and skills. Usually the older children (boy or girl) are involved but if children are of the same age, the girl child often provides the care since she is expected to have the relevant skills. The confinement of women's labour to the "reproductive economy" (the unpaid economy of domestic work, childcare, and now HIV/AIDS-related care) significantly compromises women's ability to expand their activities or engage in more productive ones. Focus group participants further indicated that not only does HIV/AIDS, increase the burden of care, but the care required is also physically and emotionally taxing as well as psychologically distressing, particularly during the terminal stages when the patient becomes bedridden. The overall effect, is reduced quality of health of the care givers. Cases 1.1, 5.6., 5.7, 5.10 and 5.14 are cases that illustrate this aspect clearly.

Other causes of limited household labour

Constraints in household labour availability predate HIV/AIDS. In fact, despite the high proportions of deaths among HIV/AIDS-affected households, none of the labour indicators are significantly different between affected and non-affected households. Factors such as the young structure of Uganda's population, the low participation of adult men in agricultural activities and the limited access to child labour due to universal primary education are responsible for causing labour constraints in rural areas (cf. Chapters 1 and 2). The limited access to income-generating opportunities in rural areas leading to male rural-urban migration has also been identified as a key factor in declining household labour availability in rural areas. The HIV/AIDS epidemic aggravates existing labour constraints. Households that are labour-poor, female-headed or poor are likely to be most affected. HIV/AIDS-related labour impacts are also likely to vary with the progression of the disease, and the rate at which the affected individual becomes completely incapacitated depends on factors such as the type of syndromes exhibited, previous health status, and ability to access health services and appropriate medication. The extent of impact is also likely to depend on who in the household gets sick or dies, or on the other hand surviving household members' capacities to cope with the effects of the disease, which is also contingent on the household's size, composition, and overall resource status. It is noteworthy that other factors such as kinship relations as well as existing institutions and structures can also influence the household's and individual members' ability to respond to reduced household labour, as will be discussed in the next chapter.

7.3.2 Depletion of household resources

Given the importance of the human resource in the mobilization and use of other resources, the losses in a household's human resource inevitably results in impacts on the household's other resources. In all the twelve case studies on AIDS-affected households, household resources are depleted. However, Cases 1.1, 5.6 and 5.7, clearly illustrate the way in which this takes place. In case 1.1 Jesica loses remittances from her son, while Maria in Case 5.7 loses her late husbands labour and off-farm income. Case 5.6 gives a vivid picture of how different resources, human, financial, physical, and social are run down in a situation of AIDS. Additionally, in all cases investigated, AIDS breaks down social connections through adult death and in Case 5.6 we see reduced community participation as a consequence of AIDS-related stigma. Findings from the survey (Table 7.7) indicate the type of assets sold in distress. These include livestock, poultry, bicycles, radio, food/produce and land when all options are exhausted.

Effects on household incomes and expenditures

HIV/AIDS-related economic impact on households is felt on both income and expenditures. On one hand, incomes that are foregone during periods of prolonged illness and/or untimely death affect the households income status and level of cash in-flow; on the other hand, savings and assets are diverted to meet medical and other related costs (for example, special foods, transport) associated with caring for

Table 7.7. Effects of sickness on household resources (n=158).

	Frequency	% responses
Sold livestock to pay for medical treatment or buy drugs	109	41.4
Financial resources have been rundown	76	28.9
Land has become bushy-not looked after	56	21.3
Sold livestock and chicken to buy food & other basic needs	13	4.9
Land and property taken by relatives after parent died	7	2.7
Others	2	0.8
Total responses	263	100

Source: Household survey.

the sick as well as funeral costs (Wakhweya *et al.*, 2002). This leaves less to spend on other household goods and services.

By retrospective questioning in the survey the respondents' perceptions of changes in household income over the period 2002-2005 was examined. The data reveal no significant difference in the proportions of income change between HIV/AIDS-affected and non-affected households, whether positive or negative (Table 7.8).

The results show no direct linkage between HIV/AIDS status and income changes observed among the survey households. This can partly be explained by some of the reasons mentioned by respondents with regard to increased or reduced household incomes (see sections 6.3.1 and 6.3.2). Apart from the reduction in family labour (which is not significantly different between affected and non-affected households), the other reasons show no direct linkage with HIV/AIDS status. The lack of linkage observed between HIV/AIDS and change in household income corroborates findings of Ainsworth and Semali (1998) and Chapoto and Jayne (2005), who reported that while poverty may increase people's susceptibility to infection or intensify impacts, AIDS affects individuals in all social economic classes.

Depletion of savings (both cash and liquid resources) was mentioned by about two-fifths of the respondents. Items that respondents reported as common household expenditures included health costs, food, school fees, scholastic materials and basic household goods (soap, salt, paraffin and sugar). Other expenditures, though reported to a limited extent, included labour hired for agriculture, agricultural inputs (mainly seeds and veterinary drugs), clothing, and payment of government taxes. As shown in Figures 7.1 to 7.4, the largest household expenses are those on food and medicine. For the majority of HIV/AIDS-affected households in Uganda, household expenditure on health care has increased (Garbus & Marseille, 2003). Because of the lack of a general health insurance, households have no alternative but to use their savings or sell productive assets to meet health costs. In a study conducted in Rakai district, for example, households were found to spend up to one-third of their annual cash income on monthly medical care or a single funeral (Topouzis, 2003). Household expenditure by wealth category and by district is presented in Table 7.9, while expenditure by wealth category and by HIV/AIDS status is presented in Table 7.10. Among poor households a significantly higher proportion reported higher annual and per capita food expenditure in Kabarole than in Masaka, while differences among the well-off are marginal. Differences are observed between HIV/AIDS-affected and non-affected households among the Poor HH with non-affected households having a higher total per capita expenditure than HIV/AIDS-affected households ($p < 0.01$). The total per capita expenditure in HIV/AIDS-affected households is 15 percent lower than in non-affected households (Table 7.10).

Table 7.9. Household expenditure by district.

Variable	Masaka (N= 302)		Kabarole (N=239)		Overall (N=541)		T-Statistic
	Mean	SD	Mean	SD	Mean	SD	
Annualexpenditure[a]							
Cluster 1	21.891	4.358	19.709	8.205	20.872	14.466	-0.972[NS]
Cluster 2	6.828	4.358	7.888	4.664	7.281	4.516	2.258**
Total per capita expenditure							
Cluster 1	1794.80	1319.76	1519.57	653.21	1666.25	1067.82	-1.671*
Cluster 2	461.04	221.82	508.13	225.75	481.19	224.43	2.016**

Source: Household survey.

[a] (X100,000 UGX).

*, ** imply significantly differtent at 10% and 5% level respectively; [NS] implies not significant.

Table 7.10. Household expenditure by whether HIV/AIDS-affected.

HH Characteristic	AIDS-Affected (n=116)		Non -Affected n=425)		Overall (N=541)		T- Statistic
	Mean	SD	Mean	SD	Mean	SD	
Annual expenditure-							
Cluster 1	19.122	10.933	21.194	15.037	20.872	14.466	0.715[NS]
Cluster 2	6.556	4.487	7.511	4.508	7.281	4.516	2.772*
Total per capita expenditure							
Cluster 1	1528.48	760.67	1691.65	1115.57	1666.25	1067.82	0.715[NS]
Cluster 2	424.54	209.70	499.14	226.30	481.19	224.43	2.772***
Per capita food expenditure							
Cluster 1	753.06	886.68	864.27	1160.48	846.96	1120.63	0.464[NS]
Cluster 2	172.04	113.01	192.64	126.11	187.68	123.26	1.384[NS]

Source: Household survey.

*, **, *** imply variables that are significantly different across the row at the 10%, 5% and 1% level, respectively.

[a] (X100,000 UGX).

[NS] implies not significant.

Similarly, analyses from earlier cross country studies on Uganda show that income loss due to HIV/AIDS ranged from 40 to 60 percent in households directly affected (UNAIDS, 1999) and per person income was about 15 percent lower in orphan households and property ownership was significantly less (World Bank, 1997).

A comparison of household expenditure between HIV/AIDS-affected and non-affected households is presented in Figures 7.1 to 7.4. While non-HIV/AIDS affected households have higher mean household expenditures, for the sample as a whole HIV/AIDS-affected households report significantly higher expenditures on medicines ($p < 0.05$) and education ($P < 0.1$) than non-affected households (Figure 7.1). The higher medical expenditures among HIV/AIDS-affected households is as can be expected. The higher expenditure on education among HIV/AIDS-affected households is likely to be associated with other factors like wealth status other than whether a household is affected by HIV/AIDS or not. Since HIV/AIDS affects both the rich and poor, aggregating the sample may be responsible for this result since the majority of HIV/AIDS-affected households are in the Poor HH category. Hence the importance of disaggregating the analysis by wealth status.

Comparison between HIV/AIDS-affected households reporting death of a productive member (63 households) and those with an adult suffering from HIV/AIDS (19 households) is presented in Figure 7.2. Households reporting an AIDS-related adult death spend more significantly ($p < 0.05$) on food than those with an AIDS patient while the latter were likely to spend more on medicines. While the latter is understandable, the first requires some explanation. A first reason may be associated with the fact that HIV/AIDS causes multiple infections in an affected household leading to increased requirement of special nutrition among the surviving household members (see Cases 5.6, 5.10, 5.15 and 5.17). Special nutrition implies more food expenditure to buy foods that are not produced by the household. Information from

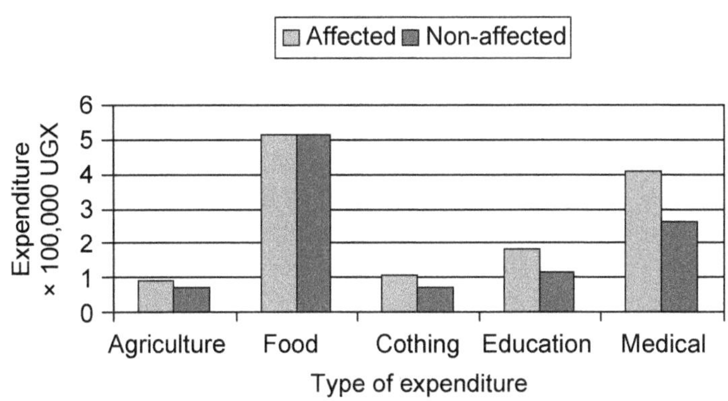

Figure 7.1. Annual HH expenditure by HIV/AIDS status.

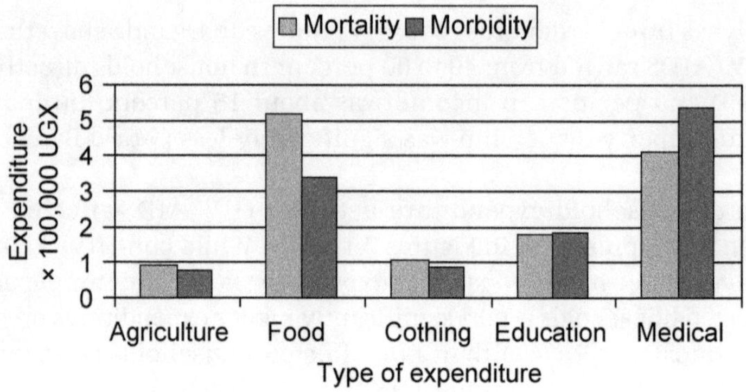

Figure 7.2. Annual HH expenditure among HIV/AIDS HH.

mixed group discussions and discussions with HIV/AIDS infected group participants indicated that infected individuals need to increase their protein and energy intake. According to Piwoz and Preble (2000), people living with HIV/AIDS have increased nutritional requirements in terms of protein (at least 50 percent) and energy (15 percent). However, proteins constitute one of the most expensive groups of foods in rural areas. It is ordinarily consumed only on festive days, especially among poor households. A more regular inclusion of such foods for an ill household member was said to strain already meagre diets and household incomes and resulted in increased food-related expenditures. Secondly, if the dead adult member was contributing significantly to food production, then his or her death may result in the remaining household members' inability to produce enough food and having to depend more on the market (see Cases 5.5 and 5.7). Given the nature of markets in the study area (Chapter 4), dependence on the market increases vulnerability to food insecurity.

In Figures 7.3 and 7.4 HIV/AIDS-affected and non-affected households in the relatively well-off and poor households are compared. As shown in Table 7.10, Figure 7.3 also shows that the relatively well-off households had significantly higher household expenditures than the poor households (Figure 7.4). Apart from medical expenditures there are no statistically significant differences observed in money spent on other household items between HIV/AIDS-affected and non-affected households regardless of wealth status. Among well-off households, for example, non-affected households report even slightly higher medical expenditures than affected-households ($p < 0.1$). However, among poor households the differences in medical expenditures between affected and non-affected households are more pronounced. HIV/AIDS-affected poor households have significantly higher medical expenditures than non-affected poorer households ($p < 0.05$). Expenditure increases associated with problems that create heightened vulnerability, such as expenditure on curative health care or increased food purchases due to inability to produce

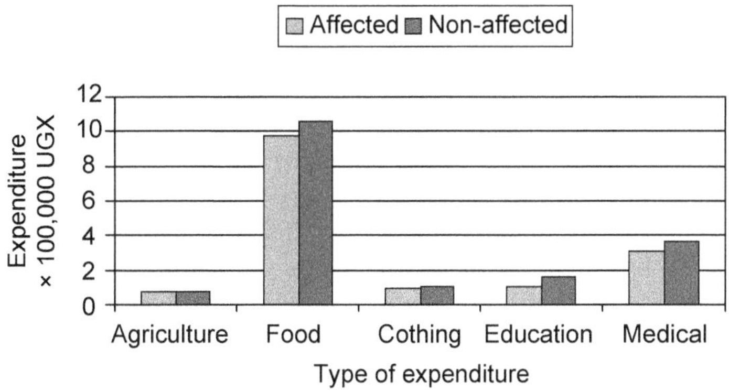

Figure 7.3. Expenditure by HIV/AIDS status in well-off HH.

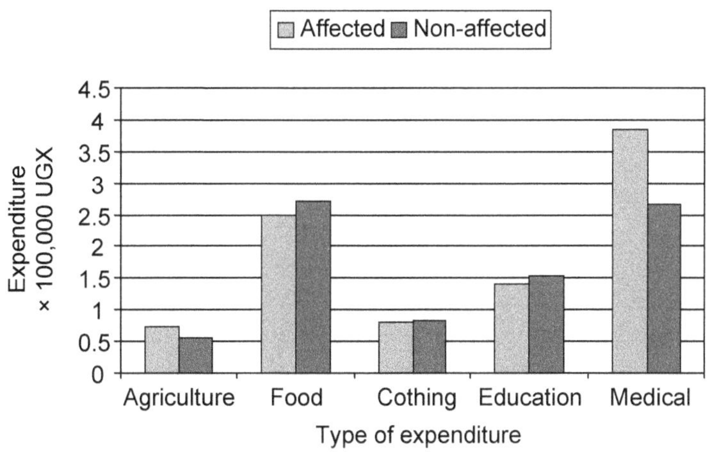

Figure 7.4. Expenditure by HIV/AIDS status in poor HH.

adequate food for own consumption should not be mistaken to mean improved well-being among affected households.

Further analysis of within cluster differences reveals that single-female-headed households had the least medical expenditure regardless of HIV/AIDS status. Additionally, among the HIV/AIDS-affected households, widow-headed households reported a significantly lower expenditure on clothing than male-headed households while among those not-affected, expenditure on food among widow-headed households was also lower than that for their male counterparts ($p < 0.10$ in both cases). These findings show that with or without AIDS, some household types, particularly female-headed households, already have little money to spend. HIV/AIDS is likely to further aggravate such constraints.

The poor usually rely on informal credit or group-based micro-finance products in times of distress. Unfortunately these types of services tend to be spatially concentrated and, hence, are vulnerable to aggregate shocks (Gillespie *et al.*, 2001). Gillespie *et al.* (2001) further argue that even when the epidemic is in its early stages, affected households are more prone to default and hence become less attractive to group-based liability schemes. Among surveyed households, no differences in access to credit are observed between affected and non-affected households (less than three percent of the respondents had access to credit). However, information obtained from group discussions with HIV/AIDS-affected individuals indicate that community members were reluctant to lend them money for fear that it would be paid back late or not at all.

Change in household assets

HIV/AIDS-affected households have been said to possess fewer physical resources because of the increased expenditure needs associated with HIV/AIDS-related care and funeral expenses that necessitate household resources to be converted to cash (Ekaas, 2003; FAO, 2003). In this study, HIV/AIDS-related effects vary with social-economic status. However, even within the same socio-economic category, differences are mixed and sometimes observed for particular resources and not for others. Nonetheless, survey data show that HIV/AIDS-affected poor households experience more significant reductions in land, small animals and chicken than non-affected poor households over the period under investigation. When household incomes drop below expenditures, households have no alternative but to cash assets and savings to meet their increased needs.

The reasons for change in small livestock and poultry are presented in Table 7.11. Mentioned by 40 percent of the respondents, small animals (goats and pigs) and poultry are the most commonly depleted household assets for purposes of obtaining food and health services. Twenty percent of the respondents reported selling land to buy food and pay for health services, while about half this proportion said they had to sell their cattle for the same reasons. There is evidence indicating that households attempt to first sell small animals and assets with the least impact on long-term production potential (Jayne *et al.*, 2005), and that land is the last asset that is disposed of in case of severe stress (IP & FAO, 2003). The higher proportions of respondents reporting sale of small animals compared to those selling cattle and land obtained in this study corroborates this. However, the higher proportion of respondents reporting land sales compared to those reporting cattle sales, is unexpected. This may be attributed to the fact that only 24 percent of households owned cattle while over 95 percent owned land. In this case, although the decision

Table 7.11. Reasons for change in small livestock and poultry numbers (N=541).

Reasons for reduction in numbers	Frequency	% response
Death due to pests and disease	233	38.1
Sold to buy food	120	19.6
Sold to pay for medical expenses	96	15.7
Sold to pay for school fees	58	9.5
Sold to buy other household assets (radio, bicycle)	48	7.8
Animals/chicken stolen	30	4.9
Sold them because couldn't afford to feed them	18	2.9
Others[a]	9	1.5
Total responses	612	100.0

Source: Survey data.
[a] other responses included; given as gifts to children, sold to pay for labour, sold because no space to keep the animals.

is likely to compromise future livelihood security, some people had to resort to selling their land.

Similar findings on asset depletion have been reported by the IP & FAO (2003) study conducted in Uganda. Asset depletion compromises the future survival capacity of those left behind. As Jayne *et al.* (2005) argue, the cumulative effect of asset depletion may cause a decline in the capability of small-scale farmers to produce a marketable surplus from farming.

Data on change in household assets (land, livestock and chicken) between 2002 and 2005 were collected. For the sake of brevity, Table 7.12 only presents assets for which there was a significant change over the study period. No differences are observed between HIV/AIDS-affected and non-affected households among the well-off households with regard to changes in the number of cattle and land owned. However, for the poor households, there was a slight reduction in land acreage owned among affected households, while non-affected households reported a slight increase in land acreage over the period ($p<0.1$). Additionally, affected poor households reported a mean increase in the number of cattle owned while non-affected ones reported a decrease, the difference being significant ($p<0.05$).

This is contrary to what would be expected but may be explained by (i) the reported high deaths of animals due to diseases and (ii) the presence of NGOs giving livestock to HIV/AIDS-affected households in the study area. As would be expected, affected

Table 7.12. Change in household assets by HIV/AIDS status between 2002-5.

Type of asset change	AIDS-Affected (n=116) Mean(SD)	Non-Affected (n=425) Mean(SD)	Overall (N=541) Mean(SD)	T-Statistic
Well-off HH				
Change in land (n=163)	-0.03 (0.15)	0.11(2.63)	0.09 (2.42)	0.267^{NS}
Change in cattle (n=43)	0 (0.71)	-1.18(2.87)	-1.07(2.78)	-0.805^{NS}
Change in small livestock (n=165)	-0.96(2.89)	-0.87(4.50)	-0.88(4.28)	-0.101^{NS}
Poor HH				
Change in land (n=364)	-0.13 (1.67)	0.13 (0.93)	0.07 (1.15)	1.830*
Change in cattle (n=79)	-0.81(3.41)	-1.36(4.33)	-1.22(4.09)	-0.528^{NS}
Change in small Livestock (n=374)	-1.72(4.03)	-0.35(3.93)	-0.68(4.00)	2.874***

Source: Household survey.
^{NS} implies not significant.
*, *** imply variables that are significantly different across the row at the 10%, and 1% level, respectively.

households reported significantly more reduction in small livestock numbers than non-affected households regardless of wealth status ($p<0.05$).

The impact of spousal death on household resources according to AIDS widows is presented in Table 7.13. Asset depletion and reduced household labour availability feature as the most important effects reported by the majority of affected widows. Only four out of the 36 HIV/AIDS widows said that the spouse's death had no significant impact on household resources.

7.3.3 HIV/AIDS impacts on agricultural activities

The impacts of the epidemic at household level have a direct effect on agricultural production and food security through a reduction in family labour and time allocated to farming (Barnett & Blaikie, 1992; Mutangadura *et al.*, 1999; Shapouri & Rosen, 2001). Among the surveyed households, abandoning of land due to limited labour was mentioned by one third of the respondents. Furthermore, 40 percent of respondents reported delayed implementation of agricultural activities as a result of ill-health-related labour shortages. And 16 percent reported an increase in prevalence and spread of plant and animal diseases. Selected banana management practices and access to hired labour and extension services, among the sampled households are presented in Tables 7.14 and 7.15.

Table 7.13. Impact of spousal death on household resources according to AIDS widows (n=36).

	Frequency	Responses(%)
Sold assets (land, livestock, bicycle) to pay hospital bills and debts, school fees and other household needs	19	39.6
Reduced household lablour & increased workload – leading to reduced production and income from agriculture	10	20.8
Land and livestock taken by late spouse's relatives	12	25.0
None	4	8.3
Depreciation of assets which cannot be replaced or repaired: house collapsed because of lack repair, children's mattresses very old.	3	6.3
Total responses	48	100

Source: Household survey.

Apart from the use of hired labour, there is no significant difference between well-off and poor households in terms of implementation of water and soil management practices, mulching, use of clean banana planting materials, access to credit and extension services (Table 7.15). The lack of significant difference with regard to mulching, use of clean planting materials or access to services (Tables 7.14 and 7.15) can be explained by the local situation where there is limited availability of mulching and clean planting materials and access to extension and credit services, as mentioned in over 60 percent of the focus group discussions (men and women's FGDs).

Table 7.14 shows that there are mixed differences between affected and non-affected households in terms of the banana management practices. It is important to note that no differences in the implementation of banana management practices are observed by gender of the household head or between affected and non-affected households among the well-off households. A slightly higher proportion of non-affected poor households in Masaka use clean banana planting materials ($p<0.10$) than HIV/AIDS-affected households. Implying the possible diversion of resources in HIV/AIDS-affected households and leaving few resources to purchase planting materials. An unexpected finding is the significantly higher proportion of poor HIV/AIDS-affected households in Kabarole ($p<0.05$) applying soil and water management practices than non-affected households. Since this is a highly labour intensive activity one would expect HIV/AIDS labour constrained households to have abandoned implementation of soil management practices. No direct explanations could be obtained for this result. It might be that, since the banana farming households surveyed had plantations older than three years, it is possible

Table 7.14. Banana management practices and access to services by HIV/AIDS status.

	HIV/AIDS-Affected (N=116)		Non-Affected (N=425)		Overall (N= 541)		X^2
	N	%	N	%	N	%	
Soil conservation methds							
Yes	45	38.8	121	28.5	166	30.7	4.565**
No	71	61.2	304	71.5	375	69.3	
Use clean planting materials.							
Yes	22	19.0	54	12.7	76	14.1	2.957*
No	94	81.0	371	87.3	465	85.9	
Mulching							
Yes	22	19.0	105	24.7	127	23.5	1.672^{NS}
No	94	81.0	320	75.3	414	76.5	
Controls pests & disease							
Yes	37	31.9	105	24.7	142	26.3	2.434^{NS}
No	79	68.1	320	75.3	320	73.7	
Used hired labour							
Yes	44	37.9	179	42.1	223	41.2	0.659^{NS}
No	72	62.1	246	57.9	318	58.8	
Access to formal credit							
Yes	15	12.9	38	8.9	53	9.8	1.642^{NS}
No	101	87.1	387	91.1	488	90.2	
Access to extension							
Yes	43	37.1	240	56.5	283	52.3	13.750***
No	73	62.9	185	43.5	258	47.7	

Source: Survey data.
*, **, *** imply variables that are significantly different across the row at the 10%, 5% and 1% level, respectively.
^{NS} implies not significant.

that implementation of soil and water management amounted to just maintenance of existing structures. The more hilly terrain in some parts of Kabarole compared to Masaka also makes it inevitable to use soil conservation methods.

No significant differences are observed between HIV/AIDS-affected households and non-affected ones in terms of change in crops grown, area under agricultural production, and change in agricultural incomes. The only difference is in change in crop yields with a significantly higher proportion ($p < 0.05$) of non-affected households

Table 7.15. Banana management practices implemented and access to services by wealth status.

	Well-off HH(N=167)=		Poor HH (N=374)		Overall (N= 541)		X^2
	N	%	N	%	N	%	
Soil conservation methds							
Yes	53	31.7	113	30.2	166	30.7	0.126^{NS}
No	114	68.3	261	69.8	375	69.3	
Mulching							
Yes	32	19.2	95	25.4	127	23.5	2.502^{NS}
No	135	80.8	279	74.6	414	76.5	
Use clean plating materials							
Yes	29	17.4	47	12.6	76	14.1	2.202^{NS}
No	138	82.6	327	87.4	465	85.9	
Used hired labour							
Yes	91	54.5	132	35.3	223	58.8	17.560***
No	76	45.5	242	64.7	318	41.2	
Access to formal credit							
Yes	14	8.4	39	10.4	53	9.8	0.546^{NS}
No	153	91.6	335	89.6	335	90.2	
Access to extension							
Yes	93	55.7	190	50.8	283	52.3	1.105^{NS}
No	74	44.3	184	49.2	258	47.7	

Source: Survey data.
*** implies variables that are significantly different across the row at the 1% level.
^{NS} implies not significant.

reporting increased yields than HIV/AIDS-affected ones. Also, a significantly higher proportion of Well-off HH ($p<0.01$) obtained incomes from sale of agricultural produce than poor households. Household level analysis reveals that the two types of female-headed households had about 1.3 times less land under annual crops than male-headed households ($p<0.01$). This may also be attributed to the fewer number of active adults in female-headed households than male-headed ones. In another study carried out in three Ugandan villages, Dolan (2002) notes that while female heads expressed a desire to cultivate new crop varieties, the majority cannot do so because of lack of resources to purchase inputs and hire agricultural labour.

Rural households tend to utilize, among others, off-farm income to purchase agricultural inputs and hire labour for farm production (Reardon *et al.*, 1995; Marenya *et al.*, 2003). However, Yamano & Jayne (2004) note that these sources of income are often jeopardized among AIDS-affected households, particularly among the asset-poor ones. Cash constraints for increasing farm production are further compounded by illness and death, when medical and funeral expenses rise and care-giving reduces income-earning potential (Jayne *et al.*, 2005). From the results obtained in this study, the effects on household income are significant among poor households. Furthermore, evidence from the IP survey (IP & FAO, 2003), shows that for the case of Uganda, the following could be observed for all households affected by HIV/AIDS: a substantial decrease in the amount of money spent on farm equipment and agricultural inputs; reduced uptake of recommended agronomic practices, such as row and line spacing, appropriate depths, compost and manure making; the storage and use of seed for sowing rather than the purchase of costly high-yielding varieties; and infrequent hire of tractors for preparing land. In this study, household expenditure on agricultural inputs is very limited, and no differences could be observed between HIV/AID-affected and non-affected households.

Finally in Table 7.14, the proportion of HIV/AIDS-affected households accessing agricultural extension services is about one-and-a-half times less than that of non-affected households ($p < 0.01$). These differences were found to be more significant among poor households ($p < 0.010$) implying that while the poor have limited access to extension services, those that are HIV/AIDS-affected have even less. It is noteworthy that the situation is worse for female-headed households which are three times more likely to be HIV/AIDS affected and about one-and-a half times less likely to have access to agricultural extension services than male-headed households.

7.4 HIV/AIDS effects on intra-household relations

This section presents findings from the qualitative data on HIV/AIDS-related impacts on intra-household relations among the study population. The data are based on experiences and perceptions obtained from group discussions held with HIV/AIDS-affected and non-affected individuals, as well as individual interviews with those affected and AIDS orphans. As William (2003:127) notes, the provision of support is a function of cultural norms and inter-generational relationships, together with economic situations to offer this support of those who are supposed. In the following sections, the ways HIV/AIDS affect the roles of different individuals within the household and how this in turn affects or changes intra-household relations are discussed.

7.4.1 Relationship between spouses

The marital relationship is expected to be a source of support for both the husband and wife throughout life until the death of either one partner or separation results in ending the relationship. Partners in a marriage tend to have different roles in household management. In Uganda, a man is expected to meet the financial needs of his household while the woman's duties involve provision of food for her household, bearing children and caring for household members.

In a situation of HIV/AIDS, the effects of chronic illness of one of the partners implies that the "still healthy" partner may take over the spouse's roles and sometimes be forced to seek external support from relatives to help with the increased work load and care-related needs. The failure to perform one's expected role as a consequence of disease induces changes in the inter-personal relations between the spouses.

The social norms that give men authority as the household head also expect them to cover their household's needs. In a situation of HIV/AIDS, this authority seems to be declining. Male group participants said that AIDS erodes one's authority as a household head. Because one cannot provide for one's household, the woman and children stop respecting you. Some men mentioned that women mistreat their ailing spouses accusing them of bringing AIDS into the family. One male participant said: "Sometimes women are very ruthless; if you become very sick and she thinks that you will not recover, she abandons you. She even makes your children hate you. This is particularly so if you are poor and the woman sees that there is even nothing to benefit from you after your death."

Information from discussions with both men and women revealed that following a spouse's death, some women take their children to their spouse's relatives, usually the grandmothers and leave them there (see Case 1.1). Two incidences were quoted where women wanted to poison their spouses in order to take the property. In addition to neglect and mistreatment, men also reported experiencing violence from their wives, mostly in the form of verbal abuse. In fact, some men gave this as one of the reasons that they never reveal their HIV/AIDS status to their spouses, because of the resulting likelihood of strained relations and harassment.

Separate discussions with women confirmed strained gender relations, characterized by mistrust, tension, disharmony and violence in the home. Female focus group participants reported violence in the form of verbal abuse, battery, sexual harassment, rape, psychological abuse and even homicide. In a couple of focus group discussions in Masaka, women mentioned being restricted from accessing medication because the spouse did not want other people to know that the couple had AIDS. Furthermore, all the eleven HIV/AIDS-affected women with whom in-depth interviews were held, said that the men refused to use condoms. One affected woman said "When a man falls sick first, he does not want to die alone. He will make sure that he infects you. Even if you do not want sex he will force you."

Alcoholism and a man's perception that the wife is no longer looking after him were raised as a cause of increased violence. In households where men consume alcohol, women experienced more violence. The Banyankole, Banyarwanda, Bakiga and Batoro were identified as ethnic groups which consume a lot of alcohol and are also known for domestic violence. Men from these ethnic groups said that taking alcohol is an expression of being a man and also gives social status: "Men drink". A man who has the money to buy others alcohol is held in high regard. From my personal observations, some cases of alcoholism, particularly among the poor, have no linkage with the aspiration to be called "a man" but can be better explained by or associated with frustration and disillusionment. This corroborates information obtained from focus group discussions with HIV-affected men in Masaka, who indicated that taking alcohol helps drowning the worries associated with AIDS, even when one is on medication and health personnel have advised not to do so. For others the shame of failure to provide for their household makes them take on drinking.

There was a consensus among female group participants that most of the violence occurs when women attempt to question their husband about issues of infidelity and the associated problems of HIV/AIDS. They said that they would fear to talk about HIV/AIDS with their spouse even if they suspected that one of them was sick. Sometimes a woman fears to propose to go for HIV/AIDS testing because the man could easily accuse her of infidelity. When asked whether they would like to know their HIV status, responses were mixed. However, all agreed that in their situation knowledge may not be useful because they would still have to live with their husbands anyway. Others said that knowing one's status just causes worries, particularly if one is poor and cannot even afford drugs. Moreover, if the man knows that his wife has gone for an HIV test, he may even divorce the wife saying that she has been unfaithful. Yet again the majority said they cannot deny sex to an unfaithful husband because it only leads to violence or divorce. Besides, they believe, that a married woman should not deny her husband sex. "Then why would you have got married?", said one female focus group participant. The following statement exemplifies women's powerlessness with regard to control over their reproductive health and sex, a situation that will continue to put women at risk of infection: "We have nothing to do, even if you know that this man is unfaithful, you have to give him sex when he demands it. What is even worse is that they (the men) do not want to use condoms when they know that they are sick. These men are going to kill us, that is, if they have not yet infected us!" Case 6.10 also illustrates women's powerlessness and subordinate situation.

One wonders why despite the fact that women are aware of the risks, they would still remain married. When asked about this, some elderly woman considered the question to exhibit ignorance of the reality of women's circumstances. She said:

> *Where do you want us to go? One is not welcome at one's natal home. With no education and skills, one can only expect to depend on men. Besides, even if one separated from her unfaithful husband, one would still need to get another man to take care of one's needs. However, we are old and those prospects are limited! Then, there is the issue of children, one would not leave one's children to suffer.*

So, while they are aware of the risk of infection, to these women, marriage offers assurance of livelihood, at least, shelter and land to grow food. That counts more than the fear of being infected by one's spouse and later dying of AIDS. As Meer *et al.* (1997) rightly note, in cases where a woman's access to resources depends on her relationship to a man, then married women are often forced to remain in problematic or even violent relationships in order to secure the income and other resources vital to their own and their children's survival. In a 1992 report, the United Nations observed that "for most women, the major risk factor for HIV infection is being married" (UNDP, 1992). However, as Farmer (1996) rightly argues, it is not marriage per se, that places women at risk, but rather the ways by which social forces, such as gender inequality and poverty interact and become transformed into risk factors for HIV infection.

Also to men, a woman's position in the marital relationship depends on whether she is able to fulfil her marital obligations. In this regard, HIV/AIDS-related infertility becomes a problem to women. For young women the inability to produce children means that you have failed as a woman as illustrated in Case 20. The man may divorce you and marry another woman. It is very problematic when a woman succumbs to AIDS earlier than her husband, in which case she cannot even be productive on the farm or look after her husband. In such cases, focus group participants said that such a woman is sent to her parent's home if she cannot look after herself or get a relative that can come to help look after her. But in most cases the woman goes to her parents' home where the man may periodically send her some financial help (Case 5.19). The cases where the woman is infected almost all result in divorce or separation. However, when the man is infected, often the woman stays and nurses him, providing care even amidst violence and risking infection herself (Case 5.10).

Discussions with health personnel and local leaders also indicated that HIV/AIDS results in unhealthy marital relations. "There is no trust between couples these days. Men start on ARVs but do not tell their wives. Some women are also on HIV/AIDS treatment but they keep their drugs with neighbours so that their husband does not find out", one elderly village chairman revealed during an interview. Cases where a man secretly sells his land to raise money for treatment without the spouse knowing it (although this is against the law), were also reported. In Cases 5.6 and 5.10, while Kamurari did not sell his land, he refused his wife access to a sufficient portion of it to sustain her and her orphaned grandsons. In this case we see that marriage may not necessarily guarantee a woman access to sufficient resources. Even before Kamurari dies, his brother and the villagers are aware of the woman's situation and there is no way she can have access to more land upon her husband's death. While one should not underestimate the role of in-laws in property grabbing, it is important to note that a man's failure to protect his wife's and children's property rights either by writing of a will or declaring his interests before elders, may indeed cause the in-laws to claim such property.

7.4.2 Relationship between children and parents

Intergenerational support is a two-way process. Parents take care of their children when they are young and when these children grow up, they are expected to take care of their aging parents. In the past, in addition to socialization, parents just had to ensure that their children had enough to eat to remain healthy. In recent times, they also must provide for their children health care, descent clothing and school fees for an extended number of years. From both men and women focus group discussions, parents feel obliged to support their children when they are young as well as provide some inheritance (at least to boys). Information from focus group discussions with children revealed that children expect their parents to look after them (sometimes taking it for granted). Furthermore, a social norm states that children have to respect their parents in order to enjoy their parents' support or else risk losing their inheritance or being disowned. For example, in the past a son had to be obedient to his father to keep entitled to his part of inheritance, these days the son needs to have his school fees paid. In the case of a daughter, in the past she had to be obedient to avoid her father disowning her while these days, additionally, she may fear losing the opportunity for education. Young and unmarried children living with their parents are expected to participate in domestic chores as well as help with farm work, depending on the sex and age of the children and their capacity.

The depletion of household resources by HIV/AIDS has affected parents' capability of being good parents, particularly among the poor. At the same time, the disease has also changed children's expectations of their parents' support. Not only are parents failing to support their children, but in addition, children are being required to support their families at a very early age. The lack of income and employment opportunities in the rural areas have sometimes driven children to migrate to urban areas to look for employment, which has resulted in loss of parental control and guidance over children's activities. Women focus group participants indicated that even children living with their parents become less respectful because there is hardly any support from their parents. "When they say they want to go and look for employment, you cannot refuse them, because you know they want shoes that you cannot provide," said one woman. They also revealed that single mothers and widows faced bigger challenges than parents in conjugal relationships. Consequently, there was a general agreement in all men and women's focus group discussions of a trend of decreasing morals among the young. However, this is not limited to children but has been observed among adults as well. As one district level woman representative said, "while in the past women used to advise their daughters to remain virgins till marriage, because of poverty some women coach their daughters to actively look for potential husbands." Thus, failure of poor parents to provide for their children because of HIV/AIDS-related impoverishment may eventually change children's attitudes towards supporting their elderly parents and relatives. There is need to investigate whether the reduced remittances from migrant family members (mentioned by the majority of households with members who had migrated) is not related to a change in social norms of reciprocity.

Among the well-off households, group participants raised other causal factors for changes in the relationship between parents and children. Among them are the exposure to new ways of thinking through education, which at times portray African culture and values to be backward, the concept of children's rights, which is foreign to the African way of socializing children, and exposure to Western films, movies and pornography. These factors have been responsible for increased engagement in sex at an early age, and taking alcohol and hard drugs which are associated with increased risk of exposure to HIV/AIDS. These changes are being seen not only among children of the affluent but also the poor. However, for poor children who drop out of school at lower levels and have no money to go to movies, such factors play a lesser role compared to those induced by poverty. Nonetheless, the values of the younger generation are diverting from those of their parents, supposedly leading to decline of social morals and cohesion.

Ideally when a child became of age, their parents would support them to get married after which they would be expected to start looking after their parents. Considering child support to parents, the social norms regarding these relationships can even be inferred from some proverbs. For example:

"*Orume kurukura rwonka abaana barwo*" Literaly meaning: when a rabbit grows old it suckles its young. (Runyankole/Rukiga). A similar one exists among the Baganda.

"*Olukula luyonka 'baana!*" Literary. "Old people suck from their children!"

HIV/AIDS-related mortality of young productive adults who normally would have been the providers for their families and their aging parents has changed parents' expectations. This is illustrated by several cases already discussed (Cases 1.1, 5.6 and 5.9). Thus, the old people now have no one to look after them and are also over-burdened with orphans. Parents are sometimes the source of care for their children even when they are terminally ill with AIDS (Case 1.1). The plight of grandmother-headed households in HIV/AIDS situation has been well elaborated by Nguthi (2007).

Focus group discussions and case study information showed that children still provide critical support to parents, except that they now do so at a much younger age. Children were said to completely take over household tasks when the mother is AIDS-affected and cannot do much work. When parents are on ARVs children remind them to take the drugs. Sometimes children sacrifice their own food for their sick parent. Many orphans look for employment and support their families by buying basic necessities like paraffin oil, salt, food and sauce. However, such children do this at the expense of their education and their future.

While the general trend was that whenever resources allowed, parents and children worked to support each other in dealing with the effects of HIV/AIDS, cases of conflict and absence of support were evident, though to a limited extent. According to key informants, in some cases, parent's have refused to look after their AIDS-affected children or take in their children because of the feeling that the affected individuals brought the problem on themselves and possibly because in the first place parents never appreciated their child's life style. For example, if parents think that their daughter got AIDS through prostitution, then they may refuse to offer support. Some feared taking in their sick children because of fear of the cost and responsibilities that it would entail, while for others, fear was associated with the stigma attached to having an AIDS patient in the family. In the latter case, some people would prefer the sick individual to go to another relative from where they could send him or her the necessary support. Cases of children being unruly, disrespectful, not participating in any household activity or leaving home altogether were also mentioned by focus group participants and local community leaders.

7.4.3 Relationships between orphaned children and other household members

Twenty-two percent of all children in the sample population lived with a relative other than the biological parents and many orphans, particularly double orphans, lived in such relationships. In over 50 percent of the cases, the children were living with a grandmother. The narratives were mixed, some being positive while others tended to child abuse. For example, about half of the orphans that participated in the focus group discussions indicated that they were very grateful to the relatives who had taken them in and offered them opportunity for education, though in many cases this ceased because of limited resources. Children used statements like "my grandmother has been good to me", "supportive", "comforting", "nice", "gives me advice", indicating a good relationship between the children and those who had taken them in. However, orphaned children also revealed that they experience discrimination. For example, they do more household chores and heavy activities than the biological children, sometimes eat less or miss meals when meals are served in their absence (cf. Cases 5.12 and 5.13). Some also said they suffered stigmatization, as is well illustrated by Agnes' situation (Case 5.13).

Key informants also described the poor conditions and discrimination that orphaned children sometimes experience. In a number of cases, orphans are taken in by host households just for purposes of exploiting their labour. Gender may be a factor, with girls being taken in for domestic activities. In such cases rarely is money spent on clothing and provision of other material needs of the children. Children also have limited power and control over the products of their labour as one Masaka orphan aged 17 related:

> *I asked my uncle to give me a small piece of land where I could grow some beans to raise money to pay for my school fees because my uncle had told me that he could no longer afford to pay for me. He gave me about half an acre of his second piece of land that is three kilometers from home. I planted beans and maize. After harvest, I gave my aunt one debe*[58] *of beans to use at home. However, before I could sell the other maize and beans, my uncle said that I should give it to him to sell and he would bring the money to me. I have never received that money and its now over a year. Every time I ask him he just says he has problems and he will refund it when he gets money. I got very disappointed because I had hoped to use that money for my school fees.*

Some relatives were said to take in orphans with a view of using them to access NGO support. However, according to key informants in Masaka, after such support is obtained many orphans have been denied access to it. Yet because of their inferior position in the household, the affected children cannot complain.

Therefore, the relationship between orphans and other relatives may be characterized by mutual support, but also by discrimination, conflict and exploitation, with the latter three scenarios seemingly dominant according to the qualitative data. The high dependence of orphans on other people for their livelihood makes them powerless and vulnerable. The age at which one becomes an orphan, double orphanhood, coming from a very poor background and having very limited options of support,

[58]One *debe* is equivalent to about 18 kg.

determine the extent of vulnerability and the intensity of orphanhood-related effects.

7.4.4 Relationship between married women and mothers-in-law

Situations where a woman lives in the same house or compound with her mother-in-law are not common in the study area. Even where it occurs, in the majority of the cases the two women cook separately. While the relationship between women and their mother-in-law varies, from women's focus group discussions, it can be inferred that it is often not a good one. The level to which a mother-in-law can exert control over her daughter-in-law depends on their relationship, the relationship between the mother-in-law and her son, the age of the married woman and the level of dependence of the couple on the mother-in-law or the nature of support that can be expected from her and other in-laws. For example, in situations where mother and son are very close or the daughter-in-law is very young or the couple significantly dependent on the mother-in-law, the mother-in-law exercises a lot of control over the daughter-in-law's activities and decisions. However, in situations where the couple is independent, the married woman is economically independent and having a good relationship with her husband, the mother-in-law's influence on household affairs is limited. Therefore depending on prevailing circumstances, HIV/AIDS may strengthen or weaken the power relations between women in the same household as Anazia's case (Case 5.14) clearly illustrates.

The case of Anazia is an example showing that not all women in male-headed households have the same access and power over resources. While gender theory often relates women's lack of access to resources to their subordinate position to men, the case shows that some women can limit and control other women's access to resources. Anazia believes that all the misfortune that has befallen her is because her mother-in-law forced her to leave her home and engage in a livelihood that created a risky environment for her children.

In Case 5.10, Veronica says that her widowed daughter-in-law does not respect her. She does not even care whether Veronica sees her with other men because they offer her a source of livelihood which Veronica cannot afford. In one interview in Kabarole, a widower told us about his widowed daughter-in-law who had three other children since her husband died, all from different men. Though the woman lives in the same compound with her father-in-law, the latter has no control over her activities because he is poor and the woman mainly gets support from her natal home and her male friends. According to the qualitative data, in the past the behaviour exhibited by the two widows would not be acceptable, regardless of whether your in-laws support you or not. In Cases 1.1, 5.4 and 5.9, however, we see relationships that are supportive. Old women supporting their daughters-in-law with childcare and looking after orphans. Survey data also reveal that in about eight percent of the households, parents sent their older children to go and visit and help their old grandparents with domestic work while in 14 percent of the households grandmothers helped out with looking after children. Therefore, whatever undercurrents may exist between women and mothers-in-law, the importance of old women for childcare support and fostering orphans in the era of AIDS cannot be over-emphasized.

7.5 Linking HIV/AIDS, wealth status and livelihood security

7.5.1 Determinants of livelihood security

Model specification

To identify determinants of livelihood security among the surveyed households, I have used per capita household expenditure instead of income as a proxy for livelihood security. This is because household income data has been widely criticised in literature to be marred with high measurement errors than expenditure data and respondents are more willing to give information on their expenditure than their income (cf. Chapter 3)

The statistical model used here is the OLS estimator (Ordinary Least Squares)since the dependent is continuous and has no truncation or censoring data as each respondent spent some money .(Gujarati, 1988). The empirical model (equation) is specified as below:

$$\text{PERCAPEXP} = B_0 + B_1X_1 + B_2X_2 + B_3X_3 + \dots B_{14}X_{14} + \varepsilon \qquad \text{Equation 7.1}$$

Where: PERCAPEXP is the dependent variable indicating the daily per capita expenditure in US$ and the Xs are the explanatory variables with a stochastic error term (ε) that measures any unobserved heterogeneity not captured by the observed factors. The explanatory variables are defined in Table 7.16.

A Chow Test was done to test whether there was an equality of coefficients for the two districts, this null hypothesis was rejected indicating that there is a difference between the coefficients of Kabarole and Masaka districts hence I presented the results for each district and also the pooled results to compare the consistency and robustness of the results. These results are presented in Table 7.17 Overall the data fitted the model well judging from the large R squared values and the small probability value of 0.000.

Table 7.16. Definition of variables used in OLS model.

Variable		Definition
X_1	hhsize2005	Household size in 2005
X_2	district	District: 1 = Masaka; 0=Kabarole
X_3	landlaboratio	Land-labour ratio: land owned in 2005/ (No. of adult equivalents)
X_4	education	Education of household head: 1= at least with education of upper primary; 0 = no education or up to primary 4.
X_5	gender	Gender of household head: male = 1; 0 = Female.
X_6	widowed	Being a widow: Widow = 1; 0=Other.
X_7	aidshh	Lost adult due to AIDS or reported having a sick individual with HIV/AIDS: Yes =1.
X_8	hiredlabour	Hired labour: Yes = 1
X_9	tot_bedridden	Total number of days bedridden by economically active household members in a period two months prior to survey
X_{10}	bansoldprop	Sold some banana to raise income: Yes = 1.
X_{11}	othcropsold	Sold maize and beans to raise income: Yes = 1.
X_{12}	hhsizegender	Interaction between household size and being a male household head. Yes = 1.
X_{13}	Well-off & aidshh	Interaction between being AIDS-affected and belonging to Well-off HH: Yes = 1.
X_{14}	Well-off & gender	Interaction between being a male household head and belonging to a Well-off HH: Yes = 1.
ε		disturbance term; B_0 is the intercept and B_{is} are the coefficients of the independent variables

Discussion of results

From the results, education, HIV and the interaction between well-off and gender appear as the main factors that significantly affect per capita consumption consistently across all regression results showing very strong robust results .

Higher formal education is associated significantly with more household consumption and hence better welfare.The impact of formal education and HIV/AIDS-affectedness on per capita household expenditure was similar in both districts. Formal education was found to be significant ($p<0.05$ for Masaka and $p<0.01$ for Kabarole) with a positive impact on per capita expenditure: moving from lower primary to upper primary increases daily per capita expenditure by 0.10 USD for households in each district. This implies that increased education is likely to lead to improved opportunities to access high income employment. This is consistent with Schultz's

Table 7.17. OLS output for daily per capita expenditure.

Variable	Masaka		Kabarole		Overall	
	Coefficient	SE	Coefficient	SE	Coefficient	SE
hhsize2005	-0.012	0.015	0.011	0.008	-0.002	0.010
district	n.a.	n.a.	n.a.	n.a.	0.040	0.030
landlaboratio	0.001	0.011	0.006	0.007	0.004	0.007
education	0.104**	0.041	0.070***	0.032	0.101***	0.028
gender	-0.117	0.127	0.052	0.076	-0.070	0.082
widowed	-0.028	0.059	-0.019	0.030	-0.029	0.032
aidshh	-0.102**	0.043	-0.085**	0.033	-0.111***	0.026
hiredlabour	0.129**	0.061	0.019	0.035	0.076**	0.037
tot_bedridden	0.000	0.001	0.002***	0.001	0.001	0.001
Bansoldprop	-0.176	0.113	-0.084	0.110	-0.132	0.082
othcropsold	0.018	0.047	0.037	0.036	0.034	0.031
hhsizegender	-0.007	0.018	-0.018*	0.011	-0.011	0.012
Well-off & aidshh	0.024	0.234	0.305***	0.091	0.202*	0.109
Well-off & gender	0.719***	0.105	0.467***	0.044	0.587***	0.056
Constant	0.556***	0.132	0.278***	0.084	0.420***	0.087
F-Statistic	7.45		21.45		21.29	
Prob.> F	0.000		0.000		0.000	
R-Squared	0.391		0.573		0.412	
Number of observations	303		238		541	

Source: Household survey.
SE is Standard Error.
*,**, *** imply significantly different at 10%, 5% and 1% level respectively.

education hypothesis (Schultz, 1975), though one needs to bear in mind that some low level income generating activities in rural areas do not require one to be highly skilled. These results underscore the importance of human development in developing countries on welfare improvement which is consistent with many empirical studies in other parts of Uganda and in other countries (Appleton *et al.*, 1999; Deininger & Okidi, 2003; Nkonya *et al.*, 2004).

As expected, HIV-AIDS is associated with lower household consumption expenditure and hence poorer welfare. This implies that the impact of an HIV/AIDS-related death or presence of a chronically sick adult member in a given household decreases the daily per capita expenditure by 0.10 US$. This is consistent with literature, that

HIV/AIDS-related labour loss due to sickness and death leads to a loss in household incomes (FAO, 2003; Haddad & Gillespie, 2001; Topouzis, 2000).

Furthermore, a combination of being a male-head and belonging to the Well-off HH category has a significant ($p<0.01$) and positive impact on per capita expenditure. This implies an increase in per capita expenditure of US$ 0.72 in Masaka and US$ 0.47 in Kabarole. For Masaka households, hiring of labour was found to increase per capita expenditure by 0.13 US$ and the effect is significant ($p<0.05$). This implies that hiring of labour is likely to increase households' production and, consequently, incomes from sales, leading to higher expenditure.

In Kabarole district, the total number of days that economically active adults are bedridden by illness was found to be significant ($p<0.01$) and with a positive impact on per capita household expenditure. An adult member being bedridden implies that they have severe illness and this leads to increased medical expenses. A combination of belonging to a Well-off HH and being HIV/AIDS-affected was also found to positively impact on per capita expenditure with the impact being significant ($p<0.01$). This implies that an additional sick household member in a well-off AIDS-affected household increases per capita expenditure by US$ 0.31. This finding is consistent with that of Ekaas (2003) and FAO (2003) who reported that HIV/AIDS-related sickness leads to increased medical, care and transport expenditure. The fact that this is observed for well-off households suggests that poor households may lack the money to spend on medicines. In Table 7.18, it is also shown for Kabarole that a combination of household size and gender causes marginal impact on per capita household expenditure ($p<0.10$) with the impact being negative. An increase in household size by one household member in female-headed households reduced household expenditure by US$ 0.02.

These results show that wealth, gender and being affected by HIV/AIDS are key determinants for livelihood security in both districts. HIV/AIDS effects on per capita expenditure are significant but mixed. On one hand, we see reduced household expenditure as a consequence of loss of income from HIV/AIDS-related death or mortality of affected household members. On the other hand, among the well-off HH in Kabarole we see increased per capita expenditure that can be associated with increased HIV/AIDS-related treatment and care. Education of the household head and access to hired labour, both of which lead to engagement in more production and income-generating activities, are associated with increase in household incomes and expenditures. Male-headed households in the Well-off HH category who have access to hired labour and are educated are likely to have more secure livelihoods and ability to cope with the effects of HIV/AIDS.

Table 7.18. Ordered logit regression estimates of determinants of household food security.

Variables	Masaka		Kabarole		Overall	
	Coefficient	SE	Coefficient	SE	Coefficient	SE
Household size	0.115***	0.053	0.004	0.063	0.052*	0.038
Cattle number	-0.070*	0.040	0.014	0.102	-0.061*	0.034
Ruminant number	-0.063*	0.036	-0.094*	0.054	-0.067**	0.027
HH head occup 2 [a]	35.041	3.04 E+07	0.636	1.230	1.001	0.833
HH head occup 3	0.365	0.586	0.464	0.506	0.295	0.436
Land-labour ratio	-0.030	0.083	-0.197*	0.119	-0.105*	0.057
HH head age	0.013	0.009	0.001	0.012	0.008	0.007
HH head educ 4	-0.034	0.332	-0.052	0.350	-0.044	0.233
HH head educ 5	-0.510	0.416	-0.109	0.585	-0.286	0.307
HH head educ 6[a]	35.526	4.43 E+07	-33.660	1.231	0.062	1.466
HH head educ 7	-0.988	0.977	-33.016	1.185	-1.227*	0.884
HH head educ 8	.	.	1.933	1.749	2.450*	1.480
HH head educ 9	0.057	0.360	0.831**	0.377	0.385*	0.253
Gender	0.070	0.273	-0.574	0.413	-0.011	0.220
Hired labour	-0.507*	0.259	0.268	0.279	-0.189	0.185
AIDS-affected HH	0.339	0.346	0.008	0.358	0.379*	0.231
Sold maize	-0.555*	0.317	0.256	0.391	-0.222	0.225
Use clean plantlets	-0.238	0.394	-0.780**	0.316	-0.515**	0.248
Pest/disease control	-0.155	0.296	0.104	0.299	-0.058	0.202
Fertilizer use	-0.358	0.250	0.137	0.297	-0.156	0.184
Soil conservation	-0.507	0.312	-0.346	0.312	-0.351*	0.204
Access credit	-0.624	0.462	-0.174	0.438	-0.403*	0.302
Dependency ratio	-0.199***	0.071	-0.120	0.135	-0.175***	0.061
Land owned (2005)	0.012	0.039	-0.002	0.069	0.023	0.029
District	.	.	.	.	2.716***	0.238
_cut1	-3.123***	0.655	-0.969	0.841	-0.513	0.502
_cut2	-0.440	0.616	2.042**	0.833	2.239***	0.518
No. of observations	303		238		541	
Log likelihood function	-245.699		-197.150		-456.226	
Prob>chi2	0.0014		0.0000		0.0000	
Pseudo R2	0.0901		0.0878		0.2110	
Brant test (P-value)					0.219	

Source: Household survey.
SE is standard error.
***,**,* implies significance at 1% , 5%, and at 10% respectively.
[a] the large error term in the Masaka model are due to the fact that there were very few respondents for these variables.

7.5.2 Determinants of household vulnerability

Model specification

HIV/AIDS, food and livelihood insecurity are closely interlinked (cf. Chapter 2). Gillespie and Kadiyala (2005) note that HIV/AIDS heightens vulnerability to food insecurity while, reciprocally, food insecurity heightens susceptibility to HIV exposure and infection. In this study, therefore, household food security is used as an indicator for livelihood vulnerability. First, a food adequacy score – a mean rank explaining adequacy of the various food categories for each household and used as a proxy for household food security – was computed (cf. Chapter 3). Second, the mean adequacy ranks were then used to categorize households into three food security status categories: food insecure, barely food secure, and food secure.

To identify factors that influence food security (and consequently livelihood vulnerability), another model was used. In this part of the analysis, the outcomes (food security status) were mutually exclusive and exhaustive and there was an ordering (hierarchy) among the responses (rankings) of the respondents. In this type an ordered choice model was required. Models of ordered choice describe settings in which individuals reveal the strength of their utility with respect to a single outcome (Green, 2003). The ordered logit model was used in this case (cf. Chapter 3). For the specification of the ordered logit regression model for livelihood vulnerability, latent variable food adequacy (adeqcat222*) was considered. The Equation is as follows:

$$\text{adeqcat222*} = f(Y_1, Y_2, Y_3 \ldots Y_{25}, \varepsilon_i) \qquad \text{Equation 7.2}$$

where; ε_i is a vector of error for the equations estimated, $\varepsilon_i \sim$ logistic. Other variables are defined as in Equation 6.3 (cf. Table 6.11)
adeqcat222 = 1 if adeqcat222* $\leq a_1$
adeqcat222 = 2 if adeqcat222* $\leq a_2$
adeqcat222 = 3 if adeqcat222* $> a_3$; Where

a_1 is a threshold parameter for each level of food security, which is estimated along with the coefficients of the explanatory variables. 1 = Food Insecure -Aggregate scores < 21; 2 = Barely Food Secure- aggregate scores = or > 21 but < 35; 3 = Food Secure-aggregate scores > 35.

Discussion of the results

The results show that a household's livelihood vulnerability, whether it is affected by HIV/AIDS or not, is highly influenced by the district in which the household is found, its ability to rear small animals (cattle, goats and pigs), and per capita land (Table 7.18).

The Masaka model shows that households of large size and small dependency ratios have a high likelihood of being food secure. This relationship is highly significant ($p < 0.01$). Although marginally significant ($p < 0.10$), households that have no cattle, pigs or goats, and no access to hired labour have a high likelihood of being food insecure. The results for Kabarole indicate that households that do not own small ruminants, have no access to clean planting materials and with a small land-labour ratio have a high likelihood of being food insecure.

Overall, a household's food security status is influenced by its location ($p < 0.10$). Food secure households have a higher likelihood of being in Kabarole, while food insecure households have a higher likelihood of being in Masaka. The prolonged drought and other weather related shocks like floods and hail that households in Masaka experienced between 2003 and 2005, declining soil fertility, high incidence of crop pests and diseases may have constituted location-specific factors that created a vulnerable environment. The interaction of this with high HIV/AIDS prevalence levels may be responsible for the higher incidence of food insecurity reported for Masaka.

The results suggest that households with cattle, ruminants, higher land-labour ratio, access to planting materials, access to credit and those that have invested in soil and water conservation are less likely to be vulnerable to food insecurity. The results also show that AIDS-affected households are more likely to be vulnerable to food insecurity, although the evidence is not very strong ($p < 0.10$).

The implication of these findings is that as long as households have cattle, ruminants, land, access to credit and better soil management, HIV/AIDS is not a significant factor in affecting the household's food security status. In other words, AIDS will have less negative impacts on households that have a strong asset base (cattle, goats, pigs, land), access to agricultural inputs (planting material, labour, credit) and with better managed soils. The results further suggest that land degradation may exacerbate the impacts of HIV/AIDS in agriculture-based livelihoods. Although the analysis has shown that HIV/AIDS-related food security impacts are marginally significant, the presence HIV/AIDS is likely to intensify food insecurity due to other factors.

7.6 Conclusions

AIDS is the leading cause of adult and spouse death in the sample. The impact is most clearly felt when considering labour. This chapter has shown that the factor labour in the context of HIV/AIDS constitutes and reflects a range of complexities. The impact of HIV/AIDS on labour is predominantly felt at the level of productivity, the reallocation of labour away from productive activities to care and the redirecting of monetary resources from production to caring for the sick. The outcome is a decrease in productivity of labour and a reduction in cultivated land. Labour shortages occur due to: (i) sickness or death or labour foregone to HIV/AIDS-related care, (ii) poor health among the remaining household members and (iii) lack of inter-generation transfer of knowledge and skills. HIV/AIDS-related impacts on household labour include poor health, increased care and orphan burden, and loss of income of sick or dead household member.

AIDS also undermines one's capacity to effectively make use of other resources or opportunities that may come by or one's ability to negotiate and obtain social support.

Effects on resource use can be summarized as asset depletion, increased medical and food expenditure, diversion or inefficient use of other household resources due to HIV/AIDS-related labour loss, abandonment of agricultural practices that are labour-intensive or require cash, reduced ability to access inputs or hire land, and disinvestment in production and child education. Through property grabbing, widows and orphans also lose land and other property.

What stands out from the analysis presented here is that the impact is clearly socially differentiated. Better off households generally access a broader range of resources to mitigate the effects of HIV/AIDS compared to the poorer households. It is important to bear in mind, however, that some of the differences observed between HIV/AIDS-affected and non-affected HH are not directly attributable to HIV/AIDS but may be associated to other socio-economic or environmental factors. Nonetheless, if those factors are associated with vulnerability, the superimposition of HIV/AIDS only intensifies such vulnerabilities.

Using daily per capita household expenditure as a proxy for livelihood security, the following determinants for livelihood security are identified: a household head having an educational level of at least upper primary, access to hired labour, gender of the household head, household wealth status, and being HIV/AIDS-affected. Well-off households headed by men with a capacity to hire labour and with no history of being affected by HIV/AIDS have higher daily per capita expenditures, that is, more disposable income.

Access to adequate land, ability to rear livestock, access to planting materials and credit, and investment in soil and water conservation, HIV/AIDS status, and residing in Masaka constitute the factors that determine a household's vulnerability status. Orphans and orphan-headed households, widow-headed households, female-headed households and households with very old or illiterate or HIV/AIDS-affected households heads are among the most vulnerable households. These households have only limited access to land or are nearly landless, limited labour for production, limited sources of agricultural income, illiterate household heads, as well as a lack of or limited social networks.

Chapter 8
Responding to HIV/AIDS and community level impacts

8.1 Introduction

The previous chapter examined the impact of HIV/AIDS at household level. This chapter explores the ways in which households and individuals respond to HIV/AIDS. Strategies that reduce or soften HIV/AIDS related effects aim at reducing one's vulnerability, in the short or in the long run, but are not developed in isolation. What happens at community level as well the strategies and plans of intervening organizations to control HIV/AIDS have to be considered. The first part of the chapter focuses on responses at household level and the second on the effects and responses at community level. This is followed by a description of existing institutional and community initiatives for the control and prevention of HIV/AIDS-related effects and an assessment of the effectiveness of existing interventions and possible ways of strengthening them.

8.2 Responding and coping with HIV/AIDS-related impacts

The discussion here focuses on how individuals and households in Masaka and Kababrole have tried to deal with and adapt to the effects of the epidemic. The discussions on the effects of HIV/AIDS with respondents revealed that the most significant impacts felt are poor health, reduced household labour availability, food insecurity, reduced household income, and increased HIV/AIDS-related expenditures. To document and analyse the responses and strategies employed to deal with these effects, I have organized them in five categories: (i) labour-based, (ii) consumption-related, (iii) income-based, (iv) social capital, and (v) health-related. It is important to note that while these response categories are separately discussed, in reality individuals pursue them in combination, sometimes simultaneously. While emphasis is given to household level strategies, in a few cases individual level strategies are highlighted.

8.2.1 Labour-based responses

Sumilar to Goudge & Govender (2000) and Sauerborn *et al.* (1996), this study found that illness and death triggers intra-household labour substitution as a way of coping with production losses. Labour-based strategies generally involve replacing lost labour by intra-household labour reallocation such as taking children out of school, bringing in new family members or hiring labour. Other studies reveal a shift in cropping mix and areas planted to adjust to labour shortages. Table 8.1.

Table 8.1. Responding to effects of spouse death according to AIDS-widows (n=33)[1].

Response	Frequency	% of responses
Intensified use of own labour	23	60.5
Received support from social networks	6	15.9
Use of child labour	4	10.5
Leaving positively with AIDS	4	10.5
Hire casual labour in plantation	1	2.6
Total	38	100

Source: Household survey.
[1] of the 36 widows interviewed, three did not respond to this question.

summarizes how AIDS-widows respond to reduced household labour due to AIDS-related mortality.

Household labour reallocation

The survey data show that about 21 percent of the households reported members having to relocate their time to caring for a sick household member. In about half of the sampled households, households members were forced to reduce time engaged in productive activities, with 20 percent indicating that household members had to completely abandon their job to be able to care for the sick. Though reported to a lesser extent (3%), sometimes household members took on an additional job to earn supplementary income. Labour re-allocation entailing changes in gender roles was observed in two cases of widowers (Cases 5.17 and 5.18) who, albeit with difficulty, cooked and cared for their young children. Similar changes in gender roles have been reported elsewhere (De Waal *et al.*, 2005). In Case 5.5 we see a shift to a less labour-intensive income-generating activity from farm work to selling alcohol.

Removal of children from school

In HIV/AIDS-affected households, children are often taken out of school for a variety of reasons including: (i) taking care of sick relatives or younger siblings when adult labour is diverted to HIV/AIDS-related care, (ii) working in the field to compensate for reduced adult labour loss, (iii) engaging in income-generating activities, and (iv) as a way of reducing household expenditure. Survey data indicates that in about six percent of the households, children had to be taken from school to care for a sick relative. Among HIV/AIDS-widows, four out of the 33 widowed households interviewed withdrew children from school to help with household activities. Among the same group of widows, eight out of 33 said that the children had altogether dropped out of school due to lack of school fees. A study carried out in Tanzania has shown that schooling for orphans in wealthier households is often protected (Beegle *et al.,* 2006), implying that withdrawal of children from school is a strategy of the poor rather than the well-off who can afford hired labour. However, as has been observed in a recent study in Zimbabwe, other socio-economic factors may be responsible for withdrawal of children from school than AIDS (Senefeld & Polsky, 2005). While HIV/AIDS has definitely increased the incidence of orphanhood with the likely consequence of missed schooling opportunities, it is important to be aware of other socio-economic factors that may cause more significant effects than HIV/AIDS or that may interact to intensify HIV/AIDS-related effects. Nonetheless, the withdrawal of children in-order to utilize their labour has serious implications for future literacy levels and the child's participation in the modern economy (Rugalema, 1999b).

Hiring labour and access to free labour

As Mutangadura *et al.* (1999) note, households with a stable income are often able to hire labour. Among the well-off HH, 39 percent of affected households hired labour. It is noteworthy that this was significantly lower than that for non-affected households (58%, $p < 0.05$). In Cases 5.15 and 5.19, in spite of being AIDS-affected, the large resource base of these household enable them to hire labour for agricultural activities. Among the HIV/AIDS widows interviewed, only one out of the 33 hired labour. Regardless of HIV/AIDS, poor households mainly rely on family labour, though free labour from relatives or the community was very limited and could not be relied upon because most households experience labour constraints (information from mixed group discussions in Phase 1). Initiatives to pool labour for agricultural activities, though at a limited scale, were reported among self-help groups of HIV/AIDS-affected women in Kabarole and AIDS-affected households under the MAHCOP programme in Masaka.

Reduction of area cultivated

According to FAO (1995) the most common strategy employed by affected households in response to HIV/AIDS-related morbidity and mortality is the reduction of the area under cultivation (De Waal *et al.*, 2005; Topouzis & Du Gueny, 1999). However, I did not find statistically significant differences in the proportions of land cultivated with annual crops between affected and non-affected households. Only the area under banana production was slightly smaller among affected households than among non-affected ones. The proportion of households cultivating less land due to illness is lower in Kabarole (13%) than in Masaka (40%), possibly due to the higher HIV/AIDS prevalence level in the latter area. Household level analysis also shows that widow-headed households are more likely to cultivate less land than the male-headed households. Mentioned by about 40 percent of the respondents, sickness-related household labour reduction is the commonest cause of failure to implement recommended agronomic practices. This may imply an increased incidence of crop neglect or delay in farming activities due to labour shortages (cf. Case 5.6, 5.7, and 5.9). So, HIV/AIDS-related effects are more likely to be related to poorly tended crops than reduction of the area under production. One third of the households in each of the two districts reported a decline in crop yields due to illness of household members.

8.2.2 Consumption-related responses and strategies

Consumption related responses include those that were discussed in Chapter 6, such as, change in the types of foods, quantities and number of meals eaten, as well as provision of special diets to HIV-infected household members. Individuals sometimes find a way to eat some special foods. For example, a boy said: "Sometimes one needs to eat good food like meat or chicken. So you go out and look for a weeding job and after you are paid you go to the restaurant in the trading centre and enjoy a good meal." This was actually more done by men than children. Whatever the economic or food security status at home, men said that once a week one should eat roast meat and have an alcoholic drink. Therefore, while there may be no food at home, men will try to make sure that they have some money to take care of their special food requirements.

For some individuals (orphaned children and adults alike) desperation forces them to steal food and livestock. Because of reduced household labour and inability to supervise one's fields, HIV/AIDS-affected households have particularly suffered from food losses through theft.

Survey data also show that HIV/AIDS-affected households that had experienced an adult death reported spending more on food than those that were nursing a chronically sick member. The latter spent more on medicines. If such households are not producing enough food of their own, reduced expenditure on food may result in malnutrition, thus triggering the HIV/AIDS malnutrition cycle. The increased dependency on the market among households that suffered an HIV/AIDS-related death is likely to increase their vulnerability because of their low purchasing power.

8.2.3 Income-based responses

Existing AIDS literature shows that rural households pursue different strategies to raise or supplement household incomes to soften AIDS effects (De Waal *et al.*, 2005; Drimie, 2002; Muchunguzi, 1999; Rugalema, 1999a). People in Masaka and Kaborole do this by selling livestock and agricultural produce, selling household assets and services, engaging more than before in petty trading, and in some cases migrating to other areas.

Sale of livestock and agricultural produce

During good times people try to accumulate different assets that they can also draw upon and sell in times of financial crisis, thus making asset sales a common way of smoothing consumption. In Masaka and Kaborole livestock sales formed an important part of raising quick cash to meet medical or other expenses. Small animals (goats and pigs) are the most commonly sold, followed by chicken. While very few households own cattle, both qualitative and quantitative data show that cattle are rarely sold. Their sale is usually a sign of severe financial distress. The social value attached to cattle is such that their sale would mean a fall in social status.

When asked about the effect of sickness on household resources, about sixty percent of the respondents said it had resulted in sale of livestock to cover medical treatment and purchase drugs. For those who sold livestock, 18 percent did so to meet medical costs, 11 percent to pay for children's school fees, while 22 percent said it was to meet the increased food requirements in the household. Among HIV/AIDS-widows, 19 out of 36 sold livestock and chicken to "cover medical and funeral costs as well as meet other household needs (Table 7.15). However, livestock and chicken deaths due to pests and diseases were responsible for larger reductions in the livestock and chicken owned than sales related to medical treatment. Therefore, livestock pests and diseases are likely to compromise households using this as a coping strategy. It is also noteworthy that in a few cases (3%), HIV/AIDS-related expenditure results in the inability of households to continue raising livestock. While HIV/AIDS leads to depletion of a given resource, in this case livestock, it also reduces the capacity of affected individuals to rear the remaining ones.

Sale of produce was particularly important among households that did not own livestock. It is important to note that households sell their produce whether they have a surplus or not. For example it is not uncommon to find households selling most of their food following a harvest (when prices are at their lowest) and then buy it back later from traders when prices have gone up. Maize and beans sales were the main source of income from farm produce. Respondents in banana-growing households said that one could not fail at any particular point in time to get a bunch to sell and address a specific need. Income from banana, albeit being little at a time, is more regular and evenly spread.

Sale of household assets

Selling household assets like radio, bicycle, motorcycle, mattress, to mention a few, helps to raise money to "cover HIV/AIDS-related increased expenditure and buy food. In a few cases, land is sold to cover medical expenses. Its worth mentioning that asset sales involving disposal of factors of production like land become problematic because of their negative impacts on future livelihood security. However, it was apparent in all households that sold land that they had no other option of raising income. Distress sales of land are an indicator of increasing vulnerability. While qualitative information indicated that men are likely to benefit more from asset sales, there was no quantitative data to support this. Similarly, Rugalema (1999b) observed trends of differential benefits from asset sales in his study in Tanzania. All the cases of HIV/AIDS-affected households discussed in this thesis provide examples of sale of different household assets.

Whereas selling different household assets as a response to unforeseen crises predates HIV/AIDS, when combined with property stripping (particularly land) from widows and orphans, it is likely to intensify the HIV/AIDS-related effects among these groups. In the sample as a whole, four percent of the respondents reported losing land after the death of the male household head. The proportion was significantly higher among HIV/AIDS-widows, with one third (12 out of 36) having lost land and livestock to the relatives of the late spouse.

Selling labour and petty trade

Sale of labour for cash or food is common among the very poor and female-headed households. As was discussed in Chapter 6, in some communities casual labouring is looked down upon and in some cases people may rather prefer to go without food than work on a neighbour's field. Income from such jobs is small and irregular. Despite being small, poor health status and physical fitness among HIV-infected individuals interferes with their capacity to sell their labour. Selling handicrafts, foods and alcohol is mainly done by women to raise additional household income. Additional information from Case 5.18 reveals that women also engage in the sale of second hand clothes (hawking). These activities are not usually regular sources of income but are started to solve a crisis situation or people get involved in them during periods that they are likely to be relatively profitable.

Women with limited sources of income sell sexual favours as a way of raising income to cover household expenditures, pay for children's school fees, or start small income-generating activities or strengthen existing ones. In addition to cash, such women were said to receive nutritious food, particularly protein-rich food (such as meat), from their male partners. However, selling of sex increases the risk of contracting HIV/AIDS.

Migration

Migration is both an individual and household level strategy (see Chapter 5). About one third of all surveyed households reported having at least one member who migrated to look for employment. No differences are observed between affected and non-affected households in this regard. However male-headed households in Masaka were more likely to have a household member migrating compared to female-headed households in Kabarole (see Chapter 5). This implies that female-headed households have limited access to this income-raising strategy, because they often have limited adult labour that can be reallocated in this manner. Qualitative data indicate that there is an increasing trend among poor households to withdraw children from school and send them to look for employment in urban areas. Some children decide for themselves to go and look for work away from home. Migration has been associated with increased risk of contracting HIV/AIDS due to, on one hand, prolonged separation between spouses which forces migrant members to get other sexual partners, and on the other, increased risk to sexual exploitation of children due to early entry into paid or unpaid labour. Case study data (Cases 1.1 and 5.3) indicate mixed results with regard to benefits from remittances, though the quantitative data show that remittances are not a significant source of household income. There are also women who have migrated after being chased from their spouse's land by in-laws following the spouse's death, while others do it to escape HIV/AIDS-related stigma.

8.2.4 The role of social networks in facilitating responding to HIV/AIDS-effects

Kinship networks

Kinship relations, neighbours and civil society organizations influence households' and individual household members' ability to cope with HIV/AIDS-related effects. As discussed in Chapter 6, close kin (parents, children and siblings) are the main source of support to affected households. The importance of kinship relations is seen by the proportion of households (over half) giving and receiving support (see section 6.4.1). Case study data reveal similar findings. In addition to receiving food, money and other necessities, other support takes the form of moving in with relatives and hosting children. Particularly grandmothers take care of the children, take in orphans and pay their school fees. While one fifth of the households sent their children to live with relatives, there is no significant difference in proportions between affected and non-affected households. Case study data clearly show that households that lack close kin are among the poorest and most vulnerable. Examples of these include widow-headed households as discussed in Cases 1.1, 5.3, 5.10 and 5.19; grandfather-headed household (Case 5.17) and the orphan households (Cases

5.14 and 5.16). In contrast, Cases 5.11, 5.15 and 5.18 have strong social networks that enable them to cope with the impacts of the epidemic.

Support from neighbours and friends often includes psychological support, provision of information on available institutional support or giving information to NGOs providing support about vulnerable people that need support. Occasional help with agricultural activities was also mentioned. An interesting aspect of support from friends is that it is likely to be given to households that are not severely affected. Severely affected households are avoided – people don't want to entangle themselves in unending responsibilities. One of the reasons for this may be that most social relations are based on reciprocal exchange, so that people may be reluctant to offer support to households where it is clear that no future benefits can be expected.

Contrary to what is normally presented in the literature about the limited role of men in HIV/AIDS-related care and support, men are also involved in HIV/AIDS-care. Through informal interactions with the community it was not uncommon to meet men who went out of their way to give food and money to old widows and orphans. Two striking encounters in Masaka include: (i) a man who took in an AIDS-widow and her four children after they had been evicted by her late spouse's relatives, and (ii) a community worker who was seeking NGO support on behalf of three orphaned children who had lost both parents to AIDS and had no relatives. Also, discussions with HIV-infected women in Kabarole revealed that some of them received support (money for drugs and school fees) from male kin. The lack of direct physical involvement of majority of men in HIV/AIDS-related care should not be interpreted as total lack of involvement. The survey data also reveal that men and women contribute to HIV/AIDS-related care with men mainly contributing cash and women physical care.

Marriage

Section 6.4.1 clearly demonstrates women's dependence on men and how marriage is not just a conjugal relationship for procreation but also a means to a livelihood. Through marriage most women gain access to productive resources like land and male labour. To continue to lay claim on access to these resources one has to behave "well" (as determined by society and the husband), be hard-working, produce enough children (most importantly boys) and be submissive to the husband. However, marriage does not guarantee women's continued access to land and other property after the death of the spouse even if they behaved "well". Women's high dependence on men has increased their vulnerability, both in terms of increased risk to HIV/AIDS (due to power relations) and increased loss of livelihood following the spouse's death (due to limited property rights).

One of the women parliamentarians I talked to in Masaka mentioned that some women have opted for widow-inheritance[59] where such customs occur. Other widows enter into casual sexual relationships with their male in-laws to retain access to land. Discussions with a group of HIV-infected women in Kabarole indicated that some women do not get into serious marriage relationships, but instead opt to have several partners who provide for different needs. However, to ensure commitment and sustained support they would bear each man a child, through which support can be negotiated. Information from a couple of men's group discussions in Masaka also revealed cases, though very few, of poor men who were "married' by rich widows. Such men had no source of livelihood and chose to lose their social status as "real men" and get married to women who could take care of them to provide for their sexual and livelihood needs.

Re-marriage after a spouse's death has long been a strategy to cope with the labour lost due to the death of the spouse. Widows face more restrictions than widowers regarding re-marriage. If a widow re-marries, she forfeits her access to the late spouse's land and property. However, HIV/AIDS has caused re-marriage to be a risky business. Furthermore, daughters who have dropped out of school are also being married off. Four out of 36 HIV/AIDS widows said that they had to marry off their daughters at a very early age, a response associated with income expected from a bride price or as a strategy to reduce household size or both.

Community-based institutions

Civil society organizations as is discussed below, have been very instrumental in helping households to deal with HIV/AIDS, thereby compensating for the very limited role of the government. It will therefore suffice to say here that some affected households and those supporting orphans and vulnerable children have received medicines (including ARV treatment) or medical costs paid for, food aid, improved maize and bean seed and other planting materials, livestock (goats, pigs and heifers), bicycles, education support for orphaned children as well as some having houses constructed for them. Pilot activities to give financial grants as start up capital for income-generating activities as well as access to credit facilities have been initiated among groups of HIV/AIDS-affected households.

[59] Widow inheritance is a custom where following a spouse's death, a brother to the dead spouse takes over the woman as his wife. It was meant to provide mechanisms that could guarantee women's and children's livelihood security. Although the practice is slowly dying out, some ethnic groups in the study areas, that is, the Banyankole, Bakiga, Banyarwanda and Batoro practice widow inheritance. Where it is practiced, refusal of the widow jeopardizes access to late spouse's property.

8.2.5 Health-related responses

Some of the strategies already discussed, such as consumption-related responses, aim at improving food intake, which is very useful for HIV-infected individuals. Income-based responses are important for raising money required for treatment, care, transport and nutrition, while individuals will also draw on available social support networks to access the necessary treatment and care. Some women have stopped giving birth after being sensitized about the hazards of pregnancy when one has AIDS. However, this strategy seemed to be only used by women who are economically independent and do not need to depend on men for survival. The three HIV/AIDS widows who decided to get pregnant even after being sensitized, did it for survival. Households employ other strategies to improve their health status. One key strategy identified by HIV infected men and women during focus group discussions was accepting one's HIV/AIDS-status and start living positively. Three out of the 33 HIV/AIDS widows interviewed (see Table 7.16) also mentioned it as a way of coping with the disease, seeing it as a first step to deal with fear and stigma and be able to seek medical and other support. Faith-based organizations have been instrumental in providing counselling and psychological support to individuals infected with HIV to enable them live positively. For those who cannot access health services, buying some drugs off the counter or using traditional herbs has been an alternative. Some people combine traditional herbs and western medicine.

Some, rich and poor alike, have resorted to witchcraft and refused to go to hospital. One key informant in Masaka said that the practice is more common among remote communities that have not received any HIV/AIDS sensitization. Another problem is the belief that AIDS can be cured through having sex with virgins, which has increased the vulnerability of girls to HIV/AIDS infection.

While there are efforts to sensitize against such beliefs, there is evidence that they still exist. Some rural institutions like church-based organizations and traditional herbalists have been found to discourage or stop HIV-infected individuals from accessing medical treatment and cases of patients who were responding well on ARVs have ended up dying after stopping their medication.

From the above discussion, it is clear that individuals adopt a range of responses and strategies to deal with HIV/AIDS sickness and death. It is noted that responses vary between communities, households and even individuals within the same household.

8.3 HIV/AIDS effects at community level and on organizations

Like Mullins (2002) this study highlights the main effects of HIV/AIDS at community level: changes in community demographic composition and structure, health status and educational attainment of community members. Also the quantity and quality of service providers comes out as a critical factor. Wiggins (2005) has pointed out that service delivery significantly affects households and communities.

The first section of this part of the chapter summarizes aspects of the relationship between HIV/AIDS and community development. Subsequently, the focus is on the changing nature of social networks and whether and how intervening organizations at community and/or village level are affected by HIV/AIDS. The analysis points at a series of critical challenges, some of which are reviewed in this chapter. But first I present a descriptive account of one case study village in Masaka district that has been affected by HIV/AIDS and pictures a real-life experience of what is taking place in some communities.

Village case study: Nyenje, Masaka district

Nyenje is a small village in Lwengo sub-county of Masaka district and is located two kilometres from Mbirizi trading centre which is about two hours from Kampala, along the Kampala-Mbarara highway. Like some other parts of Masaka district, the village has been devastated by the HIV/AIDS epidemic.

The first striking thing that attracted my attention when I visited the village was that the majority of people we passed along the road or saw in the fields were children and old women. There was no trace of young and able-bodied men. I had previously requested the area extension officer to mobilize some male and female farmers who could participate in the focus group discussions. Apart from one gentleman who happened to be the Local Council 1 chairman of the area and reported to have been in his mid-forties, all the other group participants were men and women with grey hair, in their fifties or sixties (according to self-reported age). When I asked where the young people were, we were told that the majority had died of "The disease" [AIDS].

The story as I later heard was that in the mid-nineties the banana trade boomed in the area and many young men were drawn into the trade. Young men would buy bananas from farmers in the area and transport them to Kampala, which is more profitable than selling them in Masaka town. Business was good and many young people were able to buy plots of land in Mbirizi trading centre, start construction of rental structures and also improve their own dwellings with brick walls and iron sheet roofs. However, the journey to Kampala involves night stopovers at other trading centres along the Kampala Masaka highway, points that have been identified as initial nodes of HIV/AIDS infection along this highway. The nature of the business, money and availability of cheap sex at these points, created circumstances that facilitated a quick spread of HIV/AIDS among the banana traders and their spouses, the impacts of which, ten years later, decimated the group of productive adults in the community. The widows and grandmothers in the focus group discussions identified poor eating and living standards and increased number of school dropouts as major effects of HIV/AIDS. In order to survive, many of the widows said that they had to sell the assets that their spouse left behind, but even this was not enough to educate the children. One strategy of dealing with food insecurity was to resort to less traditional staple food, *posho* (maize meal). Inter-household support was said to be almost none; because of the extent of the problem – almost every household is affected – no one has any resources to help others. So, one has to work extra hard to survive.

In this village, women have mobilized themselves and are taking a central role in community activities because no men do so. Focus group participants mentioned tasks such as spraying and cleaning of water sources as well as participation in community politics, in which women have increased involvement. Nonetheless, the village which at one point in the past seemed to be moving upward out of poverty, has lost many of its young entrepreneurs, and the strategies pursued by those remaining behind seem to be simply for survival. The situation on the ground can best be depicted by the following excerpt from the interviews with the women:

> *This disease (AIDS) has crippled development in our area. Move around the village and all you will see are old people and orphans. All our young blood, the people who were starting to develop the area died, leaving us these young children. We can only look at them. We have no future to offer them. They are being chased from the Universal Primary Education (UPE) schools because we cannot afford to buy pencils, books or pay for their lunch at school. What does the future hold for them? Indeed, some of them have started robbing us of the little food we have!* (Women FGD, Nyenje, Lwengo, Masaka District)

8.3.1 Community development and farming

Participants in a range of focus groups were asked about how they perceive the effects of the epidemic on children, men and women, as well as the community in general. Table 8.2 summarizes these perceptions. The overall picture is one of: (i) increasing number of orphans, child-headed and grandmother-headed households, and death of youthful and skilled people with the result of reduced capacity of households to cope with the large number of orphans; (ii) increases in social problems including loss of social control, unhealthy social relations between spouses with increased incidence

Table 8.2. Focus group discussions: impacts of AIDS at community level.

Level	Impacts
Demographic	Increase in number of orphans; child-headed households; grandmother-headed households; and death of youthful and skilled people.
Social	Loss of social control (cohesion/social disintegration): loss of morals- some infected men and women spread the virus to children and married couples intentionally. Also said for some cases of discordant couples, where affected-men refuse to have protected sex with the non-affected spouse, and affected male teachers defiling young girls. Belief that having sex with a virgin results in one being healed of HIV/AIDS increases vulnerability of girls to risk of infection.
	Increase in rate of separation and divorce (due to disturbed relationships as a consequence of AIDS, fear of stigma of living with an HIV/AIDS-affected spouse with women suffering most, or just because a man cannot manage to look after his sick wife so he sends her to her relatives).
	Dissolution of households following death of benefactor: children divided between relatives with associated traumatic effects. Sometimes relatives exploit the children through sexual abuse and heavy child labour, poor condition of many orphaned children.
	Delinquents: often orphaned children who have to look after themselves, lack parental guidance and therefore lack socialization into socially acceptable behaviours and livelihood skills.
	Reduced social status of community in comparison to other communities: the more progressive farmers or traders or rich individuals in a community, the higher its social standing. In one village an example was given where many of the progressive youth who had started investments in the area and putting up permanent houses, had died. People from this village are now considered very poor. "*Abali bavudeyo, bona bafa*"- all those who were progressive (had escaped poverty) died.
	Increased role of women in fending for their families and taking on community activities.
	Increase in consumption of alcohol because of fear and frustration after people know that they are HIV/AIDS-positive. Loss of hope among community members because of limited access to ARVs.
Economic	Loss of economically productive labour –people with skills and experience in various trades. The young and inexperienced and the aged who are now taking care of families are less productive.
	Loss of entrepreneurs and intellectual people leading to reduced business investments and services in the community, and reduced tax revenue – An example of a one Dr. Semakula, specialist in treating children, who had started a vibrant clinic for children died and the community lost his services. Examples of other successful traders and farmers also given.

Table 8.2. Continued.

	Tendency to lose support of those with the means, that is, the rich. Reference was made to the crucial role they have in supporting the relatively poorer segment of community members, for example through provision of employment; providing market for local products, buying inputs (mulching materials), small animals, chicken, etc.; being a source of food; and informal credit (money for business). "Since the *mugaga* (rich man) died, it is difficult to get anyone to lend you money for school fees". "The 'disease' [HIV/AIDS] is finishing those who had money to buy our chicken". "Whenever one had an emergency at night, one would run to Mr Kato's place and he would take you to the hospital in his car. But after he died, the sons mismanaged the car, besides they do not want to help the way their father used to help us".
	Increased poverty: Those with means have died – limited investments into off-farm activities. "Remittances have declined because our children who used to send us money have died". Reduced capacity of families to cope with the orphan problem.
	Some affected-households have had to sell productive resources (land) leaving orphans and widows destitute. Affected community members have re-channelled meagre resources to HIV/AIDS-related costs and care, and looking after orphans.
Agriculture	Decline in level of production and management of agricultural enterprises. A well managed banana plantation was a social status symbol. But now some plantations look like forests – with too many suckers and overgrown with weeds.
	Death of good farmers who used to be a source of knowledge for the other farmers.
	Orphans do not have agricultural skills
	Reduced food security: lost work days due to increased sickness among community members and labour lost through AIDS-related deaths.
Institutional	Reduced participation of community members in government programmes, for example, reduced participation of AIDS-affected households in agricultural extension programmes, and new technologies may not be taken in. Withdrawal of children from school as a consequence of HIV/AIDS-related labour loss.
	Death of government workers (extension service providers, teachers, health personnel).
	Difficulties experienced by local leaders in enforcing government laws. For example, girls are being married off at an early age with the consent of parents, some cases of defilement go unpunished because the offender gives the poor parents of the child money which is more welcome for their survival than him being jailed.

Source: Focus group discussions.

of physical violence among women, delinquents, and increased consumption of alcohol; (iii) loss of economically productive labour and entrepreneurs who would ordinarily initiate development activities in the community, consequently a decline in agricultural production and other economic activities and services, increased food insecurity and poverty; (iv) reduced participation of community members in government programmes and a further decline in government service provision and the quality of services delivered due to HIV/AIDS-institutional effects. Therefore, despite the initiatives during the last decade to deal with the effects of the epidemic, communities continue to experience significant effects. Some of the demographic changes observed (increased number of households headed by children and elderly) are indicators of communities on the verge of disintegration.

Farming system changes, thus, reflect a reduction in cultivated land, a decline in crop yields and the variety of crops grown; and changes in livestock (Du Guerny, 2002; Barnett & Blaikie, 1992; De Waal *et al.*, 2005; FAO, 1995); a loss of valuable agricultural skills and experience (Hurst *et al.*, 2005; Du Guerny, 2002) as well as rising labour costs due to labour shortages (Hurst *et al.*, 2005). The data in this study reveal that the effect of sickness amongst widow-headed households mainly results in reductions in area under agricultural production and yields as well as an increase in disease and pest infestation. On the other hand, a higher proportion of male-headed and single-female households experience effects associated with reduction in implementation of recommended good management practices.

Further more, poor agronomic practices due to labour shortages are usually associated with an increase in prevalence and spread of plant and animal diseases (UNDP, 1995). Likewise, this study shows poor agronomic practices for most crops because of reduced household labour input, as mentioned by about 40 percent of the respondents from each of the two districts. This was followed by a decline in crop yields occurring in one third of households in each of the districts. However, a higher proportion of respondents in Masaka (40%) reported reduced banana yields than those in Kabarole (17%). While this could be associated with the higher HIV/AIDS prevalence levels in Masaka compared to Kabarole, the interaction between HIV/AIDS and other environmental factors (particularly prolonged drought and poor soils) may have worked in synergy to lead to the observed higher proportions of Masaka households experiencing declining yields. In addition, increase in pest and diseases due to sickness was mainly reported for banana plantations with incidence of the problem higher in Masaka (24%) than in Kabarole (7%), probably for the same reasons as given above. Also, the proportion of households cultivating less land as a result of illness was less in Kabarole (13%) than that in Masaka (40%). The proportion in Masaka is higher than that reported in the Topouzis (2003) study (i.e. 25%).

The literature associates HIV/AIDS also with changes in the type of crops grown with a shift to the production of less labour-intensive crops (Barnett & Blaikie, 1992; Topouzis, 2003). This study, however, shows a mixed picture. For example, crops such as beans, cow peas, maize, Irish potato, cassava, and groundnuts, to mention a few, which were said to have been abandoned by some households are the same crops reported to have been taken on as new crops by other households. As was discussed in Chapter 5, a number of factors are responsible for farmers' decisions on whether to take up new crops or stop growing existing ones that are not associated with HIV/AIDS-status of the household. This again underscores the importance of looking at HIV/AIDS and related effects in the context of prevailing circumstances, which at particular points in time may be more influential than whether a household is affected or not.

Despite the few differences noted, there is no evidence to show that the farming system in Masaka is more affected than that in Kabarole. Differences in how generalized the epidemic is in the communities studied, population size and other environmental factors may be partly responsible for the results obtained. Nonetheless, according to my own observation, it was more common in Masaka than in Kabarole to find fields lying fallow because those who used to tend them had died of AIDS.

8.3.2 The role of and effects on social networks

Social capital has been described as one of the important assets of the poor because of its potential to function as a safety net in times of stress or crises. According to Haddad & Gillespie (2001), social capital refers to the strength of associational life, trust, and norms of reciprocity. People invest in social networks with the expectation that in case of a crisis in the future; these networks can be called upon for support.

In this study, both qualitative and quantitative data generated information on the various ways in which individuals in the study areas negotiate and establish social linkages that facilitate access to and use of productive resources, employment as well as labour. Focus group participants provided information on the ways community members invest in social capital. These include giving gifts, participating in cultural ceremonies and fulfilling expected social obligations, participating in community activities, investing material resources in various feasts (marriage, Christening), paying school fees for a relative's child, lending money to friends or relatives without expecting interest, visiting relatives or friends particularly when they are in problems (for example visiting the sick and taking food or money), and helping one's neighbour or relatives with some labour intensive agricultural tasks such as land preparation, weeding or harvesting.

Marriage was also seen as an important way of expanding one's social networks and, if possible, an individual from a poor household would hope to marry into a family of higher social status, as a strategy to link into higher social status networks. While people are aware of the challenges associated with taking care of a large family, producing children is still regarded by many as an investment for the future.

Finally, those who have money use it to establish some level of social standing that can facilitate connections to certain networks. For example, alcohol drinking joints are used by men as points of entry to socializing and developing business and political contacts or contacts with government officials. Such contacts are said to be helpful in, for example, accessing a fair tax assessment or in case one gets into legal problems. Furthermore, the way one dresses oneself and the family or the schools to which the children are sent, were said to affect which type of networks one would be able to penetrate or participate in.

Social capital also plays a significant role in people's access to resources for production, in times of food shortages, access to children's education and the type of livelihood strategies pursued. Those who have connections to friends and relatives with fallow land were able to access it without cost. Engagement in shared cropping arrangements is often between friends and close kin. This was also said to be the case with shared livestock-rearing arrangements. Members of a women's group in Kabarole said that they found it cheaper and more affordable to hire land and buy other inputs as a group and grow maize together. Indeed this approach lessens a single household's risk of crop failure. Additionally, to overcome individual labour constraints, the group pooled their labour. Thus, they were able to grow and access much more food after sharing than each would have been able to grow on her individual plot.

Mrs Mutebi, a widow in Mbirizi village Masaka, said her connection with the church enabled her to get employment. Being the leader of the mothers' union in her parish church, the parish priest put her in charge of taking care of the church gardens. Her role was to get women who could weed the gardens and help with harvesting. Mrs Mutebi is also a community worker and chairperson of Mbirizi Widows' group, a ROSCA. So she said that she gives first priority to women in her group when looking for labourers to work in the church gardens. The majority of women focus group participants also emphasized the importance of maintaining relationships with relatives in urban areas who they said become useful if one wants to send a son or daughter to look for employment. Yet still, those who have connections with rich farmers in the area can access employment for themselves and their children.

Inter-household support for the education of children was reported by about half of the surveyed households. In Cases 5.4 and 6.3 the widows were able to access their children's school fees through relatives (sisters) and an NGO. Further information from key informants showed that connections to the Catholic Church and the local leadership in Masaka are a key determinant on accessing food aid, orphan support, medical treatment for opportunistic infections and ARV treatment. In addition, those who have money to pay the responsible Local Council chairmen, are able to access support (school fees and clothing) for their children, even if they are not orphaned.

Therefore, social identity, social status, position, and gender determine whether one is able to access state, institutional or local resources. For those affected by HIV/AIDS, this has also become a determining factor in access to social capital. For example, a number of authors have linked the HIV/AIDS epidemic to social capital, showing how HIV/AIDS-related stigma, discrimination and the costs posed by care for the sick as well as for the increasing number of orphans, erode and put pressure on social capital (cf. Gaffeo, 2003; Nombo, 2007). Therefore HIV/AIDS not only reduces time and resources for building social capital, but it also breaks social connections when adults die or those affected suffer exclusion. Moore's (1978:502) observation that social cooperation and reciprocity are not innate spontaneous qualities but must be continually recreated is pertinent to our understanding on how HIV/AIDS is likely to change social relations and diminish social capital and support. Group participants indicated that the social relations and networks that they are part of are of past relationships that have been built over time. But as they emphasized, these relationships need to be maintained and kept alive. Because of social exclusion, HIV/AIDS-affected individuals find it difficult to maintain past social relations. Furthermore, people need time and resources to invest in social networks, which pose problems for affected households for whom it is difficult to mobilize resources for communal or group-based initiatives. In the study population, two groups emerged as those with the greatest vulnerability to loss of social capital: orphaned children and widows.

The way society is organized, children are provided for by their parents or guardians, and given their age and lack of experience and resources they hardly participate in social networks that are of significance for access to resources. Any benefits that children may get from society accrue by virtue of their linkage to the parents or adults looking after them. This can even be seen from the way households are referred to in the community. Apart from those headed by single females, other households are named after the male head, whether he is alive or dead. Because of their social status, men often have larger social networks than women. In a situation of HIV/AIDS, when parents die, the children lose their most important social asset. In addition, access by children to social networks that were created by their parents becomes very difficult, if not impossible.

This loss of social capital is likely to be worse for children who are still very young since they may not even be known by many people in the community. Male children may be disadvantaged, in that people do not want to take them in because they may claim inheritance. When social capital is also seen as the rules and norms that govern access to resources, double orphans have no one to ensure protection of their land rights. As the HIV/AIDS literature shows, the clustering of the disease in certain households may easily mean that some orphans are left with few or no relatives on whom to depend to protect their rights to the few resources that the parents may have left behind. The case studies in Chapter 5 show that when households lost more than one adult due to HIV/AIDS, the orphans remained with a grandmother or no one to help them.

The majority of children from child-headed households interviewed said that they were struggling on their own and had no support from anyone. This can be illustrated by a child-headed household in Mbirizi village, where three brothers, aged eleven, nine and seven had lost their father to AIDS in 2004 and their mother a year earlier. Despite the existence of an NGO providing support to vulnerable and orphaned children in their locality, these children were not receiving any support, because no one could get their names on the Local Council chairman's list (the main channel through which the NGO identified children needing support). The effort of a sympathetic neighbour who had tried to directly approach the NGO on the children's behalf, had failed. Qualitative data from discussions with AIDS orphans also reveal how relatives had taken or sold part of the orphans' land and other household resources following the parents' death, leaving the affected children with no one to turn to for help. None of the children interviewed or those who participated in the focus group discussions were aware of their property rights.

Widows' loss of social capital was related to land tenure insecurity that is dependent upon their relationship to the spouse. Women's increased constrained access to land following a spouse's death, is caused by the division of land among the sons and – to a limited extent – grabbing by the late spouse's male relatives. In their research, Barnett & Blaikie (1992) show how in patrilineal societies, widows and their dependents are in a weaker position with regard to maintaining access or control over land. Other studies have also shown that women who are widowed due to HIV/AIDS sometimes lose rights to land (Drimie, 2002; Marongwe, 2005: cited in Drimie & Gandure, 2005). Death of a spouse also means that the household loses the social support networks that the family enjoyed through the dead member.

While women also have their own support networks, old age and increased expenditures may make it difficult for women to participate in their networks. For example, Mrs Mutebi in Case 5.11 said that some of her group members who were HIV/AIDS-affected had dropped-out while others were finding it difficult to pay the weekly contributions to the group. For this particular group they have to pay group entry fees of UGX 5,000 (equivalent to slightly less than US$ 3) and subsequent weekly contributions of UGX 200 (about 10 US$ cents). As Haddad and Gillespie (2001) note and Nombo (2007) found, for those who can manage to pay the weekly fees, the group leads to the generation of social capital that may prove valuable in times of crisis. However, for those who due to HIV/AIDS fall out or do not have the means to join such a group, they face social exclusion. Furthermore, failure to pay such amounts gives an indication of the level of impoverishment experienced by some individuals in the community. Below are excerpts from an interview with an AIDS widow showing how HIV/AIDS-related sickness may interfere with agricultural labour strategies.

> *Saffina is a widow and her husband died of AIDS in 2002 and she tested HIV positive in 2003. After her husband's death, Saffina joined a group of three other women in her village (Lwera HIV/AIDS widows' group) so that they could help each other by pooling labour for various agricultural activities. Saffina says that the group worked together very well till she started falling ill more frequently towards the end of 2004. This is the period that she developed TB and had no energy to work and reciprocate what her group members were doing for her. At first, say for the first four to five months of 2005, the friends continued to work in her gardens, either weeding or harvesting. After being on medication Saffina developed some strength but she could no longer be as efficient as she used to be or manage working the whole day in the hot sun. Gradually, the other group members stopped requesting for her labour and when she would ask for help, they would give an excuse. The women have even stopped visiting her. Her three boys aged 12, 9 and 7, are the only helping hands she now has. They do most of the housework including digging in the mornings before going to school. When she is sick, the eldest boy stays at home to look after her.*
> AIDS widow, Lwera village, Kyazanga Sub-county.

Additional information from AIDS-affected women in Kabarole indicates that some women have been evicted from their homes by in-laws after the death of the husband because of stigma. In many instances, such women are forced to migrate to another area and in the process they lose the social support networks that they had built over time. As Marongwe (2005: cited in Drimie & Gandure, 2005) rightly points out, migration of women to new areas may expose them to greater socio-economic vulnerability to HIV/AIDS.

8.3.3 Effects on state institutions

HIV/AIDS affects the institutional fabric serving rural communities, making it more difficult to effectively implement various mitigation strategies. The capacity of the state to intervene declines when staff fall sick and die from AIDS-related illnesses.

Agricultural extension and research agencies have been progressively deprived of experienced people through HIV/AIDS related deaths. The death of experienced professionals presents one of the key challenges in HIV/AIDS mitigation efforts. As Cohen 2000, cited in Haddad & Gillespie 2001) put it: "How [do we] achieve sustainable development essential for an effective response to the epidemic under conditions where the epidemic is destructive of the capacities essential for the response?" Additionally, the productivity of the human resource left behind suffers due to repeated periods of illness that lead to recurrent absences from work, increased workload and reduced moral from the loss of friends and colleagues. There is also increased use of institutional resources to meet AIDS-related costs (for example, medical care, life insurance claims, burial costs, and time spent on burials) of the employees (Loevinsohn & Gilespie, 2003). The loss of institutional capacity and the expenses involved in coping with staff losses undermines public and private sector service delivery and the sustainability of sector programmes.

Discussions with senior agricultural officers in MAAIF and field staff in the study areas present a similar picture. These institutional effects need also to be seen in light of the already existing funding and staffing constraints in the agricultural extension services as well as the very low extension agent/farmer ratio. The consequences of institutional breakdown may lead to a collective and individual inability to deal adequately with the effects of HIV/AIDS. Therefore, MAAIF and NAADS need to address the institutional aspects of the epidemic in order to be effective in the context of the new challenges to the provision of agricultural extension services presented by the epidemic. To date, there seems to be limited progress in this area.

> *HIV/AIDS has reduced the number of staff working in the agricultural sector especially the field staff and this means that many farmers are left unattended. In fact, in many communities they say they do not remember when they last saw extension workers. Besides, the remaining staff's effective time has also been reduced because of the sick relatives and dependants left behind under their care. The staff are also part of the communities in which they work. So they have to be involved in burials. This also means that no work is done as farmers are away tending to the sick or at funerals. There is also an increasing drain on MAAIF's meager resources to care for the staff who are sick or contribute to the transport and burial arrangements for the staff or their close relatives who die.* Principle Animal Husbandry Officer, MAAIF.

> *There is a reduction in the number of working days because of sickness among staff. Some members of staff who have started showing signs fear to go and work because they do not want farmers to know their status. The impact of our activities is very low because staff deaths due to AIDS have further reduced the number of field extension staff, yet those remaining do*

not have transport to increase the area of coverage. Field extension officer, Kyazanga,Sub-county.

Apart from the reduced staff numbers which has resulted in even fewer farmers accessing extension services, HIV/AIDS has come with new challenges. Because of poverty, farmers were already finding it difficult to take up new technologies or buy improved seeds and other inputs. HIV/AIDS has resulted in increased impoverishment among those affected. The challenge we have is to reach out to such farmers with relevant messages. Besides being sick, the majority of clients are now young orphans with no agricultural knowledge or skills and very old women looking after orphans. This necessitates new approaches and new skills. But for those of us facing the challenges now, we do not know how to address them. Field extension officer, Ruteete Sub-county.

Between 1990 and 2000 we lost about half of our entire district health staff due to AIDS. Not only was it difficult for us to cope with the increased work load because of the reduced number of staff (there being a government policy ban on new recruitments), but the complication of ordinarily simple cases by opportunistic infections among AIDS patients further aggravated the situation. Staff morale was also low because no one knew where death would strike next. District Health Official, Masaka District.

New challenges for agricultural extension service provision

The HIV/AIDS epidemic poses a series of challenges for agricultural extension agencies. These till now have been identified as "technical", relating to issues like serious pest and/disease outbreaks, natural disasters (drought/floods) or campaigns to promote certain technologies. However, the HIV epidemic, over and above existing problems has created a completely new set of complex challenges with which extension agencies have to deal: a different clientele of extension services, the impact of the epidemic on the extension organization itself, and the very nature of the extension work. A brief discussion of these categories follows:

The HIV epidemic is changing the traditional composition of the clientele for extension services. In areas of high HIV prevalence, the category of productive men, women and youth in the late adolescence to middle age range, is one that has been most affected by the epidemic. More women, children and the elderly persons are now engaged in farming due to prolonged illness and/or death of their spouses, parents, guardians and other members of the family. Changes of this magnitude in a clientele that was already resource-limited and mostly from illiterate rural households are bound to render the existing extension strategies and methods irrelevant unless they are adjusted to the new extension clientele and their needs (Qamar, 2001, 2003). This is likely to have effect on the level of appreciation of extension messages as well as on the efficiency of adoption of recommended practices, since the very old and young may not be active seekers of extension information.

The progressive depletion of household assets associated with the epidemic, limited income, reduced household labour, as well as changes in farmers' ability to access productive resources have worked in different combinations to further make it more difficult for people to efficiently engage in agricultural production. Under such conditions of stress, short-term survival is a priority over any investments into agriculture or sustainable management of natural resources (Müller, 2004). For some farmers, these circumstances render them incapable of applying recommended practices while others (also because of the psychological impacts of HIV/AIDS) become less interested in farming. These factors coupled with increased diversion of farmers' time to tend to the sick and burials makes it difficult to plan and organize extension meetings. These changes have also rendered some of the agricultural technologies inappropriate given prevailing farmer circumstances. For example, first and second generation hybrid maize varieties require cash outlays for purchasing inputs (fertilizers and pesticides) and are technologies that are labour intensive. Such technologies become almost irrelevant in the context of labour shortages and HIV/AIDS-related monetary expenditures.

An increasing number of households are headed by children who lack basic agricultural knowledge and skills. Grandmothers, who are too old to work and/or are already overburdened by caring for their many orphans, constitute another farmer category whose needs have to be addressed. Not only is working with them challenging given their resource constraints, but it also requires new approaches to technology design and dissemination of information.

The examples highlighted above in no way provide the whole picture about the complex nature of changes that have taken place in people's livelihoods, they are useful in that they give a glimpse of the changing environment within which extension service providers have to operate and the likely technical and operational challenges that may be faced at organizational level. Presently there are very limited extension programmes and strategies to improve agricultural skills of inexperienced (young) farmers. Furthermore, the increased need to develop new technologies and equipment suitable for the new situation is difficult to address given the already weak linkages between extension, research and other relevant agencies. Moreover, the extension staff who are supposed to drive the process are themselves ill equipped to cope with the situation because of their lack of knowledge on AIDS. It is noteworthy, that the impacts of the epidemic on other institutions also have consequences for extension agencies, particularly in terms of the level of funding from the government and the type and/or effectiveness of the collaborative multi-sectoral activities.

Finally, the very nature of extension work presents challenges in terms of the increased risk of exposure of extension staff to HIV, particularly the field extension officers. This is because extension work requires field staff to travel extensively in rural areas and field officers sometimes have to spend nights away from home. Interaction with HIV positive clients exposes extension officials to the risk of acquiring HIV.

8.3.4 Role of civil society in community management of HIV/AIDS effects

Best practices in HIV/AIDS intervention: the case of Kitovu Mobile AIDS Homecare, Counselling and Orphan Programme (MAHCOP)

MAHCOP stands for Mobile AIDS Homecare, Counselling and Orphan Programme. It is a programme under the Masaka Catholic Diocese and Kitovu Hospital. The programme has two main components: AIDS-related treatment and care, and an orphan support component. The main objectives of MAHCOP are to: conduct sensitization on HIV/AIDS; provide free counselling and HIV/AIDS testing; provide HIV/AIDS-related treatment and care; equip orphans and vulnerable children with agricultural knowledge and skills; train community workers TOTs (two people at every sub-parish -one man and one woman) on HIV/AIDS and importance of HIV testing.

The HIV/AIDS prevention and support programme

Sister Ursula Sharp of The Medical Missionaries of Mary started MAHCOP in 1987 in response to the HIV/AIDS crisis in the district of Rakai. The first two nurses to work on this programme with Sister Ursula were Ms. Cortelida Nanteza and Ms. Robina Sentongo. Because of lack of drugs to treat AIDS, affected individuals would be sent away from hospital when they became terminally ill. In the beginning, therefore, MAHCOP project staff visited clients who had been sent home to give them psychosocial support. Eventually, as more and more people became infected, the project saw the need to address the HIV/AIDS problem as a community issue and started to engage the community in caring for the sick by training community workers. The responsibility of the community workers is to mobilize community members and sensitize them on HIV/AIDS, provide counselling and train patients on drug use when they come to receive their medication, conduct follow-up visits on patients or those who consult, give advice on importance of making wills as well as on how to make wills. From time to time, MAHCOP conducts refresher training for the community workers. Community workers are given gum boots, an umbrella and a bicycle each, to facilitate their work. Sometimes on festive days like Christmas, MAHCOP distributes free blankets, food (soya flour, powdered milk for the children) and soap to the community workers, as a gesture of appreciation for their work which is otherwise unpaid.

In the early 1990s, activities started with counselling services and free testing of blood for those who were willing. Those tested and HIV-positive, would then receive treatment for opportunistic infections. This included a standard pack of antibiotics, sulphur or non-sulphur ointments, which would be distributed at designated centres. From two centres in the study area, the number of centres increased to four[60], to make the drugs more accessible to patients. In 2000, in collaboration with Catholic Relief Services-Uganda (CRS-Uganda) and ACDI-VOCA, MAHCOP started food distribution to its clients and households with AIDS orphans. In 2006, the project had fifteen feeding centres in Masaka, Rakai and Sembabule districts with 1,804 infected and affected individuals benefiting from the food aid. The food supplied is pre-cooked (just needs about ten minutes cooking only) and is meant as a food supplement. Each beneficiary receives nine kilograms of corn soya blend and 0.8 litres of cooking oil per month. The largest families fostering orphans receive forty-five kilograms of corn soya and four litres of oil per month.

However, because food aid is very expensive, donors were not willing to support the programme beyond 2006. Since 2003, MAHCOP staff working with the food programme have developed other strategies to improve the food security of affected communities. At each feeding centre, people are organized in groups of 30-40 individuals through which they can be reached with agricultural extension advice. Through its Community Extension Development Officers (CEDO) MAHCOP organizes monthly meetings for its clients and trains them on various agronomic practices. Farmers have also been given simple farming equipment like hoes and watering cans as well as seeds for planting. Interviews with those who had participated in the training indicate that they each received two kilograms of maize and a similar amount of bean seeds, in addition to cassava cuttings, sweet potato vines, and a variety of vegetable seeds and fruits for planting. The farmers contribute land on which the CEDOs conduct the demonstrations of whatever technology or practice is being taught. In addition to farming and pooling labour, group members have been encouraged to start up self-help savings that members can borrow from in case of problems instead of depleting their assets. The groups meet twice a month and each time members contribute UGX 200 – 500. To a few groups that have demonstrated good management of their affairs, MAHCOP is giving interest-free credit to improve their savings and start up income-generating activities. MAHCOP and the group members work out a feasible repayment schedule for the money

[60] These are distribution centres in the three sub-counties investigated. MAHCOP has many other centres in other parts of Masaka district as well as in the districts of Rakai and Sembabule.

given to the group. For example, one group of fifteen members was given UGX 1.5 million (equivalent US$ 815). While the group does not pay interest to MAHCOP, members agree on a small interest that should be paid for money borrowed as a strategy to build their savings. Group members also receive training in book keeping and financial management from MAHCOP.

It was not until 2005, that MAHCOP enrolled its first patients on anti retro viral therapy (ARV). To improve proper usage of ARVs, the community workers and medical staff train the patients every time they go for drug refills. In addition to ARV treatment, patients are tested for meningitis[61]. MAHCOP does this in collaboration with the Medical Research Centre (MRC), a research organization based in Masaka town. MAHCOP health staff collect the blood samples from the patients and send them for testing at the MRC. Patients who test positive to meningitis are then referred to Uganda Cares Masaka where they get a full preventative package. By the beginning of 2006, MAHOP had about 300 people in Masaka on ARV (estimate obtained through personal communication with a health official at Uganda Cares, Masaka).

Other support provided by MAHCOP is of a more incidental nature. Examples are two widows who have had permanent houses constructed for them; one widower with five orphans who had a three-acre piece of land bought for him; and an orphan boy who had a house and one-acre of land bought for him. In these cases, the beneficiaries contribute labour in form of transporting building materials.

AIDS treatment and care are highly appreciated because they provide an extended lease on life, even though one may not regain previous level of productivity. It enables people (who have the resources) to plan better for their children. The palliative care also improves the quality of life of affected individuals. For some, the symptoms that were a source of stigma disappear completely, they regain their weight and one would not suspect that they are infected. As one attendant puts it: "These days people who are on treatment look even better than us, the normal ones. Such people can easily spread the disease because no one will suspect them, which is another problem that these drugs (ARVs) have brought for us."

A few individuals interviewed mentioned ARV–related side effects like severe skin reactions, mental derangement, or severe body weakness after taking the medication.

[61] According to a health officer in Masaka district, meningitis is one of the causes of mental derangement among AIDS persons and Individuals with meningitis are likely to be HIV-infected.

The orphan support programme

Ideas about the inception of an orphan programme arose from the increasing concern among MAHCOP's clients about the welfare of their children during chronic illness and after death of their parents. A children's department was therefore established in 1989 to cover children's school fees and other basic needs. With the starting of the government Universal Primary Education programme in 1997, MAHCOP cut off support for many school-going children. In the same year, an evaluation of MAHCOP activities was conducted. The key recommendation from the evaluation was that there should be a shift to activities that are geared towards capacity building of individuals and communities rather than handing out of benefits. In 1998, an orphan-needs assessment study with a view of identifying impacts of HIV/AIDS on teenage school dropouts and their coping mechanisms was undertaken. Among the key findings was the need to empower orphaned youths through vocational training and provision of financial support to achieve self reliance, the necessity to equip youth, in addition to basics literacy skills, with modern agricultural skills given the importance of farming for people's livelihoods, and the importance of putting in place mechanisms that would ensure provision of seed and other inputs to facilitate improved agricultural production. In 1998, the farm school project was initiated, with a mission to:

> *To enable the teenage AIDS orphans who have dropped out of school, improve their quality of life, within the proximity of their families, communities and cultures, by starting where they are, move at a pace they can cope with, while using existing talents and resources.* MAHCOP, orphan programme report.

The community workers identify the orphans and vulnerable children (OVC), aged between 13 and 19 in their area. Priority is given to orphans who have vulnerable and very sick AIDS parents, basic literacy skills, access to land and residence within the sub-county where the farm school is operating. Orphans who were formerly MAHCOP-sponsored but dropped out of school because of lack of school fees are also given priority. Early on in the programme, after selection, the teenagers are sensitized about HIV/AIDS prevention, good morals and then given training in various agricultural skills for a period of about six months. However, from 1998 the farm school programme became more structured and the participants had to go through a two year intensive organic farming training at any of the Mobile Farm Schools (MFS). Every month, the trainees would receive a one-week residential training at the MFS, while the remaining time was allocated to implementing the acquired skills at home during those three weeks. The technical programme staff selects community volunteers to provide the necessary back stopping during the three weeks at home. In addition to farming, the trainees also receive HIV/AIDS counselling and psychosocial support.

In 2005, an evaluation of the MFS training programme was conducted and it was recommended that the two-year programme be reduced to one year of intensive training after which the trainees would receive back-up support from the field. The one-year programme has been in implementation since 2006. Selected Orphans and Vulnerable Children undergo a one-year intensive training at the MFS. The current course contents include: agronomic practices for crops grown in district; animal husbandry practices of pigs, goats, cattle and chicken; horticulture; life skills; handcraft and carpentry; financial management of projects; making savings; HIV/AIDS prevention and counselling. The trainees still have face-to-face instruction for one week every month as in the previous programme, but the training is more intensive. On completion of the first year, exemplary trainees and those with clear project proposals receive UGX 100,000 (just about US$ 50) each as a start-up grant to implement their proposals.

After the first year, trainees graduate and start implementing the acquired skills on their own farms. Facilitators of the MFS ensure that trainees in the same locality are organized into Mobile Young Farmers Groups (MYFG). The main objective of the MYFG is to enable trainees to pool skills and resources to enhance farm productivity, have improved access to credit and saving services as well as explore opportunities for joint marketing. In these groups the trainees are encouraged to identify enterprises in which they would want to specialize and they receive further training in those particular activities. Furthermore, MAHCOP gives each group financial support as a start-up fund for the group's saving activities. During the second year, each MYFG will receive relevant training and technical support requested for from the MFS staff.

Technical backstopping and follow-up continues into the third and fourth year. It is hoped that by the end of the fourth year each MYFG will have registered itself into a CBO and will have self-sustaining projects. It is also hoped that by this time, MAHCOP will have linked the MYFGs to other service providers including government institutions from where they can seek or receive more support.

Key achievements

By June 2006, 2500 OVCs from 13 sub-counties in the districts of Masaka, Rakai and Sembabule had participated in the farm school training. The target of the programme is to train orphans in all sub-counties in the three districts. It is said that over 180,000 other people have indirectly benefited from the MFS training. Furthermore, there has been increased community support in programme activities particularly by following-up of MYFG activities.

The key benefits of the programme to the trainees interviewed included: improved self esteem, improved opinion of one's worth as an orphan, a variety of acquired skills (both farming/income generating and those to protect one against AIDS), established networks and groups that, among other things, have facilitated access to micro credit, and increased knowledge of one's rights. Some have even already realized increased incomes through improved crop and livestock (pig, goat) production and the sale of handicrafts. Others have been able to sensitize siblings or other youth in their community on how to protect themselves against HIV and the importance of hard work. Each trainee received a pair of gum boots, uniform and a hoe as part of their training equipment package. During graduations, the best trainees in terms of performance, proper application of acquired skills and discipline have received prizes comprising of various farming tools such as wheel barrows, hoes, watering cans, and so on.

Nevertheless, there are also challenges, including trainees abandoning the programme. The programme has observed a higher drop-out rate among girls compared to boys. For example, according to the Orphan's Programme Coordinator[62], for the 2004 and 2005 recruitments, 46 percent of girls compared to 19 percent of boys, dropped out. Pregnancy, early marriage, and undue influence of guardians were identified as some of the major causes of the higher drop-out rate of girls. Another problem is that only about 60 percent of the trainees are able to apply the skills acquired. Lack of land on which to work is a main cause of non-implementation of acquired knowledge and skills. However, some trainees indicated that they had been discouraged to apply the knowledge and skills acquired because they had no control over the crops grown as the guardians normally controlled sales or used the crops for household food. Finally, some orphans lack transport to go and attend farm school activities.

Because of the success of the MFS programme, there has been an increased demand for similar services among adults. MAHCOP has developed tailor-made training programmes for adults in HIV/AIDS-affected households who need extension advice.

MAHCOP provides an example of a community level organization that is committed and genuinely seeks to address people's livelihood problems as they unfold. The history of their activities shows a holistic approach to development (vulnerable people need food, shelter, education for their children, health insurance and to be facilitated to engage in income-generating activities). Willingness to listen to those being helped and to what their needs are as well as involve affected people in programme activities, are central for those aiming at achieving true development. Their approach shows that programmes have to be flexible to take on new challenges, even those not originally planned for.

---

[62] Graduation speech of Orphans Coordinator MAHCOP, 16th June 2006.

Other community-based initiatives

Community-based initiatives mainly include ROSCAs and other informal groups through which members can borrow money to solve urgent financial needs or pool labour. These groups are also involved in various income-generating activities. However, activities for the ROSCAs in particular were limited by a small capital base and their inaccessibility for those who cannot afford to pay initial membership fees or periodic subscriptions. Only 15 percent of the respondents in the survey belong to a ROSCA, the larger majority of them being men. Lack of good health and physical strength limit membership to groups formed for purposes of labour pooling. In Masaka, a few women's groups have been started with the objective of improving members' material needs. Every month the group identifies a member for whom the other members buy gifts. The gifts mainly constitute basic household utensils and assets. This has enabled members to acquire simple assets that they previously could not afford. However, it was mentioned that those who are well-off receive better and more expensive gifts than the poorer members. Most of the support received by HIV/AIDS-affected households is from close kin as has been already discussed.

8.3.5 Ways in which existing initiatives in the agricultural sector can be strengthened

As has been discussed, inadequate financial and human resources and institutional capacity continue to constrain implementation and scaling up of HIV/AIDS prevention and control. Therefore, one of the main ways to strengthen existing interventions by civil society or government will be to increase resources. Nonetheless, there are other things that can be done to strengthen the effectiveness of existing initiatives in addition to increased funding of activities.

Establishing mechanisms of information collection and monitoring of activities: There is need to establish mechanisms through which information on affected households can be collected and updated. For example it may be useful to have information on which households are affected and differentiating the different types of vulnerable groups (for example, single or double orphans, orphans in child-headed households, orphans in foster homes that are poor, households that need food aid and grants or those that maybe just need credit). In addition, there is need to have an inventory of all CBO/NGOs providing HIV/AIDS-related support, the type of support, and intended target beneficiaries. Such information will be useful in identification of those in need and the specific type of support that they need, avoid duplication of efforts by different agencies, promote better targeting of beneficiaries and use of resources, besides saving time of agencies in mapping out those in need. Such a data base will also be useful in identifying households that many people do not know about but which are vulnerable. Collection of information needs to be accompanied by an effective monitoring system that will facilitate tracking of trends and updating of relevant information. While each district has a planning unit, its activities do not reach the communities. Therefore, district level planning units need to strengthen the capacity of communities to establish and manage local level information.

Community mobilization: The success of any community intervention is likely to depend on how well the target community has been mobilized to participate in the planning and implementation of such interventions. Therefore not only will community participation increase the chances of success, but resources may be saved when communities are made to contribute time and manpower. Additionally, people in the community have a wealth of information that can be very useful in identifying those most in need. In addition to people's participation in external programs, communities can be supported in starting self-help groups or existing informal groups can be strengthened. However, it is important for one to have a good understanding of the dynamics of the communities they are working with in order to ensure that marginalized groups are equally mobilized and benefit from interventions. Despite the challenges being faced by people in rural areas, communities have potential to contribute towards efforts for mitigating AIDS effects. Sometimes external support is necessary to initiate processes that can lead to self organization. Part of the success of MAHCOP and World Vision in Masaka district has been the heavy engagement of communities in their activities. Given the respect that Faith based organizations usually enjoy from their followers, their involvement could be beneficial.

Local level coordination of CBO/NGO activities: From my own observation, there was lack of collaboration between different agencies providing HIV/AIDS-related care and this led to some households receiving the same support from different agencies or having some households receiving support from several agencies while other needy ones had no support at all. Given that all agencies complained of limited resources, coordination of activities would be one way to efficiently use agency resources to meet expected goals. Coordination could be at the level of, for example, sharing information on which households are being targeted and with what support. The other information that could be shared is on community facilitators. If two agencies are working in the same area, it makes no sense for each organization to waste resources training another set of facilitators. It may be cheaper to equip existing facilitators with the relevant knowledge and skills. Resources may also be saved through mounting of joint training programs. Of course one needs to bear in mind the varying scope of different agencies' activities but there are potential areas of collaboration. For example, MAHCOP has employed agricultural extension staff to provide agricultural extension information for their affected clients. However, the government extension worker in that area, and who has more experience than MAHCOP's staff, is redundant because the government cannot give him transport to reach the community.

Another level of collaboration would be through joint organization of activities that reinforce each other. For example, with increasing availability of ART, there will be need to teach users proper nutrition if treatment is to be successful. So health staff may need to work with agricultural extension workers in ensuring that users get all the relevant information. Collaboration can facilitate a holistic approach to AIDS prevention and control. In the later example of an agency providing ART working with extension workers, the clients may benefit more from the ART if they are also facilitated to improve their food security and income-generating capacity. Therefore if the ART provider can link their clients to another agency that provides seeds or credit, the clients will benefit more.

Sharing of experiences with regard to what has worked and what has failed can help different agencies to streamline their strategies.

Operationalization of multi-sectoral approach: While HIV/AIDS has been mainstreamed in all government ministries, activities remain fragmented both within and between ministries. For example, at the district level there was no evidence of extension agents working with the judiciary to see how people affected with HIV/AIDS can have their land and property rights protected. Many government staff do not understand the concept of mainstreaming or how they can mainstream HIV/AIDS into their programs or activities. This is a big challenge that needs to be addressed because it is likely to result in inefficient use of resources.

Its important that collaboration be not only limited between agencies but should also involve government departments and local leaders.

Chapter 9

Conclusions and discussion

In this chapter, I present the main conclusions and a discussion of the main findings from the study. In the first part, I answer the research questions that this study sought to answer followed by a discussion of the results. The second part discusses the methodological and theoretical implications, and policy implications in the agricultural sector based on the findings.

9.1 Answering the research questions

9.1.1 Resources, activities and livelihood strategies of banana farming households

The main household resources accessible to households were family labour and land. Other physical resources included both small and large livestock, chicken, and various household items like bicycle, radio, and motorcycle among others. In addition, people depended on close kin (social capital) for food, financial and other household needs.

Family labour is almost exclusively the main source of labour for agricultural activities. Results in this study show no significant difference in household size and number of economically active individuals per household between the two districts. However, households in Masaka have a significantly higher dependency ratio than those in Kabarole. Ill health is identified as the main cause of reduced household labour. No difference is observed between the districts in terms of access to land and amount of land owned. However, land is unevenly distributed with the majority owning less than a hectare (2 acres). At the same time, seasonal variation in access to land (particularly the rented or borrowed plots) as well as the processes associated with women's access to land (that is, access through marriage or male-relatives) increases tenure insecurity of individuals in poor households and more so for women.

The main source of income is agricultural, from the sale of crops followed by livestock, and to a limited extent agricultural labour. Other less important income sources include non-agricultural casual labour, remittances, salaried employment, property rents, donations or pensions. For the two districts no differences are observed in the average income earned three months prior the survey. The majority (87%) reported income change during the period 2002-2005, with two-thirds experiencing reductions. Low yields due to prolonged drought, reduced household labour due to sickness and to a lesser extent animal and crop pests and diseases are reported as main causes of reduced household incomes. For those households that reported increased income, respondent said that it was due to increased agricultural production, good market prices at the time of sale and engagement in off-farm income-generating activities.

Social capital played a significant role in people's access to employment, labour and resources. Those who have connections to friends and relatives with fallow land were able to access it without cost. Having connections with rich farmers in the area provides access to employment for one's self and one's children. Furthermore, connections to the Catholic Church and the local leadership in Masaka is a key determinant of access to food aid, orphan support, medical treatment for opportunistic infections of AIDS-affected persons and, later on, being enrolled in ARV treatment. Social status, position, and gender appeared to influence ability to access state, institutional or local resources.

The study shows that there is significant differential access to resources by wealth status and between male- and female-headed households. The well-off households have significantly higher total per capita and food expenditures than poor households (i.e. 3.5 and 10 times respectively). Also, for all the household resources investigated, the two types of female-headed households have fewer assets than the male-headed ones. The two types of female-headed households that constituted the largest proportion of poor households have the smallest total annual and per capita expenditure than male-headed households. Widowed household heads are significantly older than household heads in single-female and male-headed households by at least six to nine years, respectively. Furthermore, the household heads in the two types of female-headed households have lower literacy levels and higher incidence of HIV/AIDS-affectedness than their male counterparts. Regarding changes in amount of land owned between 2002 and 2005, significant differences are observed with male-headed households reporting increase in land acreage over the period while the two types of female-headed households reported a decrease in land size.

Households typically pursue three types of livelihood strategies that have been labelled as: (i) perennial crop producer (growing more perennial crops, less food crops, and keeping few animals) (ii) diversified smallholder farmer (less perennial crops, more food crops, and more livestock production) and (iii) staples grower (less food crops, few small livestock). Despite certain historical and contextual differences between the two districts, farmers engage in similar activities and pursue more or less similar strategies. Empirical data clearly show evidence of on-farm diversification and expansion, non-farm diversification and migration characterizing livelihood strategies in the two districts. Thirty five percent of the respondents reported having a second source of income in addition to farming.

The results show differences in the type of strategies employed by different households. Livelihood strategies mainly employed by poor households, particularly female-headed ones (subsistence production, casual labouring, marriage, transactional sex, depending on kin and charity, and consumption reduction strategies), reflect a lack of alternative options rather than initiative to capitalize on investment opportunities. While these households would have been compelled to diversify, as a response to reduced returns on their labour in farming as well as deteriorating economic options, this does not seem to be the case. Mugyenyi (1998) makes a similar observation on female-headed households in Uganda. Female-headed households are trapped in a type of farming that does not pay and when economic hardships intensify, they engage in reactive strategies that are risky and increase exposure to HIV infection. It is also important to note that hiring out of labour by poor subsistence farmers causes their own farm production (however little) to decline.

In contrast, some male-headed households that dominate the perennial crop producer and diversified smallholder clusters employ strategies that are risk-averting or proactive in nature, in the sense that they are based on a conscious plan to circumvent environmental, social or economic constraints. Both survey and case study material has clearly shown that after some households accumulate resources (purchase land) and expand agricultural production, they also start non-farm income-generating activities. This result corroborates Smith *et al.* (2001:249) observation on diversification in other parts of Uganda that "income and security from crop production, land and livestock ownership enable rural households to divide their labour between farm and non-farm economic activities, or to hire labour to work on their farms enabling them to concentrate part of their labour on non-farm activities". These finding show that different factors motivate farmers to diversify. In this case, farmers in well-off households diversify and relocate their labour to benefit from available opportunities while those in poor households are forced to hire out their labour to survive (cf. Niehof, 2004).

Empirical material on participation in non-farm employment indicate no significant difference in the proportion of household members participating in off-farm employment across the livelihood strategy clusters, regardless of wealth status. The small share of employment in non-agriculture at about five percent, that implies existence of very few employment opportunities, may partly be responsible. Bagamba (2007) notes that regardless of wealth status, the relative remoteness from markets and services also forces farmers to concentrate on agricultural and less on off-farm employment. However, the fact that female-headed households constituted the majority in the staples grower strategy with the lowest per capita expenditures, implies that female-headship plays a significant role in inhibiting the pursuit of more remunerative livelihood strategies. This study suggests that the association of gender and the occupation of a household head may be a strong indicator of poverty.

The nature of farming and associated constraints has meant that the majority of rural farmers in Masaka and Kabarole cannot produce adequate amounts of food and generate sufficient income to sustain their households by farming alone. Limited land, degraded soils, prolonged periods of drought as well as imperfect markets have worked in synergy to make returns from farming low, particularly for poor households with small landholdings. Additionally, inability to use purchased inputs (fertilizers and pesticides) and hire labour are identified as key constraints to the development of agricultural production, which is consistent with previous research findings in Uganda (cf. Pender *et al.*, 2001; 2004). The above challenges coupled with present under developed scientific methods of production and non-profitability of agriculture reduce farmers' capacity to gainfully engage in their main source of livelihood, thus implying that their livelihoods are already vulnerable before even considering the effects of environmental shocks such as HIV/AIDS. It is imperative that government urgently facilitates improved access to input markets, extension services and (agricultural) credit, as well as review land tenure legislation to address tenure-related constraints.

While agriculture remains the most important livelihood activity and the involvement in non-farm income activities is strongly linked to farming, individuals straddle different types of activities and earn income from various sources to sustain and improve their livelihood. Alternative sources of income have the potential to bolster households and individuals against shocks thus reducing the risk of increased vulnerability to such shocks. However, the limited sources of non-farm rural employment in the study area implies that farmers find it difficult to finance farming activities and buy inputs, deal with poor harvests or manage overall income risk. Improved transport and communications infrastructures as well as availability of functioning markets for agriculture inputs and products are of crucial importance. The expansion and growth of the non-farm rural sector may provide an alternative source of livelihood for households that have very small or no land.

9.1.2 The effects of HIV/AIDS-related mortality and morbidity on household resources, and overall livelihood security

Effects on labour

This study shows that labour is not simply one-dimensional. The factor labour in the context of HIV/AIDS constitutes and reflects a range of complexities. The impact of HIV/AIDS on labour is predominantly felt at the level of productivity, because of the reallocation of labour away from productive activities and the redirecting of monetary resources from production to caring for the sick. The outcome is a decrease in productivity of labour and a reduction in cultivated land. Labour shortages occur due to: (i) sickness or death or labour foregone to HIV/AIDS-related care, (ii) poor health among the remaining household members, and (iii) lack of inter-generation transfer of knowledge and skills. HIV/AIDS-related impacts on household labour include poor health, increased care and orphan burden, and loss of income of sick or dead household member. AIDS also undermines one's capacity to effectively make use of other resources or opportunities that may come by or one's ability to negotiate and obtain social support. Differences in HIV/AIDS-related effects were more significant among poor affected households than their well-off counterparts.

Empirical data reveal that AIDS in the household results in a higher reduction of labour productivity compared to malaria and other diseases. A significantly higher proportion of HIV/AIDS-affected households reported sick and bedridden productive household members and about twice as many bedridden days than non-affected households. The days lost to sickness in affected households, are likely to even be more because of the increased susceptibility to opportunistic infections among HIV/AIDS-affected individuals. Due to reduced labour availability of a sick household member, other household members are forced to reduce time engaged in productive activities or completely abandon their job to be able to care for the sick. Over two thirds of caregivers spent a week providing care for a sick member but time spent away from school or work looking after a sick household member ranged from one week to two months.

HIV/AIDS is the leading cause of death among the sampled households and the spouses, mainly affecting adults between 18-45 years of age. Regardless of wealth status, a higher proportion of HIV/AIDS-affected households experienced an adult death than non-affected ones. Case study material shows mixed effects with regard to AIDS-related death but overall changes in household labour availability and well-being of surviving members depend on changes in household composition, labour contributions of joiners or what the leavers were contributing, who takes over dead household member's roles, and the person who dies. The impact of a woman's death is more associated with reduced household food security and reduced care of the children, particularly of those below five years of age. While effects due the death of a male head is associated with reduced household labour and incomes.

A higher proportion of HIV/AIDS-affected households fosters orphans and is more likely to have more orphans than non-affected households. Because the majority of affected households are poor households, the significantly higher number of orphans being fostered is likely to further strain the few resources making effects more significant in affected than in non-affected households. Even then, the effects of taking in orphans are mixed. The gender and age of orphans, and whether an orphan is HIV-infected or not, the number of orphans being taken in, as well as the resource status of the host household influence the type and magnitude of the effects experienced. Taking in older orphans often provides extra hands for cooking, collecting water, farming and baby-sitting, while taking in younger or

HIV-infected children is associated with increased care requirements. Qualitative evidence reveals that some households have received material benefits from NGOs because they have fostered orphans.

It is noteworthy that limited household labour predates HIV/AIDS. Labour-poor households include those headed by old people, women, children, and people with AIDS (PLWHA). Nonetheless, being HIV/AIDS-affected intensifies labour-related constraints in such households.

Effects on income and expenditure

HIV/AIDS-related economic impact on households is felt on both income and expenditures. With regard to changes in household income over the period 2002-05, the results show no direct linkage between HIV/AIDS status and income changes observed among the surveyed households. Furthermore, there is no significant difference in the proportion of HIV/AIDS households that reported increased or reduced incomes over the same period. The lack of linkage observed between HIV/AIDS status and change in household income points to the fact that AIDS affects individuals in all social economic classes (cf. Chapoto and Jayne,2005; Ainsworth and Semali, 1998).

The largest household expenses are those on food and medicine. HIV/AIDS leads to increased medical expenditure but reduces total per capita expenditure. Apart from medical expenditures, there are no statistically significant differences observed in money spent on other household items between HIV/AIDS-affected and non-affected households regardless of wealth status. However, among the poor households, the differences in medical expenditure are more pronounced than among the well-off, implying that HIV/AIDS has limited effects on well-off households. Additional information reveals that among affected households, those reporting an AIDS-related adult death spend more on food than those with an AIDS patient while the latter were likely to spend more on medicines.

Expenditure increases associated with problems that create heightened vulnerability, such as expenditure on curative health care or increased food purchases due to inability to produce adequate food for own consumption, should not be mistaken to mean improved well-being among affected households. Because of lack of general health insurance, households have no alternative but to use their savings or sell productive assets to meet health costs when expenditure exceeds income. The poor also usually rely on informal credit or group-based micro-finance products in times of distress. Among surveyed households, no differences in access to credit are observed between affected and non-affected households, but less than three percent of the respondents have access to credit. However, community members are reluctant to lend HIV-infected individuals money for fear that it would be paid back late or not at all.

Effects on other household assets

Reported by more than half of the AIDS-widows interviewed, asset depletion featured as one of the most important effects of spousal death on household resources. HIV/AIDS-related effects on household assets vary with social-economic status. However, even within the same socio-economic category, differences are mixed and sometimes observed for particular assets and not for others. Survey data show that HIV/AIDS-affected poor households experienced more significant reductions in land, small animals and chicken than non-affected poor households over the period under investigation. Goats, pigs and poultry were the most commonly depleted household assets for purposes of obtaining food and health services. The sale of land and cattle for the same purpose was reported to a lesser extent. The higher proportions of respondents reporting sale of small animals compared to those selling cattle and land indicate that households attempt to first sell assets with the least impact on long-term production potential.

Change in household assets (land, livestock and chicken) between affected and non-affected households over the period 2002 to 2005 also vary by wealth status. Among the well-off households, no differences are observed between HIV/AIDS-affected and non-affected households with regard to changes in the number of cattle and land owned. However, for the poor households, a slight reduction in land acreage owned among affected households could be noted, while non-affected households reported a slight increase in land acreage over the period. HIV/AIDS is also leading to landlessness. In the period 2002 to 2005, one third of the HIV/AIDS-widows interviewed lost their land and property to relatives of the dead spouse. Lack of access to land implies that individuals in these households have to subsist on casual employment and petty trading which are found to be very unreliable sources of income. Possibly due to the presence of NGOs giving livestock to HIV/AIDS-affected households in the study area, results show that affected poor households reported a mean increase in the number of cattle owned while non-affected ones reported a decrease. However, with regard to goats and pigs, affected households reported significantly more reduction in small livestock numbers than non-affected households regardless of wealth status.

Effects of HIV/AIDS on intra- and inter-household relations

HIV/AIDS-related effects on the relationship between spouses have, in most cases, resulted in conflict, mistrust and disharmony, increased violence, separation or divorce. Women's inferior and subordinate position in the household, and their limited access to resources, forces some women to remain in risky marriage relationships that expose them to HIV infection. Though few men suffered HIV/AIDS-related verbal abuse or physical violence, among women this was a more common occurrence. HIV/AIDS-induced poverty has reduced parents' capacity to meet their natural obligation of taking care of their children as evidenced with increased school dropouts among orphans and early entry into the job market by children. The study also shows that many AIDS orphans are discriminated against and exploited by relatives who take them in. Some orphans have had support meant for them diverted and used for other children. However, cases of mutual support where men and women looked after their infected partners and gave them all the possible support also exist. Children provide the first line of support to sick parents, in some cases taking over adult roles. The relationship between orphans and other relatives can be one of mutual support, but also one of discrimination, conflict and exploitation, with the latter three scenarios seemingly dominant.

While inter-household support through exchange of food, money and gifts was reported in over 50 percent of the surveyed households, HIV/AIDS has eroded some of this social support. As affected households contend with increasing expenditures while earning less income, it becomes more and more difficult for them to provide or maintain support to other households. Sickness also increases care-related time thus reducing time to participate in or engage in reciprocal exchanges. In the study population, two groups emerged as those with the greatest vulnerability to loss of their social capital: orphaned children and widows in poor households.

AIDS erodes the social networks that are supposed to act as safety nets for rural people in times of crisis. HIV/AIDS-related death of productive adults has left some households with old grandmothers as the only relatives to support orphans. Following the death of a household head, the practice in the study area is that close kin agree on how the orphans and widows are to be cared for and who would provide what kind of support or take in which orphans. Evidence from the study shows that due to the clustering effects of HIV/AIDS many orphans find they have no relatives to look after them. The few who may still be alive may be too poor to take in orphans or are just reluctant to do so. The reluctance is associated with the fact that many AIDS orphans are double orphans or will be double orphans. Additionally, people are afraid of the responsibility involved in taking in young children or those that have AIDS. Where grandmothers are still alive, this has lead to the burden falling on them. Death of parents also implies that children's access to any social networks that had been created by their parents becomes very difficult, if not impossible. The loss of social connections is likely to be greater for children who are still very young because they may not be known by kin or the children are not aware of which friends or relatives to seek support from.

Death of a spouse also means that the household loses his/her social support networks. While women also have their own support networks, the debilitating effects of the disease and increased expenditure makes it difficult for some women to participate in networks, particularly those that require regular payments. HIV/AIDS-affected impoverished households cannot join such networks. Thus, AIDS leads to social exclusion. HIV/AIDS-affected individuals find it difficult to maintain past social relations or create new ones. Widows' loss of social capital also relates to land tenure insecurity that is dependent upon their relationship to the spouse. Their problematic access to land following the death of a spouse comes about by subdivision of land for the sons, and to a limited extent, land and property grabbing by the late spouse's relatives. Stigma and conflict between relatives of the dead spouse and the widow lead to some women being evicted from their homes by in-laws after the death of their husband. In many instances such women are forced to migrate to new areas and in the process they lose the social support networks that they had built over time.

HIV/AIDS has also led to a breakdown of social cohesion and a degeneration of morals among children and adults. Children experience increased violence as a consequence of HIV/AIDS. The custom of cultural cleansing increases a girl's vulnerability to risk of infection. In addition to the risks of sexual exploitation some orphans are badly treated. Cases of women and men that have abandoned their children and spouses were reported. There is also an increase in the number of delinquent children who do not help old parents with work and, because of stealing, have become a nuisance in their community. Some relatives have taken or sold part of the orphans' or widows' land and other household property, leaving the orphans and widows with no means of survival. The breakdown in social cohesion and the degeneration in morals are likely to create an environment of increased risk to infection, particularly for orphaned children.

9.1.3 Differences in HIV/AIDS-related effects

The study found out that HIV/AIDS-effects are different for people of different wealth status and gender. And that gender and wealth status influence the way people respond or cope with the effects of the epidemic.

Widowhood and labour constraints

There is a high level of widowhood in the study area with two-fifths being caused by AIDS. Also notable in this study is that all widow-household heads in Kabarole are HIV/AIDS positive and widowhood is more prevalent among women than men. Some ethnic groups in the study area practice widow inheritance. However, because of the fear of AIDS, it has become difficult for widows to be inherited by the relatives of the late husbands or obtain a potential man interested in marriage and for widowers to get substitutes from their in-laws. Therefore, for those women to whom remarriage (whether through wife inheritance or otherwise) is the only option to survival, the HIV/AIDS-related risk thus alters such socio-cultural relations. Widowers are less affected by widowhood because men face fewer restrictions in remarrying than women and when one wife dies, the man still has another wife to look after him. Therefore, restrictions on remarriage and factors such as harassment and stigma or refusal of widow inheritance, have in some cases forced women to migrate either to their natal home or to new areas where people do not know them. When they do so they lose their rights to the late spouse's land and property. Migration of widows increases their vulnerability.

While widowers easily re-marry, and are therefore able to replace lost labour, most widows do not remarry and have labour constraints. Not only do widow-headed households suffer from the loss of the dead member's labour, but because in many cases the widows are also HIV infected, they are also less productive. Empirical data reveal that labour is the main constraint to production among female-headed households. Over two thirds of the HIV/AIDS-widows interviewed reported intensifying their own labour to cope with the loss of spousal labour. The two types of female-headed households also have a higher proportion of young children (aged 10 and below) than the male-headed ones. Therefore, HIV/AIDS is likely to further constrain women's mobility through increased labour constraints.

Case study material shows that HIV/AIDS-widowers who did not remarry also experience labour constraints. The biggest challenges they face are learning to cook, clean and care for their children, roles that they were not socialized to do. However, HIV/AIDS-widowers never experience threat to lose their land and they have a choice to remarry if they want. It is noteworthy that HIV/AIDS-widowers (particularly the very old) are more likely to suffer from depression and social exclusion because they lack the kind of social support networks women have.

Differences between male-headed and female-headed households

Over the period of study (2002-5), female-headed households experienced greater asset depletion than male-headed ones. The assets that the two types of female-headed households were likely to own (goats, pigs and chicken) significantly declined over the period of study. This may imply that fewer assets are depleted to care for sick women in male-headed households or households experience more asset depletion if the male household head gets infected. While one would need more data to substantiate this conclusion, there is documented evidence to this effect elsewhere (cf. Rugalema, 1999b). The decline in household assets among female-headed households (from an already very low base) is a sign of increased impoverishment and vulnerability. This also partly explains why some women resort to risky behaviour like transactional sex or having multiple partners. The study shows that households that have the least household assets and the smallest per capita expenditure also lack access to other agricultural inputs, such as, improved seeds, fertilizers, pesticides and have the highest vulnerability to food insecurity.

While men, women and children participate in HIV/AIDS-related care provision, both qualitative and quantitative data show that the burden of care falls disproportionately on women.

Orphanhood and violence among children

Child orphanhood increases the risk of poverty in adulthood, especially when the affected children fail to acquire an education. HIV/AIDS has exacerbated the prevalence of orphanhood. Results from this study clearly show how HIV/AIDS-related labour shortages result in the substitution of adult labour by child labour, leading to less schooling time or sometimes complete withdrawal from school. Children who have lost parents due to HIV/AIDS are stigmatized and discriminated against or experience psychological trauma. For such children, if they are still at school, this may affect their health and performance. Because many orphans come from poor backgrounds, their prospects for education are often already limited. Coupled with dependence on other people for survival, this makes orphans very vulnerable. Orphans in well-off households continue education. A few vulnerable orphans in Masaka who were targeted for NGO support were able to continue their education as well. Disillusionment from economic hardships, redundancy, alcohol and drug abuse, as well as loss of social control create a mix of risk factors that increase orphans' vulnerability to HIV/AIDS infection. For some older orphans trying to earn a living from farming, the crisis in agriculture frustrates their efforts, while there are already limited income-generating opportunities in the area.

Children experience increased violence as a consequence of HIV/AIDS. Orphaned girls have suffered rape and defilement and in most cases have no one to help them to seek justice. There is also evidence of sexual exploitation of boys by rich women in the urban areas (Seeley *et al.*, 2003). In a way, this increases the vulnerability of boys because it is the boys that are under pressure to start earning at an earlier age in poor households. Therefore, HIV/AIDS not only impoverishes orphans through the death of their parents, but leaves them also with limited options for survival given that any strategy they would think of taking to break the poverty cycle increases their risk of infection. The age at which one becomes an orphan, sex, double orphanhood, having AIDS, coming from a very poor background, having very limited options of support, and whether the orphan is benefiting from any form of support determine the extent of vulnerability and the intensity of orphanhood-related effects.

Differences by wealth status

With regard to characteristics of HIV/AIDS-affected households, the majority are poor with uneducated heads, reside in Kabarole and about half are female-headed. Among the well-off households, there is no significant difference between affected and non-affected households with regard to the education and age of the household head and differences in assets are marginal or non-existent. Variables for which marginal differences are observed such as the amount of land under cultivation or extent of hired labour use do not impact directly on people's survival. However, the differences observed among poor households are significant. Poor and affected households have significantly lower per capita food expenditures, lower access to extension services, and reduced involvement in activities to improve production (pest and disease control, soil and water management - issues directly related to one's livelihood) than their non-affected counterparts. This implies that poor households experience more significant impacts of HIV/AIDS than well-off households.

The low levels of HIV/AIDS among the well-off households contradicts the AIDS literature on Uganda that shows that HIV prevalence levels among the rich are higher than those among the poor (Ministry of Health and ORC Macro, 2006; UBOS, 2006). This could be due to HIV/AIDS-related-asset-eroding effects such that some well-off households that get affected become poorer and move from the well-off to the poor household category. This shows that while wealth status influences people's response to the effects of HIV/AIDS, HIV/AIDS-related effects also influence one's wealth status. Therefore, HIV/AIDS is likely to affect social differentiation. Furthermore, the higher proportion of affected households among poor households may also be linked to the very low asset base observed among widow-headed households. Almost half of the affected households are male-headed. One could argue that poor men who cannot access health services or afford good nutrition are likely to succumb to the effects of HIV faster, thus leaving their widows with very few or no assets to live on. The small asset base observed for widow-headed households may therefore be an indicator of broader social inequality that maintains unequal resource distribution.

Differences between affected households

Regardless of wealth, gender, and age, other location specific factors influence the magnitude of HIV/AIDS-related effects and the ability of individuals and households to respond to these effects. Affected households that: (i) have close kin capable of providing financial, food or care-related support, (ii) have connections to institutions or NGO's providing HIV/AIDS-related care and support or are located in areas served by these organizations, (iii) have access to health services that provide (free) treatment for opportunistic infections and/or ARVs, (iv) are personally known to or have kinship relations with local village chairmen, or (v) belong to informal social networks, are better off than affected households that do not have such access or connections. For example, affected households in Mbirizi and Kyazanga in Masaka had more rings of social support (relatives, informal networks, local NGO, and government) than in other villages in Masaka and in Kabarole. For some, this dampened the effects of the epidemic and improved, for example, people's food security or opportunities for orphan education. Comparing the two districts, this study shows that the interaction between the high HIV-prevalence levels and longer duration of the epidemic in Masaka with location specific factors like drought, declining soil fertility and pests and diseases, has increased the vulnerability of affected households in Masaka.

The results show that HIV/AIDS causes differential impacts for different categories of households and individuals and different epidemics in different localities therefore the need for different strategies and interventions when targeting affected households.

9.2 Effects of HIV/AIDS on household food and livelihood security

This study shows that a household's wealth or socio-economic status, changes in resources over time, and its demographic characteristics substantially influence the extent of the effects of AIDS on the members' livelihood. In the overwhelming majority of affected cases the effects of AIDS are negative and lead to increased impoverishment and vulnerability. However, for some households, the severity of HIV/AIDS-related effects are not so great as to be unmanageable, for others there was no impact, while in some cases HIV/AIDS produced a positive impact. For example, Appleton *et al.* (1995), cites case studies showing distress sales of land and labour by the poor to the rich. Others have benefited from the exploitation of cheap labour of widows and orphaned children (UNDP, 1995). The differences and the magnitude of effects experienced are associated with factors both at household level and beyond.

Using daily per capita household expenditure as a proxy for livelihood security, the following significant factors could be identified: education and gender of the household head, access to hired labour, household wealth status, access to credit and extension services and NGO support, and district of residence in addition to being HIV/AIDS-affected. Also using food (in)security as a proxy for household vulnerability, households that have a wide asset base (cattle, goats, pigs, land), access to agricultural inputs (planting material, labour, credit), and with better-managed soils are food secure. The results show that HIV/AIDS is not a significant factor affecting household food security, implicating that HIV/AIDS will have less negative effects as long as households have access to production resources and services, and good soils.

These results point to the fact that HIV/AIDS is just one factor among a variety of factors that make households vulnerable. The differences or similarities observed between affected and non-affected households are not due to HIV/AIDS alone but to the interaction between HIV/AIDS and other environmental factors. This also implies that one cannot talk about direct causality due to HIV/AIDS. The effects observed among HIV/AIDS-affected households are a result of a complex set of interactions between different factors, including AIDS. This study shows that other factors may cause more significant effects on people's food and overall livelihood security than HIV/AIDS. Nonetheless, because of the negative effects associated with HIV/AIDS, its presence is likely to intensify food insecurity due to other factors as exemplified by the higher food insecurity experienced by households in Masaka.

The following categories of households and individuals are, therefore, identified as some of the most vulnerable to HIV/AIDS-related effects: orphans, orphan-headed households, widow-headed households, female-headed households and households with very old or illiterate or HIV-infected household heads. They are characterized by limited or no access to land, limited labour for production and sources of (agricultural) income, illiteracy, as well as a lack of or small social networks. Thus, vulnerability depends on a combination of factors and processes. It is noteworthy that these different factors and processes may converge differently at different points in space or time, creating a very different manifestation of vulnerability for different households and even for individuals within the same household. Results from the study demonstrate that both a wide asset base and opportunities to diversify activities help protecting a household against external shocks, such as HIV/AIDS. Thus underscoring the relevance of intra-household analysis.

9.3 Effects of AIDS on agriculture and the role of agriculture extension services

Both for Masaka and Kabarole, the most significant effect of ill health on agricultural production is related to poor agronomic practices for all crops because of reduced household labour. This is followed by a decline in crop yields, increase in banana pests and diseases, and a reduction in cultivated land, the latter being reported more for Masaka than Kabarole. While this could be associated with the higher HIV/AIDS prevalence levels in Masaka, the interaction between HIV/AIDS and other environmental factors (particularly prolonged drought and poor soils) may have worked in synergy to lead to higher proportions of Masaka households experiencing the aforementioned effects. With regard to changes in the type of crops grown, a mixed picture and no differences are observed between affected and non-affected households in terms of change in the type of crops grown, area under agricultural production, and change in agricultural incomes obtained. However, a significantly higher proportion of non-affected households reported increased yields than HIV/AIDS-affected households. Despite the differences noted, there is no evidence to show that agricultural production in Kabarole is more affected than in Masaka or vice versa. The differences in the results may be attributed to differences in the level of HIV prevalence, population size and other environmental factors.

Household level analysis reveals that HIV/AIDS-related effects vary by wealth status and household type. Among the well-off households, no differences in banana management practices by gender of the household head or HIV/AIDS status are observed. However, the picture is mixed among the poor households, with a higher proportion of non-affected households unexpectedly showing less engagement in certain banana management practices (for example, soil and water conservation) than affected households. This points to the fact that some of the differences observed between affected and non-affected households are due to other causes other than HIV/AIDS status. Furthermore, the effect of sickness amongst widow-headed households mainly results in reduction of area under agricultural production and yields as well as an increase in disease and pest infestation. Conversely, a higher proportion of male-headed and single-female households experience effects associated with reduction in implementation of recommended crop management practices.

Apart from the use of hired labour, there was no significant difference between the well-off and poor households with regard to mulching, use of clean planting materials or access to services, with the lack of significance being attributed to the local situation that is characterized by limited access to these materials and services. However, the proportion of HIV/AIDS-affected households accessing agricultural extension services is lower than that of non-affected households, with the differences being more significant among poor households. This implies that while the poor have limited access to extension services, those that are HIV/AIDS-affected have even less. It is noteworthy that the situation is worse for female-headed households which are more likely to be HIV/AIDS affected and less likely to have access to agricultural extension services than male-headed ones. HIV/AIDS therefore challenges current development trends to reform extension service provision through privatization (Qamar, 2001). How would farmers that have been struggling to maintain production and have now depleted their meagre resources to deal with HIV/AIDS-related effects be able to pay for extension services? Such policy reforms need to be re-examined.

Regardless of HIV/AIDS, the factors that have been identified as crucial in limiting households' capacities to increase agricultural production include land scarcity and tenure-related constraints, dependence on rain-fed agriculture, pests and diseases, declining soil fertility, limited household labour, limited use of modern inputs as well as limited availability of appropriate technologies. In addition, the low levels of education among household heads, limited access to agricultural information and financial services due to few institutions operating in the area, make it difficult for farmers to adopt labour or capital-intensive technologies. The high labour requirements associated with some banana management practices (corms removal and splitting stems, soil and water conservation, and de-suckering) and the lack or limited availability of resources to hire labour by certain households has resulted in the majority of farmers abandoning such practices. Yet these are also identified as key banana management practices. The superimposition of HIV/AIDS on existing constraints is likely to make banana-farming households vulnerable to effects of reduced production.

Given the mandate of agricultural extension organizations to facilitate agricultural development, they clearly have an important role to play in preventing and mitigating the effects of the epidemic. However, agricultural extension services have also experienced the brunt of HIV/AIDS. Effects include the loss of experienced staff, reduced productivity among HIV-infected staff, an increased workload among the remaining staff and rise in institutional resources to meet HIV/AIDS-related costs, and an overall decline in the level and quality of service provision. In addition to HIV/AIDS-related institutional changes, the epidemic has introduced new challenges and demands for the extension organizations. Some of these include: (i) a new clientele characterized by old women and orphaned children that are resource-constrained, less interested in farming, incapable of applying recommended agricultural practices or investing in agriculture and natural resource management; (ii) limited knowledge and skills on the part of extension staff to address HIV/AIDS-related effects; and (iii) risks associated with working in high HIV-prevalence areas. The change in composition of clientele implies that some of the existing extension methods and technologies are rendered irrelevant (Nguthi, 2007). The increased diversion of farmers' time to attend to their sick and burials also makes it difficult to plan and organize extension services.

As a government response to mitigate the impacts of HIV/AIDS in the agriculture sector, MAAIF has mainstreamed HIV/AIDS in its programs and established focal point officers to coordinate HIV/AIDS activities, initiated sensitization of staff on HIV/AIDS, developed a policy and strategic framework to guide the mainstreaming of HIV/AIDS in the agricultural sector and also developed a training guide on HIV/AIDS for field extension agents. In addition to government initiatives, civil society has played a significant role in improving people's capacity to deal with the effects of HIV/AIDS. Specific activities targeting the agricultural sector have included: provision of agricultural extension services and training, provision of improved seeds (mainly maize, beans and vegetable) and other planting materials, provision of livestock (local and improved breeds of goats, pigs and heifers), food aid and to a limited extent, financial support in form of grants and credit. Furthermore, community awareness-raising on AIDS, provision of VTC services, orphan support and home-based care (HBC), as well as psychological support have been provided in selected communities.

In spite of prevailing challenges, the role of extension and other advisory agencies in educating the farming population about AIDS, as well as in developing new strategies, methodologies, materials, technology and equipment to address new extension needs can be significant. I propose the following areas for extension agencies to act on.

1. Prevention of further spread of HIV/AIDS through community mobilization and sensitization with emphasis on self protection against infection, improved nutrition, dealing with HIV/AIDS-related stigma and discrimination as well as how to ensure protection of rights of widows and children over productive resources.
2. Supporting food production and introducing profitable agro-income generating activities, intensifying promotion of nutrition education programs, facilitating development of local food banks and labour pooling arrangements, promoting labour-saving technologies, and reinforcing community-based mechanisms to preserve local agricultural knowledge. This needs to be in addition to facilitating affected households to link up with other relevant service providers.
3. Provision of education, life skills and vocational training for AIDS orphans and vulnerable children through formal and informal channels.
4. Conducting research on HIV/AIDS and specific aspects of extension with emphasis on area specific research and interventions. This needs to be in addition to periodic monitoring of impact trends.

A key issue that emerges from this research is the need to work beyond traditional "agricultural focused" interventions to those that are more holistic and integrated in manner. This also calls for the establishment of linkages or strengthening of existing ones with other organizations providing support to HIV/AIDS-affected communities. These linkages have the potential to provide an environment of experience, sharing and learning on how to deal with the effects of HIV/AIDS as well as facilitate better use of scarce resources. The above notwithstanding, farmers must be facilitated to use new technologies and improve their production. Therefore as some authors have proposed, it is necessary, for example, to distribute improved seeds and tools, provide agricultural input grants, subsidies or credit and strengthen income generating activities as well as local saving initiatives like ROSCAs (Wiggins *et al.*, 2005).

The proposed recommendations above will obviously require additional human, financial and physical resources. It is therefore imperative that national extension systems receive the financial and technical assistance they need. In addition to increased funding for service provision and AIDS activities, review of existing curricula of agricultural training institutions, appropriate training of agriculture staff, establishing mechanisms of information collection and monitoring of activities at community level, community mobilization, better coordination of local level interventions as well as effective operationalization of the multi-sectoral strategy at the local level are likely to strengthen existing initiatives.

9.4 Gender: women's position and access to resources

Women's subordinate position in society entails inferior status in the household and access to land and other resources. In this study, for all assets investigated the two types of female-headed households on average have a weaker asset base than their male counterparts, regardless of HIV/AIDS status. This implies that in order to deal with issues of women's limited access to resources, we must consider factors that perpetuate inequalities in asset ownership among the rural poor, particularly female-headed households.

In this study, land is identified as one of the most important assets and source of livelihood for the majority, but women's claims to land remains problematic. While the government of Uganda has shown commitment to addressing issues of women's empowerment and has put in place structures, laws and systems to ensure that it is achieved, many customary and statutory laws discriminate against women in areas of marriage, divorce and inheritance. Even where the legal system is non-discriminatory, the degree to which women can exercise their rights in practice remains constrained by a number of factors (Eilor & Giovarelli, 2002). Some of them include the necessity for male mediation, persistent reluctance among men to associate women with the notion of individual rights, corruption in the legal system, women's lack of economic autonomy and the dominance of customary practices. The 1998 Land Act, intended to address historical gender imbalances in land ownership, failed to provide for spousal co-ownership of land. Thus, inequalities in marital status and property ownership perpetuate women's dependency on men, resulting in increased vulnerability to HIV infection when women have to remain in unfaithful relationships. As the study shows, for some these inequalities have led to women's impoverished status and having to engage in prostitution or transactional sex for survival.

HIV/AIDS exacerbate gender inequalities (Müller, 2005a). Women's inferior and subordinate position, their lack of power to negotiate safe sex or recourse to "survival sex", the inequalities in access to resources, and barriers to women's effective control over what they own, have been responsible for women's vulnerability to the epidemic. While HIV/AIDS-related health impairment is not gender-specific per se, when superimposed on the debilitation of old age among widows, and exacerbated by other gender-related constraints of limited labour, land and other resources, the resulting circumstances can only be those of severe distress and vulnerability, as qualitative findings in the study illustrate. The study also shows that women's lack of or limited access to land also constrains their access to other resources such as credit and agricultural inputs and marketing facilities, which in turn limits their decision-making over agricultural production. Regardless of HIV/AIDS, it is imperative that women's limited land and property rights are redressed because they have direct implications for women's survival as well as for agricultural and overall national development.

However, women are not a homogenous group, and the study has shown that women in different households, same household or of different wealth status own different levels of assets and have different life opportunities. Thus, it is relevant to identify the specific resource needs of different categories of women.

9.5 Methodological issues

In this study, the household is used as the unit of analysis. While results have shown that a household is an arena of cooperation and conflict, with members that have different capabilities and access to resources, and that sometimes individual rather than household livelihood strategies are pursued, the concept remains relevant. Its relevance is illustrated by the way household members care for the sick and orphans (even with the least of resources), socialize the young and provide a sense of belonging. Some orphans and other individuals living alone reiterated the desire to belong to a household. The study also shows that household level factors seemed more important in influencing vulnerability than location specific factors. However, an appreciation of the different capabilities, interests and needs of different household members is imperative for effective programme and policy design. This study also shows that while the concept of headship is useful, because of existing gender inequalities, a focus on households that are vulnerable (whether male- or female-headed, affected or non-affected) may be more useful in identifying households that need support in situations of crises.

The livelihood framework was used to investigate the effects of HIV/AIDS on banana-farming households and the ways individuals and households respond to these effects given the resources they have. The framework proved useful for looking at livelihoods in a holistic manner. It facilitates the understanding that people's livelihoods are created and constrained by a complex set of factors and processes that interact at different scales and levels. This framework is, however, static and does not capture the dynamic nature and process dimension of livelihoods. It also tends to have a bias towards tangible assets such that intangible assets like social relations, claims, power, or the qualitative aspects of assets (for example, emotional or psychological aspects of humans, capability of individuals or meanings attached to different assets) are difficult to capture and receive less attention. Even for the tangible assets, the framework does not facilitate assessing the changing quantity and quality of these assets. In practice, it is difficult to capture the value attached to different assets by different individuals in the same terms and on the same scale for one to make useful comparisons.

Furthermore, the framework is limited with regard to the analysis of the internal dynamics of households such as gender and power relations, gender inequalities and the differential access to resources by different household members. As this study shows, differences in access to and use of resources vary between households headed by males and females and between men and women within the same household. Beyond the household, there is also a failure to explicitly address issues of social differentiation. Finally, the livelihood framework portrays a positivist outlook on the way people make their living. The notion of "sustainable" livelihoods is questionable. Not all livelihood strategies result in positive livelihood outcomes and many households struggle to survive and when they experience a shock like AIDS, get trapped in a cycle of poverty and increased vulnerability. This calls for further research in the development of a more comprehensive framework that can facilitate capturing of the various dimensions of assets and issues such as power at household and institutional level.

In this study a combination of research methods was used to improve the validity and reliability of the results. The survey was used to collect data that could be quantitatively analyzed to facilitate comparisons between affected and non-affected households. However, it is limited in as far as capturing of processes in concerned. Through retrospective questioning in the survey and looking at life history accounts of case study subjects, an attempt was made to assess and understand processes through which HIV/AIDS and other environmental factors influence livelihoods. The combining of gender analysis and livelihood analysis during qualitative data collection and analysis illuminated gender differences within and between households. The analysis in this study follows as much as possible a comparative approach. This was useful to highlight the differentiated nature of the impact of HIV/AIDS. A distinction was made between male-headed and the two types of female-headed households as well as between households that are considered to be well off and those that are considered to be poor.

Livelihoods are complex and the multi-dimensional nature of the interactions between different factors and processes in the environment, and between and within households make them difficult to investigate. Nonetheless, results from this study provide insights into the processes that take place as individuals in Masaka and Kabarole strive to make their living.

Disentangling the impacts of HIV/AIDS is difficult and this is aggravated by the incremental nature of the impacts such that even longitudinal studies are unlikely to enable isolating of HIV/AIDS effects. Small location-specific studies (conducted on a regular basis) on how HIV/AIDS-affected households and individuals are responding to the epidemic are likely to be more useful than large scale surveys to find ways in which to support these people. Such studies must, however, be linked in a comprehensive framework. Improving people's livelihoods will not be viewed in simplistic terms with focus on single and discipline specific initiatives. Rather, there is a need for a holistic multi-disciplinary and multi-sectoral approach to dealing with livelihoods vulnerable to shocks such as HIV/AIDS.

9.6 Areas for future research

The following are proposed:

- Identification of different vulnerable groups and their needs to enable effective targeting of affected rural populations.
- Assessment of the impacts of HIV/AIDS on existing agricultural technologies, inputs and factors of production, and institutional changes, and supply and demand for agricultural services and implications for agricultural extension service delivery (cf. Karuhanga, 2007).
- HIV/AIDS is accelerating the process of rural transformation and causing intergeneration transfer of disadvantage and inequality. An assessment of existing (agricultural) policies (for example, land, privatization of extension services, agricultural subsidies) for their relevance of in a context of HIV/AIDS is recommended.

9.7 Conclusion

I conclude that an interplay of diverse factors have contributed to the creation of a high risk and vulnerable environment for many Ugandans. These factors include ecological crises, economic hardship, negative effects of structural adjustment programmes, war and instability, the loss of agricultural profitability, the absence of income-generating opportunities and the HIV/AIDS epidemic. While HIV/AIDS is not the only factor influencing vulnerability, this study has shown that HIV/AIDS seriously exacerbate the livelihood problems of those who get infected as well as their households and communities. This it does through its asset-eroding effects, reduction of productivity of income earners and impacts on policies, institutions and processes in the environment. At the same time, environmental factors and processes have increased susceptibility to HIV/AIDS and intensified HIV/AIDS-related vulnerability (Müller, 2005b). Stillwaggon (2006) refers to this as HIV/AIDS being a part of the ecology of poverty. This study has also shown how individuals and rural households are being affected by the disease and the different ways in which they try to respond. This understanding is crucial not only for the development of relevant policies and intervention programs, but also for ensuring that responses are better targeted. Furthermore, one needs to bear in mind that there are historically specific social practices, policies, and ideologies that continue to maintain or reproduce distinct forms of inequality, with certain social groups being marginalized and others being privileged. Regardless of whether the shock that individuals experience at any given time is HIV/AIDS or not, these processes will continue to be a cause of people's vulnerability if they are not addressed. Besides the issues raised, there is need to scale up existing HIV/AIDS activities especially community based services and ART to reach under served areas.

References

Abdalla, Y.A. & K.A. Egesa (2005). Trade and growth in agriculture: A Case Study of Uganda's Export Potential within the Evolving Multilateral Trading Regime. BOU Working Paper, WP/05/01.

Adato, M. & R. Meinzen-Dick (2002). Assessing the impact of agricultural research on poverty using the sustainable livelihoods framework. FCND discussion paper 128. APTD discussion paper 89. Washington: International Food Policy Research Institute.

Ainsworth, M. & I. Semali (1998). Who is most likely to die of AIDS? Socioeconomic correlates of adult deaths in Kagera Region, Tanzania. In: M. Ainsworth, L. Fransen, M. Over, (Eds.) *Confronting AIDS: evidence from the developing world*, Brussels: European Commission, pp: 95-109.

Ali, A. (2005). *Livelihood and food security in rural Bangladesh*. PhD Thesis Wageningen University, The Netherlands

Alwang, J. & P.B. Siegel (1994). Rural poverty in Zambia: An analysis of causes and policy recommendations. Washington DC, Human Resources Division, Southern Africa Department, World Bank.

Appleton, S., A. Balihuta, P. Bevan, J. Mackinnon, A. Ssewaya & G. Ssemwogerere (1995). Poverty in Uganda in 1994. A research report. Centre for the Study of African Economies (CSAE) Mimeo.

Appleton, S., T. Emwanu, J. Kagugube & J. Muwonge (1999). WPS/99.22. Changes in Poverty in Uganda, 1992-1997. Centre for the Study of African Economies, Oxford, University of Oxford.

Arce, A. & E. Fisher (2003). Knowledge interfaces and practices of negotiation: Cases from a women's group in Bolivia and an oil refinery in Wales. In: J. Pottier, A. Bicker and P. Sillitoe (Eds.) *Negotiating local knowledge: power and identity in development*, London: Pluto Press, pp.74-97.

Ashley, C., D. Start, R. Slater & P. Deshingkar (2003). *Understanding livelihoods in rural India: diversity, change and exclusion*. Norwich: Overseas Development institute.

Asingwire, N. (2001). *The impact of HIV/AIDS on agricultural production and mainstreaming AIDS messages into agricultural extension*. Kampala, Uganda, Ministry of Agriculture, Animal Industries and Fisheries. Accessed at: http://www.livelihoodoptions.info (12th August, 2006).

Asingwire, N. & S. Kyomuhendo (2003). *An analysis of policy gaps*. Report compiled for Uganda AIDS Commission.

Babbie, E. 1995. *The Practice of social research*. Leiden: Stenfert Kroese.

Badcock-Walters, P. (2001). HIV/AIDS as a management challenge in the education sector. Paper presented at the training workshop of the Senior Staff of the Department of Social Development, Government of South Africa at the Aloe Ridge Hotel, Johannesburg, 11-15 November.

Bagamba, F. (2007). *Market access and agricultural production: The case of banana production in Uganda*. PhD Thesis Wageningen University, The Netherlands.

Bagchi, D.K., P. Blaikie, J. Cameron, M. Chattopadhyay, N. Gyawali & D. Seddon (1998). Conceptual and methodological challenges in the study of livelihood trajectories: Case studies in Eastern India and Western Nepal, *Journal of International Development 10*: 453-468.

References

Bahiigwa B.A.G. (2002). Rural household food security in Uganda: an empirical analysis, Eastern Africa, *Journal of Rural Development 18*(1):8-22.

Barnes, C. (1983). Differentiation by sex among small-scale farming households in Kenya, *Rural Africana 15*(16): 41-63.

Barnett, T. & A. Whiteside (2002). Poverty and HIV/AIDS: Impact, coping and mitigation policy, In: G.A. Cornia (Ed.) *AIDS, Public Policy and Child Well-being*, Florence: UNICEF, Chapter 11.

Barnett, T. & P. Blaikie (1992). *AIDS in Africa: Its present and future impact.* London: Belhaven Press.

Barnett, T., A. Whiteside & J. Decosas (2000). The Jaipur paradigm: A conceptual framework for understanding social susceptibility and vulnerability to HIV. *Journal of the South African Medical Association* 90: 1098-1101.

Barnett, T. & A. Whiteside (2002). *AIDS in the Twenty-First Century: Disease and globalization.* Basingstoke UK: Palgrave Macmillan.

Barnett, T., J. Tumushabe, G. Bantebya, R. Sebuliba, J. Ngasongwa, D. Kapinga, M. Ndelike, M. Drinkwater, G. Mitti & M. Haslwimmer (1995). The social and economic impact of HIV/AIDS on farming systems and livelihoods in rural Africa: Some experiences and lessons from Uganda, Tanzania and Zambia. *Journal of International Development 7*:163 – 176.

Barraclough, S.L. & M.F. Scott (1988). The Rich Have Already Eaten. In: Roots of Catastrophe in Central America" Working Paper No. 105. University of Notre Dame, USA: Helen Kellog Institute for International Studies.

Barrett, C.B., D.R. Lee & J.G. McPeak (2005). Institutional arrangements for rural poverty reduction and resource conservation, *World Development* 33:193-197.

Barrett, C.B., M. Bezuneh, D. Clay & T. Reardon (2005). Heterogeneous constraints, incentives and income diversification strategies in rural Africa. *Quarterly Journal of International Agriculture* 44 (1): 37–60.

Barrett, C.B., T. Reardon & P. Webb (2001). Non-farm income diversification and household livelihood strategies in rural Africa: Concepts, dynamics and policy implications, *Food Policy* 26 (4): 315–331.

Baser, H. (1988). *Technology, Women, and Farming Systems.* Ottawa: Agriculture Canada.

Baylies, C. (2002). The impacts of AIDS on rural households in Africa: A shock like any other? *Development and Change,* 33(4): 611-632.

Bayliss-Smith, T. (1991). Food security and agricultural sustainability in the New Guinea highlands: Vulnerable people, vulnerable places. *IDS Bulletin* 22:5-11.

Beall, J. & N. Kanji (1999). Households, livelihoods and urban poverty, Theme Paper Three, ESCOR-Commissioned Research on Urban Development: Urban Governance, Partnership and Poverty.

Bebbington, A. (1999). Capitals and capabilities: A framework for analyzing peasant viability, rural livelihoods and poverty, *World Development 27*(12): 2021-2044.

Beegle, K., J. de Weerdt & S. Dercon, (2006)). Orphanhood and the long-run impact on children, *American Journal of Agricultural Economics* 88(5):1266–1272.

Beijuka, J. (1999). Microfinance in post-conflict countries. The case of Uganda. Paper presented at the joint ILO/UNHCR Workshop, 15–17 September, ILO, Geneva.

Bekunda, M. (1999). Farmers' response to soil fertility decline in banana-based cropping systems of Uganda, *Managing African Soils* 4:1-20.

Bevan, P. & A. Ssewaya (1995). Understanding poverty in Uganda: Adding a sociological dimension, The Centre for the Study of African Economies. Working Paper Series; Paper 28.

Bigstein, A. & S. Kayizzi-Mugerwa (1995). Rural sector responses to economic crisis in Uganda, *Journal of International Development* 7(2), 181–209.

Bikaako, W. & J. Ssenkumba, (2003)). Gender, land and rights: Contemporary contestations in law, policy and practice in Uganda. In: L.M. Wanyeki (Ed.), *Women and Land in Africa: Culture, Religion and realizing Women's Rights,* Cape Town: David Philip Publishers, pp. 232-277.

Blaikie, P., T. Cannon, I. Davis & B. Wisner (1994). *At Risk: Natural Hazards, People's Vulnerability and Disasters.* New York: Routledge.

Bohle, H.G. (1993). *The Geography of Vulnerable Food Systems.* Germany: Universitat Freiburg.

Bond, G.C. & J. Vincent (2002). The moving frontier of AIDS in Uganda: Contexts, texts, and concepts. In G. C. Bond & N.C. Gibson. (Eds.) *Contested Terrains and Constructed Categories: Contemporary Africa in Focus.* Oxford, Westview Press, pp.345-364.

Brant, R. (1990). Assessing Proportionality in the Proportional Odds Model for Ordinal.

Breitmayer, B.J., L. Ayres & K.A. Knafl (1993). Triangulation in qualitative research: Evaluation of completeness and confirmation purposes. *Journal of Nursing Scholarship* 25:237-243.

Brocklesby, M. & E. Fisher (2003). Community development in sustainable livelihood approaches - An Introduction, *Community Development Journal* 8 (3):185-197.

Brons, J., T. Dietz, A. Niehof & K. Witsenburg (2007). Dimensions of vulnerability of livelihoods in less-favoured areas: Interplay between the individual and the collective. In R. Ruben, J. Pender & A. Kuyvenhoven (Eds.) *Sustainable Poverty Reduction* Less *Favoured Areas, Wallingford: CAB International,* pp.91-110.

Brown, D.R., E.C. Stephens, J.O. Ouma, F.M. Murithi & C.B. Barrett (2006). Livelihood strategies in the rural Kenyan highlands. *African Journal for Agricultural and Resource Economics 1*(1): 21-36.

Calon, M.L.H. (1990). *Population, farming systems and food security.* Paper No. 7 (E). International Course for Development Oriented Research in Agriculture. Farming Systems Analysis.

Cardona O.M. (2004). The need for rethinking the concepts of vulnerability and risk from a holistic perspective: A necessary review and criticism for effective risk management. In G. Bankoff, G. Frerks & D. Hilhorst (Eds.) *Mapping Vulnerability: Disasters, Development and People.* UK and US: Earthscan, pp.37-51.

Carletto, C. (1998). Household food security and the role of women: IFAD's Experience in Guatemala. Accessed 3rd March, 2007 at http://www.ifad.org/gender/thematic/guatemala/guat_toc.htm .

Carney, D. (Ed.) (1998). *Sustainable Rural Livelihoods: What Contributions can we Make?* London: Department for International Development.

Carney, D. (1999). *Approaches to sustainable livelihoods for the rural poor. ODI Poverty Briefing No.2.* London: ODI.

Carney D. (2002). *Sustainable Livelihoods Approaches: Progress and Possibilities for Change.* London: Department for International Development.

References

Carter, M.R & C.B. Barrett (2006). The economics of poverty traps and persistent poverty: An asset based approach, *Journal of Development Studies* 42(2):178–99.

Carter, M.R. & J. May (1999). Poverty, livelihood and Class in Rural South Africa. *World Development 27* (1):1-20.

Chambers, R. (1989). Editorial introduction: vulnerability, coping and policy. *IDS Bulletin* 2(2): 1-7.

Chambers, R. & R. Conway (1992). Sustainable rural livelihoods: Practical concepts for the 21st Century. IDS Discussion Paper, No. 296.

Chambers, R. (1990). Editorial introduction: Vulnerability, coping and policy, *IDS Bulletin 20* (2): 1-7.

Chambers, R. (1997). *Whose Reality Counts? Putting the Last First.* London: Intermediate Technology Publications.

Chant, S. (1997). *Women Headed Households: Diversity and Dynamics in the Developing World.* London: MacMillan Press Ltd, pp:1-29.

Chapoto, A. & T.S. Jayne (2005). Socio-economic characteristics of individuals afflicted by AIDS-related prime-age mortality in Zambia. *Policy Synthesis* No.10. Food Security Research project – Zambia. Ministry of Agriculture and Cooperatives, Agriculture Consultative Forum, Michigan State University. Accessed at *http://www.aec.msu.edu/agecon/fs2/zambia/index.htm* (12*th* September, 2007).

Cheal, D. (1989). Strategies of resource management in household economies: Moral economy or political economy. In: R.R. Wilk. (Ed.). *The Household Economy; Reconsidering the Domestic Mode of Production*. London: West View Press, pp.11-22.

Chin, J. (1990). Current and future dimensions of the HIV/AIDS pandemic in women and children. *The Lancet* 336:221-224.

Clay, C.D. & H.K. Schwartzweller (1991). Introduction: Researching household strategies, *Research in Rural Sociology and Development* 5:1-11.

Collins J. & B. Rau (2000). *Aids in the Context of Development.* Geneva: United Nations Research Institute for Social Development.

Corbett, J. 1988. Famine and household coping strategies, *World Development* 16(9): 1099-1112.

Crabtree, B.F. & W. Miller (Eds.) (1992). *Gender, Family and Household in Tanzania*. Avebury: Aldershot.

Cutter, S. (1996). Vulnerability to environmental hazards. *Progress in Human Geography* 20**:** 529-539.

Davies, S. (1993). Are coping strategies a cope out? *IDS Bulletin* 24:60-72.

Davis, G. (1995). Banana and Plantain in the East African Highlands.In: *Banana and Plantain* S. Gowen (Ed.). London, Uk: Chapman and Hall.

De Haan, L. & A. Zoomers (2005). Exploring the frontier of livelihoods research, *Development and Change 36* (1): 27-47.

De Waal, A. & J. Tumushabe (2003). HIV/AIDS and Food Security in Africa, A report for DFID.

De Waal, A., J. Tumushabe, M. Mamdani & B. Kilama (2005). HIV/AIDS and changing vulnerability to crisis in Tanzania: Implications for food security and poverty reduction, Paper Presented at the International Conference on HIV/AIDS and Food and Nutrition security, Durban, 14-16 April.

Deaton, A. (1989). Saving in developing countries: Theory and review, Proceedings of the World Bank Annual Conference on Development Economics. Washington, DC: World Bank.

Deininger, K. & J. Okidi (2000). Rural Households: Incomes, Productivity and Non-farm Enterprise, Washington DC: World Bank.

Deininger, K. & J. Okidi (2003). Growth and Poverty Reduction in Uganda1999-2000: Panel Data Evidence *Development Policy Review* 21 (4): 481-509.

Devereux S. (2001). Livelihood insecurity and social protection: A re-emerging issue in rural development, *Development Policy Review* 19(4):507-519.

Devereux, S. (1993). Goats before ploughs: Dilemmas of household response sequencing during food shortages. *IDS Bulletin* 24:52-59.

DFID. (2000). *Sustainable livelihood guidance sheets*. Department for International Development. Accessed at www.livelihood.org/info/info_guidancesheets.htm. (17th June, 2007)

DFID. (2007). Uganda fact sheet. http://www.dfid.gov.uk/countries/africa/uganda.asp. Accessed 26th August, 2007.

Dietz, T., (2000)). Poverty and land degradation. Paper for the conference on World poverty: A challenge for the private sector. October 3-4, 2000, Amsterdam.

Dolan, C. (2002). Gender and diverse livelihoods in Uganda. LADDER Working Paper No.10. ODG/DEV February.

Doss, C.R. (1999). Twenty-five years of research on women farmers in Africa: Lessons and implications for agricultural research institutions, with an annotated bibliography. International Maize and Wheat Improvement Center (CIMMYT). Paper No. 99-02. Mexico D. F.: CIMMYT.

Dreze, J. & A.K. Sen (1989). *Hunger and Public Action*. London: Clarendon Press.

Drimie, S. & S. Gandure (2005). The Impacts of HIV/AIDS on rural livelihoods in Southern Africa: An inventory and literature review. FAO Sub-regional Office for Southern and Eastern Africa.

Drimie, S. (2002). *The Impact of HIV/AIDS on Rural Livelihoods and Land Issues in Southern and Eastern Africa* – A Background Paper Presented for the FAO Sub-regional Office for Southern and Eastern Africa.

Du Guerny, J. (2002). *Agriculture and HIV/AIDS*. New York: United Nations Development Program (UNDP).

Eicher, C.K. & J.M. Staatz (1986). Food Security and policy in Sub-Saharan Africa. In: A. Maunder (Ed.) *Agriculture in a Turbulent World Economy*. Gower: Aldershot. pp.215-229.

Ekaas, S. (2003). Gender HIV/AIDS and food security. Paper prepared for ECOSOC Ministerial Roundtable on Gender and Rural Development, New York: UNIFEM.

Ellis, F. (1993). *Peasant Economics: Farm Households and Agrarian Development*. Cambridge: Cambridge University Press.

Ellis, F. (1998). Household strategies and rural livelihood diversification, *Journal of Development Studies 35*(1): 1-38.

Ellis, F. (2000). *Rural Livelihoods and Diversity in Developing Countries*, Oxford: Oxford University Press.

Eilor, E. & R. Giovarelli (2002). Land sector analysis: Final report for the government of Uganda. Rural Development Institute.

Elson, D. & B. Evers (1997). Gender Aware Country Economic Reports: Uganda.

References

Engberg, L.E. (1990). Rural Households and Resource Allocation for Development: An Ecosystem Perspective. FAO, Rome.

Evans, A. (1991). Gender issues in household rural economics, *IDS Bulletin 22* (1): 51-59.

FAO (1992). *The effects of HIV/AIDS on farming systems in Eastern Africa.* Rome: Food and Agriculture Organization.

FAO (1995). *The effects of HIV/AIDS on farming systems in Eastern Africa*, Rome: Food and Agriculture Organization.

FAO (1996). United Nations Food and Agriculture Organization, "Rome Declaration on World Food Security, Proceedings from the World Food Summit, November 13–17, .Rome, Italy. Accessed from <http://www.fao.org>. (15th March, 2007)

FAO (2001). *The impact of HIV/AIDS on food security*, Rome: Food and Agriculture Organization.

FAO (2002). *The State of Food Insecurity in the World 2001 and 2002*, Rome: Food and Agriculture Organization.

FAO (2003). *The Impact of HIV/AIDS on the Agricultural Sector and Rural Livelihoods in Uganda. Baseline Report.* Kampala: National Agricultural Advisory Services (NAADS).

FAO (2004). HIV/AIDS and the food crisis in Sub-Saharan Africa: The impact of HIV/AIDS on food security, Twenty-third Regional Conference for Africa, 1-5 March, Johannesburg, South Africa.

Farmer, P. (1996). Social Inequalities and Emerging Infectious Diseases. *Emerging Infectious Diseases* 2, 1996c.

Farrington, J., D. Carney, C. Ashley & C. Turton (1999). Sustainable Livelihoods in Practice: Early Applications of Concepts in Rural Areas', ODI Natural Resource Perspectives No. 42.

Flyvbjerg, B. (2006). Five misunderstandings about case-study research, *Qualitative Inquiry 12*(2): 219-245.

Fontana, A. & J.H. Frey (1994). Interviewing: The art of science. In: N.K. Denzin and Y.S. Lincoln (Eds.) *A Handbook of Qualitative Research.* Thousand Oaks, Sage Publications. Chapter 22.

Forest Department (2002). National biomass study technical report. Kampala: Ministry of Water, Lands and Environment (MLWE).

Francis, E. (2002). Rural livelihoods, institutions, and vulnerability in North West Province, South Africa, *Journal of Southern African Studies 28* (3): 531-550.

Frankenberger, T.R. (1992). Indicators and data collection methods for assessing household food security. In: S. Maxwell & T. Frankenberger, (Eds.) Household food security: concepts, indicators, and measurements: a technical review. Rome: International Fund for Agricultural Development and New York: United Nations Children's Fund..

Frankenberger, T.R., (1992)). *Indicators and data collection methods for assessing household food security.* Rome: International Fund for Agricultural Development and New York: United Nations Children's Fund.

Frankenberger, T.R. (2001). The role of non-governmental organizations in promoting nutrition and public health. Paper presented at the 17th International Congress of Nutrition, August 27 - 31, 2001. Vienna.

Frankenberger, T.R. & M.K. McCaston (1998). The household livelihood security concept. Food Nutrition and Agriculture No. 22, Rome*: FAO.*

Fuwa, N. (2000). The poverty and heterogeneity among female-headed households revisited: the case of Panama, *World Development 28*(8):1515- 1542.

Gaffeo, E. (2003). The economics of HIV/AIDS: a survey, *Development Policy Review 21* (1):27-49.

Garbus, L. & E. Marseille (2003). HIV/AIDS in Uganda. San Francisco: Regents of the University of California.

Gillespie, S.R. & S. Kandiyala (2005). HIV/AIDS and food and nutrition security: from evidence to action, Food Policy Review 7. Washington, DC.: IFPRI.

Gillespie, S., L. Haddad & R. Jackson (2001). HIV/AIDS, food and nutrition security: impacts and actions. Paper presented at the 28th Session of the ACC/SCN Symposium on Nutrition and HIV/AIDS 1 May, Geneva.

Gittleson, J. & S. Mookherji (1997). The application of anthropological methods to study intrahousehold resource allocation. In L. Haddad, J. Hoddinot & H. Alderman (Eds.) *Intrahousehold Resource Allocation in Developing Countries: Models, Methods, and Policy,* Baltimore and London: The Johns Hopkins University Press, 193-212.

Gladwin, C. H., A. Goldman, A. Randall, A. Schmitz & G. E. Schuh (1997). Gender and Soil Fertility in Africa. In: Replenishing Soil Fertility in Africa, SSSA Special Publication Number 51: 219-236.

Glewwe, P. & G. Hall (1998). Are some groups more vulnerable to macroeconomic shocks than others? Hypothesis Tests Based on Panel Data from Peru, *Journal of Development Economics 56*:181 - 206.

Goetz, A.M. (1995). Macro-meso-micro linkages: understanding gendered institutional structures and practices. A contribution to the SAGA Workshop on Gender and Economic Reform in Africa, Ottawa, 1-3 October.

Green, E.D., (2005)). Ethnicity and the politics of land tenure reform in Central Uganda. Development Studies Institute London. Working Paper Series No. 05-58.

Greene, W.H. (1997). *Econometric Analysis.* New York: Prentice Hall.

Greene, W.H. (2003). *Econometric Analysis.* New York: Prentice Hall

Gujarati, D.N. (1988). *Basic Econometrics.* 2nd edition. New York: McGraw-Hill.

Guyer, J.I. (1980). Household budgets and women's incomes. African Studies Center Working Paper 28. Boston, Massachusetts: Boston University.

Guyer, J. (1981). Household and community in African studies. *African Studies Review* 24:87-137.

Guyer, J.I. and P.E. Peters (1987). Conceptualizing the household: issues of theory and policy in Africa, *Development and Change* 18(2):1197-1214.

Guyer, J. (1988). The multiplication of labour; Historical methods in the study of gender and agricultural change in modern Africa, *Current Anthropology 29*(2): 247-273.

Haddad, L.J. 1997. Achieving Food Security in Southern Africa: New Challenges, New Opportunities. Washington DC: IFPRI.

Haddad, L., J. Hoddinott & H. Alderman (Eds.) (1997)).*Intrahousehold Resource Allocation in Developing Countries: Models, Methods and Policy.* Washington DC.: Johns Hopkins University Press for IFPRI.

References

Haddad, L. & S. Gillespie (2001). Effective food and nutrition policy responses to HIV/AIDS: what we know and what we need to know, *Journal of International Development* 13:487-511.

Hebinck P. & L. Smith (2001). Livelihoods and rural transformations in the Central Eastern Cape: from production to consumption? A case of the two rural villages Guquka and Koloni, Paper Given at the Development Studies Association Conference: Different Poverties, Different Policies, Manchester, 10-12 September.

Hebinck, P & M.F.C. Bourdillon (2001). Analysis of livelihood. In: M.F.C. Bourdillon and P. Hebinck (Eds.) *Women, Men and Work: Rural Livelihoods in Central-Eastern Zimbabwe*, Harare: Weaver Press, pp.1-13.

Hebinck, P., W. van Averbeke, N. Monde, L. Smith & J. Bennet (2007). Life histories and livelihood trajectories. In: P. Hebinck & P.C. Lent (Eds.) *Livelihoods and Landscapes: The people of Guquka and Koloni and their resources*. Leiden and Boston, Brill, pp.307-334.

Hoddinott, J. (1999). Operationalizing household food security in development projects: an introduction. Technical Guide no.1. Washington DC: International Food Policy Research Institute.

Hoddinott, J. & L. Haddad (1995). Does female income share influence household expenditures? Evidence from Côte d'Ivoire, *Oxford Bulletin of Economics and Statistics 57*(1): 77-98.

Hougham, D.A. & F. Sturrock (1973). The farms, present day organization. In: A.I. Richards, F. Sturrock and J.M. Fortt (Eds.) *Subsistence to Commercial Farming in Present-day Buganda,* Cambridge: Cambridge University Press, pp.150-178.

Human Rights Watch (2003). Just die quietly: domestic violence and women's vulnerability to HIV in Uganda. August Vol.15, No. 15 (A).

Hunter, S. (1990). Orphans as a window on the AIDS epidemic in Sub-Saharan Africa: initial results and implications of a study in Uganda, *Social science and Medicine 31*(6): 681-690.

Hurst, P., P. Termine & M. Karl (2005). Agricultural Workers and their Contribution to Sustainable Agriculture and Rural Development. FAO-ILO-IUF.

Hussein, K. & J. Nelson (1998). Sustainable livelihoods and livelihood diversification. Institute of Development Studies, IDS Working Paper 69. University of Sussex.

International Network for Improvement of Banana and Plantain (INIBAP) (1989). Worldwide importance of bananas. Annual Report pp 9-11.

IP & FAO (2003). *HIV/AIDS and Agriculture: Impacts and Responses Case studies from Namibia, Uganda and Zambia.* Rome: FAO.

Jackson, C. (1985). *The Kano River Irrigation Project.* West Hartford, Connecticut: Kumarian Press.

Jameson, J.D. (1970). *Agriculture in Uganda*. London: Oxford University Press.

Jansen, H.G.P., A. Damon, J. Pender, W. Wielemaker & R. Schipper (2003). Policies for sustainable development in the hillsides of Honduras: A quantitative livelihoods approach. Discussion paper. Washington, DC.: International Food Policy Research Institute (IFPRI).

Jayne, T., M. Villarreal, P. Pingali & G. Hemrich (2004). Interactions between the agricultural sector and the HIV/AIDS pandemic: implications for agricultural policy. ESA Working Paper No. 04-06. Rome: FAO Agricultural and Development Economics Division.

Jayne, T.S., M. Villarreal, P. Pingali & G. Hemrich (2005). HIV/AIDS and the agricultural sector: implications for policy in eastern and southern Africa, *Journal of Agricultural and Development Economics 2*(2):158-181.

Jayne, T.S., A. Chapoto, E. Byron, M. Ndiyoi, P. Hamazakaza, S. Kadiyala & S. Gillespie. 2006. Community-level impacts of AIDS-related mortality. Panel survey evidence from Zambia. *Review of Agricultural Economics 28* (3): 440-457.

Judge G. G., W.E. Griffiths, H. Lütkepohl & T.C. Ee (1985). *Theory and Practice of Econometrics.* New York: John Wiley and Sons.

Juteau, D. (Ed.) (2003). *Social Differentiation. Patterns and Processes.* New York: University of Toronto Press.

Kabeer, N. (1991). Gender, production and well-being: rethinking the household economy. Institute of Development Studies, IDS Discussion Paper 288. University of Sussex.

Kabeer, N. (1994). *Reversed Realities: Gender Hierarchies in Development Thought.* London: Verso.

Kabeer, N. (1997). Editorial: Tactics and trade-offs. Revisiting the links between gender and poverty, *IDS Bulletin* 28(3): 1-13.

Kabeer, N. (1999). Resources, agency, achievements: reflections on the measurement of women's empowerment, *Development and Change 30*(3):435-464.

Kabeer, N. & T.V.A. Tran (2002). Leaving the rice fields but not the countryside: gender livelihood diversification and pro-poor growth in rural Vietnam. In: S. Razavi (Ed.) *Shifting Burdens. Gender and Agrarian Change under Neoliberalism.* Bloomfield: Kumarian Press, pp.109-150.

Kabonesa, C. (2002).Gender relations and women's rights to land in Uganda: A study of Kabarole District, *East African Journal of Peace and Human Rights* 8 (2): 227-249.

Kakuru, D.M. (2006). *The Combat for Gender Equality in Education: Rural Livelihood Pathways in the Context of HIV/AIDS*, Wageningen: Wageningen Academic Publishers. [AWLAE Series No.4].

Kamjathy, K. & E. Nicholas (2001). Women's access to land-FIG guidelines. principles for equitable gender inclusion in land administration. Background Report and Guideline.

Karamura, D. (1998). Numerical taxonomic studies of the East African Highland Bananas (Musa AAA-East Africa) in Uganda. Unpublished Ph.D. Thesis, University of Reading.

Karuhanga M.B. (2007). Impact of HIV and AIDS on agriculture and rural livelihoods in Uganda: implications for agricultural extension services. In: M.N. Mangheni(Ed.) *Innovations and Issues in Agriculture Extension in Uganda: Lessons and prospects.* Kampala: Fountain Publishers. 144-173

Katwijukye, A.K. & W. Doppler (2004). The socioeconomic analysis of land use changes and soil conservation in Central and Western Uganda, *Uganda Journal of Agricultural Sciences* 9:303-311.

Keller, A., R. Sakthivadivel & D. Seckler (2000). Water scarcity and the role of storage in development. IWMI Research Report No. 39. Colombo, Sri Lanka: International Water Management Institute.

Kharono, E., (2001)). Women's Land Rights, Agricultural Productivity and Food Security in Uganda: A Case Study of Lira and Mbale Districts. Research report commissioned by the Food and Agricultural Organization (FAO), Sub-Regional Office for Southern and Eastern Africa, Harare.

Kollmair, M. & St. Gamper (2002). The sustainable livelihood approach. Input Paper for the Integrated Training Course of Kollmair North-South. Aeschiried, Switzerland 9-20 September.

Kwesiga, J.C. (1998). Central yet peripheral: The rural women farmer and issues of African development. *IITA Seventh lecture in the Distinguished African Scientist Lecture Series.* Ibadan: *International Institute of Tropical Agriculture (IITA).*

Little, P.D., K. Smith, B.A. Cellarius, D.L. Coppock & C.B. Barrett (2001). Avoiding disaster: diversification and risk management among East African herders, *Development and Change,* 32(3):401-433.

Loevinsohn, M. & S. Gillespie (2003). HIV/AIDS, food security and rural livelihoods: understanding and responding. RENEWAL Working Paper No. 2. Washington DC: IFPRI.

Long, N. (1997). Agency and constraint, perceptions and practices. A theoretical position. In: H. de Haan and N. long (Eds.) *Images and Realities of Rural Life,* Assen: Van Gorcum, pp.1-20.

Ministry of Agriculture Animal Industry and Fisheries (MAAIF) (2000). National Agricultural Advisory Services (NAADS) Program. Master Document of the NAADS Task Force and Joint Donor Group.

Ministry of Agriculture Animal Industry and Fisheries (MAAIF) and Ministry of Finance Planning and Economic development (MFPED) (2000). Plan for Modernization of Agriculture (PMA): Eradicating Poverty in Uganda.

Ministry of Agriculture Animal Industry and Fisheries (MAAIF) and Ministry of Finance Planning and Economic development (MFPED) (2000). Plan for Modernization of Agriculture (PMA): Eradicating Poverty in Uganda. Kampala, Uganda.

Mobile AIDS Homecare, Counselling and Orphan Programme (MAHCOP) (2005). Kitovu Mobile AIDS Homecare, Counseling and Orphan Program. Unpublished Project Report.

Makokha, K.A. (2001). Structural adjustment participatory review initiative (SAPRI). Uganda Country Report: A Synthesis of the Four SAPRI Studies Prepared for the National Steering Committee. Accessed July, 31, 2007 from http://www.saprin.org/uganda/research/uga_country_rpt.pdf

Mamdani, M. (1992). Class formation and rural livelihoods: a Ugandan case study In: H. Bernstein, B. Crow and H. Johnson (Eds.) *Rural livelihoods. Crises and Responses.* Oxford: Oxford University Press in association with The Open University.

Mann, J., D.M. Tarantola & T.W. Netter (Eds.) (1992). *AIDS in the World.* Cambridge: Harvard University Press.

Marais, H. (2005). *Buckling Up. The Impact of AIDS in South Africa.* M. Crewe (Ed.). Pretoria: University of Pretoria, Centre for the Studies of AIDS.

Marenya, P., W. Oluoch-Kosura, F., Place & C. Barrett (2003). Education, Non-Farm Income, and Farm Investment in Land-scare Western Kenya, BASIS Brief 14, Department of Agricultural Economics, Madison: University of Wisconsin.

Marshall, C. & G. Rossman (1995). *Designing Qualitative Research.* London: Sage

Masanza, M. (2003). *Effect of Crop Sanitation on Banana Weevil (Cosmopolites Sordidus) Populations and Associated Damage.* PhD Thesis, Wageningen University, The Netherlands.

Maxwell, D. (1996). Measuring food insecurity: the frequency and severity of coping Strategies, *Food Policy 21*: 291-303.

Maxwell, S. & T.R. Frankenberger (1992). Household food security: concepts, indicators, measurements: a technical review. New York and Rome: UNICEF and IFAD.

Maxwell, S. (1988). National food security planning: first thoughts from Sudan, Paper Presented to Workshop on Food Security in the Sudan, Institute of Development Studies, Sussex, 3-5 October.

McFadden, D. (1973). Conditional logit analysis of qualitative choice behaviour. In: P. Zarembka (Ed.) *Frontiers in Econometrics*. New York: Academic Press, pp.105-142.

Mechlem, K. (2004). Food security and the right to food in the discourse of the United Nations. *European Law Journal 10*(5): 631–648.

Meer, S. (Ed.) (1997). *Women, Land and Authority, Perspectives from South Africa*. Cape Town: Oxfam/David Philip.

Mettrick, H. (1967). *Aid in Uganda: Agriculture*. London: Overseas Development Institute.

MFPED (2000). Uganda participatory poverty assessment report: learning from the poor. Kampala: Ministry of Finance, Planning and Economic Development, June.

MFPED (2001). Uganda poverty reduction strategy paper progress report: summary of poverty status report. Kampala: Ministry of Finance, Planning and Economic Development, 8 February.

MFPED (2003). Uganda Poverty Status Report, Kampala: Ministry of Finance, Planning and Economic Development

MFPED (2004). Poverty Eradication Action Plan 2004/5 – 2007/8. Kampala: Ministry of Finance, Planning and Economic Development

Miller, R.L. (2000). *Researching Life Stories and Family Histories*. London and New Delhi: Sage

Mitchell, J.C. (1983). Case and situation analysis. *The Sociological Review 31*(No. w new series):187-211.

MWLE, Forest Department (2002). National Biomass Study Technical Report. Kampala: Ministry of Water, Lands and Environment.

MOH and ORC (2006). *Uganda HIV/AIDS Sero-behavioural Survey 2004-2005*. Calverton, Maryland, USA: Ministry of Health and ORC Macro.

MOH (2003). *STD/HIV/AIDS* Surveillance Report. Kampala: Government of Uganda,
Ministry of Health (STD/AIDS Control Programme).

Moore, H. (1988). *Feminism and Anthropology*. Minneapolis: University of Minesota Press.

Moore, S.F. (1978). Old age in a life-term social arena: some Chagga of Kilimanjaro in 1974. In: B.G. Myerhoff & A. Simic (Eds.) *Life's Career – Aging*, Beverley Hills: Sage, pp.23-75.

Moser, C.O.N. (1993). *Gender Planning and Development: Theory, Practice and Training*. London: Routledge.

Moser, C.O.N. (1998). The asset vulnerability framework: reassessing urban poverty reduction strategies. *World Development 26*(1): 1-19.

Muchunguzi, J.K. (1999). The impact of HIV/AIDS on smallholder agriculture: The experience of Muleba District, Tanzania. In: G. Mutangadura, H. Jackson and D. Mukurazita (Eds.) *AIDS and African Smallholder Agriculture*, Harare: Southern African AIDS Information Dissemination Service (SAFAIDS). pp.36-40.

Mujer y desarrollo (2004). Understanding poverty from a gender perspective. *Serie* mujer y desarrollo No. 52. Santiago, Chile, June 2004.

Mugyenyi, M.R. (1998). Towards the empowerment of women: a critique of NRM policies and programmes. In: H.B. Hansen & M. Twaddle (Eds.) *Developing Uganda*, Oxford: James Currey, pp.133 -144.

Mukiibi, J. (Ed.) (2001). *Agriculture in Uganda.* Kampala: Fountain Publishers/ CTA/NARO.

Müller, T.R., (2003)). Moving Beyond 'Capitalization': A resource Profile Approach as Alternative to the Livelihood Framework. (Unpublished paper)

Müller, T.R., (2004)). *HIV/AIDS and Agriculture in Sub-Saharan Africa,* Wageningen: Wageningen Academic Publishers. [AWLAE Series No.1]

Müller, T.R., (2005)a). HIV*/AIDS, Gender and Rural Livelihoods in sub-Saharan Africa,* Wageningen: Wageningen Academic Publishers. [AWLAE Series No. 2]

Müller, T.R., (2005)b). *HIV/AIDS and Human Development in Sub-Saharan Africa,* Wageningen: Wageningen Academic Publishers. [AWLAE Series No. 3]

Mullins, D. (2002). *What Can it Look Like to Mainstream HIV and AIDS?* Oxford: Oxfam UK.

Murray, C. (2002). Livelihood research: transcending boundaries of time and space. *Journal of Southern African Studies 28*(3): 489-509.

Murry, C. (2000). Family histories and "Household" Livelihoods', Multiple Livelihoods and Social Change working paper series, 7, Manchester: Institute of Development Policy and Management, University of Manchester.

Mutangadura, G, H. Jackson & D. Mukurazita (Eds.) (1999). *Aids and the African Smallholder Agriculture,* Harare: Southern African AIDS Information Dissemination Service (SAFAIDS).

Muwanga, R.O.M., C.N. Ocitti p'Obwoya, B. Odongo & G.M. Turyamureba (2001). Sweet potatoes *(Pomoea batatas(l.)Lam).* In: J. Mukiibi, (Ed.) *Agriculture in Uganda.* Kampala: Fountain Publishers/ CTA/NARO, pp.233-278.

NAADS (The National Agricultural Advisory Services) (2003). *The impact of HIV/AIDS on the agricultural sector and rural livelihoods in Uganda.* Rome: Integrated Support to Sustainable Development and Food Security Programme (IP), FAO.

Narayan, D., J. Patel, J. Schafft, A. Rademacher & S. Koch-Schulte (1999). Can Anyone Hear Us? Voices from 47 Countries. *Voices of the Poor,* Volume 1. Washington DC: World Bank.

Negash, A. (2001). *Diversity and conservation of enset* (Ensete ventricosum Welw. Cheesman) *and its relation to household food and livelihood security in South-Western Ethiopia.* PhD Thesis, Wageningen, The Netherlands: Wageningen University.

Negash, A. & A. Niehof (2004). The significance of Enset culture and biodiversity for rural household food and livelihood security in South-western Ethiopia. *Agriculture and Human Values* 21**:** 61-71.

Nelson, M.K. & J. Smith (1999). *Working Hard and Making Do: Surviving in Small Town America.* Berkeley: University of California Press.

National Environment Management Authority (NEMA) (1998). State of the Environment Report for Uganda.

National Environment Management Authority (NEMA) (2001). State of the Environment Report for Uganda.

Netting, R. McC. & R.R. Wilk (1984). Households: Changing forms and functions. In: R. McC. Netting, R.R. Wilk, and E.J. Arnould (Eds.) *Households.* Berkely: The University of California Press, 1-28.

Newman, C. & S. Canagarajah (1999). Non-Farm Employment, Poverty, and Gender Linkages: Evidence from Ghana and Uganda, Working Draft, Washington DC: World Bank.

Nguthi, F.N. (2007). Adoption of agricultural innovations by smallholder farmers in the context of HIV/AIDS: The case of the tissue cultured banana in Kenya. PhD Thesis Wageningen. The Netherlands: Wageningen University.

Niehof, A. & L. Price (2001). *Rural Livelihood Systems: A Conceptual Framework*. Wageningen: WU-UPWARD Series on Rural Livelihoods, No. 1.

Niehof, A. (2004). The significance of diversification for rural livelihood systems. *Food Policy* 29: 321-338.

Nkonya, E., J. Pender, C. Kaizzi, E. Kato & S. Mugarura (2005). Policy Options for Increasing Crop Productivity and Reducing Soil Nutrient Depletion and Poverty in Uganda. Washington D.C: International Food Policy Research Institute.

Nkonya, E., J. Pender, P. Jagger, D. Sserunkuuma, C. Kaizzi & H. Ssali (2004). Strategies or Sustainable Land Management and Poverty Reduction in Uganda. Research Report No. 133. Washington D.C: International Food Policy Research Institute.

Nombo, C. (2007). *When AIDS meets poverty: Implications for social capital in a village in Tanzania*. Wageningen. The Netherlands: Wageningen Academic Publishers.

Nowakunda, K. & W. Tushemereirwe (2004). Farmer acceptance of introduced banana genotypes in Uganda. *African Crop Science Journal 12*(1): 1-6.

Ntozi, J.P.M. (1997). Widowhood, remarriage and migration during the HIV/AIDS epidemic in Uganda, *Health Transition Review* 7:125-144.

Ntozi, J. & I. Nakanaabi (1997). The AIDS epidemic and infant and child mortality in six districts of Uganda, *Health Transition Review* 7:189-205.

Nuwagaba, A. (1994). Household Formation Pattern in Uganda. An Illustrative Analysis of Modern Contraceptive Use. Kampala: Makerere University.

Nzioki, A. (2001). A Synthesis Report. Sub-Regional Study on Women's Ownership and Access to Land. Eastern African Sub-Regional Support Initiative for the Advancement of Women, Kampala: Eastern African Sub-Regional Support Initiative for the Advancement of Women (EASSI).

O'Leary, Z. (2004). *The Essential Guide to Doing Research*. New Delhi: Vistaar Publications.

Opiyo, P. (2001). HIV/AIDS, Gender and livelihood in Siaya District, Kenya: an analysis of AIDS impact on rural hHouseholds. Unpublished MSc. Thesis. Wageningen University.

Opio, F., M.A. Ugen, S. Kyamanywa, S. David & M. Mugisha-Mutetika (2001). Beans. In: J. Mukiibi (Ed.) *Agriculture in Uganda*. Kampala: Fountain Publishers/CTA/NARO.pp: 162-191.

Orubuloye, I.O., P. Caldwell and J.C. Caldwell (1993). The role of high-risk occupations in the spread of AIDS: truck drivers and itinerant market women in Nigeria, *International Family Planning Perspectives 19*(2):43-48, and 71.

Otim-Nape. (1990). Root Crops in Uganda. In: Hartmans (Ed.) Agricultural Research in Uganda: Five Year Research Plan. Vol. 1. Kampala: USAID.

Ovonji-Odida, I., F.E. Muhereza, L. Eturu & L.A. Wily (2000). *Land, Gender and Poverty Eradication, Is There a Case for Spousal Co-Ownership of Primary Household Property?* Kampala: Land Act Implementation Project.

Pena, C., P. Webb. & L. Haddad (1996). Women's economic advancement through agricultural change: A review of donor experience. Food Consumption and Nutrition Division (FCND) Discussion Paper No. 10.

Pender, J., F. Place & S. Ehui (1999). Strategies for Sustainable Agricultural Development in the East African Highlands. Washington D.C: International Food Policy Research Institute.

Pender, J., P. Jagger, E. Nkonya & D. Sserunkuuma (2001). Development pathways and land management in Uganda: causes and implications. EPTD Discussion Paper No. 85. Washington D.C: International Food Policy Research Institute.

Pender, J., P. Jagger, E. Nkonya & E. Kato (2004). *Livelihood and Land Use Options in Northwestern Uganda.* Washington D.C: International Food Policy Research Institute, Mimeo.

Pennartz, P. & A. Niehof (1999). *The Domestic Domain: Chances, Choices and Strategies of Family Households.* Aldershot, Brookfield: Ashgate.

Piwoz, E. & E. Preble (2000). HIV/AIDS and nutrition: A review of the literature and recommendations for nutritional care and support in Sub-Saharan Africa. SARA Project, Washington, D.C: USAID.

Price, N.S. (1995). The origin and development of banana and plantain cultivation. In: S. Gowen (Ed.) *Banana and Plantains.* London: Chapman and Hall, pp.1-13.

Prudencio, Y.C. and R. Al-Hassan (1994). The food security stabilization roles of cassava in Africa, *Food Policy* 19:57-64.

Purseglove, J.W. (1988). *Tropical Crops: Monocotyledons.* London: ELBS/Longman.

Qamar, M.K. (2001). The HIV/AIDS epidemic: an unusual challenge to agricultural extension services in sub-Saharan Africa, *Journal of Agricultural Education and Extension 8* (1): 1-11.

Qamar, M.K. (2003). *Facing the Challenges of an HIV/AIDS Epidemic: Agricultural Extension Services in Sub-Saharan Africa.* Rome: FAO.

Quisumbing, A.R., L. Haddad & C. Pena (2001). Are Women Over-represented among the Poor?" Food Nutrition and Consumption Division (FNCD) Discussion Paper No. 115. Washington DC: International Food Policy Research Institute.

Rakodi, C. (2002). A livelihood approach. conceptual issues and definitions. In: C. Rakodi and T. Lloyd-Jones (Eds.) *Urban livelihoods. A People Centred Approach to Reducing Poverty.* London: Earthscan Publications, pp.3-22.

Reardon, T. (1997). Using evidence of household income diversification to inform study of the rural non-farm labor market in Africa, *World Development 25*(5):735-747.

Reardon, T., C. Delgado and P. Matlon (1992). Determinants and effects of income diversification amongst farm households in Burkina Faso, *Journal of Development Studies 28*(2): 264-296.

Roberts, P. (1989). The sexual politics of labour in Western Nigeria and Hausa Niger. In: K. Young (Ed.). *Serving Two Masters: Third World Women in Development,* New Dehli: Allied Publishers, pp.27-47.

Rudie, I. (1995). The significance of eating: cooperation, support and reputation in Kelantan Malay households. In: K. J. Wazir (Ed.). *Male and "Female" in Developing Southeast Asia*, Washington D.C: Berg Publishers, pp.227-247.

Rugalema, G. 1999a. Adult Mortality as Entitlement Failure: AIDS and the Crisis of Rural Livelihoods in a Tanzanian Village. PhD Thesis. The Hague: Institute of Social Studies.

Rugalema, G. (1999)b. It is not only the loss of labor: HIV/AIDS, loss of household assets and household livelihood in Bukoba District, Tanzania. In: G. Mutangadura, H. Jackson and D. Mukurazita (Eds.) *AIDS and African Smallholder Agriculture,* Harare: Southern African AIDS Information Dissemination Service (SAFAIDS).pp.41-52.

Ruspini, E. (1996). Lone mothers and poverty in Italy, Germany and Great Britain. Evidence from panel data, *Working Paper*, N° 99-10, Colchester: University of Essex, Institute for Social and Economic Research.

Saito, K.A. (1992). Raising the productivity of women farmers in sub-Saharan Africa. (Vol. 1) Overview Report. Washington DC: World Bank, Population and Human Resources Development Department.

Saito, K.A. (1994). Raising the productivity of female farmers in sub-Saharan Africa. Washington D.C: World Bank Discussion Paper.

Saito, K.A. & C. J. Weidemann (1990). *Agricultural extension for women farmers in Africa.* Washington D.C: World Bank.

Sauerborn, R., A. Adams & M. Hien (1996). Household strategies to cope with the economic costs of illness, *Social Science and Medicine* 43: 291-301.

Schlager, E. & E. Ostrom (1992). Property-rights regimes and natural resources: a conceptual analysis. *Land Economics* 68:249–262.

Schmink, M. (1984). Household economic strategies: review and research agenda. *Latin American Review 19*(3):87-101.

Schrimshaw, S. (1990).Combining quantitative and qualitative methods in the study of intra-household resource allocation. In: B.L. Rogers and N.P. Schlossman (Eds.) *Intra-household Resource Allocation: Issues and Methods for Policy and Planning,* Tokyo: United nations University press, pp.86 - 99.

Schultz, T.W. (1975). Human capital and disequilibrium. *Journal of Economics Literature,* 13: 287-846.

Scoones, I. (1998). Sustainable rural livelihoods: a framework for analysis. Working paper No. 72, Sussex: University of Sussex, Institute of Development Studies.

Sebina-Zziwa, A.J.N. (1995). Gender Perspectives on Land Ownership and Inheritance in Uganda. Access to Land and Other Natural Resources in Uganda: Research and Policy Development Project, Research Paper 16. Kampala: University of Wisconsin, Kampala University, Makerere Institute of Social Research, and the Land Tenure Centre.

Sebina-Zziwa & A.J.N. (1998). *The Paradox of Tradition: Gender, Land and Inheritance Rights among the Baganda.* Kampala: Makerere University.

Seeley, J., U. Wagner, J. Mulemwa, J. Kengeya-Kayondo & D. Mulder (1991). The development of a community-based HIV/AIDS counseling service in a rural area in Uganda, *AIDS Care* 3:207-217.

Seeley, J. (1993). *Searching for Indicators of Vulnerability: A Study of Household Coping Strategies in Rural South West Uganda.* London: Medical Research Council/Overseas Development Agency Research Programme..

Seeley, J., Sutherland, K., Dey, R. & Grellier, R. (2003)). *Mitigation of gender- specific impact of HIV/AIDS on rural livelihoods.* Norwich, unpublished report to DFID, August.

Seeley, J., R. Grellier & T. Barnett (2004). Gender and HIV/AIDS impact mitigation in Sub-Saharan Africa–recognizing the constraints, *Journal of Social Aspects of HIV/AIDS 1*(2):87-98.

Sen, A.K (1980). Equality of what? In *The Tanner Lectures on Human Values*, edited by S. McMurrin. Salt Lake City: University of Utah.

Sen, A.K (1981). *Poverty and Famines: An Essay on Entitlement and Deprivation.* Oxford: Clarendon Press.

Sen, A.K. (1985). *Commodities and Capabilities*. Amsterdam: Elsevier.

Sen, A.K. (1990). Gender and cooperative conflicts. In: I. Tinker (Ed.) *Persistent Inequalities: Women and World Development*. New York and Oxford: Oxford University Press, pp.123-149.

Sen, B. (2002). Risks, vulnerability and poverty in Bangladesh: issues and evidence: variations on a theme. Accessed August 2, 2007 at http://www.bids.org/sen2002.doc

Senefeld, S. & K. Polsky (2005). Chronically ill households, food coping strategies in rural Zimbabwe. Working Paper No. 2, Manchester: University of Manchester.

Shapouri, S. & S. Rosen (2001). Toll on agriculture from HIV and AIDS in sub-Saharan Africa, *Agricultural Information Bulletin* Number 965-9, United Nations Department of Agriculture, Economic Research Service.

Smith, D.R., A. Gordon, K. Meadows & K. Zwick (2001). Livelihood diversification in Uganda: patterns and determinants of change across two rural districts. *Food Policy* 26:421-435.

Start, D. & C. Johnson (2004). Livelihood options? The political economy of access, opportunity and diversification. Overseas Development Institute Working Paper 233. London: (ODI). Accessed at: http://www.odi.org.uk. (15 April, 2007).

Stillwaggon, E. (2006). *AIDS and the Ecology of Poverty*. New York. Oxford University Press.

Strauss, A. & J. Corbin (1990). *Basics of Qualitative Research: Grounded Theory and Procedures and Techniques.* London and New York: Sage Publications.

Subbarao, K., A. Mattimore & K. Plangemann (2001). Social protection of Africa's orphans and other vulnerable children: issues and good practice program options. Human Development Working Papers Series: Washington D.C: World Bank.

Swift, J. (1989). Why are rural people vulnerable to famine? *IDS Bulletin 20*(2):8-16.

Tallis, V. (2002). Gender and HIV/AIDS. overview report. Institute of Development Studies.

Tanzarn, N. and C. Bishop-Sambrook (2003). The dynamics of HIV/AIDS in small-scale fishing communities in Uganda. Draft Report. Rome: FAO.

Tenkir B. (2000). Resources, poverty and human development in rural Uganda. *Africa Development 20*(3/4): 31-76.

Tibaijuka, A. (1983). Competition between banana and coffee on smallholder in Tanzania: A Case Study of the Kagera Region and Central Africa. In: Banana Production and Research in East and Central Africa. Proceedings of a regional workshop held in Bujumbura, Burundi. 14-17 December 1983. Ottawa: IRDC, pp.83-101.

Tibaijuka A. (1997). AIDS and economic welfare in peasant agriculture: case studies from Kagabiro Village, Kagera Region, Tanzania. *World Development* 25: 963-975.

Bass, E. (2006). "Uganda is learning from its Global Fund grant suspension".The Lancet, Volume 366, Issue 9500, Pages 1839-1840.

Topouzis, D. & J. Du Guerney (1999). *Sustainable Agriculture: Rural Development and Vulnerability to the AIDS Epidemic.* UNAIDS Best Practice Collection, Geneva: UNAIDS and FAO.

Topouzis, D. (2000). *Measuring the impact of HIV/AIDS on the Agricultural Sector in Africa.* Geneva: UNAIDS Best Practice Collection.

Topouzis, D. (2003). *Addressing the Impacts of HIV/AIDS on Ministries of Agriculture: Focus on Eastern and Southern Africa.* Rome: FAO and UNAIDS.

Tushemereirwe, W., D.A. Karamura, H. Sali, D. Bwamiki, I. Kashaija, C. Nankinga, F. Bagamba, A. Kangire & R. Sebuliba, (2001)). Bananas (*Musa spp).* In: J. Mukiibi, (Ed.) *Agriculture in Uganda.* Kampala: Fountain Publishers/ CTA/NARO.

Uganda Bureau of Statistics (UBOS) (2001). *Statistical Abstract* 2001. Kampala. Uganda Bureau of Statistics.

Uganda Bureau of Statistics (UBOS) and ORC Macro. 2001. *Uganda Demographic and Health Survey 2000-2001.* Calverton, Maryland: Uganda Bureau of Statistics and ORC Macro.

Uganda Bureau of Statistics (UBOS) (2003)a. National Household Survey 2003, Report on the Labour Force Survey. Kampala: Uganda Bureau of Statistics.

Uganda Bureau of Statistics (UBOS) (2003)b. 2002 National Census Report. Kampala: Uganda Bureau of Statistics.

Uganda Bureau of Statistics (UBOS) (2004). 2002 Uganda Population and Housing Census Main Report. Kampala: Uganda Bureau of Statistics.

Uganda Bureau of Statistics (UBOS) (2006). *Uganda National Household Survey 2005-2006.* Kampala: Uganda Bureau of Statistics.

Uganda AIDS Commission (2003)a. The HIV/AIDS Epidemic: Prevalence and Impact. Kampala: Uganda AIDS Commission.

Uganda AIDS Commission (2003)b. The National Strategic Framework for HIV/AIDS, Activities in Uganda: 2000/1 – 2005/6. Mid-Term Review Report. Kampala: Uganda AIDS Commission.

Uganda AIDS commission (2006). The Uganda HIV/AIDS Status Report. July 2004 –December, 2005. Kampala: Uganda AIDS Commission.

UNAIDS (1999). The UNAIDS Report. Accessed 7th December, 2006 from http://158.232.20.26/ UNAIDS/projects/repluly99.pdf .

UNAIDS (2000). *Report on the global HIV/AIDS epidemic.* Geneva: UNAIDS.

UNAIDS (2004). *Report on the global AIDS Epidemic.* Geneva: UNAIDS.

UNAIDS (2006). Report on the Global AIDS Epidemic. Geneva. UNAIDS. Accessed 7th December, 2006 from www.unaids.org/bangkok2006/report.html

United Nations Development Program (UNDP) (1992). Young Women: Silence, Susceptibility and the HIV Epidemic. New York.

UNDP,1995. Quoted in Human Development Report 1997. New York: Oxford University Press.

United Nations Development Program (UNDP) (2002). Uganda Human Development Report. The Challenge of HIV/AIDS: Maintaining the Momentum of Success. Kampala.

United Nations Development Program (UNDP) (2004). *Uganda Human Development Report 2002. The Challenge of HIV/AIDS: Maintaining the Momentum of Success.* Kampala: UNDP.

United Nations Development Program (UNDP) (2005). *Uganda Human Development Report. Linking Environment to Human Development: A Deliberate Choice.* Kampala: UNDP.

UNFPA (1995). *UNFPA State of World Population 1995. Advocating change: Population, empowerment, development.* New York: UNFPA.

UNFPA (2005). *State of World Population 2005, The Promise of Equality, Gender Equity, Reproductive health and the Millennium Development Goals,* New York: UNFPA.

UNFPA (2006). UNFPA State of World Population 2006. A Passage to Hope, Women and International Migration. New York: UNFPA.

UNIFEM (2000). Progress of the World's Women. New York: UNIFEM.

UPPAP (1999). Uganda Participatory Poverty Assessment Report – *Learning from the Poor*. Kampala: Ministry of Finance Planning and Economic Development.

Upton, M. (2004). The Role of livestock in economic development and poverty reduction. Pro-Poor Livestock Policy Initiative, Working Paper No. 10. Accessed from http://www.fao.org/ag/pplpi.html (7th April, 2007)

Urassa, M., T.J. Boerma, R. Isingo, J. Ngalula, J. Ng'weshemi, G. Mwaluko & B. Zaba (2001). The impact of HIV/AIDS on mortality and household mobility in rural Tanzania, *AIDS 15*(5):2017-2023.

Van Averbeke, W. & P. Hebinck (2007). Contemporary livelihoods. In: P. Hebinck and P.C. Lent (Eds.) *Livelihoods and Landscapes: The People of Guquka and Koloni and their Resources*. Leiden and Boston: Brill, pp.285 – 305.

Van Braun, J., H. Bouis, S. Kumar & R. Pandya-Lorch, 1996. *Improving Food Security of the poor: Concept, Policy and programs.* Washington D.C: International Food Policy and Research Institute.

Van der Geest, K. & A.J. Dietz (2004). A literature survey about risk and vulnerability in dry lands with a focus on the Sahel. In: A.J. Dietz, R. Ruben and A. Verhagen (Eds.) *The Impact of Climate Change in Dry Lands, With a Focus on West Africa*. Dordrecht: Kluwer Academic Publishers, pp.117-146.

Wakhweya A., C. Kateregga, J. Konde-Lule, R. Mukyala, L. Sabin, M. Williams & H.K. Heggenhougen (2002). Situation analysis of Orphans in Uganda. Orphans and their Households: Caring for their Future Today. Final Report. Kampala: Ministry of Gender, Labour and Social Development.

Wallace, C. (2002). Household Strategies: Their Conceptual Relevance and Analytical Scope in Social Research. *Sociology 2002 36*(2): 275-292. Accessed April 5, 2007 at http://soc.sagepub.com.

Wallmann, S. (1984). *Eight London Households.* London: Routledge.

Warde, A. (1990). Household work strategies and forms of labour: conceptual and empirical issues, *Work Employment and Society 4*(4): 495-515.

Watts, M.J. and H.G. Bohle (1993). The space of vulnerability: The causal structure of hunger and famine, *Progress in Human Geography* 17: 43-67.

West, H.W. (1972). *Land Policy in Buganda*. Cambridge: Cambridge University Press.

White, J. & E. Robinson (2000). HIV AND AIDS and Rural Livelihoods in Sub-Saharan Africa. Chatham, UK: University of Greenwich, Natural Resources Institute.

Whitehead, A. (1981). I'm hungry, mum: The politics of domestic budgeting In: K. Young, R. McCullugh and C. Wolkowitz (Eds.) *Of Marriage and the Market*. London: CSE Books, pp.88-111.

Whitehead, A. (2001). Trade, trade liberalisation and rural poverty in low-income Africa: A gendered account, Background Paper for the UNCTAD 2001 Least Developed Countries Report.

Whitehead, A. (2002). Tracking livelihood change. Theoretical, methodological and empirical perspectives from North-East Ghana, *Journal of Southern African Studies 28*(3): 575-598.

Wiggins, S. (2005). Southern Africa food and humanitarian crisis 2001-04: causes and lessons. Discussion Paper, Agricultural Economic Society Annual Conference, Nottingham, April 4-6.

William, A. (2003). *Ageing and Poverty in Africa. Ugandan Livelihoods in a Time of HIV/AIDS.* Aldershot: Ashgate.

Winchester, P. (1992). *Power, Choice and Vulnerability: A Case Study in Disaster Management in South India.* London: James and James.

Wisner, B. (1993). Disaster vulnerability: geographical scale and external reality. In: H. Bhole (Ed.) *Worlds of Pain and Hunger: Geographical Perspectives on Disaster Vulnerability and Food Security.* Fort Lauderdale and Saarbrucken: Verlag Breitenbach, pp.13-55.

World Bank (1986). Poverty and hunger: issues and options for food security in developing countries. World Bank policy study. Washington DC: World Bank.

World Bank (1993). *Uganda: Agriculture.* Washington DC: World Bank: Accessed December, 2006 at www.fao.org/hivaids.

World Bank (1997). *World Development Report 1997: The State in a Changing World,* Oxford: Oxford University Press.

World Bank (2000). World Development Report 2000/2001: Attacking Poverty. New York: Oxford University Press for the World Bank.

Worthington, E.B. (1955). *A development plan for Uganda.* Entebbe: Government Printer.

Yamano, T. & T.S. Jayne (2004). Measuring the impacts of working-age adult mortality on small-scale farm households in Kenya, *World Development 32*(1): 91-119.

Yamano, T. & T.S. Jayne (2005). Working age adult mortality and primary school attendance in rural Kenya, *Economic Development and Cultural Change 53*(3): 619-653.

Yin, R. K. 2002. *Case Study Research: Design and Methods.* 3rd edition. London: Sage.

Zake, J.Y., M.K. Magunda & C. Nkwiine (1997). Integrated soil management for sustainable agriculture and food security. The Ugandan Case. Paper presented at the FAO Workshop on Integrated Soil Management for Sustainable Agriculture and Food Security in Southern and Eastern Africa, Harare, Zimbabwe December. 8-12.

Appendices

Appendix I. Statistical notes

The models

1. In Chapter 6, in order to identify the determinants of choice of a particular livelihood strategy, a multinomial logit regression was used. The choice of the mlogit model was based on its ability to perform better with discrete choice studies (McFadden, 1974; Judge *et al.*, 1985). The probability that a household chooses a given livelihood strategy, lies between zero and one. The model assumes that a household makes a choice that maximizes its utility (McFadden, 1974) and that the random disturbance terms are independently and identically distributed (McFadden, 1974), which is popularly known as the Independency of Irrelevant alternatives assumption (iia). I failed to reject this assumption indicating that the mlogit is the appropriate statistical model for data. The model can be expressed as follows:

$$\Pr(Y_i = j) = \frac{\exp(\beta'_j X_i)}{1 + \sum_{k=1}^{J} \exp(\beta'_j X_i)} \qquad \text{for } j = 1,2, \ldots, J \qquad 1$$

where:

$\Pr(Y_i = j)$ is the probability of choosing either perennial crops producer or Staples grower livelihood strategies, with the diversified small-holder as the base category.

J is the number livelihood strategies

j = 0 is mixed farming strategy

X_i is a vector of household-specific characteristics (variables)

β_j is a vector of the estimated parameters.

Algebraic rearrangement of equation 1 above results into a regression equation 2:

$$P_i = \frac{e^{(b_0 + b_1x_1 + \ldots\ldots + b_nx_n)}}{1 + e^{(b_0 + b_1x_1 + \ldots\ldots + b_nx_n)}} \qquad 2$$

Finally, the equation used to estimate the coefficients (by maximum livelihood) is

$$\ln \frac{P_i}{1-P_i} = b_0 + b_1x_1 + \ldots\ldots + b_nx_n \qquad 3$$

where $\frac{P_i}{1-P_i}$ is the odds ratio; the log odds are expressed as a linear function of the independent factors independent factors (x_j and j = 1...25). i = 1 = Perennial crop producer and i = 3 = Staples grower strategy. i = 2= diversified small-holder strategy is the reference group. There are two sets of coefficients because strategy

1 and 3 each have to be compared with the reference group. Estimated coefficients measure the estimated change in the logit for a one-unit change in a given variable while the other variables are held constant. A positive estimated coefficient indicates an increase in the likelihood that a household will choose to be in an alternative livelihood strategy. A negative coefficient indicates that there is less likelihood that a household will change to an alternative livelihood strategy. The definition of variables used in the model are shown in Table 6.11 while a summary of their statistics is presented in Appendix 8.

2. In Chapter 7 another model is estimated to identify factors that influence livelihood vulnerability. In this part of the analysis, the outcomes (food security status) were mutually exclusive and exhaustive and there was an ordering (hierarchy) among the responses (rankings) of the respondents. In this type, an ordered choice model was required. Models of ordered choice describe settings in which individuals reveal the strength of their utility with respect to a single outcome (Green, 2003; Greene forthcoming).

In literature, two standard cases appear for ordered choice models: ordered probit model and ordered logit model. For instance if error () term has a normal distribution, an ordered probit model emerges while if it has the standardized logistic distribution, the ordered logit model is produced (Greene forthcoming). The probability of choosing a given outcome is given by;

$$\text{Prob}(y_i = j|X_i, Z_i) = prob(U_i^* \leq \mu_j) - \text{Prob}\ (U_i^* \leq \mu_{j-1}) = F(\mu_j - X_i' - Z_i'\gamma) - F(\mu_j - X_i' - Z_i'\gamma) \qquad 5$$

where is assumed either to be normal or logistic. Since the dependent variable is ordered, the appropriate statistical model is the ordered probit regression. This model is also known as the Proportional-odds model because the odds ratio of the event is independent of the other categories. The model provides only one set of coefficients for each independent variable, hence there is an assumption of parallel regression, that is, the coefficients for the variables in the equations would not vary significantly if they were estimated separately. The intercepts would be different, but the slopes would be essentially the same. I tested for this assumption using the Brant test but failed to reject the null hypothesis which justified the appropriateness of the model. The specification of the model is given below.

$$\text{adeqcat222}^* = f(X_1, X_2, X_3 \ldots X_{25}, \varepsilon_i) \qquad 6$$

where; ε_i is a vector of error for the equations estimated, ε_i ~logistically. Other variables are defined as in Equation 6.3 (cf. Table 6.11)

adeqcat222 = 1 if adeqcat222* $\leq a_1$
adeqcat222 = 2 if adeqcat222* $\leq a_2$

adeqcat222 = 3 if adeqcat222*> a_3

a_i is a threshold parameter for each level of food security, which is estimated along with the coefficients of the explanatory variables. 1 = Food Insecure with Aggregate scores < 21; 2 = Barely Food Secure with aggregate scores ≥ 21 but < 35; and 3 = Food Secure with aggregate scores > 35.

Appendix 2.

Summary statistics for the explanatory variables used in the ols model

Variable	Mean	SD	Minimum	Maximum
TotalExpenditure	0.458	0.448	0	4.0
hhsize2005	6.283	2.653	1	15.0
district	0.560	0.497	0	1.0
landlaboratio	1.656	2.198	0	20.3
education	0.488	0.500	0	1.0
gender	0.725	0.447	0	1.0
widowed	0.187	0.390	0	1.0
aidshh	0.214	0.411	0	1.0
hiredlabour	0.412	0.493	0	1.0
tot_bedridden	11.464	16.531	0	130.0
Bansoldprop	0.882	0.323	0	1.0
othcropsold	0.665	0.472	0	1.0
hhsizegender	4.732	3.714	0	15.0
Well-off & aidshh	0.048	0.214	0	1.0
Well-off & gender	0.242	0.429	0	1.0

Summary statistics for the explanatory variables used in the mlogit and ologit models

Variables	Mean	SD	Minimum	Maximum
Household size	6.283	2.653	1	15
Cattle number	0.963	3.137	0	32
Ruminant number	2.628	4.046	0	45
HH head occup 2	0.013	0.113	0	1
HH head occup 3	0.048	0.214	0	1
Land-labour ratio	1.656	2.198	0	20.3
HH head age	43.168	13.727	18	90
HH head educ 4	0.340	0.474	0	1
HH head educ 5	0.128	0.334	0	1
HH head educ 6	0.004	0.061	0	1
HH head educ 7	0.009	0.096	0	1
HH head educ 8	0.004	0.061	0	1
HH head educ 9	0.257	0.437	0	1
Gender	0.725	0.447	0	1
Hired labour	0.412	0.493	0	1
AIDS-affected HH	0.214	0.411	0	1
Sold maize	0.806	0.396	0	1
Use clean plantlets	0.140	0.348	0	1
Pest/disease control	0.262	0.440	0	1
Fertilizer use	0.638	0.481	0	1
Soil conservation	0.307	0.462	0	1
Access credit	0.098	0.298	0	1
Dependency ratio	1.260	1.536	0	14
Land owned (2005)	2.933	4.676	0	75

Appendix 3. Table showing causes of death in past three years

Cause of death	Percent HH reporting death of a member (N=118)	Percent widow-HH reporting spousal death (N=36)
HIV/AIDS	28.8	41.5
Malaria	22.9	7.7
Unknown	13.6	18.6
Cholera	6.8	3.1
Pneumonia	6.1	6.1
Tuberculosis (TB)	4.2	7.7
Old age	3.4	0.0
Witch craft	2.6	0.0
Cholera	0.0	3.1
Hernia	2.5	3.1
Un-known persistent fever	1.7	1.5
Typhoid	1.7	0.0
Excessive bleeding	0.8	0.0
Brucellosis	0.9	0.0
Measles	0.8	0.0
Severe headache	0.8	0.0
Accident	0.8	3.1
Diabetes	0.8	1.5
Epilepsy	0.8	0.0
Poisoned	0.0	1.5
Alcohol	0.0	1.5
Total	100	100

Summary

The HIV/AIDS epidemic is undoing decades of economic and social development in sub-Saharan Africa and its impacts on rural populations – their livelihoods, their farming systems and food security – have been especially severe. While a lot of studies have been undertaken, research in the social sciences lags behind, particularly (intra-)household level analysis of HIV/AIDS impacts. Such research is essential for the development of relevant policies and intervention programs. The 'livelihood' approach was used to facilitate understanding, in a holistic manner, about how people's livelihoods are created and constrained by a complex set of factors and processes in a context of HIV/AIDS. The main objectives of this study were to:

1. contribute towards the livelihood conceptual framework by focusing on the role of social differentiation in livelihood generation and in dealing with livelihood shocks, and
2. identify critical factors that need to be taken into consideration in the development of relevant policies for HIV/AIDS-affected agriculture-based households or those that are at risk.

Specifically the study examined how the effects of HIV/AIDS on banana-farming households influence household resource use and consequently the food and livelihood security of rural farmers in the study area. A gender perspective was applied throughout the study. The study was carried out in the districts of Masaka and Kabarole that have high and medium-level HIV/AIDS prevalence, respectively. The study is descriptive in nature. A cross-sectional study design and a combination of qualitative and quantitative research methods were employed.

The main source of livelihood for people in Masaka and Kabarole is agriculture. They derive their income mainly from the sale of crops, followed by livestock and, to a limited extent, agricultural labour. Less important income sources include non-agricultural casual labour, remittances, salaried employment, property rents, donations and pensions. However, limited land, degraded soils, prolonged periods of drought, inability to use purchased inputs (fertilizers and pesticides) and hire labour, as well as imperfect markets, have worked in synergy to make returns from farming low, particularly for poor households with small landholdings. While agriculture remains the most important livelihood activity, households straddle different types of activities and try to diversify their sources of income to sustain and improve their livelihood. On-farm diversification and expansion, non-farm work and migration are part of the livelihood strategies in the two districts.

The study shows that there is no significant difference in access to resources between the two districts; farmers engage in similar activities and pursue more or less similar strategies. However, significant differences by wealth status and between male- and female-headed households could be observed. Well-off households have significantly more assets and higher per capita food expenditures than poor households. For all household assets investigated, female-headed households, whether headed by widows or single females, have fewer assets than the male-headed ones. In addition, limited access to production resources among poor households, particularly the female-headed ones, forces them to pursue activities that yield low returns or are risky (subsistence farming of staples, casual labouring, transactional sex), locking them into poverty traps. In contrast, better-off male-headed households may engage in proactive strategies such as accumulation of resources (purchase land), expansion of agricultural production, and initiation of non-farm income-generating activities.

The study shows that HIV/AIDS causes significant negative effects on the lives of those affected and their resources. HIV/AIDS is the leading cause of death among the sampled households. HIV/AIDS-related sickness and death result in reduced household labour availability, an increased care and orphan burden, and loss of income of sick or died household members. Effects on resource use can be summarized as asset depletion, increased medical and food expenditures, diversion or inefficient use of other household resources due to HIV/AIDS-related labour loss, abandonment of agricultural practices that are labour-intensive or require cash, reduced ability to access inputs or hire land, and disinvestment in production and child education. Impacts on agricultural production are associated with poor agronomic practices for all crops, a decline in crop yields, increase in banana pests and diseases, and a reduction in cultivated land. HIV/AIDS-related effects on intra- and inter-household relations lead to conflict and increased violence between spouses, reduced capacity of parents to care for their children and discrimination and exploitation of orphans by their relatives.

However, HIV/AIDS effects are differential. Gender and wealth status influence the way people respond to or cope with the epidemic's impacts. HIV/AIDS-related effects are more significant among poor affected households than their well-off counterparts, implying that HIV/AIDS has limited effects on well-off households. There is also a high level of widowhood in the study area, with two-fifths of it being caused by AIDS. While most widowers do not experience losing land or property and easily remarry, which enables them to replace lost labour, most widows face restrictions on remarriage and have labour constraints. Retrospective questioning showed that during the period 2002-5, female-headed households experienced greater asset depletion than male-headed ones. Additionally, HIV/AIDS-related care provision falls disproportionately on women. While orphans in well-off households continue education, those in poor households are likely to have less schooling time or drop out completely. Orphaned girls may also suffer rape and defilement.

This study shows that a household's wealth or socio-economic status, changes in resources over time, and its demographic characteristics substantially influence the livelihood effects of AIDS. Using daily per capita household expenditure as a proxy for livelihood security, the following significant factors could be identified: education and gender of the household head, access to hired labour, household wealth status, access to credit and extension services and NGO support, and district of residence in addition to being HIV/AIDS-affected. Using food (in)security as a proxy for household vulnerability, households that have a wide asset base (cattle, goats, pigs, land), access to agricultural inputs (planting material, labour, credit) and better-managed soils, are food secure. The following categories of households and individuals could be identified as the most vulnerable to HIV/AIDS-related effects: orphans, orphan-headed households, widow-headed households, female-headed households and households with very old, illiterate or HIV-infected household heads. They are characterized by having little or no land, limited labour and sources of income, illiteracy, as well as small social networks. Results from the study show that both a wide asset base and opportunities to diversify activities help protecting a household against an external shock such as HIV/AIDS.

While in the overwhelming majority of affected cases the effects of AIDS are negative and lead to increased impoverishment and vulnerability, for some households the HIV/AIDS-related effects are manageable. The differences and the magnitude of effects experienced are associated with factors both at household level and beyond. Results from the study also show that household-level factors seem to be more important determinants of livelihood security than location-specific factors. However, the higher level of food insecurity experienced by households in Masaka points to the fact that AIDS produces different epidemics in different locations. This highlights the need for location-specific interventions.

While the government has put in place a number of policy and institutional mechanisms to prevent and control the impacts of AIDS, the epidemic has introduced new challenges and demands for agriculture extension. In addition to HIV/AIDS-related institutional changes, the epidemic has resulted in a change in the composition of extension clientele, implying that some of the existing extension methods and technologies are rendered irrelevant. AIDS also challenges the currently promoted development paradigm of privatization of extension services. Existing HIV/AIDS initiatives could be strengthened through (i) equipping staff with skills to enable them integrate AIDS in their work, (ii) establishing mechanisms of information collection and monitoring of activities at community level, (iii) community mobilization, (iv) better coordination of local level interventions, (v) up-scaling of activities, and (vi) effective operationalization of multi-sectoral approaches at the local level.

It can be concluded that the differentiated nature of HIV/AIDS impacts calls for different strategies and interventions for different categories of vulnerable households, groups or individuals in the affected areas. But HIV/AIDS is not the only factor influencing vulnerability. Environmental factors and processes, like ecological crises and economic hardship, also make people vulnerable and increase susceptibility to HIV/AIDS, thereby intensifying HIV/AIDS-related vulnerability. While it is imperative that these problems be dealt with, there are historically specific social practices, policies, and ideologies that continue to maintain or reproduce distinct forms of inequality, with certain social groups being marginalized and others being privileged. Unless these are redressed, they will continue to aggravate people's vulnerability regardless of the type of shock that individuals are exposed to or experience.

About the author

Monica Karuhanga Beraho was born in Itendero-Kagango Sheema, Bushenyi District in Western Uganda. She holds a bachelor of Veterinary Medicine from Makerere University (1991), and a Masters of Agronomy and Farming Systems (majoring in agricultural extension and agribusiness) from Adelaide University, South Australia (1996). She obtained her doctorate from Wageningen University, the Netherlands. Her PhD research in Uganda focused on HIV/AIDS impacts on banana-farming households and implications for food and livelihood security. Her PhD was part of the AWLAE (African Women Leaders in Agriculture and Environment) research program on gender, food systems and HIV/AIDS in Africa.

She has six years of community level agricultural extension work with Mukono District Local government in Uganda. In 1991 she joined Makerere University as a lecturer and has taught several undergraduate courses related to agricultural extension, participatory research, rural development and gender. In addition to teaching she coordinated students' internship programs for the Department of Agricultural Extension Education, Faculty of Agriculture (2001-2003). During the same period she was part of a task force that spearheaded integration of gender into the curricula of the Faculty of Agriculture, Makerere University. Her areas of research interest include issues of gender and rural development, livelihood studies, and participatory research.

She has held several leadership positions in professional organizations. She has been Chairperson and later Executive Committee Member of the Association of Uganda Professional Women in Agriculture and Environment (AUPWAE); Treasurer of the Association of Uganda Professional Agriculturalists; Member of the Agricultural Committee for the National Council of Science and Technology; and Member of the Gender Budget Program Management Team for Forum for Women in Democracy (FOWODE).

www.ingramcontent.com/pod-product-compliance
Lightning Source LLC
Chambersburg PA
CBHW061156240926
51846CB00006B/1032
* 9 7 8 9 0 8 6 8 6 0 6 4 7 *